CIRCLING THE ELEPHANT

**Comparative** / *Thinking Across*
**Theology** / *Traditions*

SERIES EDITORS:

*Loye Ashton and John J. Thatamanil*

This series invites books that engage in constructive comparative theological reflection that draws from the resources of more than one religious tradition. It offers a venue for constructive thinkers, from a variety of religious traditions (or thinkers belonging to more than one), who seek to advance theology understood as "deep learning" across religious traditions.

# CIRCLING THE ELEPHANT

## A Comparative Theology
## of Religious Diversity

JOHN J. THATAMANIL

*Fordham University Press* NEW YORK 2020

Chapter 6, "The Hospitality of Receiving: Mahatma Gandhi, Martin Luther King, Jr., and Interreligious Learning," was originally published in Lewis V. Baldwin and Paul R. Dekar, eds., *"In an Inescapable Network of Mutuality": Martin Luther King, Jr. and the Globalization of an Ethical Ideal* (Eugene, OR: Cascade Books, an Imprint of Wipf and Stock Publishers, 2013), 131–151. Used by permission of Wipf and Stock Publishers, www.wipfandstock.com.

An abbreviated version of Chapter 7 was published as "God as Ground, Contingency, and Relation: Trinitarian Polydoxy and Religious Diversity," in Catherine Keller and Laurel Schneider, eds., *Polydoxy: Theology of Multiplicity and Relation* (New York: Routledge Press, 2011), 238–257. It is republished here with permission from Taylor and Francis (Books) Limited.

Fordham University Press has no responsibility for the persistence or accuracy of URLs for external or third-party Internet websites referred to in this publication and does not guarantee that any content on such websites is, or will remain, accurate or appropriate.

Fordham University Press also publishes its books in a variety of electronic formats. Some content that appears in print may not be available in electronic books.

Visit us online at www.fordhampress.com.

Library of Congress Cataloging-in-Publication Data available online at https://catalog.loc.gov.

Printed in the United States of America

22  21  20    5  4  3  2  1

First edition

*to*
*Catherine Keller and*
*Kate & Kate*

# CONTENTS

# PREFACE: AUTOBIOGRAPHY AND COMPARATIVE THEOLOGY

Theologians who work comparatively face a peculiar challenge: Why does the theologian work with just these traditions and texts? Why should anyone engage in Buddhist-Christian-Hindu trialogue? Who is the author, and for what community or communities does he write? Such questions about selection are inevitable.[1]

One possible response is through an autobiographical turn. The author offers an existential account for the choices made. Some arbitrariness remains, but readers will have some sense of why just these traditions were selected.

I begin with the number 1.5. Neither a first-generation immigrant nor a second-generation child born in the United States, I am a member of the 1.5 generation, someone born in India who came to the United States as a child, along with my immigrant parents. This fact marks me as a child of two worlds, belonging wholly to neither but caught somewhere in between. Having emigrated from India and arrived in Brooklyn as an eight-year-old, I can speak a largely "unaccented" American English with occasional lapses. Something more than a lapse transpires when I am with family. There, without self-awareness, I speak a combination of my mother tongue, Malayalam, and a heavily accented English. I did not know that I made this shift in accent until my college roommates told me. Even then, I protested—perhaps driven by a young person's desire to fit in and pass—and stopped my protestations only after hearing a recording, surreptitiously made, of me in phone conversation with my parents. Sometimes we come to hear ourselves only when others overhear us, others who can tell us more about who we are than we can know in isolation.

Such experiences lead me to reject the notion that understanding is likely to run aground on the shoals of difficulty only when we cross the boundary line between one religion and another. Often, habitual familiarity with our own symbols, myths, practices, and theologies prevents us from understanding what we are up to. We fail to hear our own accents. This lack of self-awareness even marks speculative theological labor so long as that labor operates within homogeneous communities of conversation. It is not clear to me that Christian theologians know what we are doing when we speak about God, Trinity, incarnation, and salvation until we are compelled to articulate the meaning of our vocabulary to others who do not share it. We need others[2] even to hear ourselves and thereby come to self-understanding.

Another lesson I take from my still malleable accent is that my identity remains fluid as I move across and inhabit different communities. I do not now take my failure to maintain a single and standard American English accent to be a sign of confusion or a mark of unstable identity; rather, my variable accent is a mark of an internal multiplicity that makes possible differing authenticities. I can be consistent without aspiring to be homogeneously self-identical.

Both in India and in the United States, I grew up as a member of the Mar Thoma Church. The Mar Thoma Church is an Indian Christian community that calls the South Indian state of Kerala home. It is just one among the many communities of St. Thomas Christians who believe that St. Thomas, the doubting Apostle, came to India in 52 CE to preach to Jewish traders in Kerala. According to tradition, Thomas had little luck with the Jewish community but succeeded with South Indian Brahmins. Already in this routinely narrated nugget of tradition, the problematic affiliation between caste status and Kerala Christianity is sadly evident. This community of St. Thomas Christians eventually came under the care of the Syrian Orthodox Church. The complex history of Christianity in South India is too complex to narrate here.[2] Eventually, this community of Syrian Orthodox Indian Christians was subjected to Catholic Inquisition and subjugation in the wake of Vasco Da Gama's arrival. In time, Indian Christian communities resisted Catholic control, and a variety of splinter groups emerged.

The Mar Thoma Church was formed in the nineteenth century when a segment of the Indian Syrian Orthodox community came under the influence of Anglican Church Missionary Society (CMS). The founder of the Mar Thoma Church, Abraham Malpan, is regarded as Kerala's Martin Luther, because he refused the CMS missionaries but sought instead, albeit unsuccessfully, to reform the Syrian Orthodox Church by surrendering devotion to icons and saints and adopting the indigenous language of Malayalam rather than Syriac for worship. The failure of his reformation efforts led to a division within the Orthodox community and the formation of the Mar Thoma Church, which retained Syrian Orthodox liturgical style, a commitment to episcopal succession, but adopted a Protestant and evangelical theological sensibility. The emphasis, above all, was on reading the Bible in Malayalam and worshipping in Malayalam.

The Mar Thoma Church in the twentieth century was characterized—especially in its leadership—by a socially progressive evangelicalism. M. M. Thomas's integration of liberation theology and interreligious dialogue, well before either of those terms was in common circulation in the global church, found a home and eventual recognition within the Mar Thoma community.[3] However, among the laity, and certainly in my family, Mar Thoma devotional life is evangelical, a combination of born-again piety and a commitment to justice even though that commitment is imperfectly realized because of the community's insufficient attention to the question of caste.

To grow up with an Indian version of evangelical piety in the seventies and eighties in the American Northeast was an oddity, not because of my Indianness, but rather because such evangelical sensibilities are more likely to be found in the American South than in New York or Connecticut. Growing up Christian in North America is hardly special. Hence, my desire to discover what it means to be distinctively Indian led to interest in Indic religious traditions. That interest was nourished by early exposure in Sunday school to Huston Smith's book *The Religions of Man*. Strangely, my first conscious encounter with Hinduism in my teenage years was neither through friends nor by way of exposure to the larger Indian community. Neither during my childhood years, despite years lived in an important temple town like Trichy, nor in my youth, did I experience living encounter with Hindu communities. The Mar Thoma community in America lived its life without substantive interchange with Hindu communities. Meetings take place on major Kerala holidays like Onam and other Indian community gatherings.

The interest awakened by Huston Smith's book continued unabated during my undergraduate years. Indian traditions evoked a passion because, through these traditions, I began to acquire a sense of what it means to be Indian in a way that being Indian Christian alone could not. My love for Indic traditions was not occasioned by immigrant displacement alone. I have come to see, albeit in retrospect, that my interest in

Hindu and Buddhist traditions, even in college, was motivated by spiritual affinities.

Throughout my college years, my religious life was unusually full, not because I was given to extraordinary religious experiences, but rather because I had a continuous felt sense of divine presence. I did not then have the language to describe this sense. A musical analogy may be most apt. I liken my sense of divine presence to the drone in a classical Indian raga, there in the background, available to ear and mind, establishing the basic tonality for the rest of the piece, but rarely the focus of explicit attention. The only Christian language that comes close to capturing this sense—I cannot call it an experience as it was neither discrete nor episodic but rather something beneath all experiencing—are the lyrics of Horatio Spafford's poem set to music by Philip Bliss, "It Is Well with My Soul": "When peace, like a river, attendeth my way/When sorrows like sea billows roll/Whatever my lot, Thou has taught me to say/It is well, it is well, with my soul." This sense of wellness was rooted in something more than the assurance that I was embraced by the forgiving grace of God through Christ's sacrificial atonement. Those convictions were integral to Spafford's experience. My intuition of wellness was rooted in a sense of divine intimacy. What mattered was not that God forgave me from *without* but that God was present *within*, right in the midst of quotidian life. In language that I did not then have at my disposal, I would say that I had a sense and taste for the nondual.

I did not take this sense of immanent presence to be in tension with or in contradiction to God's transcendent greatness as more conventionally named and experienced in evangelical Mar Thoma piety. As I recall, my favorite hymn from those days was not Spafford's "It Is Well with My Soul," but rather Boberg's "How Great Thou Art." The sense of lofty divine grandeur present in nature and far beyond may not be easily reconcilable with the nondual, but, nonetheless, both were vital to my somewhat idiosyncratic Christian experience in young adulthood.

The only discrete experience that I have had that might be characterized as "religious" or "mystical" took place on the campus of Washington University in St. Louis. The campus, although lovely, was not then and is not now a nature preserve but contains instead just the usual sort of campus greenery, albeit in abundance. On a routine walk to Olin Library from my dorm, on a path I had traversed dozens of times before, something occurred—I cannot now recall what triggered the experience—that brought into heightened awareness the intimate nearness of things.

More than the vividness of color, and beyond the sense that I was seeing the bushes and trees with greater clarity—as though someone had unbeknownst to me substituted my glasses with a stronger pair that sharpened acuity of vision—what I remember most is an intense proximity to nature. I was granted an intimacy with each leaf, branch, and twig that I have not experienced before or since.

The passing of time has erased many details of that encounter. What abides is a feeling of vitality and luminosity, not because anything about the day or space was somehow more extraordinary, but rather just because I was somehow nearer to everything, and, with that closeness, felt a sense of communion and joy. I would have then found the term "religious" strange to deploy for this experience because the experience lacked a discrete religious object. I experienced neither God nor any sort of transpersonal ultimate. Instead, I met the usual objects of daily experience, only they did not stand outside or over against me. For the duration of that experience—a duration that I could not measure—what I encountered could not rightly be described as a series of "objects." I cannot recall now whether I then knew the categories and language of William James's notion of pure experience, but that language does now seem appropriate.

By way of retrospection, I can say that the feeling tones of these distinct dimensions of my religious life were markedly different. The continuous subliminal awareness of nondual presence I enjoyed was marked by calm, assurance, peacefulness, and a subtle and constant joy, available to reflection should I tune into it, but otherwise present in the background, conditioning my surface experiences regardless of whether they were pleasant or painful. The second and more traditional mode of Christian piety was marked by devotion that cannot be characterized as nondual. What feels to me most vital in such piety is wonder at God's creative and sustaining power that is "throughout the universe displayed." The third, indeed the only event that is sufficiently individuated to be marked as a distinct experience, was neither transtheistic nor devotional. This experience, too, can be characterized as nondual. The boundary lines between experiencer and the experienced were erased, but I had no experience of union with any transpersonal or personal ultimate reality.

My fondness for certain strands of Hindu, Christian, and Buddhist traditions is because of the way in which elements from each of these traditions shed light on these various dimensions of my religious life. Within the Hindu family, the Advaita Vedanta tradition's[4] emphasis on the presence of Brahman, not so much as the content of a discrete mystical experience (although some Advaitins, like Ramana Maharishi, do report mystical experiences of Brahman) but rather as that which makes experience itself possible, affords me the best language for the transpersonal divine presence within and beneath all experiencing.

Although I came to understand my experience at Washington University with the help of Martin Buber's I-Thou language, Buddhist categories now seem more adequate. In Buber's I-Thou encounter, there is always a Thou that evokes and becomes the focus of encounter, whether a horse, tree, or another human being. In my experience, there was no such focal Thou but rather a momentary dissolution of ego-identity, an unpracticed, undisciplined, and therefore transient opening, a brief nondual experience of relation.

Christian devotion remains the core and basic plumb line of my religious life. For that reason, I have never thought of my love for other traditions as calling for conversion. I am willing to speak of multiple religious participation though not multiple belonging, as the latter term seems too rich; I am inclined to reserve the latter term for persons who have been formally welcomed into more than one religious community. Paul Knitter notes, at the conclusion of his marvelous book, *Without the Buddha, I Could Not Be a Christian*, that he has made just this transition. He has recited the Bodhisattva vow in the presence of a recognized teacher within an established Buddhist teaching lineage while continuing in his life as a lay Catholic.[5] The notion of multiple religious belonging is appropriate in his case. In my case, the term multiple religious participation is most apt.

In recent years, my own religious life has moved in a far more social direction and is no longer a matter of isolated experiences or textually mediated encounters with non-Christian traditions. During my fieldwork in India as a graduate student, I became a student of an Advaita guru, Swami Paramarthananda of Chennai. I came to regard Swamiji with genuine devotion because he mediated to me the truth of Advaita Vedanta as found in the Upanishads and in Sankara's commentaries. Even during that time in India, I continued to attend the Mar Thoma Church and preached on occasion.[6] In my years at Vanderbilt Divinity School (VDS), in addition to regular worship life at St. Augustine's Episcopal Chapel, I became a part of the Nashville Insight Meditation Group led by Gordon Peerman and Kathy Woods. Quite fortuitously, this group met for some years in the Divinity School's All Faith Chapel on Wednesday afternoons.

On Wednesday mornings, that same Chapel was the worship site for the Divinity School community.

Moreover, some members of the Nashville Insight Meditation Group were also regular worshippers at St. Augustine's Chapel. Because I taught courses in Buddhist-Christian dialogue at VDS, a number of my students also meditated with this group. Hence, about a dozen of us regularly participated in Eucharist upstairs and engaged in *vipassana* downstairs. Communities like ours face a deep theological question: Can we give a coherent account of the difference but also profound resonance between these two very different kinds of practice? I doubt that any among us would say that we were doing the same thing upstairs as we did downstairs.

I offer a brief sketch of this community in order to describe an emerging core community of practitioners who are serious about both Buddhist practice and Christian Eucharistic life. Because I was, during my Vanderbilt years, a regular preacher and member of the pastoral team for the St. Augustine community, I felt keenly the obligation to think rigorously about the meaning of our life together.

For some in the group, although the vibrant life of our progressive and justice-seeking Christian community continues to be meaningful, the practical power of Buddhist disciplines for structuring everyday life, breath by breath, is so immediately accessible that life is more richly illuminated by means of Buddhist practice than through Christian narratives and theology. As Peerman likes to say, Buddhists are better at operationalizing and implementing Buddhist wisdom than Christians are at doing likewise.[7] Hence, many face a temptation to live their practical lives as Buddhists while retaining a deep love for Christian worship without being able to articulate the reasons for the continuing power of Christian Eucharistic life. But because a core group still continues to participate with regularity in both modes of practice, I am confident that all involved find a rich complementarity between insight meditation and Christian worship, even if hard-pressed to give a theological account of the meaning of that complementarity.

Some years ago, I moved from Vanderbilt to my new institutional home, Union Theological Seminary. I continue Buddhist practice and Christian worship, again within the walls of the Seminary itself. Buddhist practice at Union is shaped by Tibetan and Zen traditions rather than by *vipassana*.

Increasingly, communities and not just individuals share practice across religious lines. Given the existence of such communities, characterizations of multiple religious participation as individualistic, undisciplined, and shallow consumerist pop eclecticism are questionable. We now need theological projects that seek to explore the meaning of such modes of practice. How can traditions that seem to be guided by different theological intuitions inform the same persons and communities? Is complementarity possible?

*Circling the Elephant* is one provisional attempt to articulate the nature of that complementarity. It is written, in part, for those who seek to remain within sacramental Christian communities even as we seek also to cultivate Buddhist mindfulness or yoga practice. This book is also a brief on behalf of comparative theology as the discipline best suited for such work, the work of nurturing hybrid communities in a time of multiple religious participation and belonging.[8]

# NOTE ON TRANSLITERATION

This book dispenses with diacritical marks. Scholars do not need them, and general readers may find them unhelpful and cumbersome. Foreign-language terms are given in the form most likely to be familiar to English-language readers—hence nirvana, not *nibbana*. Also, when a term (for example, "nirvana" in the previous sentence) has become a familiar English-language term, it is presented without italics. The aim in all such decisions is reading ease for the nonspecialist reader rather than philological exactitude for Indological experts who already know the relevant terms.

# Introduction:
# Revisiting an Old Tale

*Is it really our desire to build a monolithic society: one party, one view, one leader, and no opposition? Is religious uniformity desirable or even possible? . . . Does not the task of preparing the kingdom of God require a diversity of talents, a variety of rituals, soul-searching as well as opposition? . . . In this aeon diversity of religions is the will of God.*

—ABRAHAM JOSHUA HESCHEL

## Revisiting an Old Tale: The Elephant and the Blind(folded) Men

Is religious diversity fundamentally a problem? Religious diversity may *give rise* to problems—conflict, for example—but that is a different matter than thinking of religious diversity as intrinsically problematic. A thing might be good but nonetheless bring in its wake deep challenges. What about religious diversity? I pose this question because recourse to talk about "the problem of religious diversity" has become so commonplace in Christian theological discourse that few have stopped to ask whether reflection about religious diversity might begin from an altogether different point.[1] Can we imagine theological reflection that begins with a "delight in multiplicity," reflection that even invites us to "grow an appetite" for religious difference?[2] Might we begin to think of religious diversity as promise rather than as problem? That is the question that *Circling the Elephant* sets out to explore.

To think of religious diversity as a problem is to fall all too neatly into a larger global pattern in which allergy to difference and a love for a nationalistic monolithic are everywhere on the rise. In a time of ecological crisis, nationalists hell-bent on diminishing ecological diversity aspire to do the same with religious diversity too. Islamophobia, anti-Semitism, and allergies also to sexual difference—all are expressions of an international axis of xenophobia in a time of diminished economic expectations. Hence, a great deal is at stake should religious communities uncritically fall into the habit of thinking of religious diversity as problem rather than promise. Giving into such habits is a capitulation to those who wish to characterize religious diversity as intrinsically dangerous. To imagine religious diversity as promise instead of problem is to refuse those who seek to turn diversity into divisiveness.

The US context, the one in which I write, is marked by profound contradiction. On the one hand, there is immense appreciation for religious diversity and even openness to multiple religious participation, and not just among theological progressives. Even as the pews empty out, there is a profusion of religious experimentation. SBNRs, the "spiritual but not religious," are growing in number, as are those who take up multiple religious participation.[3] On the other hand, the nation's president foments Islamophobia and anti-Semitism and endorses policies that do the same. The Muslim ban still stands. Hate crimes skyrocket in number, and the Far Right is emboldened as never before.

Christian theologians, indeed religious thinkers from all traditions, bear special obligations in so dire a season. Their obligation is not merely to plead for national policies of tolerance. Tolerance is a limited imaginative register, at best a stopgap first step, at worst a failure to ask why some hold the upper hand and so have perks, power, and privilege to tolerate those they'd rather not. What is required instead is a celebration of diversity, not as frilly ornamentation, but as essential to life itself. Might we come to imagine that we desperately need religious diversity just as we do ecological diversity? Might we come to believe that a loss in religious diversity diminishes us too? Abraham Joshua Heschel's work remains unfinished, the work of showing that religious diversity is an intrinsic good and indeed the very "will of God." That is the call that ought to animate interreligious theology.

If religious difference receives theological endorsement and not just acceptance, another possibility presents itself: a holy desire, even a holy envy, for the wisdom of our religious neighbors.[4] We can learn to love and love to learn from what is not already our own. After generations of seeking to convert the world and thereby erase religious diversity—a project that has underwritten all manner of colonial violence—the time has come to receive rather than to propagate, to reorient Christian communities toward the virtues of humility and hospitality rather than an aggressive "giving" that believes that it has nothing to receive. What is a closed hand that is unwilling to receive but a fist?

Standing in the way to such a reorientation is that, for many, a love for the "*unum*" triumphs still over the "*pluribus*" out of which the *unum* is to arise. We have not yet learned to cherish the many and the multiple; that shortcoming is both an ethical and a theological failure. No robust vision of justice is possible as long as we remain in the thrall of the monolithic and allergic to difference, not an uncritical and indifferent letting be of difference, but a welcoming of demanding difference, even difference with which we must wrestle. That sort of theological *eros* is an unmet need of this historical moment.

In the time of the postmodern, diversities are celebrated. The creative instability of language and the proliferation of meaning generated thereby are recognized as unavoidable for sign-using creatures. Few would speak with regret about cultural diversity or variety in artistic or musical styles. And no one thinks to begin a conversation about ecology with the phrase "the problem of ecological diversity." The core ecological problem that confronts us is not biodiversity but rather its radical diminishment. In these spheres, reflection is not, from the start, imprisoned within a cast of mind that regards diversity as regrettable or problematic. So an obvious question presents itself: Why is religious diversity routinely perceived to be different from other modes of diversity? Christians have been able to affirm natural diversity as a divinely created good but not religious diversity.

Is religious diversity unique in this respect, or do other modes of difference also beget suspicion? How about the diversity of philosophical, moral, and political judgments? In these domains also, diversity is difficult to characterize as unambiguously good. Diversity in the philosophical, moral, and political spheres is often a source of deep discord, division, and even violence. In these domains, it will not do to shrug and say, "You say po-tay-toh; I say po-tah-toh." Is that the reason why some diversities are celebrated whereas others are not? Perhaps diversity is likely to be treated as problematic in just those domains in which difference might trigger discord.

In still other cases, the sheer presence of difference suggests that something has gone awry as is the case in matters of perception. If you say, that chair is blue, and I see it as green, at least one of us is wrong. Diver-

sity, in this case, is an unwelcome sign of error. Correction, not celebration, is the appropriate response. Is religious diversity likewise the
result of cognition gone wrong?

But suppose that what is going on in interreligious debate, at least in
some cases, is tantamount to the following conversation: One interlocutor says, "The chair is green!" and the other responds, "No, you fool, it's
made of wood." In this case, both are in dispute about the same object,
but the conflict is apparent, not real. Both parties might be correct. The
conflict becomes real rather than apparent only if disputants are comparing the object, in this case the chair, *in the same respect.*[5]

Of course, when the argument is about chairs or other mundane objects, it is a simple matter to discern that we are not arguing about the
same object in the same respect. To make similar determinations when
arguing about ultimate reality is a trickier proposition. Do the various
parties even have the same reality in mind when engaged in conversation or debate? Is it even right to think of religious traditions as largely
given over to determining the nature of some extramundane ultimate
reality(ies)? After all, those traditions we have come to classify as religions
are as much concerned about death, marriage, economics, politics, and
society as they are in arguing about the diverse conceptions of divinity.
Our ideas about "religion" often distort what these traditions are about;
we fail to recognize and even marginalize the very mundane, indeed secular, concerns of religious traditions and focus attention instead on the
postmortem condition of human souls, forgetting the tragic premortem
conditions under which over a billion of us live.[6]

Still, among the projects that religious persons undertake—at least
when they are intellectuals within their respective traditions—are arguments about how rightly to understand the nature of reality, and especially if there might be some feature or features of the real that might be
characterized as ultimate. Buddhists and Hindus have had millennia long
arguments about this question.[7] Moreover, many of these arguments have
also been *intra*religious and not interreligious, a truth often overlooked
by those who suppose that religious conflict takes place primarily across
religious traditions rather than within them.

Given that such arguments take place, how might we come to think
of religious diversity as gift and promise rather than as a mark of error?
One answer to that question rests in positing, as a hypothesis, that ultimate reality is at least as complex as the chair in our earlier thought experiment. If so, then differences within and across religious traditions

might persist because they register distinctive dimensions of divine life. We might then imagine religious diversity not just as a de facto but as a de jure good. We need religious diversity in order to register and receive the rich multiplicity of the divine life.

Might it not be the case that partisans in debate find themselves caught up in conflict because they believe that they are speaking of ultimate reality in the same respect when in fact they are not? Of course, not all cases of religious conflict are merely apparent, but some surely are. Moreover, conflict itself may be vital to the work of truth-seeking inquiry. Not every conflict is a sign that conversation has collapsed. Much depends on sustaining meaningful conflict for the sake of a larger vision than any single interlocutor or tradition might find alone.

That very possibility is registered in the ancient but now much beleaguered Indian parable of "the blind men and elephant."[8] The fortunes of this extended allegory as a tool for thinking about diversity have been mixed; the allegory has fallen out of favor in contemporary reflection for a variety of reasons—some good, some bad. But the allegory, despite its shortcomings, remains good to think with, and, like any interesting allegory, might be read in a variety of productive ways. I believe that allegory should survive even if some of its uses are problematic.

First a fundamental concern must be raised about the tale itself. In a lecture at the Queen's Foundation for Ecumenical Theological Education, the practical theologian John M. Hull worried about how the tale depicts blindness.[9] In conventional narrations, each blind man jumps to a conclusion about the nature of the entire elephant after grasping just a part. Hull, who lost his vision in middle age, said, "This is precisely what the blind do not and cannot afford to do." Hull notes that vision as a sense gives the impression of taking in the object of sight comprehensively and instantaneously. Tactile knowing, by contrast, is incremental, patient, and must proceed deliberately.[10] Vision gives the impression of being synchronic; touch is perforce diachronic.

In conversation after his lecture, Hull explained, "If I am placed before an engraving of Joseph and Mary traveling with Jesus on a donkey, it will take me some time to make out just what it is that I am touching. Is it a horse? Is it a donkey? I could not hazard a guess all at once. I would have to proceed with care." Hull argues that, given the long schooling in the gradual ways of tactile knowing, no blind person would leap to such conclusions. Hence, this story, he says, "can only be about sighted people fumbling about an elephant in a darkened room or blindfolded sighted persons. The blind know better." Sighted persons project onto the blind what the sighted imagine about how the blind proceed, but the projection discloses only the prejudgments of the sighted. So Hull recommends that if we choose to keep telling this tale, it would be wise to retell it as one about blindfolded persons, lest we continue to mischaracterize the blind as ignorant and foolish.

Fair enough, but for the sake of metaphorical consistency, we must confront a problem with the new allegory. Why not simply take off the blindfold? Indeed. Wisdom calls us to remember that we are working provisionally and allegorically. One way to deal with the problem introduced by this contemporary riff on an ancient tale is to imagine that our blindfolded persons have forgotten that they are blindfolded. In any case, might not those who affirm that the divine is marked by an excessive "brilliant darkness" affirm that no eye, terrestrial or angelic, is equal to the divine, that no one can grasp the infinity of the divine plenitude?[11]

Still, the tale, suitably reformulated, is appealing because it gives theologians a way to imagine real diversity as a positive good. The tale begins with a king who brings together seven blindfolded men and an elephant. Each approaches the elephant from a particular direction and grasps hold of a different part of the elephant. Jeffery Long offers the following concise retelling, which I will not seek to improve:

> One grasped the ear and declared, "Elephant is like a large fan." Another grasped a leg and declared, "Elephant is like a great pillar." Another found the trunk, and feeling it, proclaimed, "Elephant is like a snake." Another grasped the tail and declared, "Elephant is like a rope hanging from the sky," while another, grasping only the tuft of the tail, said, "Elephant is like a broom." A sixth encountered the side of the elephant and maintained, "Elephant is like a wall." The seventh insisted that the others were all wrong, for he had grasped the tusk. He proclaimed, "Elephant is not any of those; elephant is like a spear." Each being certain of the truth of his own experience, they began to fight.
>
> A person who was not blindfolded chanced to come by and found them quarrelling. After listening to their individual perceptions from their different points of view, he gently explained that there was no need for fighting over the issue, for each was partially right. But to have complete knowledge of the nature of the elephant, he said, one would have to be able to be aware of and combine all the different aspects of the creature.[12]

Crucial to my reading of the tale is that each blindfolded man truly registers some aspect of the elephant and so rightly says, "It's like a rope" (tail), or "It's like a wall" (the side), and so on. The diversity of perspectives is a positive good. Each is right about what he affirms but wrong about what he denies. Error results from overreaching. Conflict arises for a variety of reasons: (1) each cannot imagine the possibility that he might be only partially in the right; (2) each, therefore, assumes that he wholly knows the whole; (3) each cannot imagine that the elephant might be a complex reality with many aspects; and (4) consequently, each one cannot imagine that the others might also be in the right in a way that does not entail that he himself is mistaken. To each blindfolded man, diversity of judgment is a sign of error. (5) Each also fails to register the limitations of the sign-concept he employs. The ear is not a fan; it is only *like* a fan. The use of "like" should serve to signal a certain tentativeness about the adequacy of words like "fan" or "rope." Yet, in the narrative there is no tentativeness among disputants. They are not much slowed down by the "like." Nonetheless, despite the inadequacy of the sign-concept, provisionally true knowledge is granted, and the seeker grasps an important feature of the elephant.

Great care must be exercised when this allegory is employed as a means for thinking about religious diversity. Perhaps the primary reason that the allegory has been dismissed as a viable tool is that the tale is told from the perspective of the sighted observer who finds the blindfolded men in conflict. Theologians such as Lesslie Newbigin note that no one can claim to stand in the position of the all-seeing passerby or king and thereby to know the whole when it comes to ultimate reality.[13] Newbigin writes,

> The story is told from the point of view of the king and his courtiers, who are not blind but can see that the blind men are unable to grasp the full reality of the elephant and are only able to get hold of part of the truth. The story is constantly told in order to neutralize the affirmation of the great religions, to suggest that they learn humility and recognize that none of them can have more than one aspect of the truth. But, of course, the real point of the story is exactly the opposite. If the king were also blind there would be no story. The story is told by the king, and it is the immensely arrogant claim of one who sees the full truth which all the world's religions are only groping after. It embodies the claim to know the full reality which relativizes all the claims of the religions and philosophies.[14]

Newbigin is right but only partly so. All, without exception, stand within some partial and limited vantage point, but the one who proposes the allegory appears to violate the constraint of particularity. Hence Bishop Newbigin levels the charge of arrogance. However, the allegory is meant only to suggest how it might be that the traditions are warranted in the claims they advance and still have something to learn from others who propound claims that seem radically incompatible. The allegory might best be understood not as a claim to secure knowledge but rather as a *pictorial hypothesis* that, if sustained, can help us to imagine how persons within various traditions can hold onto their own claims even as they learn from very different ones.[15] Read in that way, the tale does not "neutralize the affirmation of the great religions." The tale suggests that many, if not all, of these affirmations are likely to be true, even if only partly so.

There is a second reason that many dismiss the power of this tale: some readings fail to register a central point of the narrative—namely, that each blindfolded person has true, albeit partial, knowledge of the elephant. If you begin from an abstemious Kantian perspective, one that asserts that all conceptions of ultimate reality fail to access the noumenal real, if there is an opaque curtain between the phenomenon and the thing in itself, only then would you be right to conclude that no tradition's claims arrive at the real. Parity between traditions is secured by invalidating the knowledge claims advanced by each.

If you wish to make that claim, this tale is not for you. This allegory is ill-suited for Kantian readings, although it is often so misread. Contrary to the perspective imputed to the philosopher John Hick, who acknowledges his Kantian commitments, this story affirms that each blindfolded person arrives at some true knowledge of the elephant. The thing in itself is known, although not exhaustively. By extension, I posit that several religious traditions do likewise.[16] Each arrives at true knowledge of the real from some particular vantage point. Like the blindfolded men, traditions err when they overreach. When traditions, or, more accurately, thinkers within them, claim wholly to know the whole and then reject contrary claims, conversation breaks down. Diversity is dismissed.

For these reasons, this tale cannot be read as a defense of what Newbigin calls "religious agnosticism."[17] Each blindfolded man truly knows. All have knowledge but might yet learn more.

This hope for learning from religious neighbors, in their difference, is the animating impulse for this book. The core promise of religious diversity rests in interreligious learning, learning that can be both personal and social with consequences of civilizational scope. Think, for example, of the ramifications of Gandhi's learning from a variety of religious interlocutors and then the learning of Martin Luther King, Jr., from Gandhi (Chapter 6). To prepare the ground for such learning, traditions must discover resources for "the hospitality of receiving"—reasons that articulate why Christians qua Christians have much to gain from other wisdoms. While traditions have long cultivated postures of giving— taking the form of superiority claims that fund arguments for the missionary enterprise—few have cultivated reasons for believing that they have much to learn from other traditions. Religious thinkers have gone to great lengths to conceal that they always have been learning with and from others. In this historical moment, few tasks are more important for religious thinkers than this labor of finding reasons, internal to their traditions, for being receptive to religious neighbors. The allegory serves to free the mind for the possibility of such learning and, therefore, as a goad toward a posture of hospitable receptivity.

This tale also invites traditions to humility and suggests that no tradition can claim to know ultimate reality exhaustively. Indeed, thinkers *within* traditions routinely make such claims on internal grounds, especially in their apophatic modes.[18] The allegorist, therefore, need not make claim to special or comprehensive knowledge. Furthermore, the hope that the various traditions refer to the selfsame reality is a working and contested hypothesis. Traditions may, after all, be oriented to entirely different realities. Of course, every allegory falls short. In the case of religious diversity, the point must be readily granted: there are no omniscient knowers.

A third problem with this tale is that the elephant is silent. The elephant seems incapable of communicating anything about its nature to the blindfolded men.[19] But at the heart of the various religious traditions are claims of revelation: ultimate reality discloses itself to human beings. It does not stand by as seekers paw at it. Many thinkers within these traditions insist that elephant *must* communicate if it is to be known: all efforts on the part of human beings will fall short apart from divine self-communication because of human limitation or sinfulness. At this point, the promise of the tale is at risk because thinkers within traditions often insist that the elephant has disclosed itself exhaustively to them. That is why they are wholly in the right whereas others are mistaken or at best partially true.

Such claims for plenary revelation lead some philosophers to reject appeals to revelation altogether. When claims to comprehensive knowledge are grounded in appeals to revelation (e.g., you cannot be in the right because God has disclosed Godself exhaustively to me), intractable conflict seems inevitable, and diversity of perspectives is reduced to evidence of error. Might there be some way to insist that the elephant does communicate without also claiming that the elephant has made itself known entirely and only to just one religious community? Must we dismiss claims to revelation in order to generate epistemological parity among traditions?

Other strategies are available—strategies that affirm revelation without disabling the possibility of interreligious learning. A variety of theological strategies in the modern and postmodern period do just that. Paul Tillich, for example, contends that the mystery discloses itself as mystery. Revelation neither removes nor eliminates mystery because then what is revealed is no mystery but a mere puzzle.[20] One can affirm that revelation grants genuine knowledge but without asserting that it affords exhaustive knowledge. When such strategies are deployed, we can allow that the elephant does speak but still preserve the power of allegory.

A fourth problem with certain readings of the allegory is that no tradition is like an isolated blindfolded person who holds only one position on the elephant. Each tradition is a long-standing, historical, and ongoing run at the elephant. Contrary to the way in which religious traditions are far too frequently characterized in theological discourse, no tradition is a singular interpretive scheme—a point I make in Chapter 5. Each tradition houses multiple interpretive schemes. As such, there is no single Christian reading of the elephant and no one Buddhist reading either. Contrary to custodians of orthodoxy within each tradition who assert that their dogmatic stance stands in for the entire tradition, historically and contextually sensitive readings demonstrate that every tradition is polydox in character.[21] No tradition affords a single perspective and hence cannot, strictly speaking, be compared to an isolated blindfolded person.

Moreover, each and every tradition has come to be what it is through conversation with others. As Abraham Joshua Heschel wisely noted, "No religion is an island." Theologians have yet to appreciate his claim that "the religions of the world are no more self-sufficient, no more independent, no more isolated than individuals or nations. Energies, experiences and ideas that come to life outside the boundaries of a particular religion or all religions continue to challenge and to affect every religion."[22] Hence, multiplicity is embedded in every tradition, not least because each has been formed by its interactions with others. Therefore, no tradition and no person within a tradition can be imagined as standing in just one location alone. To reject omniscience is to not foreclose on the promise of multiple angles of vision. The simplest way to manufacture conflict between traditions is to eliminate from view their rich internal multiplicity. Only then can traditions be understood to stand in stark opposition. If you make the whole of a Western tradition stand in for transcendence and an entire Eastern tradition stand in for immanence, then, of course, conflict will seem intractable.[23]

A fifth problem has to do with the nature of the relationship between the blindfolded men and the elephant. In the allegory, the blindfolded men are external to the elephant. In conversations about ultimate reality/ies, matters are more complex. Panentheism, pantheism, and nondualism all disrupt the notion that human beings stand over against ultimate reality. On these accounts—and here I extend the allegory in unpardonable fashion—one may be inside the elephant or even just be the elephant. Only the flattest forms of theism, which take ultimate reality to stand in discrete and spatial transcendence to the world and humanity, conform to the pictorial logic of this allegory.

Do these many qualifications vitiate the allegorical promise of the tale of the blindfolded men and the elephant? I think not. The tale stands because, these qualifications notwithstanding, it still manages to propel thought along a trajectory that can recognize diversity as a positive good. Although no tradition is fixed, singular, and homogeneous, nonetheless, persons within a tradition typically think by means of this particular vocabulary rather than that, this set of practices and not that, and this set of conceptual tools rather than the other. The tale reminds us that there is considerable promise in learning to think about ultimate reality by way of conversation with other blindfolded persons, other valid, albeit partial, perspectives on ultimate reality.

This book is a *Christian* exercise in pachyderm perambulation. Recognizing that there is no omniscient king or passerby who can tell us what the elephant is, this book calls for interreligious circumnavigation. As one walks around the elephant, the Christian qua Christian begins to make a guess at what she is seeing. The categories we use to formulate our hypothesis are necessarily Christian. In my case, these categories are trinitarian. However, the categories and the vision they seek to articulate are transformed in the very process of circumnavigation. I not only hope to add to the wisdom I have, but I stand prepared to revise my tradition's wisdom and categories in light of newly acquired knowledge. This process is complex, multidirectional, fluid, subject to revision, and always unfinished.

As I walk around the elephant with the guidance of others and learn from them (*comparative theology*), I retain elements of my warranted belief that the elephant is like a giant fan, but I am prepared to supplement that belief as necessary. I see now that others' judgments are also warranted. That recognition compels me to revise my initial account of other elephant surveyors and their claims (*theology of religious diversity*).[24] As I begin to recognize the validity and truth of other accounts of the elephant, I acknowledge that my account of ultimate reality, as first formulated, was partial even if that knowledge was granted to me by way of revelation. I am compelled to recognize that my earlier account of ultimate reality stands in need of revision (*constructive theology*). When others told me that I was mistaken to say that the elephant was a fan, they were right even though they were wrong to dismiss the truth of my position. There are good grounds to hold that my neighbors can often see me not only better than I can myself, but they are sometimes in a position to discern the limitations of my seeing. Now, I can also see how they came to believe that the elephant was a rope.

Here, I pause to register my reasons for speaking of "theology of religious diversity" (TRD) when referring to the subfield that seeks to make theological sense of the meaning of religious difference. The customary term, "theology of religions," risks taking the term "religion" for granted—something I refuse to do. On the other hand, the newer term, "theology of religious pluralism," is incurably ambiguous as the term "pluralism" is routinely employed in three distinct ways: (a) "religious pluralism" is sometimes employed as a synonym for "religious diversity" (e.g., "the world is marked by religious pluralism"); (b) "theology of religious pluralism" sometimes stands in as the name for the entire subfield within theology which assesses the meaning of religious diversity; and (c) "pluralism" is also used as the name for one set of options within that subfield, the one which posits parity between religious traditions. Given these multiple usages, confusion is inevitable. The term "theology of religious diversity" should, therefore, be the preferred term for that project that seeks to make theological sense of the reality and meaning of religious diversity.

One final word about the limits of this allegory and my use of it: thoughtful readers are sure to recognize that a battery of epistemological questions might be posed, questions that appear to threaten the easy promise of the tale. Put simply, human beings may not be able to shift perspectives on ultimate reality as easily as blindfolded persons can circumnavigate the elephant. Traditions hold that religious knowledge is made possible only by taking up specific practices that are written into the bodies of practitioners. We know because we are enabled to know by means of the therapeutic regimen we follow. Hence, it is no simple matter to be formed otherwise so as to know otherwise. Given the intimate connection between practices of knowing and religious knowledge, some also raise questions about whether we not only see the world as we take it to be (an uncontroversial claim) but also partially constitute the world by our modes of knowing. John Hick's appeal to the wave-particle duality of light and his observation that what we see is determined by the apparatus we bring to bear is the most telling instance of how our ways of knowing may shape what we take ultimate reality to be.[25] In any case, there is no way of standing outside of all such particular accounts to check on their relative merits from some neutral vantage point.

Several complex responses to these challenges can be offered, none of which entails recourse to epistemological naivete. One can appeal, for instance, to some mode of critical realism that suggests that the world is rich enough to speak back to and so correct the perspectives we bring to bear on our world interpretations. Moreover, without underestimating the difficulty of bearing out such a claim, as I have already been suggesting, our world interpretations are neither impermeable nor monolithic. They are porous to and revisable by the real and by other traditions. Our traditions and our worldviews are neither like clothing that we don and doff at will nor straightjackets into which we are forcibly bound.

In any case, the allegory itself does not make appeal to a flat objectivity. It suggests only that we are not locked into monocular vision. Persons can and routinely do learn to see the world otherwise; they can learn to see the world, at least to some extent, as others see the world and thereby acquire what might be called binocular vision—the capacity to see the world through more than one set of lenses and be enriched. The empirical reality of multiple religious participation and multireligious identity demonstrates as much. If such multiplicity is possible, then we can hope to correct for and revise our interpretations of the world by appealing to other interpretations thereof. We need only open the door to that possibility to see how we can learn from and with persons of other religious traditions. Such interreligious learning is the promise of religious diversity.

## The Itinerary for Our Journey

The coming chapter expands on this highly compressed allegorical account by describing the relationship between theology of religious diversity (TRD), comparative theology (CT), and constructive theology. In terms of my pachyderm imagery, theology of religious diversity is the religion-specific work of giving an account of other elephant surveyors and the status of their claims about the elephant. What do they say about the elephant, and what should we make of their claims? Comparative theology is the detailed, slow, partial, and patient work of elephant circumnavigation. It is the labor of learning with and from persons who stand on some other side of the elephant than our own. Constructive theology is the work of generating revised accounts of the elephant and our relationship to it in light of what has been learned by way of TRD and CT. The goal of the book as a whole is to show that these three projects can and must be integrated. The book shows how this might be done. It also offers a sustained analysis of obstacles that have thus far prevented such integration.

This chapter also invites readers into an alternative starting point or stance for examining religious diversity. Might not prejudices built into an inquiry's beginnings predetermine the outcome? If so, it stands to reason that if we begin by taking religious diversity to be a problem to be resolved rather than as a promise to be celebrated, the tenor and conclusions of the theological project are sure to be constrained by such assumptions. Certain options will be foreclosed, and we will walk the path wishing that the world were otherwise, that this problem did not belabor and beleaguer us from the first.

Chapters 2 and 3 introduce and assess theologies of religious diversity, albeit in a new key. To date, most theologies of religious diversity have been preoccupied by questions of soteriology and parity. The driving goal has been to determine which TRD can most vigorously affirm the saving presence of God outside the Christian tradition. With respect to parity, the driving concern has been the desire to affirm that many, though not all, religious traditions are *equally* salvific and truth-bearing. Theologies of religious diversity are mapped on a sliding scale from those that are most soteriologically restrictive and least willing to affirm parity to those that are most optimistic on questions of salvation and religious parity. These are not the goals that drive my presentation of TRD.

My concern is whether any particular TRD can offer compelling reasons for interreligious learning. I hold that some varieties of pluralism appear to make such learning neither possible nor necessary, and quite surprisingly, some recent exclusivist positions leave room for interreligious learning. To the degree that any given TRD recognizes interreligious learning as possible and commendable, then that TRD is not without some merit. We might find it wanting for other reasons, but we can celebrate the promise of such theologies for opening the door to interreligious learning for traditionalist religious communities. Questions will remain about whether the possibility of interreligious learning is only begrudgingly acknowledged. My hope is for a robust TRD that celebrates diversity and hence interreligious learning as positive goods. I offer just such a trinitarian theology of religious diversity in Chapter 7. Chapter 3 also builds to a notion of "relational pluralism" that seems closest to my own position.[26]

A recurrent theme in Chapters 2 and 3 is that on every occasion that a particular TRD stops short of making room for interreligious learning or actively opposes such learning, without fail, indefensible assumptions about religion and the religions are at play. Sometimes these assumptions function in the background, but quite often, they are explicitly articulated and defended. Where do these theoretical accounts come from? What are their sources? Chapter 4 answers those questions by presenting a survey of genealogical investigations of the category religion. This literature raises concerns about the way in which the category "religions" bears troubling similarities with the notion of "races." This unsettling resonance should make us worry about discourses developed to engage difference by means of these categories—namely, "theology of religions" and race relations theory. Just as talk about race relations presupposes and reinforces the notion that race is biologically or ontologically real, talk about "religions" and "interreligious dialogue" can function in like manner. It, too, can give the impression that there are real, impermeable boundaries between religions and thereby obscure from vision the constructed nature of the border lines between traditions. By contrast, interreligious learning and mutual transformation are only possible if traditions are porous, permeable, and perpetually fluid realities. Unfortunately, too much talk about "religions" is marked by reification and not porosity.

Chapter 4 demonstrates that we have not always thought of the world as divided into a set of seven or eight impermeable world religions along with several lesser primal or local religions. With Talal Asad, Arvind Mandair, Tomoko Masuzawa, and others, I believe that it is impossible to think of "religion" in our modern and contemporary sense apart from the invention of its companion contrast term—namely, "the secular." These terms co-arise. The invention of religion is simultaneously the invention of the secular and vice versa. An examination of this narrative shows just how recent, how problematic, and how contestable our bounded conception of religion is.

We then proceed to examine how our conception of "religion" is carried over into what "the religions" are. Of fundamental interest with respect to this genealogy of "religion" and "religions" is how both concepts function in the construction of identity. Having defined multiple spheres of Western life as secular and hence not "religious," and then defining the religions as clearly demarcated and reified entities, our customary modes of discourse assume that singular religious identity is the norm and that religious multiplicity is an aberration. Our configuration of the category "religions" tutors us to imagine that we live within a prison house of bounded homogeneity and face radical incommensurability only when we step outside our religion.

Chapter 5 offers definitions of "religion" and "the religions" that are meant to disrupt reifications that impede interreligious learning. My definitions are tutored but not hemmed in by a genealogical sensibility. Yes, every definition is a product and intervention in social processes, but that does not mean we should simply refrain from offering new definitions. I offer a stipulative definition of *the religious* as the work of comprehensive qualitative orientation. I argue that comprehensive qualitative orientation is a cross-cultural constant even though the organization of sociocultural space into religious and secular realms is not. Not all cultures have religions, but all take up the work of comprehensive qualitative orientation.

The religious, so understood, cannot be contained within the religions even in those secular societies that invent and strive to cordon off privatized religions from the public domain. For example, neoliberal visions of capitalism and their confidence in the power of the market as the sole effective means to secure a prosperous human future are most assuredly religious in character. If that is true, then every Christian living in a capitalist society is already religiously multiple; no one can escape the market's capacity to tutor desires by means of its therapeutic regimes. Religious multiplicity doesn't appear on the scene only when a Christian turns to Buddhist or Hindu practices.

Once our reified, static, impermeable, and monolithic configurations of the religious and the religions are disrupted, many conceptual hindrances to interreligious learning will have been removed. Removing hindrances is all well and good, but the theologian must also offer *positive resources* for openhearted learning. I do just that in Chapter 6 by calling for the "hospitality of receiving." Building on the work of Mohandas Gandhi and Martin Luther King, Jr., two of the twentieth century's exemplary interreligious learners, I argue that if Christians are to exercise a virtue that lies at the core of Christian tradition—namely, hospitality—we must be prepared to receive as well as to give. So argued Gandhi, who found this virtue missing in most missionaries with whom he interacted.

When such receptivity is exercised, profound theological and even large-scale social transformation may come to pass, which is what transpired when King and others set out to learn from Gandhi. The nonviolent Civil Rights Movement of the 1950s and 1960s was a major moment in the history of interreligious receptivity and a vivid enactment of the promise of religious diversity. In sum, this chapter contends that the work of receiving wisdom from other religious traditions is not novel and has already proved to be of great significance for Christian life and the culture at large.

Having set forth a conception of the religious and religions that makes comparative theology integral to the work of constructive theology, I offer in Chapter 7 a brief exercise in Hindu-Christian-Buddhist trialogue on the way toward generating a new trinitarian theology of religious diversity. Through this exercise in comparative theology, three distinctive conceptions of ultimacy emerge—namely, ground, singularity, and relation. Closer examination suggests that these different conceptions of ultimacy show up *within* traditions and not just *across* them.

Very quickly, this exercise becomes not just a conversation across traditions but also within them. An account of ultimate reality as transpersonal ground is especially prominent in Hindu Advaita, but also emerges in some positive accounts of Buddha-nature as an infinite and bottomless resource for compassion. In Christian traditions, God is construed not only as being-itself, and hence as transpersonal ground, but also as creative source of the world of *singularity*. Such accounts posit a distinction between the source and the world that is sourced, a difference that undergirds personal theologies of God as an Other, as One who is the source, evocation, and object of desire. By contrast, Madhyamikas refuse accounts of ultimate reality as transpersonal ground or personal source but instead speak of ultimate reality as emptiness (*sunyata*) understood as *relation* (*pratityasamutpada*). Ultimate reality is neither an eternal and immutable world ground nor a world creator. Indeed, ultimate reality is not an absolute of any sort but the very denial of absoluteness. Nothing whatsoever exists apart from relation, and it is relation that is the ungrounded medium of compassion. On this account, ultimate reality is neither personal nor transpersonal and so cannot be designated as either. In what is likely the most distinctive account of ultimate reality available in any of the world's religious traditions, ultimacy is just conventional reality rightly understood as relation.

I draw upon these three accounts of ultimate reality as ground, singularity, and relation to shed new light on trinitarian discourse. I show how Christian theology can receive and be transformed by these resources from non-Christian traditions. This discussion refuses to gloss over the different ways in which various traditions and the strands within them describe ultimate reality. Nor do I assume that these differences are due solely to culturally variant points of origin. Ultimate reality is understood differently across traditions because these differences are rooted in the divine life itself. Ultimate reality, like the elephant, is complex. We experience ultimate reality diversely because ultimate reality is marked by multiplicity.

The promise of drawing intimate connections between comparative theology, theologies of religious diversity, and constructive trinitarian theology is considerable. On the one hand, such comparative theology can contribute to a TRD that refuses both underlying sameness (all traditions point to the same ultimately inaccessible reality) and radical incommensurability (differences between traditions are so sharp that they point to different ultimate realities). Moreover, a trinitarian TRD can take seriously the differences between traditions and within them; we differ not simply because of culture, biology, or biography but because ultimate reality is itself internally differentiated. It is no simple matter to determine just how these different religious accounts hang together, but a trinitarian account gives reasons for confidence that such coherence or co-inherence is possible.

This trinitarian TRD can also account for how multiple religious participation can afford access to dimensions of ultimate reality that are inaccessible through dominant practices found within one's own home tradition. Vipassana and Zen are not the same as Christian prayer; each aims at and grants access to dimensions of ultimate reality that are not well attended to in mainstream Christian traditions. Some such account is surely preferable to perennialist philosophies that cannot say much about why differences between forms of practice may be religiously and even ontologically significant.

Finally, this interchange between theology of religious diversity, comparative theology, and constructive theology can help Christian theologians to appreciate the promise of comparative theology for Christian theology, thereby diminishing what still appears to be a stubborn divide between comparative theology and systematic/constructive theology which restricts itself to Christian sources, traditions, and norms alone. Indeed, the result is an integration of three intellectual projects that yields a constructive trinitarian comparative theology of religious diversity.

Chapter 8 draws what may be the most significant learning from this entire project: interreligious learning is holy labor. There is no moving toward God that is not also a movement toward one's neighbors and our neighbors' wisdom. Indeed, we need our neighbors' religious traditions even to understand our own. We must practice the hospitality of receiving if we are to understand each other, ourselves, and if we are to move into the very life of God.

# 1 Religious Difference and Christian Theology

## THINKING ABOUT, THINKING WITH, AND THINKING THROUGH

*Only on the wide basis of universal revelation could the final revelation occur and be received. Without the symbols created by universal revelation the final revelation would not be understandable. Without the religious experiences created by universal revelation no categories and forms would exist to receive the final revelation. The biblical terminology is full of words whose meaning and connotations would be completely strange to listeners and readers if there had been no preceding revelations in Judaism as well as in paganism.*

—PAUL TILLICH, *Systematic Theology, Vol. I*

### Should Religious Diversity Be a "Problem" for Christians?

This book sets out to answer a single overarching question: How can Christian communities and Christian theology best flourish in a world marked by deep and enduring religious difference? What must transpire in Christian imagination to ensure that positive engagement with religious difference is recognized as essential to and constitutive of constructive theology? Just as no one imagines that a systematic project that fails to address Christology, pneumatology, or soteriology is adequate, theological labor that fails to address the question of religious diversity is partial at best, and negligent at worst. At present, specialist theologians engage in the work of theology of religious diversity (TRD) and comparative theology (CT), but those tasks are understood as optional rather than integral to Christian theology. The joke seems to be that comparative theologians are only comparatively theological. Comparison is understood to belong to the descriptive labor of religious studies whereas the normative work of constructive theology is expected to operate from resources drawn from within the boundaries of a single tradition alone. Such boundedness is even taken to be the hallmark of theology: philosophy of religion can be universal, but theology must be confessional and particular. The philosopher of religion is the free-range chicken who can wander about and eat what she wants; the theologian, by contrast, must live and eat within the coop of tradition. Hence, the term "comparative theology" seems oxymoronic. If a project is comparative, it cannot be theology; if a project is theological, it must not be comparative. That sensibility is changing, but slowly.

Moreover, when Christians engage the theme of religious diversity, that labor is often framed as a problem to be solved rather than as a promise to be fulfilled. The prompting impulse is rarely a sense of hopeful expectation that Christians have much to learn from their religious neighbors but is instead motivated by a feeling of unease about the recalcitrant persistence of religious diversity. Difference seems to weaken the "plausibility structures" that might otherwise make one's own faith seem like the only game in town.[1]

Consider the subtitle of a volume that appears to betray a longing for another world than the one we have—namely, Gerald McDermott's *God's Rivals: Why Has God Allowed Different Religions?*[2] Although McDermott intends to take religious diversity seriously and positively—and I argue below that he succeeds in some important ways—the question posed by his subtitle suggests that God not only might have created a world devoid of religious diversity but that some wish He—and only a hypermasculine deity can be imagined to wield such controlling omnipotence—had.[3] Theology and, surely, life itself would have been simpler. The cast of the question is a telling instance of what it means to frame religious diversity as problem rather than as promise.

Imagine how non-Christian readers might read McDermott's subtitle. Might not a Hindu or a Buddhist wonder, "Is the author really asking why the Christian God permits my tradition to exist? Is my very existence a problem for Christian life and thought?" I am reminded of W. E. B. Du Bois's question about the tragic nature of black experience in the American context: "How does it feel to be a problem?"[4] I draw no flat parallel between the violence of black life in America and the challenges posed by religious diversity, but only a massive case of historical amnesia could lead Christians to forget the degree to which we have sought by way of conquest, colonization, and conversion to dissolve the problem of religious diversity by erasing it. A long and tortured history teaches us that no group fares well when it is treated as a problem in need of a solution.

By contrast, to think of religious diversity as a de jure and not merely a de facto good is to imagine with Abraham Joshua Heschel that "in this aeon diversity of religions is the will of God." Rather than imagine the divine as reluctantly permitting religious others to be, can we imagine instead a God who seeks to be known in, through, and by way of difference and multiplicity? Such an imagination empowers Christians not to regard religious diversity begrudgingly as a reality that must be navigated but as a promise to be received. When we affirm that we need the other in order to arrive at God, we affirm not only an *ethical* obligation to, and need for, the neighbor but also a *theological* desire for her. Religious neighbors must be hallowed because we need them to arrive at a deeper encounter with and understanding of divinity. The practices and insights of others can even, in some cases, become sacraments for our way into the divine life, earthy mediations that enable us to access the more.

Can we imagine constructive reflection that begins with just such a sense of promise and expectation, a theological vision in which religious diversity is celebrated rather than reluctantly accepted? Can we imagine theological systems in which every loci within Christian theology is treated with an eye to difference—projects in which Christology is done in conversation with Buddhology and the doctrine of God is formulated in conversation with accounts of ultimate reality as Brahman or Buddha-nature?[5] What must happen for such modes of theological practice to be recognized as "normal science" rather than as an elective and fringe exercise?[6] Must we usher into being an entirely new theological paradigm before construction and comparison can be understood as inseparable?

The reality of religious diversity has impinged upon Christian communities from the inception of the Jesus movement. In the earliest stages of that movement, Jewish followers of Jesus were just a small and fragile community in a sea of religious difference. In that historical moment, and for several subsequent centuries, the labor of constructing the Christian tradition required explicit and ongoing conversation with a variety of communities and traditions. Christians rarely pause to reflect on the meaning of an obvious truth: every intellectual resource for articulating the meaning of the Christ event came from the non-Christian milieu in which Jesus followers sought to understand the meaning of the life, death, and resurrection of the one whom they called Lord. The only distinguishing mark of the early Jesus movement was its peculiar insistence that Jesus the crucified was the Messiah. Everything else was inherited or borrowed. Christian tradition is, *ab initio*, "a hybrid affair."[7]

This hybridity is not merely a matter of cultural significance; it has theological import. As Paul Tillich observed, apart from the language, symbols, rituals, and metaphysical resources of other traditions, Christians would lack the means to articulate their distinctive convictions. Even the core narratives of the New Testament are products of conversations with a dizzying array of extra-Christian religious resources, most obviously the inheritance of Ancient Israel, the various mystery religions, Hellenistic philosophical schools and, of course, the implicit patterns of sense and meaning-making embedded in the Greek language itself. To learn to think Christianly required thinking with, and sometimes against, those who were not part of the church to such an extent that it is impossible to draw neat lines between "internal" and "external." What could these terms mean in a period in which tradition itself was under construction?

Tillich was clear about the meaning of Christianity's indebtedness to other religious traditions: the Christ event and our capacity to receive the meaning of that event stand in need of a larger history of revelation that prepares the ground for the coming of the New Being. For Tillich, Christian life and thought stand in *theological* debt to the religious history that precedes and makes possible the Christ event. As he put it, final revelation requires and presupposes universal revelation.[8] In sum, Christian reflection cannot proceed without the help of non-Christians. For these reasons, it seems a truism to say that constructive theology was, for the first four centuries of the church, also comparative theology. Perhaps, then, we do not need to create a new theological paradigm. We need only to discern how what once was seen as integral to theology came to be regarded as optional, or worse, as superfluous.

A critical question is whether other traditions continue to have positive meaning for themselves and for Christian communities *after the Christ event and the establishment of the church*. Or does "final revelation" supplant universal revelation? Do Christians still stand in ongoing need of other religious traditions? Do other religious traditions continue to have a place in the divine economy even after the coming of the Christ?

Answering these questions with a decisive yes—and in that sense leaving behind the long-standing *praeparatio evangelica* tradition—is a central goal of this book.

Over time, especially after Constantine's conversion, Christian communities came to understand themselves as a separate imperially sponsored religious tradition. Recognition by empire was taken to be divine vindication of Christianity's superiority. Eventually, the border lines between Christianity and its others were understood to be clearly demarcated, giving rise to the possibility of a reflective process that proceeds by appeal to a body of materials—scripture, creeds, and the writings of the church fathers—internal to an independent and self-standing tradition.[9] Only then does it become possible to imagine theological reflection as an activity that proceeds without borrowing from and being indebted to larger groups of religiously diverse interlocutors, a process that remains a vital need even today.

A part of this process of tradition constitution is the willful forgetting of the internal multiplicity of our texts, a peculiar (un)learned ignorance which obscures the truth that virtually every line in scripture and the foundational texts of tradition are meaningful only when understood as part of an interreligious conversational matrix in which they came to have meaning at all. When these texts are further secured by claims to special revelation—claims that sever Christian traditions from the broader history of divine revelation—then conditions are in place to imagine that Christian theology can operate by appeal to a deposit of faith that is in no way indebted to religious neighbors.

After imperial recognition, Christians, at least in the West, were rarely compelled to encounter persons from other traditions on a level playing field. Christianity's religious others lacked the prestige that accrues to a tradition by way of political patronage. This is not to say that Christian traditions were impervious to a variety of philosophical and religious traditions. Far from it! A careful exploration of Christian traditions would reveal a steady stream of moments in which Christian thinkers were shaped by encounters with a variety of non-Christian interlocutors—Jews and eventually Muslims, but also with the "discovery" of the New World, the various indigenous traditions of North and South America. Even the variety within European Christianities shows that there has never been a singular and pristine Christianity without admixture. "Pagan" traditions have always shaped the ritual lives and theological sensibilities of every local form of Christianity.[10]

The history of Christian theology can be read as a sustained conversation with a variety of non-Christian philosophical traditions starting with Greek and Hellenistic thinkers, the reintroduction of Aristotle in the medieval period by way of encounter with Islamic tradition, and subsequently the secular philosophical traditions of the Enlightenment. The history of Christian reflection is incomprehensible apart from its philosophical conversation partners. It is unclear why contemporaries do not recognize this conversation, especially early engagements with pagan thinkers, as part of the history of interreligious encounter. Much rests on which traditions are regarded as "religious" as opposed to "philosophical." Perhaps it is safer to think of pagan wisdom traditions as narrowly philosophical rather than as religious because their reception into Christian traditions need not then be recognized as itself a kind of religious hybridization.

Unfortunately, it is anachronistic in the extreme to suppose that there was a neat separation between philosophy and religion in antiquity. Early Christian teachers often styled themselves as philosophers and their communities as philosophical schools. Also, as Pierre Hadot has shown, ancient philosophical schools are better understood as "ways of life" rather than the desiccated exercises in technical reason that sometimes pass for philosophy today.[11] The failure to appreciate the porosity between philosophy and religion, generated by an unwillingness to see Christian traditions as hybrid and polydox, gives the impression that interreligious encounter and comparative theology are new realities for the church.[12] So much depends on what counts as a "religion."

There have been moments in the history of European Christianity in which encounters with religious others have been especially jarring. The voyages of exploration and the "discovery" of the New World administered a shock to the theological system. Theologians were compelled to ask, "What does it mean that so many in so much of the world have had no access to saving knowledge of the Christ?" What, then, of the traditional Christian affirmation that God desires to save all, that God so loves the world, if much of that world has lived apart from the saving knowledge of the Christ?

The periodic eruption of these questions notwithstanding, it is hard to detect in premodern Christian theology reflection that dares to imagine that other "religions" might themselves be vehicles of salvific divine agency. That way of framing soteriological questions is hardly possible in historical periods that did not construe the world as composed of a

delimited set of religions that might or might not be salvific. When soteriological questions were posed about those "outside the church," they
were framed within another imaginative matrix, one in which the crucial questions were about how the Word or the Spirit operates upon those
who are not followers of the Christ. And when questions were raised
about the status of other traditions, they were not yet understood as religions in any contemporary sense. Few have thought to examine the
metamorphosis of soteriology when it falls under the influence of the
modern category "religion." There is a vast difference between asking
about whether the word in seed form (*logos spermatikos*) or the Holy
Spirit is present to other communities and quite another to ask about
whether something called a "religion" is salvific.

Even today, the idea that other religions may be, on their own terms,
salvific remains contested. But the question "Do other religions save?" is
recognized as self-evidently meaningful; liberals offer various affirmative answers against theological conservatives who say no. However, the
question only became meaningful in the late nineteenth century, after
the establishment of a "world religions discourse."[13] But just what is a "religion" anyway? Does any religion, even Christianity, save?

Aren't liberals and conservatives buying into a broad range of assumptions that make the very terms of their contestation possible? What do
we presume when we classify Hinduism, Buddhism, Judaism, and Christianity as "religions" and each of these religions as ways to salvation?
These questions are rarely posed and when posed are often treated with
insufficient rigor. Thankfully, a growing chorus of voices is slowing down
the conversation in theology of religions to pose these critical queries.
The work of thinkers like Jenny Daggers and Paul Hedges and their interrogations of the category "religion" are important landmarks.[14] With
them, I am mindful that by the time we rank-order religions with respect
to their relative soteriological merit—whether we argue for the superiority of our own or the relative parity of all in properly pluralist fashion—
we have taken for granted the work of "religion-making," which renders
these traditions into religions, into entities of the same kind.[15]

It is time to interrogate these processes of religion-making because
theology has been impeded by the ways in which we have imagined religion. Any theology of religious diversity that envisions religions as hermetically sealed, tightly integrated conceptual and soteriological systems
is mistaken and so bound to go awry. That's just not what religious traditions are. Working within such a broken conceptual framework is sure

to raise more problems than it resolves. Our traditions are porous and constituted by their interactions with others. Imagining religions as reified entities that can be weighed for their relative soteriological merit or for their truth potential is a curious proposition. Just how does one weigh religions? On what scale? Don't Christians have grave reservations even about their coreligionists on matters of truth and salvation? Does Christianity save? If so, which Christianity? The Christianity of the crusaders, the Christianity of Dorothy Day, or, to be more disruptive still, the Christianity of Mohandas Gandhi?

Often unmindful of these questions, a robust literature has emerged, variously called theology of religions or theology of religious pluralism. Virtually all of this literature emerged after World War II.[16] The various independence movements in which Western colonial incursions were pushed back and the subsequent migration of formerly colonized peoples into the heart of the metropole have generated a situation in which Christianity is once again becoming just one tradition among many, but now without the questionable prestige that comes from imperial support. One consequence of the world wars and the various independence movements is the fraying of a cultural imaginary in which Christianity is taken to be the self-evidently superior religion of the paramount culture. In our time, Hegelian narratives that depict Western cultures and nations as standing at the apex of human cultural evolution seem incredible. Those evolutionary narratives were themselves strategies to contain the disruptive power of a serious encounter with religious traditions of great antiquity and intellectual power. The weaving of these tales was arguably integral to the constitution of many forms of Western modernity.[17]

Such constructions have not disappeared: a variety of secular thinkers and Christian theologians continue to advance metanarratives in which some Western cultural formation or Christianity itself is regarded as the sole hope for the human future, the sole hope for genuine peace. Whether that narrative is a secular deliverance of political science—Huntington's clash of civilizations rhetoric—or a theological claim that Christianity is the sole religion that is capable of imagining difference peaceably—the claim made by John Milbank's radical orthodoxy—ours is a time in which these attempts to build walls against difference smack of a reactionary nostalgia.[18]

Christians in the West have had to face up to the reality of their postcolonial and post-Constantinian situation for only six decades or so. It is no coincidence that these decades have witnessed the growth of a theological literature dedicated to questions about the meaning of religious diversity for Christian faith. Beginning with the ground-breaking proclamations of Vatican II, Christian theologians in the West have been compelled to give accounts of the meaning of religious diversity in a world in which it is no longer possible to imagine that Christianity will eventually replace other religious traditions. What to make of those religious traditions thus becomes a fundamental theological challenge.

The task of Christian theology in this moment of cultural flux is to imagine theologies that make it possible for the faithful to conceive of religious diversity as promise rather than problem, as resource rather than as rupture. Having arrived at a historical moment that is similar to the pre-Constantinian period, can theologians come to see that any credible theology must go about its business in sustained conversation with other religious traditions?[19] Can we imagine theologies that see religious traditions as standing in positive need of each other, even to accomplish their own distinctive goods? This book aims at precisely that task: to track a path toward a speculative trinitarian theology of religious diversity that offers robust reasons for believing that we need not only our neighbors but also their traditions if we are to move more fully into the life of God.

We are once again in a historical moment in which it will be impossible to separate constructive theology from comparative theology. To understand the meaning of Christian faith in our time, we will have to think with the theological resources of other traditions. In a social milieu in which the credibility and intelligibility of Christian discourse will require discerning just what Christian claims and practices mean in relationship with and in contradistinction to the broader interreligious milieu, comparative theology will, once again, have to become a constitutive part of the work of constructive theology. Moreover, our theologies of religious diversity, too, will have to be worked out in collaboration with persons from other traditions. It will not do to speculate about the truth and salvific efficacy of other traditions apart from sustained relationship and conversation with persons from those traditions. Only a "relational pluralism" in which the salvific power of our various traditions are mobilized and animated through relationship and mutual transformation can serve as an adequate foundation for a theology of religious diversity.

## Christian Theological Engagements
## with Religious Diversity

What is the state of Christian theological engagement with religious diversity at this historical moment? Christian theological writing about religious diversity has largely coalesced in the North American context into two distinct subfields: theology of religions/theologies of religious pluralism and comparative theology.[20]

Christian theology of religious diversity asks about the presence of truth and saving power in non-Christian traditions. Exclusivist theologies hold that other traditions, regardless of their venerable history, intellectual sophistication, and ethical power, do not save and are not finally true.[21] Other Christian theologians and their communities wonder whether religious diversity might be part of the divine providence, and if so, what that might mean for how Christians ought to think about the meaning of the Christ event itself. Are other religious traditions salvific because Christ or the Holy Spirit is present in some hidden way in those traditions (inclusivists), or are other religious traditions independently efficacious paths to the divine (pluralists)? These are the sorts of questions that theologians of religious diversity take up.

Comparative theology takes itself to be a very different enterprise. Comparative theology is constructive reflection that aims at religious truth by learning from the resources of more than one tradition. If Christian TRD is the work of thinking *about* religious others in light of Christian faith, comparative theology is theology *with* religious others, even when the theologian is working alone in her study reading the scriptures of a tradition other than her own. Although the comparative theologian is usually, but not necessarily, rooted in one home tradition, she does not imagine that her tradition is alone in having thought about normative questions regarding the nature of ultimate reality, the human condition, and the prospects for human fulfillment. Comparative theologians believe that we can learn *more and better* by learning *from and with* theologians and their analogues in other religious traditions. The hallmark of CT is attention to detail. Generally eschewing questions about religious diversity as such, the comparative theologian attends to specific thinkers and texts rather than attempting the impossible task of comparing traditions in their entirety.

As these fields have developed over the last several decades, new questions have arisen about the nature and prospects of TRD and comparative theology. While some theologians argue that TRD and comparative theology can be pursued independently, the comparative theologian James Fredericks argued in 1999 and 2004 that comparative theology must replace and supersede TRD. He maintained that we simply do not know enough about other traditions to venture sweeping claims about the nature and meaning of religious diversity. Fredericks also argued that every then available theology of religious diversity had serious problems. Finally, Fredericks argued that engaging in the intra-Christian debate about formulating a proper TRD keeps Christians talking among themselves rather than with neighbors of other faiths.[22] Francis X. Clooney, S.J., one of the founders of comparative theology in its contemporary incarnation, also evinces little enthusiasm for theoretical questions about the relationship between TRD and comparative theology because he, too, is eager for theologians to get about the business of interreligious learning.

Despite Fredericks's brief on behalf of comparative theology as an alternative to theologies of religious diversity, the latter discipline continues to be marked by considerable productivity. Indeed, the pendulum has now swung in the other direction as theologians of religious diversity like Kristin Kiblinger have convincingly demonstrated that every comparative theology presupposes and is guided by at least some implicit theology of religious diversity. Theologians of religious diversity ask, What gives comparative theologians confidence to believe that knowledge about God can be deepened through the study of other traditions other than some implicit conviction that "God has not left Godself without witness" outside the church? Best to render such implicit theologies explicit and hence vulnerable to correction as comparative theology proceeds.[23] Hence, it no longer seems plausible to place a moratorium on TRD. We need help from both theological projects if we are to negotiate the meaning of Christian life in the twenty-first century, a life that is unavoidably interreligious.

Although I recognize the importance of the conversation between Kiblinger and comparative theologians, my concerns lie elsewhere. I want to see to it that the good work done by both theologians of religious diversity and comparative theologians is not relegated to the status of technical subfields to be pursued only by a very few. True, as any area of research grows in scope and complexity, specialist scholars will be needed to master the relevant literature and languages. But any province of theology that remains an optional specialist project rather than the mandatory general responsibility will not thrive. Not all theologians, for example, will write treatises on ecotheology, but any theology that does not make a place for ecological concerns is shortsighted. Likewise, the time has come to recognize that questions about religious diversity are indispensable for constructive Christian theology.

This book is a venture in constructive Christian theology that is enriched by the work of theologies of religious diversity and comparative theology. It hopes to demonstrate that Christian reflection about our religious neighbors (theologies of religious diversity), Christian learning with and from those neighbors (comparative theology), and Christian reflection about ultimate matters (constructive theology) can and must be integrated. These theological tasks cannot flourish in isolation. When Christians think about other traditions without being informed by them and informed also by how they interpret Christianity, Christian reflection becomes spectatorial in posture. Christians remain always in the subject position, ever the interpreters gathering data about our religious neighbors who remain only native informants rather than interpreters in their own right.

Such theologies of religious diversity lack an ethos of mutuality and appear to assume that Christian categories, without revision or enrichment, are adequate to the task of registering what is true and important about the convictions of our neighbors. Christians even claim to understand other traditions better than their adherents do when we maintain, for example, that they are implicitly oriented toward the Christ or the church. Moreover, what we prize in other traditions is what resonates best with our own intuitions.

Should Christians seek to interpret others without being tutored by them? I contend that learning from and with religious neighbors must shape Christian theologies of religious diversity. TRD must be ventured in conversation with comparative theology. Moreover, Christians must open up to being interpreted, challenged, and changed by our religious neighbors. Christian categories for interpreting others must be revised, at least in part, after conversation with them. Even if, at the outset, Christian interpretations of our religious neighbors begin with our internal categories, in the course of comparative theological learning, those categories will be enriched and transformed by what we have come to learn about other traditions.

Christians should also stand prepared to learn from a reversal of the interpretive gaze. We must hospitably receive wisdom about our tradition from close readings of Christian materials offered by non-Christians. Finally, what is the point of comparative theology if it fails to contribute to the work of constructive theology? Does comparative theology even count as theology proper if it fails to venture constructive proposals and thereby advance theological learning? Comparative theology, which stops short of advancing constructive proposals, is merely an exercise in comparing theologies, work which can be done just as well by historians of religions. *Comparing* theologies is not comparative *theology*. Thinking *about* religious diversity (theologies of religious diversity) and thinking *with* our religious neighbors (comparative theology) must ultimately fund our attempt to think *through* religious diversity in our reflection about God (constructive theology).

Constructive theology runs multiple risks when it severs itself from theologies of religious diversity and comparative theology. First, constructive theology fails to address fundamental practical and pastoral obligations. What does it mean to live in a world of abiding religious difference? How do you live Christianly with your Muslim wife and your Hindu coworkers? Am I obliged to seek their conversion, or can I recognize their traditions as truth-giving and salvation-bearing? Communities urgently need answers for such questions. Any constructive Christian theology that fails to answer these questions no longer serves as a guide to life in pluralistic societies.

Second, constructive Christian theology that does not take up comparative theology runs the risks of provinciality, fideism, and even sheer unintelligibility. A theological project that proceeds as though other traditions have not thought about the human predicament, about the world, and about ultimate reality, and does not engage those claims is provincial. What justifies the theologian from ignoring meaningful counterclaims about the nature of the human predicament and the aims of human life?

If the answer is that the theologian is obliged to the service of one religion alone, we must ask why. Even if the theologian holds that only one religion is true, how might the truth of that claim be demonstrated apart from comparison? Any other strategy risks fideism (e.g., It's true because I believe it; I believe it because it's true). How can Christians hope to communicate the meaning of Christian discourse apart from elucidating that meaning in conversation with a range of religious alternatives? What does commitment to Christ entail, and how does it differ from being a follower of the Buddha? Might the two be compatible, and if so, how? A constructive Christian theology that does not answer such questions will become irrelevant and even unintelligible.

What might emerge when these three projects are integrated? This book articulates the hope for a *comparative theology of religious diversity*. Just what is a comparative theology of religious diversity? A comparative theology of religious diversity is a TRD that emerges in, through, and after comparative theology. Christian theologians of religious diversity will surrender recourse to sweeping claims about religions in general that have not been first tested and refined by the careful work of comparative theology. By contrast, a comparative theology of religious diversity is constructive theology seeking to understand the meaning and significance of religious diversity *after* sustained ventures in close comparative study. Gone, therefore, is the tidy and troubling distinction between theology of religious diversity as an a priori project and comparative theology as a posteriori venture rooted in the thick details of particular texts, thinkers, and traditions. A comparative theology of religious diversity is one promising fruit of the integration of TRD, comparative theology, and constructive theology.

So much can go awry when these three projects fail to be interwoven, and yet they rarely are. Why? I believe that the trouble rests largely with our ideas about religion. Prevailing notions about "religion" and "religions" play a critical role in marginalizing these subfields. Hence, this moment requires nothing less than a vision of constructive theology "after religion." If we (mis)understand religions to be characterized by a high degree of internal coherence, impermeable boundaries, and relative self-sufficiency, then Christian theological claims, even Christian claims about religious diversity, can be formulated in isolation from the symbols, myths, ideas, texts, and practices of other religions. We can give an *account of the other* without being *transformed by the other*. After all, such transformation risks that troublesome contamination that goes by the name of syncretism. The thought that self and other are mutually co-constituted need not arise. We need not entertain the possibility that what we say about others and what they say about us may change how we think about ourselves. We need not entertain the possibility that constructive theology might become porous to and shaped by the claims and aims of other traditions. We can work to prevent the coming of a day when the distinction between constructive theology and comparative theology will cease to be meaningful save as an exercise in the division of labor.

Our unexamined ideas about "religion" and "religions" play a critical role in erecting, maintaining, and policing the border lines between religious traditions. Sadly, even theology of "religions" can be made to serve the work of fence building.[24] TRD can serve either to reify religious traditions or to disrupt the problematic notion that religions and the persons who belong to them can be neatly separated from each other. We have known for quite some time that for most of human history and in most regions of the planet persons have belonged—putting aside for the moment the very notion of "belonging" as itself a complicated notion— to more than one religious tradition.

Can we imagine a theology of religious diversity that moves beyond mere boundary preservation and maintenance because it has come to critical self-consciousness about the category religion? Might we imagine a TRD that would offer theological warrants for believing that our tradition stands in positive need of others for its own enrichment and fulfillment? Might we propose that one important criterion for a successful Christian TRD is that it can articulate a Christian need and *eros* for the religious other as integral for our movement into the divine life?[25] Can we imagine that such an *eros* might long for the other not for the sake of subsuming and digesting the other but for the sake of learning and self-transformation? I will argue that such a TRD is indeed possible, but only if we revise our ideas about what we take religion and the religions to be. That, in brief, is a highly compressed summary of the formal goals to which this book is committed.

The emphasis on demonstration rather than assertion is a key feature of this book. Although considerable space is given to theoretical considerations, the primary goal here is to show and not only to say that these three projects can be carefully integrated. Hence, Chapter 7 generates a constructive theological vision in which a novel trinitarian theology of religious diversity emerges from and out of comparative theological labor. Hence, the chapter is simultaneously an exercise in TRD, comparative theology, and constructive theology.

I am by no means the first to call for a cross-pollination between TRD and comparative theology for the sake of service to constructive theology. However, few have ventured such a task.[26] Why? Uncovering reasons for the ongoing disjunction between TRD and comparative theology requires no great speculative power. Differences in preparation, goals, and even temperament pull theologians of religious diversity and comparative theologians in different directions. To begin with, comparative theologians typically refuse to make grand claims about how religions might relate to each other but choose instead to engage in close, careful, and nuanced readings of particular religious texts and thinkers. Comparative theologians therefore seem disinclined from and wary of proposing sweeping theologies of religious diversity. The risk that general theories of religious diversity might constrain and limit acts of comparative reading—or, worse still, that the work of formulating such general theories may substitute for comparative learning itself—is an important worry. Moreover, modesty about the delimited and very particular kinds of comparisons that fuel comparative theology have led some to refrain from making developed constructive arguments after comparison.[27]

Theologians of religious diversity, on the other hand, feel compelled to ask broader questions about the relationship between religious diversity and divine grace. Is God's saving power available beyond the boundaries of Christian tradition? If so, is divine grace available to others *because* of the traditions to which they belong—that is to say in and through those very traditions—or *despite* the traditions to which they belong? Theologians of religious diversity wonder how the project of comparative theology can get under way without working out answers to such questions.

Given the divergent goals and motivations that have driven theologians of religious diversity and comparative theologians in the past, one might argue that the difference between these two projects should lead to a division of labor but not to any incommensurability. Thus, one might contend that nothing in principle prevents the weaving together of these projects. However, as noted earlier, James Fredericks did more than argue for a division of labor; Fredericks commended comparative theology because he believed that no then available options in TRD were workable. His reservations were comprehensive, theoretically well formed, and went far beyond calling for a mere division of labor, and hence his call for a moratorium on TRD for the sake of comparative theology.

Fredericks was right to be apprehensive about the prospects for most then extant forms of TRD, but he failed to identify the enervating root cause for the failures of the field—namely, problematic conceptions about the nature of religion. As mentioned earlier, treatments of religion as bounded, impermeable, and monolithic realities have made it difficult for Christians to receive resources from other traditions for fear of admixture and impurity. What we need are new theologies of religious diversity that are chastened, corrected, and enriched by insights from other traditions garnered by the work of comparative theologians. *Comparative theology must not replace TRD; comparative theology must enrich TRD and yield comparative theologies of religious diversity.* Theologians of religious diversity need insights from comparative theology to ensure that their claims about others are well grounded in and transformed by knowledge of (at least some) other traditions. Theologies of religious diversity that are informed and even transformed by insights from other traditions garnered by comparative theology can overcome the problems that have, to date, beset most forms of TRD.[28]

Without the help of comparative theology, Christian theologians of religious diversity will gaze over the boundaries and hedges of tradition at the religious activities of their neighbors and try to give an account of what they take others to be up to without asking about whether Christian categories are up to the task. Might it be possible to imagine a TRD in which Christian categories are reformulated in and through the work of comparative theology? Might we even be willing to surrender ownership of Christian categories—especially those we employ to interpret and understand religious neighbors—to just those neighbors?

This book builds toward a trinitarian theology of religious diversity that does just that. My approach is distinctive because I do not begin with a trinitarian vision derived purely from intra-Christian resources, which I only subsequently bring to bear on the reality of religious difference. My approach is, in some respects, akin to the work of Paul Tillich and Raimon Panikkar inasmuch as both maintain that trinitarian structures are likely to be evident in non-Christian traditions because they are part of the very fabric of reality. Instead of deploying a fully articulated doctrine of the Trinity as the basis for a theology of religious diversity, I turn first to Hindu-Christian-Buddhist trialogue and only then turn to a trinitarian formulation. This counterintuitive movement from other traditions to trinity is part of a larger argument that Christian theologians must be prepared not just to read other traditions—and in doing so claim to understand those traditions better than they do themselves—but also *to be read by those traditions.* I suggest that Christians can gain a deeper feeling for trinity from non-Christians than they might from intra-Christian resources alone.

Each of the religious traditions under study is committed to troubling fixed and reified notions of identity, personal as well as communal. And yet these traditions are being depicted in regnant cultural and geopolitical analyses, and sometimes with good reason, as generating rigid identities that will mark out the terrain of human conflict for generations to come. The "clash of civilizations" forecasted by Samuel Huntington is ultimately grounded in the conviction that civilizations are incommensurate and incompatible precisely because they are funded at the core by different and incommensurable religions. If this latter picture of the religions is accepted, then religious traditions function simultaneously as abiding sources of fixed and nonnegotiable communal identity even when those traditions are themselves committed to disrupting such identity configurations. Being attached to a rigid notion of being Buddhist is anti-Buddhist. Such attachment runs headlong against the core soteriological aim of Buddhist traditions. Analogous claims can be made for other traditions as well.

What roles do our theologies of religious diversity and comparative theologies play in the work of identity constitution and identity disruption? What is the relationship between these theological projects and the core soteriological purposes of Christian traditions? TRD is especially vulnerable to the charge that it operates under the assumption that religious difference is a *problem* to be accounted for rather than a *resource* for the human future. A case can be made that Christian theologies of religious diversity were ventured in earnest only after Christian communities belatedly concluded that a world without religious diversity, a world that had been won entirely to Christ, was no longer imaginable. One might well argue that the very project of TRD was, at least initially, driven by the challenge that religious diversity poses to Christian communal identity. That billions of people, or, more acutely, those few who are dear to us, choose to live by practices and commitments different from our own threatens the plausibility structures that might make Christian life seem entirely natural.

Inasmuch as TRD is meant to manage the anxiety and identity threat generated by religious diversity, theologians of religious diversity would do well to suspect that their work might fall prey to nostalgia and temptation, the nostalgia for a bygone Christendom and the temptation to externalize difference. Our definitions of "religion" play a critical role in determining whether a given TRD works to separate human communities or to bring them closer together. Indeed, some ways of theorizing religion work at cross purposes to and even sabotage what religious traditions aim to accomplish.

Some theories of religion are not just conceptually questionable but also soteriologically compromising. The work of TRD and comparative theology, as with all theology, cannot be assessed by neutral academic criteria alone; although these projects are surely exercises in second-order reflective work, they also contribute to the first-order shaping of religious lives of Christians. As such, theologies of religious diversity and comparative theologies must also be assessed to determine whether they contribute to or impede the soteriological aims of Christian traditions. If a given TRD generates conceptions of self and other that impede and obstruct charity, then such a TRD runs counter to Christian purposes.

Particularly disconcerting is a powerful formal resonance between the project of interreligious dialogue and race relations discourse. Critical race theorists Robert Miles and Malcolm Brown have pointed out that the very notion of "improving race relations" hinges on the presupposition that races are biologically real. Without discounting the multiple material forms of violence generated by the construct of race, critical race theorists remind us that race is not ontologically real; the category was invented for the purpose of privileging some groups at the expense of others. To take for granted the category of race and to hold that the human community can be divided into races is to acquiesce to just those processes of othering that must be called into question.[29]

The work of critical race theorists can be a vital resource in interrogating and disrupting cultural projects that aim to use the category "religion" to mirror and reproduce forms of othering generated by the notion "race." We must find ways of engaging in interreligious dialogue without adopting a problematic understanding of religions as: a) internally homogeneous, b) marked by rigid and impermeable boundaries, c) marked by radical difference that amounts to utter incommensurability, and d) so likely to be caught up in conflict. We need theological projects that remind us that the invention of "religions" and the invention of races were historically coterminous and part of a single, albeit multifaceted, imperial project. The fact that religions, once invented, were then rank-ordered on evolutionary schemes in which Western Christianity, or more specifically German Christianity, stands at the very apex of cultural evolution demonstrates that "religion," like "race," is not an innocent, neutral, and descriptive category. The rise of Islamophobia and the way in which racism and religious prejudice coincide therein are further indication that theologians need to be vigilant about the uses to which the category "religion" is put.[30] We must be wary of the often taken for granted assumption that religions are bound to be in antagonistic relationships and the further assumption that because religions are deep wellsprings that nourish, fund, and inspire civilizations, the civilizations themselves are bound to clash. Hence, this book is dedicated to thinking about the nature and meaning of religious diversity after a thoroughgoing critique of the category "religion."

Before turning to a critical genealogy and reconstruction of our notions about "religion," I want first to offer an assessment of contemporary Christian theologies of religious diversity. In the next two chapters, I show that whenever Christian TRDs are constructed around questionable configurations of the category religion, they run into conceptual dead ends. By contrast, whenever theologies of religious diversity show flexibility and creativity in how they think about "religion" and "religions," such theologies show openness to learning from other religious traditions and can, in doing so, begin to imagine religious diversity as promise rather than as problem. The task at hand is not to dismiss TRD but to formulate a theology of religious diversity that makes interreligious learning and mutual transformation possible. A successful comparative theology of religious diversity will itself be the outcome of such learning and transformation.

# 2 The Limits and Promise of Exclusivism and Inclusivism

## ASSESSING MAJOR OPTIONS IN THEOLOGIES OF RELIGIOUS DIVERSITY

*[I]t is not only the other religions that are fulfilled in (and in one sense, radically transformed) their* preparatio *being completed through Christianity, but also Christianity itself that is fulfilled in receiving the gift of God that the Other might bear, self-consciously or not.*

—GAVIN D'COSTA, *The Meeting of the Religions and the Trinity*

## Criteria for Assessing Theologies of Religious Diversity

This chapter and the one to follow offer a new treatment of theologies of religious diversity. I make no attempt to do justice to the whole of this enormous literature. Thankfully, Paul Knitter and Paul Hedges have already written fine monographs that treat the major problems and controversies within this subfield.[1] I am in material agreement with their core arguments. My intention is to assess theologies of religious diversity with view to two questions: (1) Does this particular TRD make interreligious learning possible and desirable, and, (2) When a TRD refuses interreligious learning, what are the operative assumptions behind that refusal?

Hedges lists me among a number of comparative theologians who "take what could be seen as a pluralistic style in their writing and theologizing" even though we cannot be classified as conventional pluralists.[2] He is right to suspect that I am not a conventional pluralist. Mine is a trinitarian version of "relational pluralism," to use the recent language of Roland Faber and Catherine Keller.[3] I hold that any pluralism that imagines religious traditions flourishing (or even existing) apart from mutual encounter and transformation is mistaken because it indulges in ahistorical fiction. Our traditions have always needed each other and always will. And if that's true, then we must surrender theologies of religious diversity, including forms of pluralism, that imagine a world in which nothing material would be lost if all other traditions but our own cease to exist. Far too many such theologies persist.

What sort of TRD results in a maximally appreciative account of religious diversity? For comparative theologians committed to interreligious learning, that's the interesting question. TRD must do more than resolve a problem of Christian conscience and theodicy—namely, how can a gracious and loving God permit the vast majority of the world's population, living and long gone, to perish eternally if faith in Jesus Christ is needed for persons to be saved? That question is not trivial; it is of great pastoral urgency. But resolving it need not make Christians *open to learning from other traditions*, nor does it affirm the enduring worth of those traditions in the divine economy. After affirming that God saves non-Christians, one might still wish to live in a world without religious diversity.

Christian theologians have generated a variety of theological solutions to the soteriological quandary. Indeed, Christian TRD has become identified almost entirely with the soteriological problem, one that is simply uninteresting to many other traditions. Even rigorous exclusivists have found ways to affirm the possibility of universal salvation by appeal to postmortem scenarios in which persons encounter the Christ after death in purgatory, limbo, or upon a general resurrection. But such soteriological solutions offer no reason to believe that Christians have anything to learn from other traditions. That is not their concern, but it is mine.

I seek a TRD that welcomes the hospitable reception of wisdom and the ongoing mutual transformation of traditions. If a TRD offers reasons for and commends interreligious learning, then other traditions may become more than stubborn facts to which I must be reluctantly reconciled or soteriological problems I must resolve. A tradition from which I can learn and be transformed might even become, for me, a blessing. A theology of religious diversity that celebrates attentive learning might move away from regarding religious diversity as a problem to be solved and recognize religious diversity as a promise to be received.

For a theology of religious diversity to affirm that genuine interreligious learning is possible, the following conditions must obtain. First, that TRD must affirm that traditions are different enough that we have something new to learn from them, but not so different as to be incommensurable. If this analogical relationship between traditions does not empirically hold—at least for some traditions—then, interreligious learning is impossible. Let us call this *the difference without incommensurability criterion.*

Second, a TRD must affirm that at least some of the claims made by traditions must actually be true. If theologians hold to a rigorously Kantian position that all religious claims fall so far short of ultimate reality as it is in itself that nothing positively can be learned from those claims— then why be seriously interested in the specific claims of other religious traditions? Where there is no such interest, there can be no learning. Let us simply call this *the truth criterion.*

Third, if particular truth claims of other traditions are to matter to me and my tradition, a given TRD must offer an account of "religion" and "the religions" that does not make interreligious learning impossible. Counterfactual theories that treat religions as monolithic, impermeable, tightly systematic, and unitary wholes will not suffice. If that is what religions are, then how can my tradition receive something new from my religious neighbors? Every instance of learning could lead only to incoherent syncretism and thereby violate the internal logic and pristine integrity of my tradition. Hence, we must ask a vital question: How does a given TRD theorize religion, and does that theory make interreligious learning possible? Does it have such a theory on offer? If no such theory is available, then what tacit accounts of religion are at play, and do they enhance or impede interreligious learning? This complex of questions is a way to speak of our *critical theory of religion criterion.*

It has long been taken for granted that whereas comparative theologians are interested in thick particularities, theologians of religious diversity explore questions of broader scope, questions about whether other "religions" as such are salvific. But are religions as a whole salvific? Should theologians of religious diversity keep speaking in this generalizing fashion? As a Christian, can I even affirm that Christianity saves? And if so, *which Christianity*? The Christianity of the enslaved or the Christianity of the slave master? Can religions be placed on a scale and weighed for their relative soteriological efficacy? Moreover, *which salvation*? Does any religion have on offer only one salvation? Just what is a religion anyway? Are all the traditions we have come to think of as religions entities of the same kind? And have they always been "religions"? One wonders whether, in becoming religions, traditions have to present themselves as apolitical, transcendentalized, and abstracted from the worldly concerns that are also very much a part of religious traditions. If so, does this mean that interreligious learning must be confined to matters otherworldly or about the nature of ultimate reality? Or can we learn from other traditions about political matters like the work of nonviolent resistance? Without a critical account of religion, we are likely to skip over the centrality of these questions.

Finally, I propose a fourth *intrinsic religious interest criterion*. Can I be interested in another tradition, while remaining a member of my own, for properly religious reasons? What I mean by the term "religious" is spelled out at length in Chapter 5. Here, I will posit only that religiousness demands the integration of truth and transformation. To be religious requires right orientation (truth) and proper comportment (transformation) to the nature of reality as understood by a given tradition. Intrinsic religious interest in another tradition would take seriously the intimate connection between the specific claims, practices, and *the aims* of that tradition.

By contrast, a Christian might be interested in the claims and practices of another tradition—claims about interrelatedness of all things (*pratityasamutpada*) or the practices of mindfulness, for example—but only because she believes that such claims and practices might deepen *her own Christian quest for salvation*. This is a mode of *extrinsic religious interest*. Although I do not rule out the legitimacy of such interests, by *intrinsic religious interest*, I wish to name the possibility that a Christian might desire Buddhist enlightenment by coming to understand *pratityasamutpada* through the specific contemplative disciplines which make enlightenment possible. So, the kind of religious interest I wish to affirm is interest in another tradition's *own* aspirations, not merely how that tradition's claims and practices might supplement religious ends to which I am already committed prior to encounter. The question is not just, "Can the Buddhist help me be a better Christian?" but instead, "Can I desire to know *what* Buddhists know *as* they come to know it?"

Why ask about intrinsic religious interest and posit that as a criterion for assessing theologies of religious diversity? First, I hold that extrinsic religious interest can run the risk of disfiguring the intentions of the traditions in question. One might, for example, practice yoga for better sex or vipassana for putting in longer hours at the weapon's manufacturing plant and be entirely indifferent to the soteriological and ethical aspirations behind these practices in Hindu and Buddhist traditions respectively. Hence an extrinsic religious interest may become a narrowly *instrumental interest.*

Less negatively, those whose interests are extrinsic (but not instrumental) might hold that everything is related to every other thing, as many Buddhists affirm, but in no way believe that insight to be of transformative or healing import. Hence, a dividing wall is erected between the Buddhist claims on the one hand and the practices and aspirations that those claims are meant to serve. Such walls forestall intrinsic religious interest in another tradition.

And what's wrong with a delimited and piecemeal mode of religious interest? Just that—it is delimited and piecemeal. Such circumscribed interests do not go far enough in affirming religious diversity as such. It runs the risk of diminishing, dismissing, or perhaps just being uninterested in the aims of other traditions. My engagement with the other remains confined to the ambit of my interests and aspirations; I may learn from religious others but only for religious ends and purposes that were already my own prior to encounter. I am not genuinely challenged to encounter other traditions *on their own terms as they pursue their own goals.* Hence, extrinsic religious interest, even when it is appreciative rather than reductive or instrumental, is a limited and limiting way of approaching religious difference.

That is why my fourth criterion asks, "Does the TRD in question make possible a religious interest in the religious aims and aspirations of other traditions?" Can I be interested in another tradition because I believe that the claims, practices, *and aims* of the other tradition might lead to transformative truth?[4] Let us now bring these four criteria to bear in assessing some current theologies of religious diversity. The current chapter will examine exclusivist and inclusivist positions. Chapter 3 will focus primarily on pluralism but will also engage briefly with the post-pluralist position of S. Mark Heim.

## Assessing Exclusivisms

Theologies of religious diversity have long been classified under a threefold rubric of exclusivism, inclusivism, and pluralism. More recently, Paul Knitter has added a fourth category called the acceptance model, one that Paul Hedges names the particularities model. Mark Heim is usually placed within this newest camp. In Chapters 2 and 3, I bring to bear the four major criteria outlined earlier to general formulations of these models and treat some exemplifications thereof.

Talk about these models customarily begins with exclusivism—or what Paul Knitter calls the replacement model.[5] Exclusivists hold that only their tradition leads to salvation. In the case of Christian exclusivists, only explicit faith in Jesus as the Christ suffices for salvation. But Paul Griffiths has pointed out that talk about exclusivism is often unsubtle. To begin with, he argues that we must begin by making the critical distinction between questions of truth and questions of soteriology.[6] He notes that one can be an exclusivist in two senses: (1) on the question of truth, my tradition is the only one that offers truth on matters religious, or (2) on the question of salvation, my tradition is the only one that affords access to salvation. Exclusivists need not assert both. He contends that few can be exclusivists in the first sense because traditions share at least some overlapping truth claims. I cannot deny that your tradition contains truth because your tradition makes some of the same claims as mine. But shared truth claims need not lead me to affirm that other traditions afford access to the salvific end commended by my home tradition. Hence, Griffiths believes that one can be a soteriological exclusivist without being an exclusivist on the question of truth.

Moreover, he takes care to note, as others after him have also done, that there need not be a correlation between soteriological exclusivism and the question of *how many* are saved: one can hold that only Jesus the Christ saves and yet hold that, regardless of religious affiliation, all will be saved by the Christ's salvific work. Soteriological exclusivists need not be "restrictivists" who contend that the number of those who will be saved is restricted and so quite small. These critical distinctions are useful in any discussion of theologies of religious diversity.

Over the last several decades, the conversation within TRD has mainly been between inclusivists and pluralists, giving the impression that exclusivism is no longer an intellectually serious option. But more recently, a robust literature has emerged defending varieties of Christian exclusivism, not least because it is possible to make the kinds of conceptual distinctions that Griffiths makes. Advocates of exclusivist positions now come from a variety of denominational traditions and include more than the usual suspects from fundamentalist and evangelical circles, but also important Catholic voices like that of Gavin D'Costa.[7] Some of these new modes of exclusivism enjoy a prestige and credibility that older forms do not. Hence, it will not do to leap over exclusivism.

The questions, as noted previously, that I would like to bring to old and new forms of exclusivism are these: (1) Does this form of exclusivism hold other traditions to be different enough to learn from but without falling into talk about incommensurability? (2) Is the exclusivism in question capable of taking particular truth claims seriously and in such a fashion that new learning is possible? Or is the recognition of truth in other religions limited only to overlapping claims? If only the latter is possible, then new learning seems limited at best, or impossible at worst because I count as true only those truths in your tradition already affirmed by mine. (3) Is the form of exclusivism in question grounded in a nuanced theory of religion? (4) Can this exclusivism commend intrinsic religious interest in other traditions, or must it rule out such interest?

To anticipate my conclusions, I hold that some exclusivists can and do answer the first two questions in such a fashion that interreligious learning becomes possible. Exclusivists generally have no trouble recognizing the deep differences between traditions. Thankfully, not all hold that such differences lead to incommensurability. Hence some exclusivists can pass nuanced judgments about truth and falsity of elements of religious traditions other than their own without dismissing those traditions in their entirety. The third test seems more challenging for some exclusivists who often hold to deeply problematic and counterfactual accounts of religion. The fourth criterion, however, is a decisive obstacle for exclusivists *by definition*. Exclusivists regard religious interest in the aims and ends of other traditions as illicit. The ends of other traditions are either not the same as the Christian *telos* (namely, salvation) or, if other traditions strive after the same end that Christians seek, they will not reach that end other than by way of Christ or the Holy Spirit. Other religions do not save! And because other religions do not save, it is improper to take their aims with religious seriousness.

Exclusivist commitments also bear on the mode in which elements of another tradition can be affirmed as true, good, or beautiful. Exclusivists deny that other traditions can mediate saving truth to their adherents. If persons who belong to other traditions are saved, they are saved *despite* the traditions to which they belong and not *because* of them—that is, because the Spirit or the Word is operative in the hearts of such adherents. Exclusivists may be prepared to recognize elements of truth, goodness, and beauty in other religions and even learn from them, but exclusivists assert that these elements do not suffice for salvation. If they took some element of another tradition to be true, good, or beautiful in a saving way, then they would, by definition, no longer be exclusivists. Hence, exclusivists cannot affirm many of the core claims, practices, and especially the aims of other traditions as true in the way that adherents of that tradition take them to be true.

Exclusivists come in many varieties. Gavin D'Costa explicitly argues that genuine interreligious learning is possible.[8] By contrast, Daniel Strange, his former doctoral student, formulates a strident exclusivism that rules out any interreligious learning other than for missiological purposes.[9] Strange is so extreme that he seems to be the sort of exclusivist that Paul Griffiths believes cannot exist. Here is Strange in his own words:

> ... Christian scripture describes there to be principially [sic] a funda-mental discontinuity between the truth of Christian faith, built on the foundation of God's revelation, and the falsity of all other worldviews/philosophies/pseudo-gospels, built on the foundation of human imagi-nation. Indeed the exclusive truth of Christianity means the impossibil-ity of the contrary.[10]

Within the framework of Strange's exclusivism, interreligious learning is neither possible nor desirable. First, religions are unalterably opposed; the relationship between Christianity and other religions is one of truth and error, of revelation and idolatry. Religions are neither merely differ-ent nor even incommensurable; they are contradictory. Second, the truth claims of other traditions are taken seriously, but learning is ruled out because those claims are false. Third, Strange, as we shall see, has a deeply problematic and mistaken understanding of religion. Finally, for Strange, Christians must not entertain religious interest in other traditions.

If Strange's position is made to stand in for exclusivism as such, ex-clusivism can be dismissed as a viable framework for the encounter be-tween religious traditions. The notion that Christian traditions, which have always learned from a host of others, could then claim that those others are flatly mistaken strains credulity. Strange is aware of the po-rosity of traditions and Christian appropriation of resources from other traditions. How, then, can he draw this stark opposition between truth and falsity? Here, Strange's indebtedness to and use of the missiologist J. H. Bavinck is telling. Bavinck maintains,

> The missionary exhales many pagan ideas with every word that he speaks. He cannot do otherwise, since he has no other vocabulary at his disposal, but he will shudder at times when he is conscious of what he is doing. . . .

We must never lost [*sic*] sight of the dangers involved, and we must endeavor to purify terms we have borrowed from their pagan connotations. This is what the apostles did with concepts such as salvation, redemption, "logos," and many others, which could easily have led to a world of misunderstanding.[11]

Here Bavinck recognizes that many of the central categories of Christian vocabulary are borrowed, but when they are borrowed, they must also be "purified." Presenting the Christian message to contemporary non-Christians will likewise require adopting pagan vocabulary because "the Gospel does not find anywhere in the world a ready language that fits completely and absolutely like a garment."[12]

Might this lack of perfect fit be a theological sign that in the world we are given no fictive purities? Might not this insight lead to a delight in and openness to the impure? Might not the Christ who embraced with his body those whom others considered impure teach us how to live in the world without the need for the stable, the fixed, the cleaned up, and the purified? For Bavinck and Strange, apparently not. Instead, the thoughtful missionary must "shudder" as Bavinck and Strange do. The encounter with religious others is a source of fear, not expectation. Tragically, fear of impurity grasps those who confess an incarnate God who constitutes Godself of dirt and clay. Should disciples of an earthy God be so fastidious and fearful of admixture, impurity, and contamination?

What, then, of all that is borrowed from other religious traditions? Strange follows Bavinck who insists,

> The Christian life does not accommodate or adapt itself to heathen forms of life, but it takes the latter in possession and thereby makes them new. . . . Within the framework of the non-Christian life, customs and practices serve idolatrous tendencies and drive a person away from God. The Christian life takes them in hand and turns them in an entirely different direction. . . . Such is neither "adaptation" nor "accommodation"; it is in essence the legitimate taking possession of something by him to whom all power is given in heaven and on earth.[13]

Tragically, Christians have been motivated over the centuries by just this spirit of "possession" to lay claim not only to pagan vocabularies and thought forms but also to pagan lands and bodies, all to subvert the "distorted" and "idolatrous" life of the pagan other. That the language of possession should still be so nakedly employed without the slightest awareness of imperialist dangers lurking in such rhetoric speaks for itself.

Also telling is the way in which Strange speaks about the encounter between his own theology of religions and rival Christian positions such as Paul Knitter's pluralism. He characterizes such encounters as the meeting of "hermetically sealed, and often incommensurable theological worlds" that are "on a trajectory for a head-on collision."[14] Such language is customarily used not of other Christian positions but of other religions. But upon closer examination, it turns out that Strange does not consider Knitter's pluralism to be Christian at all. Conversation with pluralists is, for Strange, an instance of interreligious dialogue, dialogue that is by no means irenic! Strange hereticizes and excludes Christians with whom he disagrees. It is ever so with those who strive assiduously after purity.

Unsurprisingly, Strange uses the same language to characterize other religions: "Phenomenologically religions are hermetically sealed interpretations of reality (worldviews) and as such are incommensurable, defying superficial comparison."[15] Strange cites Bavinck, who maintains, "False religion always presents itself as, and in actual fact invariably constitutes, a monolithic aggregate. Consequently, all ideas it absorbs become amalgamated with and deformed by the whole. In other words, it is not possible for isolated elements of verity, sparks of divine truth to exist in the midst of falsehood and error—in fact, if such sparks were present, they would lead to friction in and destruction of the very essence of pseudo religions."[16]

Just what sort of "phenomenology" generates such wildly counterfactual claims about religions as "monolithic aggregates" or "as hermetically sealed interpretations of reality" is hard to say. No religion is a monolith but is instead a terrain marked by robust internal contestation. No religion *is* a worldview. Religious traditions are communities of argumentation, arguments that, in some cases, have lasted for more than two millennia. Strange and Bavinck are captive to these profoundly mistaken notions about what religions are, notions that make interreligious learning impossible. Finally, it goes without saying that Strange believes that Christians must not take any intrinsic religious interest in the traditions of others. In sum, Strange's exclusivism violates every criterion I commend for a positive theology of religious diversity. As such, his position can serve as an ideal type—a summation and exemplification of what theology of religious diversity must seek to avoid.

Thankfully, other exclusivists are subtler and some are, albeit cautiously, open to interreligious learning. Gavin D'Costa is one such figure. D'Costa, a Roman Catholic, classifies himself as an exclusivist, but, unlike his student, D'Costa is open to the possibility of learning from other religious traditions. He holds that salvation comes only through Jesus Christ, and all must be positively related to the Catholic Church, which is the body and sacrament of Christ. No one is saved by any other means. If non-Christians are to be saved, then they must be saved by an encounter with the Christ, if not in this life, then in some postmortem scenario. Other religions are not as such salvific. In this sense, he is, strictly speaking, an exclusivist.

Does this exclusivist assertion mean that interreligious learning is impossible? Is all darkness outside the church? No. D'Costa argues that three affirmations have always been central to Catholic theology: "(1) the necessity of Christ and his Church for salvation; (2) the justice of God towards the righteous before (and obviously after) the coming of Christ . . . ; (3) the possibility of goodness, truth, and beauty being present in pagan traditions, but never in a manner equal to Christ and his sacramental presence in his Church in kind or degree."[17]

D'Costa's third affirmation opens the door to learning from other traditions. He affirms our religious truth criterion; elements of the true, the good, and the beautiful are present in other traditions but, of course, "never in a manner equal to Christ and his sacramental presence in his Church in kind or degree." Does this declaration mean that every element of goodness, truth, and beauty found in another tradition will already be found in superlative fashion within the Christian tradition? Here, readers of D'Costa are in for a surprise. The answer turns out to be no. D'Costa offers, by way of a close reading of conciliar documents and papal writings, a powerful argument that the church has much to learn from other religious traditions. His writing is moving, and his insights are profound; he is not a conventional exclusivist!

His argument proceeds by the following steps. He first notes that *Gaudium et Spes* explicitly acknowledges that the secular world has access to elements of truth. Not only that, but secular cultures contain truth that will *"challenge and even change elements within the church,* in its structure, formulations, and practice."[18] Of course, caution compels him to add the qualification that "none of this is to be regarded as detracting from the claim that God's fullness is known in Jesus Christ through his Spirit within the church, but is rather understood as the church deepening its own understanding and practice of the gospel, and even coming to see the ways in which it has obscured the gospel."[19]

Then, he proceeds to ask, What do such claims about learning from secularity mean for how we are to think about other religious traditions? Why can't analogous claims be made about the church's obligation to learn from, and hence her need for, other religious traditions? If the church can acknowledge that its own mission, structure, and even its understanding of the gospel can be deepened by secular others, why not also from religious others? D'Costa suggests, "It is perhaps a matter of time before similar acknowledgments regarding other religions enter into post-Conciliar documentation. . . ."[20] One can only hope. In any case, D'Costa is emphatic in drawing the right conclusions. The church would be wise to refuse unilateral and unidirectional claims about the church fulfilling elements of truth found outside the church. He invites the church to leave behind "the undialectical and therefore impoverished manner in which fulfillment is sometimes understood and the way in which *praeparatio* is in danger of domesticating the Other."[21] He argues that it is not enough to regard what truth there is outside the church merely as preparation for the fullness of the gospel. Such claims diminish the possibility of mutual learning and enrichment.

And lest one wonder if the elements of truth to be found outside the church are present to religious others *despite* rather than *because* of the traditions to which they belong, D'Costa hastens to add that one finds in John Paul II's *Redemptoris Missio* "an unambiguous acknowledgment that the Spirit's activity in other religions has important structural and cultural dimensions, and does not take place solely in the secret of the heart, or in some asocio-cultural location."[22] He quotes from the document: "The Spirit's presence and activity affect not only individuals but also society and history, peoples, cultures, and religions."[23] What more, one might wonder, might tolerant pluralists ask for?

D'Costa's response is swift: "However, *Redemptoris Missio* then makes it absolutely clear that this recognition of the Spirit's transforming activity within other religions does not confer *independent legitimacy* upon other religions (in terms of their own self-understanding), because this very positive judgment is itself a Christian theological recognition (hetero-interpretation). . . ."[24] There's the rub: the affirmation of the Spirit's activity in other religious traditions does not confer upon them *independent legitimacy.* D'Costa believes that Catholics cannot cross that line. Of course, were he to cross that line, he would no longer be an exclusivist. Moreover,

D'Costa is clear that what Christians take to be signs of the Holy Spirit in other traditions may not be what those traditions would themselves find most important on internal grounds. "Hetero-interpretation" remains in the driver's seat even if he concedes that the church can and must learn from the auto-interpretations that traditions advance.

My response to D'Costa is to call into question, albeit cautiously, the very notion of independent legitimacy for *all* traditions, Christianity included. If all of our traditions have needed each other to become and be what they are, and if the church itself needs both secular and religious others to deepen its own understanding of the gospel, then perhaps, *interdependence* rather than *independence* is the appropriate lens for understanding the relationship between religious traditions, not to mention reality as such. Is it not a fiction to imagine the world as composed of a number of discrete "religions" when in truth each is radically shaped by the other? Can the religions accurately be imagined as planets orbiting the same sun, each in its own orbital—as one of the popular metaphors in the literature envisions them—when history shows them to be in routine contact with and even constituted by interactions with each other? Perhaps the only kind of legitimacy *any* tradition enjoys is an interdependent one. On the one hand, we can affirm that a variety of religious traditions do, in fact, afford access to the divine; on the other, we can assert that every tradition's knowledge of ultimate reality can and must be challenged, clarified, deepened, and enriched by conversation. Making such claims would, of course, move us in the direction of a "relational pluralism."

D'Costa evinces a qualified opening to such a posture of mutuality when he writes that,

> the church . . . in propounding the notion of other cultures as "preparation for the Gospel" . . . is in danger of domesticating the activity of the Spirit in that religion, for the Spirit within that culture may call for an even deeper penetration, understanding and application of the truth of God's triune self-revelation entrusted to the church. That is, if the church is not attentive to the possibility of the Spirit within other religions, it will fail to be attentive to the Word of God that has been entrusted to it. . . . [I]t is not only the other religions that are fulfilled in (and in one sense, radically transformed) their *preparatio* being completed through Christianity, but also Christianity itself that is fulfilled in receiving the gift of God that the Other might bear, self-consciously or not.[25]

Costa ventures here a striking statement. I myself do not wish to go much further than D'Costa does here. John Cobb's language of mutual transformation and Faber's and Keller's discourse of relational pluralism celebrate just this notion of mutual fulfillment. D'Costa's Spirit-rich exclusivism comes surprisingly close to positions that he himself dismisses. But, regrettably, the last phrase in this quotation demonstrates that it is the Christian who alone can determine what in the other tradition is Spirit-filled and what is not. Others may not even self-consciously know what in their tradition is a sign of the Spirit and what is not. The world's religions are not explicitly set on the Christ or Spirit or the triune God, and hence, for D'Costa, we cannot expect them to share the same goals that Christians do. Again, in this sense, they are in and of themselves inadequate, no matter how much Christians may stand in need of them. Here, we part company with D'Costa.

In later writing, he argues rigorously that other religions cannot be affirmed to have a *de jure* place in the divine economy.[26] That position he believes is dogmatically forbidden to the Catholic theologian. He cannot affirm that other religious traditions might be saving in their own right even though he concedes that the Spirit's presence may be available in elements of other traditions. The presence of the true, the good, and the beautiful in other traditions cannot replace the fullness of their presence in the incarnate Christ and the church that proclaims the Christ. Non-Christians may be saved, and D'Costa's "universal access exclusivism" holds open the possibility of postmortem encounter with the Christ for righteous pagans in limbo, but they are not saved by means of other traditions as such.

D'Costa's hope of an escape hatch after death seems a fanciful, implausible, and unpersuasive way to resolve questions about religious diversity. While such a position is a theological possibility permitted by the tradition, it leaves human beings who have had the bad luck of being born in non-Christian traditions in the lurch for a lifetime, having to make do with what elements of the Spirit may be present in their traditions. Such a position does not do justice to the power, profundity, and promise of the world's religious traditions.

Thankfully, the limitations of D'Costa's account of other religious traditions are not due to a faulty theory of religion. He does not subscribe to dubious and uncritical accounts of religion that would rule out interreligious learning or posit that traditions are radically incommensurable. In fact, his book *Christianity and World Religions* includes an extended theoretical and theological treatment of the category of "religion" and "religions," a critique that resonates with some of the claims I advance in Chapter 4. D'Costa, like me, is suspicious of radical orthodox theology's penchant to see religions as homogeneities. He is rightly critical, for example, of John Milbank's ahistorical characterization of Hinduism as "seamless narrative succession."[27] He is suspicious of any account of religion that would, by definition, insist that traditions are either essentially the same or fundamentally incommensurable. The relationship between traditions, he insists quite rightly, must be understood instead as analogical.[28] In these ways and others, D'Costa's exclusivism is marked by openness to other traditions and their concrete wisdom. Those who hold to faulty accounts about the nature of "religion" brook no compromise and even go so far as to rule out interreligious learning; by contrast, theologians who hold to critical and genealogically informed theories of religion find ways to open doors to interreligious learning. D'Costa belongs to this latter camp.

To summarize, D'Costa meets virtually all of the criteria that are required for a theology of religious diversity that would make interreligious learning possible: First, he most assuredly meets the difference without incommensurability criterion. Second, he genuinely affirms the presence of the true, the good, and the beautiful in other religions. Third, he rejects untenable theories of religion and is richly aware of the genealogy of the very category. All this is to the good.

Finally, what then about the question of intrinsic religious interest in another tradition? Teasing out a definitive answer from a survey of D'Costa's work proves to be a complex task that cannot be undertaken here. We must take our cues and draw inferences from his extended discussion of interreligious prayer, a matter that D'Costa approaches with caution. The reader gathers therefrom that because the praying and the prayers of other traditions might be motivated by the promptings of the Holy Spirit, D'Costa believes that Christians should, albeit carefully, risk praying with persons from other traditions. What is the nature of that risk? The Christian, D'Costa believes, runs the risk of infidelity by substituting covenantal love for the triune God with idolatry. Nonetheless, D'Costa is not only open to interreligious prayer but also the possibility that Christians can learn from other traditions about such matters as the importance of breath and posture to prayer, as in those cases when Christian monastics have learned from Hindu and Buddhist contemplative traditions.

Nonetheless, he is careful to raise the question of "co-intentionality." Do persons from other traditions and the Christian who prays with them have the same intentionality? How could they, given the very different metaphysical frames within which traditions practice prayer? D'Costa believes that co-intentionality is especially challenging in the encounter with nontheistic traditions in which the religious object cannot properly be called God. Matters are different with Jews and Muslims. Where there is clear indication that traditions do not share the same intentions, prayer cannot be shared. Nonetheless, D'Costa insists that all genuine prayer exceeds our conscious intentions because the true agent of prayer is the Holy Spirit and not the persons who are praying. For this reason, he believes that Christians should remain open to the profound mystery of divine-human communion that can happen in interreligious prayer.

This argument can be pressed and stretched in service of taking seriously the religious aims of other traditions, even in the case of nontheistic traditions. Trusting the reports of the most serious and disciplined practitioners of interreligious encounter would seem to require an openness to the possibility that what is encountered by persons from other traditions, despite and even because of serious difference, are dimensions of ultimate reality, of the divine life, that are not well appreciated in our own tradition. While there are grounds to believe that D'Costa might be brought to such a conclusion, it does not seem to be a position that D'Costa adopts. In sum, D'Costa insists that Christians have an obligation to respectfully and reverentially listen for the witness of the Holy Spirit in other religions. That openness may even extend to actually engaging in the practices of other traditions. But, on the whole, even when these practices are taken up, D'Costa would want to have the intentions and meaning of those practices installed within a trinitarian framework.

So we find ourselves in a peculiar position with respect to D'Costa's overall position. Other religions are not valid *de jure*, and yet, Christians stand in need of these traditions, perhaps even eschatologically.[29] And yet, even when most generously read, D'Costa holds that other religions are in and of themselves deficient. They are not ways of salvation, and what of the Spirit may be present in them points toward the fulfillment of divine disclosure in the Christ. And only an encounter with the Christ, in this life or beyond it, can lead to salvation. Hence, I believe that D'Costa cannot commend an intrinsic religious interest in the aims and aspirations of other traditions. To do so would be to grant them intrinsic validity, something he refuses to do.

D'Costa opens important doors to interreligious learning, and this openness must be celebrated. D'Costa is willing to learn from and even to revere other traditions, but his commitment to magisterial authority prevents him from moving to pluralism. Nonetheless, by articulating his distinctive and generous exclusivism, D'Costa offers Christians who hold traditionalist convictions a way into comparative theology that might otherwise not be available to them. For this gift, we ought to be most grateful, its limits notwithstanding.

Because some exclusivists hold out the possibility of robust learning from other traditions, comparative theologians must be careful not to dismiss all exclusivisms. What is called for, instead, is theological judiciousness. But why be patient with a family of positions, the ethical ramifications of which have been devastating for interreligious relations? Knitter aptly renames the exclusivist model as the "replacement model" for compelling reasons because most forms of exclusivism seek to replace other religions. Conversion, not dialogue, is the normative goal. The quest for replacement has led to devastating human consequences. Wayne Morris notes, for example, the deep entanglements between exclusivist positions and imperialism. It's hard to refuse his contention that,

> Christian claims to have sole access to universal truths about the human condition and how it might be saved, with reference to its beliefs about God, has [*sic*] usefully supported religious and political agendas that have sought to force those who do not share such beliefs to conform and be normalized to Christian beliefs and practices. This has invariably had devastating consequences for people of other faiths and has led to wars, violence and the genocide of millions of people of other faiths in the name of Christianity.[30]

Christian exclusivism has, no doubt, had grave consequences over the course of history, and contemporary exclusivists walk a fraught and dangerous path. Still, if proponents of interreligious learning through comparative theology wish to draw a broad range of Christians to the work of dialogue, they must welcome *any who are prepared to listen and learn*, and to the degree that some exclusivists are prepared to acknowledge truth and even holiness in other religious traditions, as D'Costa does, then to that extent exclusivists must be welcomed. Or is interreligious learning an option only for those who fly properly pluralist flags? And isn't such learning precisely what may transform persons toward a more capacious stance toward other traditions?

Exclusivists must be welcomed to the work of interreligious learning because respectful disagreement can also be a genuine mode of interreligious encounter. To take the other seriously enough to contend that the other is mistaken—rather than merely regard the other with a detached ethnographic gaze—is an expression of theological interest and seriousness of purpose. Moreover, we are all exclusivists toward some elements in other traditions and indeed even of our own. To the degree that every tradition is not only an ongoing conversation but is an ongoing argument, serious theological interest in other traditions is bound to make us partisans in the arguments that others are having. We are sure to favor some positions over others.

For example, it is logically impossible to agree with Ramanuja, Sankara, and Madhva as these Vedantins disagree on matters ontological and soteriological. Any Christian conversation partner is sure to have commitments that draw her in the direction of one of these thinkers at the expense of the other two. As soon as nuanced judgments of this sort are ventured, it becomes impossible to speak in flat-footed terms about Hinduism as a whole. Instead, we are compelled to make discriminating judgments, at least some of which will be negative and even exclusivist. Hence, we are all bound to be exclusivists in some respects, if only with respect to questions of truth and not salvation.

Such nuanced judgments should make it plain that many of our current conversations about religious diversity are unsubtle and even obtuse. How is it possible to pass judgments about any other religion *in toto*, as though religions were homogeneous monoliths? To ask if Hinduism or Buddhism is, as such, salvific is to pose a blunt, misleading, and wrongheaded question. After all, what Christian theologian is prepared to speak of every form of Christianity as salvific? Just as some Christian theologians are likely to have grave reservations about supercessionist and anti-Semitic forms of Christianity or any Christianity that sanctifies the neoliberal economic status quo, so, too, any theologically interested and ethically committed theologian is sure to reject toxic Buddhist nationalisms and Hindu casteism as neither true nor saving. Not one of our traditions is innocent. Resonances and dissonances on crucial theological questions—salvation by grace through faith or about conceptions of the divine as personal or transpersonal—will generate crosscutting affirmations and negations between theologians of different traditions. As knowledge of the particularities of traditions deepens, we can no longer keep speaking in unsubtle fashion about religions in their entirety.

And when we recognize that Christians are who we are by way of learning and absorbing core resources from other traditions, a theological discourse that takes for granted sharp-edged distinctions between self and other will also come to seem obsolete. The natural question that next comes to mind is, "Just how can I draw clean lines of separation between my tradition and yours?" How can we ask whether your tradition is saving when my tradition is what it is because of what we have learned from yours? These are questions that theologies of religious diversity have yet to formulate well, let alone answer well.

What then should we conclude about exclusivism as a theological stance? How do we account for the fact that virtually any theologian will want to pronounce an emphatic no to some features of other traditions and even her own? And what are we to make of the fact that we now have some exclusivists who stand prepared to learn from other traditions? We must acknowledge that we are all likely to be exclusivists with respect to some features of other traditions, even traditions from which we have learned and by which we have been transformed. A strident and emphatic no must sometimes be said to elements of our own tradition and the traditions of others too.

That said, the fact that some exclusivists leave room for interreligious learning is insufficient reason to affirm that exclusivism is the most compelling option within TRD. To the degree that any TRD views other religious traditions with profound suspicion, severe constraints are placed in the way of robust learning. Most soteriological exclusivists who affirm that only encounter with Jesus the Christ, either in this life or after death, can save are unlikely to regard the specific claims, practices, and especially the aims of other religious traditions positively or even to take much interest in them, save for apologetic or missiological reasons. Because exclusivists often regard other traditions as fraught with error and even spiritual risk, it is hard to be disposed to other traditions in a generous and hospitable spirit. For these reasons, exclusivist positions will largely be found wanting by those interested in advancing interreligious learning in a spirit of generous hospitality.

## Assessing Inclusivisms

I want now to transition from my discussion of exclusivism to inclusivism with someone who is difficult to classify because he believes that the typology is problematic, and for good reasons. Gerald McDermott's own position is best characterized as a hybrid position that combines strongly exclusivist and inclusivist elements. A discussion of McDermott therefore marks the beginning of my brief analysis of inclusivist positions.

McDermott begins by advancing a troubling contention: other religions traffic with real spiritual powers that are false gods. More precisely put, "If the biblical and early church thinkers were right, 'the gods' are the remnants of primeval angelic powers, once created by Yahweh, but who later turned in rebellion against the Creator. Therefore they may be acknowledged as real and formidable creations of God, while at the same time only Yahweh is to be worshiped as the true God."[31] Other religions are, on this account, under the partial inspiration and influence of false but genuinely real supernatural powers.

This appears to be as strong an exclusivist claim as one can imagine, hardly a promising candidate for advancing interreligious learning, and yet, surprisingly, McDermott holds open just that possibility. Despite the Father's contention that demonic powers may be at work in other traditions, he rightly notes that Paul affirmed that Greek poets "spoke the truth about God." Most significantly, he observes "that Justin Martyr went a step further. He argued that some parts of some pagan religions— in his case, Greek philosophical religion—are actually inspired by Christ. According to Justin, all poets and philosophers who teach truth are followers of Christ insofar as they follow those truths. But they don't have full knowledge of God because they don't have personal knowledge of Jesus Christ."[32] With this appeal to Justin Martyr and his notion of the word in seminal form (*logos spermatikos*), McDermott strikes a cautiously inclusivist note about "some parts of some pagan religions." The presence of this note demonstrates how difficult it is to neatly classify any creative theologian into one of the boxes offered by the classical tripartite typology. Indeed, his appeal to Martyr's *logos spermatikos* leads to surprisingly strong claims about the possibility of interreligious learning. Here, McDermott must be cited at length:

> God has often used other religions to help his people better understand Christ and his gospel.... It may be that some of today's religions *portray aspects of the divine mystery that the Bible does not equally emphasize*: for example, the Qur'an's sense of the divine majesty and transcendence, as well as the human being's submission to the holiness of God's eternal decrees. Hindu traditions can help remind Christians of God's immanence when deistic tendencies have obscured it.

Theravadin Buddhists may be able to show us dimensions of the fallen ego that will shed greater light on what Paul meant by "the old man." Philosophical Daoists may have insights into nonaction that can help Christians better understand "waiting on God." Confucius's portrayal of virtue may open new understandings of radical discipleship, and the Qur'an's attention to the physical world's "signs" of God's reality can enrich our belief that the cosmos is the theater of God's glory.[33]

These claims are remarkable, not least because they are characterized throughout by specificity. McDermott does not engage in mere hand-waving about the generalized possibility of interreligious learning. He points to specific teachings from a host of traditions and suggests that these traditions hold promise for Christian learning. To the degree that he can do so, McDermott demonstrates that he has engaged in such learning himself. Other religions may be under the direction of dangerously seductive supernatural powers, but these religions are also more than that. God has not abandoned the world to destruction but has implanted seeds of wisdom and truth in other traditions—truth, it must be noted, that is not equally emphasized in the Bible. Hence, McDermott suggests the possibility that Christians have new things to learn from other traditions. But then he retreats a bit from a full-throated affirmation of that possibility:

> I am not saying that these are new insights not presently taught by the biblical revelation. *They are in the Bible, either explicitly or implicitly.* But many of us in the church have not seen them, or we see them less clearly than we could. God can use other religions to help us see what he put there long ago—just as he used Greek philosophy to help Christians in the first three centuries see with some clarity the biblical data about God being both one and three. Or think of the way God used Neoplatonism to show Augustine things about Christ that he and church had not previously seen. And the way God used Aristotle to shed light for Thomas Aquinas on certain aspects of Christ and life with him.[34]

How is one to assess such a remarkable set of apparently contradictory claims? McDermott seems constrained by principle to contend that the Christians cannot learn something genuinely new if by "new" we mean something that is not taught at all by "the biblical revelation." All truth and wisdom must be in there somehow even if the Bible does not emphasize certain truths that other traditions do. While nothing can be added to biblical revelation, Christians can learn new things with the help of other religions. But what is the nature of that new learning? We might call it "explicitation," the work of rendering explicit what is merely implicit in biblical revelation.

The constraints under which McDermott operates, or believes he must operate, can permit him to go only so far. He cannot suggest that the Christian tradition has always been growing and learning from what the Bible has never taught. If that latter claim were made, one might well tumble down the slippery slope that leads to affirming other revelations, other disclosures of God that might also be salvific, and it would no longer be possible to confess that biblical revelation is complete. For if there is truth other than or different from what the Bible teaches, then Christians may have to learn what they did not know before. This possibility points in the direction of pluralism, something that McDermott cannot affirm.

But should it matter to comparative theologians that McDermott must insist that every possible truth is already contained in scripture? True, such claims strain credulity. However, if McDermott and his community of readers must operate under the proviso that all learning is merely explicitation, let it be so. The important thing is that Christians learn what they had not appreciated before from a wide variety of other religions and philosophical traditions. To the degree that such learning is possible, one can affirm—as McDermott does—that other religions are part of the divine economy. They serve as preparations for the gospel, they prevent persons from other cultures from falling entirely into error, they are signs that the *logos* is present in other traditions, and they are means by which the Spirit "can judge and purify the church."[35] If Christians can learn from other traditions, these traditions cannot be dismissed. Still, McDermott is clear: these other religions are too fraught with error and genuine spiritual danger to save. They do not and cannot. In this sense, he strikes stridently exclusivist notes even as he has opened himself to a kind of inclusivism by affirming the possibility of deep interreligious learning.

McDermott's cautious inclusivism—we already possess the truth in full even if we need other traditions to render explicit what revelation has bequeathed—suggests that most inclusivisms are unlikely to offer substantive motivation for persons to engage in interreligious learning. Inclusivisms typically rest on a part-whole logic: even if other traditions offer possibilities for truth and/or salvation, other traditions are deficient as they offer in part what the home tradition enjoys in full. Let us call such versions "hierarchical inclusivisms." Hierarchical or part-whole forms of inclusivism are customarily unable to affirm religious diversity as a positive *de jure* good. After all, nothing material is lost should other traditions cease to exist as my tradition fulfills what is partially expressed elsewhere. Hence such inclusivisms are unpromising for those who affirm and celebrate religious diversity as a positive and necessary good.

Recent TRD literature, however, points to new kinds of inclusivism that open the door to interreligious learning. Paul Griffiths was among the first to articulate this possibility by making the distinction between closed and open inclusivism. Griffiths holds, "Inclusivism is closed if it claims that all alien religious truths (should there be any) are already known to and explicitly taught by the home religion in some form." By contrast, an inclusivism is "open if it permits the possibility that some of the truths not (yet) explicitly taught or understood by the home religion might be known to and taught by some alien religion."[36] Griffiths notes that the consequences of holding to this newer vision of inclusivism are vast. For those who adhere to closed inclusivism, "nothing new can be learned by studying and coming to know what it is that any particular alien religion teaches."[37] Hence interest in the particularities of other traditions will be severely truncated. Not so for open inclusivists! By this definition, it is plain that McDermott's position contains features of an open inclusivism inasmuch as he holds that the Christian tradition does not already and *explicitly* teach all possible religious truth.

With Griffiths, I hold that open inclusivism is a very promising option for those interested in interreligious learning. The Christian open inclusivist need not hold that the church teaches all religious truth. As Griffiths puts it, ". . . since the Church already acknowledges that she needs to learn some of what she must teach from those outside her boundaries, and that alien religions teach truths, there would need to be pressing reasons to deny that some of what the Church needs to learn is already to be found among the teachings of alien religions. . . . And, so far as I can tell, there are no such reasons."[38] I offer an enthusiastic Amen!

How, then, does open inclusivism differ from pluralism? Griffiths believes that pluralists are compelled to find some way to posit parity between the truth claims of various religions, either on Kantian or Wittgensteinian grounds, both of which he rejects.[39] Having rejected parity claims, Griffiths believes he has rejected pluralism as such, a conclusion that I take to be mistaken. By contrast, open inclusivists do not posit parity between traditions either on questions of truth or soteriology. Open inclusivists can hold that the home tradition is superior to others with respect to claims to religious truth and salvation. But superiority claims do not eliminate the possibility of learning from other traditions; Christians can take a serious and respectful interest in them. Open inclusivists can take particularity seriously. Moreover, insofar as open inclusivism is willing to learn from other traditions in specific detail and depth, open inclusivists need not be committed to counterfactual accounts of religions as tightly integrated systematic wholes or radically incommensurable language games. For all these reasons, open inclusivism represents a promising and relatively underexplored option within theologies of religious diversity.

As with certain exclusivisms, the fact that open inclusivism is compatible with interreligious learning does not offer sufficient reason for maintaining an inclusivist position. If at least some strands from a variety of religious traditions are recognized as leading persons to true and transformative "comprehensive qualitative orientation"—a definition of the religious that I advance in Chapter 5—then, some variety of pluralism is to be preferred to the superiority claims advanced by inclusivists. Moreover, we have no reason to believe that any tradition exceeds all others, not least because traditions cannot be ranked. Theological judgment is always a matter of nuance, detail, and particularity. All our traditions are, to use Paul Tillich's language, deeply ambiguous. Each contains what is life-giving but also what is death-dealing. Given the catastrophic and even genocidal suffering that those confessing Christian convictions have inflicted on countless human beings and the planet, it is difficult to make claims about unilateral Christian superiority. If truth rests not just in propositions alone but is also in embodied forms of life, Christian forms of life, as they have been actually performed, stand under indictment. In sum, we simply do not have reason to hold to the unmitigated superiority of any tradition over the other.

Furthermore, contra Griffiths and D'Costa, I hold that pluralists need not posit parity between traditions. One need not advance parity claims in order to be a pluralist. Pluralists need only posit that transformative truth is available in a variety of traditions without proceeding to a questionable discourse that weighs "religions" against each other. Pluralists can reject inclusivist claims to superiority without committing themselves to a parity discourse. Parity claims are as questionable as superiority claims, especially when they neutralize the possibility of revelation and truth by appeal to questionable Kantian strategies.[40] Religions are not the sort of realities that can be weighed comparatively. If you do believe that religions can be so measured, then you are likely committed to an untenable account of just what religions are. The version of pluralism that I commend in the next chapter, relational pluralism, does not posit parity because it regards religious traditions as complex and porous historical flows that have always been shaped by each other. They are not discrete objects, like bowling balls, for example, that can be placed upon a scale.

But what about the question of truth? Doesn't the sheer fact of belonging to a tradition or some strand thereof commit one to a set of claims one takes not only to be relatively adequate but actually superior to the claims of others? Just that contention appears to be built into Griffiths's definition of a religion. He defines a religion as,

> a form of life that seems to those who belong to it to be comprehensive, incapable of abandonment, and of central importance to the ordering of their lives. It is the great circle that seems to religious people to contain all the small circles representing their noncomprehensive forms of life; it is a form of life the abandonment of which seems to those who inhabit it to be tantamount to the abandonment of their identity; and it is a form of life that permits address to the questions that seem to those who belong to it to matter more than any others.[41]

I am deeply divided about this definition; I am appreciative of some elements but suspicious of others. A particularly problematic conclusion follows as a direct consequence of his definition—namely, that no one can belong to more than one religion, at least at one time:

> [N]o one can inhabit more than one form of religious life at a time. Religions bear the relation of noncompossibility one to another. This is because a form of life that seems to you comprehensive, incapable of abandonment, and of central importance to the ordering of your life . . . *by definition* provides answers to (or at least a mode of addressing) those questions that seem to you of central importance to the ordering of your life.[42]

By definition indeed! Griffiths's claim entails that the vast majority of human beings who have ever lived have been engaged, unbeknownst to themselves, in the impossible. Any definition of religions that builds into it the requirement that human beings can belong only to one religion at a time is akin to proposing a definition of marriage that specifies that only the monogamous can properly be said to be married. Now, while a given social group might elect to subscribe to and defend a *normative* notion of marriage that holds that marriage can only mean monogamy—in other words, marriage *must* mean monogamy—no such definition can be accepted as *descriptively* valid. Human beings have had all kinds of marital configurations, and monogamy is just one. Likewise, multiple religious participation and belonging have been constant features of human experience, particularly in East and even South Asia. Therefore, any definition of what a religion is that imposes on life what is wildly refused by widespread human behavior across various cultures and times is profoundly wanting. Griffith proposes a normative claim by sleight of hand. Definitions must fit life, not the other way around, and life in all its riotous exuberance rarely conforms to constricted definitions.

To be religious is, I will argue in Chapters 5 and 6, to aspire to comprehensive orientation. It is unclear that any finite human project can deliver on that aspiration. Traditions try. But religious traditions, at least when they are at their best, routinely remind adherents of their own failures, limits, and inadequacies at plumbing the depths of divine and worldly mystery. Thinkers within traditions and even formal teachings call to mind the limitations of every "religion." Comprehensiveness is a goal and not a given. Moreover, the religious quest for comprehensive qualitative orientation is likely to require collaborative effort of a variety of traditions working together so that the peculiar insights of each tradition, insights made possible by the particular vocabularies, conceptual forms, and spiritual disciplines of each tradition can, when taken together, generate a truer and more encompassing sense of orientation than any tradition can deliver alone.

Griffiths's other markers also seem only partially on point. While a tradition may seem incapable of abandonment, it is nonetheless true that persons adhere to their traditions in a variety of ways. A religion may well be taken seriously but not exclusively. Moreover, no one accepts a religion *in toto*, not even Griffiths; we are always selecting from, revising, contesting, and committing ourselves to particular strands of our traditions. In doing so, we abandon some versions of our tradition for others. Also, just what would it mean to maintain fidelity to an entire "religion?" The answer is hardly clear.

Nor is any religion a form of life—a root error in many postliberal imaginations. As should be apparent from the slightest empirical investigation, multiple forms of life can be and have been generated using only Christian ingredients, many of which are mutually irreconcilable. Pacifist forms of life, just war forms of life, slaveholder Christianity, liberationist Christianity—this list could go on and on. So to characterize any religion as a comprehensive and singular form of life that seems incapable of abandonment is unjustifiable on empirical grounds.

Further, few inhabit one form of life alone. This is just as true in contemporary America as in East Asia. We are always borrowing from and indebted to ingredients from several different cultural and religious repertoires. Contemporary American Christians are, whether they elect to or not, more likely to be shaped, if not co-opted, by neoliberal market forces than by their Christianity. More positively, many contemporary Christian forms of life show signs of creative incorporation of ingredients from Hindu and Buddhist religious repertoires such as yoga or vipassana. Talk of inhabiting a single form of life that is comprehensive, incapable of abandonment, one that poses all the critical questions and answers by which a human life can be lived, seems fanciful. The questions and answers offered by a religious tradition are central but therefore not incapable of contestation, revision, and even supplementation by resources borrowed from other philosophical and religious traditions.

To believe that the strand of the tradition to which I belong is true, I need not believe that it is unsurpassably true. I need only believe that it registers important dimensions of reality and divinity that are life-giving and salvific. Other traditions may also be onto something and likely are. It will take considerable conversation and engagement, perhaps even over the historical long haul, to discern how the truth claims of various traditions can be held together. In the course of that conversation, I may be compelled to revise and, if necessary, abandon elements of my tradition by which I am no longer persuaded. Hence, there is no reason to believe that the set of Christian convictions to which I currently adhere is unsurpassably true.

Nor does this more modest claim entail epistemological relativism—what D'Costa calls "indifferentism." Because I am persuaded in the truth as I have come to know it from my tradition, I am prepared to engage in an apologetic defense of the truth as I know and understand it. Griffiths's argument that apologetics has an important role to play in interreligious encounter is compelling.[43] Interreligious contestation can play a vital role in energizing religious thought and life. But apologetics ought not to be thought of solely as contestation. Apologetics is necessarily also a matter of dialogue. When I attempt to persuade you of the truth of my convictions, I must formulate and give expression to those convictions in ways you can understand. To do so, I must, at least in part, express my ideas in idioms and thought forms that you find comprehensible and cogent.

Apologetics, so understood, presupposes that the relationship between traditions is analogical, that I can articulate what I believe by using some ideas from your tradition. If so, then I am perforce acknowledging that sharp opposition and incommensurability cannot mark the relationship between my ideas and yours. Even if I believe that my convictions capture elements of truth that you do not currently appreciate, I can well imagine that the converse might also be true: you see things I do not. In this landscape of gradations and analogy, it seems hardly credible to maintain that my tradition is unilaterally unsurpassable when compared to yours.

All of this leads me to ask the following questions about Griffiths's or any version of open inclusivism: what would happen if open inclusivists surrendered implausible accounts of religion as tightly integrated and comprehensive forms of life?[44] What might transpire if open inclusivists admitted that religious traditions are malleable, porous, always internally multiple, and never discrete from other forms of life, religious and nonreligious? What if they forthrightly acknowledged that deep learning from another tradition transforms the learner and her tradition? And if there is deep learning to be had from other traditions—as open inclusivists affirm—doesn't that suggest that other religious traditions hold precious resources that are intrinsically true and transformative in their own right? What if a more empirically sustainable understanding of how traditions work softened claims to unsurpassability, deep grammars, and finality? Would not an open inclusivism, when set free from such conceptual baggage, move in the direction of robust pluralism?[45] The answer must be yes.

To conclude our conversation on inclusivism, I hold that open inclusivism is a genuinely promising option in TRD. Open inclusivists can affirm (1) that religious traditions are genuinely different but therefore not incommensurable. Griffiths, however, holds that they are "incompossible." Griffiths may be right *in some cases* but not globally so. To live within certain strands of certain traditions simultaneously is impossible, but to posit incompossibility across all religions, by definition, is theoretical overreach. The question of incompossibility must always be determined on a case-by-case basis. Other open inclusivists need not follow Griffiths's assertion. (2) Open inclusivists affirm that religions do make truth claims and that at least some of those truth claims are not already found in Christian traditions. So, open inclusivists affirm the possibility of inter-religious learning. (3) If we take Griffiths to stand in for open inclusivism in general, we run into problems with respect to our third criterion—namely, a critical theory of religion. Griffiths fails this test by subscribing to accounts of religion that are empirically unsustainable. (4) Finally, having built into his theory an account of religions as incompossible, it's hard to see how an open inclusivist can take an intrinsic religious interest in the aims of another tradition. What learning takes place across traditions is likely to be in service of the prior aims and aspirations of the learner's home tradition. Once more, we see how a constricted theory of religion limits the promise of an important option in TRD.

Although my own trinitarian comparative theology of religious diversity, outlined in Chapter 7, is pluralistic, I have a genuine sympathy and appreciation for open inclusivism. However, I refuse claims to superiority and hold that other traditions have transforming and true access to distinctive dimensions of the divine multiplicity, a multiplicity that I describe in trinitarian terms. My commitment to pluralism does not mean that I believe that pluralism is invulnerable to critique. Some forms most assuredly are, as we shall now see.

# 3 No One Ascends Alone

## TOWARD A RELATIONAL PLURALISM

*Given the precarity of planetary cohabitation, a relational pluralism happens not over and against the variously separative Ones. It breaks through their walls of mutual contradiction from within a cloud that they may im/possibly recognize they share. . . . [T]he One is one not opposed to any many: "Identity is enfolded difference." So the Supreme Complication also enfolds—in their diversity—the multiple faith practices of the world. They cannot be forced or tricked into unity, but in conversation explicate, and in practice, unfold, the ecumenical religio in which they are* already *unknowingly tied together. The folds of difference, heretofore cut into a history of catastrophe, thus unfold into peaceable conversation.*

—CATHERINE KELLER, *Cloud of the Impossible:
Negative Theology and Planetary Entanglement*

## How Pluralistic Is Pluralism?

Pluralism has come in for withering criticism in recent decades. Thankfully, some pluralists have been chastened by their critics and have advanced alternatives that escape the major challenges put to earlier versions. It's not clear that critics have noticed. In this chapter, I build toward a version of pluralism that Roland Faber and Catherine Keller call "relational pluralism." Relational pluralism answers the call advanced by Paul Hedges for a TRD that marries the best of pluralist and particularist wisdom while avoiding the excesses of each.[1] Hedges and Paul Knitter both have offered compelling critical surveys, assessments, and reformulations of pluralism; hence, I need not reinvent that wheel.[2] I wish only to situate relational pluralism as the most compelling option within a larger family of alternatives. Relational pluralism bears strong similarities to what Knitter has come to call the mutuality approach and what Hedges calls particularist pluralism. It also shares features with what David Ray Griffin and John Cobb have called "differential or deep pluralism," a position with which Mark Heim has also recently expressed "an elective affinity."[3] My version of relational pluralism affirms the recent pluralist turn toward particularity while insisting that religious differences can never be reified as they often seem to be when some pluralists posit multiple ultimate realities.

Two key features mark relational pluralism. The world's religions are not taken to be cleanly bounded isolates pursuing incommensurably different projects in isolation from all others—an account in which communal solipsism wins out. Nor are religions understood to be variations on a common and even essentially identical theme—an account in which sameness wins out. I would highlight three themes: (1) real difference, or better, distinctiveness, but never in splendid isolation; (2) distinctiveness but not incommensurability; and (3) distinctiveness catalyzed by being brought into relation. The energetic flows between traditions have always been integral to their constitution; this claim is true as a simple empirical matter. But for relational pluralism, cross-fertilization through relation is also a normative desideratum. Traditions that came to be what they are only in relation will only become what they are meant to be and fulfill their promise through relation. Relational pluralism so construed can meet the rigorous challenges leveled at older formulations.

But first, let me say more about the challenges posed by pluralism's critics. These challenges can be sorted into two kinds: one an immanent critique that accepts the basic parameters of the pluralistic project but contests pluralist answers, and the other an extrinsic critique that challenges the very terms and parameters of pluralism. I wish to account for both kinds of challenges. Extrinsic critiques of pluralism reject the very framing of the pluralist proposal, which seeks to ask whether the various "religions" are paths up the same mountain before, of course, answering yes. That way of framing the question—the labeling of our various traditions as religions and then defining religions as "soteriological vehicles"—has been sharply questioned for imposing a peculiarly Christian conception on global traditions.

Immanent critiques accept the classical framing but contest the pluralist answer. Such positions may concede that religions are, among other things, soteriological vehicles, but then proceed to hold that they do not arrive at the same soteriological destination. Or they may hold that religions are indeed projects that seek to orient persons toward ultimate reality, but there is more than one.

Both critiques are worth addressing, but the extrinsic challenge is far more serious. Those who proffer such critiques hold that pluralists impose similarity on other traditions as a condition for dialogue. You must become a religion before you can participate in "interreligious dialogue." Your tradition must be configured as a "religion," a Western category emerging from a particular provincial history that has gone global by way of colonial misadventures. My theoretical work in this book is a matter of describing and responding to this extrinsic critique (see Chapters 4 and 5). The true gravity of the problem will not be addressed apart from a perspicacious understanding of the operation of the categories "religion" and "religions." We generate conceptions that privilege *sameness* when we describe the various traditions as instances of the same universal and generic kind: religion. And we tend to privilege *difference* when we see the various traditions as a set of cleanly bounded entities, each up to its own fundamentally different, even incommensurable, project: religions. The operations of power, usually under the asymmetric and distorting influence of colonialism, have often compelled traditions to adopt the features of religion/s. That very process precedes and sets the terms for claims of sameness or difference.

Theologians of religious diversity and comparative theologians, who are alert to the problems generated by world religions discourse, face numerous challenges. Do we cease and desist? Do we jettison the work of formulating theologies of religious diversity once we realize the numerous problems that surround the notion of religion? Do we stop comparing traditions or strands thereof once we realize that we—or rather our scholarly predecessors—have played a role in reconstructing complex cultural traditions into religions? My answer is a resounding no. Even (or perhaps especially) pluralists—who have been the special object of this charge of imposing sameness—must not pack it up and go home.

Our traditions, even before they were compelled to become religions, have always given accounts of each other—evaluative accounts marked by mutual learning even if apologetic motivations played a disproportionate role. True, comparison and evaluation are changed by the ways in which communities have come to think of their traditions as religions.

But the presence of encounter and assessment well before modernity, East and West, suggests that something like the work of TRD and comparative theology has long been a feature of inter-tradition encounter. For that reason, among others, I persist in asking the key questions of TRD even as I seek to account for the ways in which that labor has been distorted by problematic accounts of the category religion.

In this chapter, I attend to both extrinsic as well as immanent critiques but with a primary focus on the latter. The distinctive feature of extrinsic critique revolves around the complications that arise around category formation. The set of issues around the category religion are so severe that the next two chapters are given over to (a) diagnosing the problems generated by the category and (b) proposing an alternative theory of the religious that hopes to avoid those problems. This chapter attends to those problems as well but only en passant as they present themselves in theories of religious diversity.

But immanent critiques matter too. It is surely true that we must take note of problems introduced by processes of religionization as they take varying global and local expressions. That said, not all but many of those traditions that we have come to think of as religions do in fact pose questions of soteriology and ultimacy. Christian preoccupation with these concerns may have to do with our focus on the notion of "religion," but theologians of religious diversity are not inserting soteriological themes into other traditions out of whole cloth, nor are concerns about ultimacy alien impositions.

Cultural traditions that we have come to call religions include far more than these themes. Moreover, those traditions that we tend to think of as non-religious also entertain soteriological concerns and ultimate commitments; hence, a focus on religions alone narrows the theologian's conversation partners. Reality is far messier than our categories—hence the need for the theoretical reformulation that follows in the chapters to come. Nonetheless, this chapter continues the humbler task of working within the frame of current questions even while pointing toward reframing those questions as we proceed.

When engaged in immanent assessment, I employ the same four criteria articulated in the previous chapter: (1) the difference without incommensurability criterion; (2) the truth criterion; (3) the critical theory of religion criterion; and (4) the intrinsic religious interest criterion. I pay special attention to the fourth criterion because pluralists have been accused, with some justification, of failing to give reasons for taking seriously the particular claims, aims, and practices of other traditions. If all traditions are but various paths to the selfsame destination, why bother engaging in the particularities of other traditions? I argue that relational pluralism passes these tests whereas neighboring forms of pluralism come close but show signs of strain.

## Current Forms of Pluralism: Assessing Strengths and Weaknesses

The most influential form of pluralism to date is John Hick's version—so influential, in fact, that often he is taken to stand in for pluralism as such. When pluralism is attacked, almost always Hick's version is under assault. Pluralists hold that a variety of religions are independently efficacious means to salvation, which Hick defines as the transformation of persons from self-centeredness to reality-centeredness. He holds that none of the major traditions performs this work any better than any other. Hence, there is relative parity between traditions on questions of salvation and truth.[4]

David Ray Griffin has rightly argued that the reduction of pluralism to Hick's formulation is a disservice to pluralism understood as a larger family of distinct options. I concur. Griffin argues that (1) pluralism comes in many forms and that (2) some forms of pluralism, those that he calls "differential pluralism" or "deep pluralism," escape the problems that beset John Hick's formulation.[5] Griffin and John Cobb, to whom Griffin is indebted, rightly hold that there are other more compelling forms of pluralism available. The key to their deep pluralism is the claim that there is more than one ultimate reality and hence also a variety of religious ends. The various religions are not planets orbiting the same sun. There are many suns! Hence religious truth cannot be singular. Nor can religious ends, or salvations, be the same.

Although I agree that Hick's mode of pluralism is not very pluralistic, I hold that talk about multiple ultimates is neither coherent nor necessary. My trinitarian version of relational pluralism is an alternative to both John Hick's pluralism and that of Cobb and Griffin. There is multiplicity *within* the divine life but no multiple ultimates. But here, I am getting ahead of myself (all the way to Chapter 7). Given Hick's prominence in the literature, any discussion of pluralism must begin with him.[6] But first a more general and basic question: What makes one any kind of pluralist at all?

The core affirmation of pluralism is that a variety of religious traditions offer access to salvation and religious truth. Still more, pluralists take the position that (1) the degree to which religions offer access to salvation and religious truth is on par, and (2) each tradition is independently efficacious in making such access possible. Both these claims are problematic. As I have already indicated, religions are not unitary and reified entities of the sort that can be weighed against each other so as to warrant either superiority claims or parity claims. Some strands of my own tradition and that of others are not merely problematic but pernicious. Theological attention to specific features and strands within religious traditions weakens the plausibility of claims about any "religion" being either superior or equal to another. Hence, pluralism cannot be defined by appeal to parity claims.

What, then, about the second feature of pluralism, the notion that religions are independently efficacious in bringing persons to salvation and religious truth? This claim is more promising but also problematic. What does it mean to affirm that any tradition is "independently efficacious?" It means, at the very least, that what makes your tradition effective in delivering truth and salvation is not a principle or power that is explicitly named and recognized in mine but is operative only in implicit, hidden, or diminished ways in yours (inclusivism). Your tradition is not independently efficacious (let's suppose that you are a Buddhist) if your tradition saves because the Christ is anonymously at work in Buddhism even though you believe it is the truth of emptiness that liberates. In metaphoric language, each tradition is its own path up the mountain. It is not the case that you are on my path without knowing it.

But if all our traditions have been informed and transformed by each other, if the history of religions is one of mutual encounter, then how can I claim that each "religion" is its own independent way of ascending the mountain of religious truth? What can independence mean over the historical long haul? Within the space opened up by the mountain climbing metaphor, would it not be closer to the mark to say our paths often cross? May we not share the very same track for a time but then diverge? Are not the outcroppings and footholds to which we make recourse sometimes the same and sometimes not? Haven't religious communities taught each other some of the practices necessary for religious mountain climbing even if each community then improvises on those practices, modifying them as befits their special needs, skills, and particular terrain?

None of our traditions can be independently efficacious because none exists independently. I do not deny that religious communities can and do serve as contexts for healing and transformation without outside assistance. I mean only to suggest that the repertoire of any tradition is historically fluid and never a discrete, bounded, and self-existent reality. Pluralists need not build reification into their definitions of pluralism. When they do, they fall afoul of the "critical theory of religion" criterion by being in thrall to inadequate notions of what religious traditions are.

Pluralists would do well to stipulate that what each tradition has to offer is not reducible to or better or best articulated in the terms of another tradition, usually the home tradition of the interpreting theologian. Each tradition, because it is itself a confluence of many streams of influence, offers liberating access to ultimate reality. The kind of access afforded depends on the language, categories, and practices that make that access possible. Even if what you come to know of ultimate reality is resonant with, and in some cases, profoundly similar to what I have learned by way of my tradition, your tradition is not just mine wearing a different cloak. "The way is not separate from the goal."[7] Something is known or appreciated by the specificities that each tradition offers, even when those specificities are also the result of religious cross-pollination.

The irreducibility of the insights of others to what we have already come to know of ultimate reality by way of our tradition should not prohibit theological attempts to capture what others have seen by way of our native vocabularies, even if those vocabularies are ruptured and reformulated in that very process. In Chapter 7, I advance a trinitarian reading of certain features of Hindu and Buddhist traditions. However, even though I use trinitarian formulations to interpret other traditions, the meaning of these terms is disrupted, supplemented, and transformed by what I have learned from other traditions.[8] This work of interpretation by way of comparative theological learning is a hallmark of "relational pluralism," a pluralism that surrenders conceptions of reified religions working in isolation. With this formulation of pluralism in hand, let's survey and assess some pluralist and post-pluralist options.

One organizing metaphor has shaped the questions taken up by theologians working within this field. The metaphor imagines religious life as akin to a venture in mountain climbing and takes the religions to be paths up a mountain. The metaphor generates a basic question that has served to set the terms for debate: Are the world religions paths up the same mountain? When we move from metaphor to concept, that question takes the following cast: Are the different religions independent means for arriving at the same saving end? Do the different religions all lead to healing because they all lead to God or ultimate reality?

We have seen that most Christian exclusivists say no: Jesus is the only way to salvation, and so other religions cannot as such lead to God. There is only one path up the mountain. Christian inclusivists offer a more nuanced answer. Persons from other religious traditions may arrive at God, but only because Christ or the Holy Spirit is at work in the lives of religious neighbors or even in their traditions. Hence, religions are not independent paths leading to the religious summit. Hick answers the question affirmatively: the religions are independently efficacious paths up the mountain. Hick's own preferred metaphor is planetary: the religions are planets orbiting (equidistantly, of course) around the same sun—hence his call for a Copernican revolution in religion away from a "geocentric view" in which one religion sits at the center.[9]

Hick contends that religious traditions are "soteriological vehicles" that lead us from self-centeredness to reality centeredness. All major religious traditions make this transformation possible, and no tradition is so exceptional at this work that it might justifiably claim to be superior to all others. All paths lead to the summit and none more swiftly than any other. Hence, Hick is a pluralist because of his commitment to a parity position.

What, then, of the various understandings of ultimate reality found in the world's religious traditions? How are the sharp differences to be correlated with Hick's contention that the traditions are engaged in the selfsame project? Hick claims that they are phenomenal "manifestations" of a noumenal Real that always exceeds all concepts that we may form about that reality. The differences between these conceptions do not bear on the soteriological work that the traditions accomplish. Ultimate reality or the Real is *neither* personal nor impersonal.[10] This is not to say that the religions are wrong to imagine the Real as personal or impersonal because the Real does give itself to be experienced in these ways. On their own terms, the religions are incompatible; traditions that claim that ultimate reality is personal really are in conflict with traditions that say that ultimate reality is impersonal. But from Hick's pluralist perspective, all fall short of the nature of ultimate reality as it is in itself.

How does Hick know that the various religions are oriented to one and the same ultimate reality? He offers a pragmatic answer: the major religious traditions all lead persons from narrow self-centeredness to reality-centeredness. They accomplish the same transformative work. Every tradition generates saints, none better than any other. Although each tradition depicts the specific features of this transformation in different ways, generically speaking all do the same thing. Hence, on both the anthropological side and the theological side, Hick asserts that there is an underlying identity between traditions. There is but one mountain to climb and one summit to reach.

## John Hick's Pluralist and Post-Pluralist Critics and Defenders

Hick's proposal fails to offer a deep motivation for interreligious dialogue. Religious traditions have little to learn about God or ultimate reality in and through dialogue. If every account of the Real is equally true and equally false because none are adequate to the nature of the Real *an sich* which infinitely transcends all concepts, then the only reason remaining for dialogue can be neighborliness. Neighborliness ought not to be trivialized; relations of care between communities can be regarded as salvific inasmuch as the work of justice and reconciliation amounts to healing labor. But, on a Hickian account, dialogue with other traditions does not lead to more knowledge about ultimate reality. We can only learn more about how our neighbors *conceive* of ultimate reality out of their own differing religio-cultural repertoires. That work is anthropological and not theological. No traditions know *anything* about ultimate reality as it is in itself. Why then assume that learning about other equally inadequate and culturally variable concepts would have anything to teach us?

Likewise, if the differences between accounts of human healing do not matter because they all generate the same generic result, we need not be *religiously* interested in the concrete disciplines and practices of other religious traditions. The Christian who partakes of the Eucharist is generically doing the same thing as the Buddhist who engages in vipassana or Zen. Each is but a tradition-specific way of moving from self-centeredness to reality-centeredness. The means differ but the end is the same. Hick fails to offer reasons for serious interest in the textured differences between traditional practices or between Christian conceptions of God and Buddhist accounts of Buddha-nature. Might the concrete spiritual disciplines of another tradition offer access to dimensions of ultimate reality that are not well accessed in our strand of our home tradition? Hick does not pose such questions because he cannot. His commitment to one unknowable ultimate reality trumps diversity. There is but one ultimate reality and just one worthwhile religious end. Hick's pluralism turns out to be not so pluralistic at all.

Hick's program gains parity but at considerable cost. All traditions are rendered on par with each other by relativizing every tradition's claim to special knowledge of ultimate reality. He believes that it would be impossible to sustain parity between traditions if one tradition makes claims to superiority by appeal to special revelation granted to it alone. If my tradition has special access and yours does not, mine is superior. To eliminate the possibility of such special pleading, Hick installs an opaque Kantian boundary between religions and ultimate reality. No one knows anything about what ultimate reality is in itself, and yet, ultimate reality makes itself present somehow to make transformation possible. We are transformed by what we cannot know.

If this reading of Hick holds—and there are followers of Hick who contest this Kantian reading—then Hick's account of religious diversity runs afoul of several of the criteria I have enumerated.[11] Of the four criteria named for a productive TRD, Hick's account meets only the first criterion: difference without incommensurability. Yes, the religious traditions are different in their own terms, but because those terms operate only at a phenomenal level, there can be no real final incommensurability between them. Or, on a slightly variant formulation, even if there is incommensurability on their own terms, that does not matter. Religious traditions serve the same general work of transformation—the movement toward reality-centeredness.

The trouble is that if religious traditions don't have access to ultimate reality—if the other has no genuine knowledge of ultimate reality—then what do I stand to learn from other traditions? Learning in a constructive key requires the assumption that some strands of some traditions are truth-granting and that some of that truth is not already available in the home tradition. Hick cannot affirm that, as all claims to truth seem to be disabled. Hick fails to meet our second criterion for any successful TRD.

Hick has generated a religious theory of religions that is (1) realistic— the various religious traditions point to a common referent; (2) egalitarian— all the religious traditions are on par with respect to salvation and truth; and (3) unitary—there is but one ultimate reality to which these traditions refer. But if there is just one ultimate reality about which the religious traditions say incompatible things, how then is a realist theory sustainable over against a projectionist account? Hick's strategy for solving this problem is striking and stark. Save realism by sacrificing truth to transformation. Posit the absolute unknowability of ultimate reality but affirm the practical validity of truth claims insofar as those claims advance the work of religious transformation.[12]

How do we know that there is *any* ultimate reality behind the screen onto which we project our diverse concepts arising from our various cultural and linguistic frames? Hick responds, "So the Real is that which there must be if human religious experience, in its diversity of forms, is not purely imaginary projection. It is, in Kantian terms, a necessary postulate of religious experience in its diversity of forms."[13]

And how do we know that there is *only one* ultimate reality rather than more than one? Hick's answer again is strikingly practical. The theoretical reasons have to do with the conceptual problems generated by a functional polytheism or by affirming one personal ultimate and one transpersonal ultimate, a position he discerns in John Cobb. Hick wonders how a diversity of realities can be ultimate if there are many. But what really drives Hick is the practical motivation: the traditions transform and they transform in the same way. There is an ultimate reality because the various traditions generate practical fruits, and there is *only one* because of the "striking similarity" in the fruits of transformation that each tradition generates.[14]

What about the differences in transformations generated and the distinctive personal excellences sought by traditions? Is love (*agape*) the same as compassion (*karuna*)? Is being awakened the same as being saved? Hick would surely respond with an of course not; he claims similarity, not identity. I say more: the distinctive goals sought by the various traditions matter because they resonate with different dimensions of the divine life. There is a correspondence between what we become and what we come to know about distinctive features of the divine life.

Defenders of Hick suggest that genuine interreligious learning is possible even within the frame of his pluralism. Notable in this regard is Perry Schmidt-Leukel, whose work is of signal importance. His defense of interreligious learning and comparative theology is convincing. Also persuasive are his ripostes to standard objections leveled against pluralism. There is also considerable overlap between his three requirements for "interreligious learning and enrichment" and mine for any adequate TRD. He writes as follows:

First, no religion must be seen as perfect; otherwise there would be nothing to learn. Second, there must be genuine difference and otherness; otherwise nothing new could be learned. Third, difference must nevertheless be related to some common ground; otherwise nothing new could be learned about the theologically crucial reality. Pluralist theologies meet these requirements by emphasizing a distinction that, as Hick has often said, lies at the centre of religious pluralism: the distinction between ultimate reality (the Real) as such (or *an sich*) and ultimate reality as humanly thought of and experienced. . . . It is this distinction which meets the three requirements. In pointing out the transcategoriality, and hence ineffability, of the Real *an sich*, the first requirement is met: it is ensured that no religious system can justifiably claim to possess the fullness of truth, a complete and accurate picture of the ultimate, which would leave no space for learning anything meaningful about the Real from others. Further, the distinction relates the various conceptions of the ultimate, its different personifications and impersonal representations, to one and the same ultimate reality, so that these conceptions can also be meaningfully related to each other. The distinction is not to sever the concrete personal and impersonal absolutes of the religions from the true yet inaccessible ultimate, but rather to see these absolutes as possibly united in a common ultimate ground. This is how pluralism meets the third requirement."[15]

If I see my religion as already perfect, I have nothing to learn; insofar as pluralists reject such a claim, they leave room for learning. Schmidt-Leukel rightly celebrates this virtue of pluralism. However, even some versions of exclusivism and inclusivism leave sufficient room for interreligious learning. Those formulations, even when sounding pluralist notes, have no need for Hick's Kantianism. One needs only some way of affirming "genuine difference and otherness," but there are many ways to get there.

With Hick and Schmidt-Leukel, I also posit a common ground. I do so because it is the most economical hypothesis. Where Hick and (possibly) Schmidt-Leukel run aground is in the next step: the claim that one must posit a distinction between an absolutely unknowable Real *an sich* and "ultimate reality as humanly thought of and experienced." Positing an impermeable wall of separation between the two is problematic. Hick argues that all conceptual claims about ultimate reality arise from out of our cultural and historical matrices. We experience ultimate reality differently because our cultures, languages, and concepts differ, and not because there is anything in the divine life that corresponds to those differences; if there were an objective correlate to such particularities, there would be no way to know. Ultimate reality appears to act as a blank screen that reflects back to us what we project onto it. *We* bring to the Real all that we claim to know about the Real; the Real in itself remains absolutely unknowable.

Contra Hick, I broach an alternative position. Not all of our diverse accounts regarding the Real are the result of culturally variant conceptual frameworks; some have a *fundamentum in re*. The Real gives itself in a multiplicity of ways because it is a multiplicity. *Some* of what we say about the Real is projection, but not *all*. No genuine interreligious learning is possible otherwise.

Interreligious learning cannot be reduced to the study of what the various traditions imagine the Real to be. That would be comparative anthropology and not comparative theology. Consider the possibility that the Real can show itself *both* as personal and as transpersonal just because there is something in the Real that grounds both showings. One might argue that the ultimate reality is *both* personal and impersonal (rather than *neither* as Hick himself argues) but in different respects and thereby avoids contradiction. The *Bhagavad Gita* makes just that affirmation. Not everything that is said about ultimate reality can be true, but far more might be admitted than Hick allows.

What about the critical theory of religion criterion? Hick has comprehensive theory of religions as soteriological vehicles. Despite this theoretical sophistication, Hick's work displays minimal awareness of genealogy of religion. He takes for granted that there just is a certain set of world religions, each of which serves as a vehicle for ultimate transformation. That such ways of thinking are of recent historical vintage goes unrecognized. On the contrary, Hick ascribes the soteriological character of religion to the transformations inaugurated by the Axial Age. He writes, "Whilst archaic religion accepted life as it is and sought to continue it on a stable basis, there came through the outstanding figures of the axial period the disturbing and yet uplifting thought of a limitlessly better possibility. Among the new streams of religious experience by no means every wave and eddy is soteriologically oriented. Nevertheless a clear soteriological pattern is visible both in the Indian religions of Hinduism, Buddhism and Jainism, and in the Semitic religions of Judaism, Christianity and Islam, as well as in their modern secular offspring, Marxism."[16]

Several features of this claim are remarkable: (1) there is a general soteriological structure present in a variety of religions (explicit premise); (2) there are several religions that exist and have existed since the axial period (taken for granted implicit premise); and (3) even the secular offspring of Semitic religions, Marxism, has a soteriological structure. Of these claims, the one that is most problematic is the second. Would these traditions recognize themselves as "religions"? Even today there are many Jews who would challenge the applicability of this descriptor. Leora Batnitzky has argued that the first Jew to describe Judaism as a religion was Kant's eighteenth-century contemporary, Moses Mendelsohn, and he was immediately challenged on that score.[17] Hence, to talk of "religions" as existing since the Axial Age seems a questionable anachronism. Ancient traditions, yes; ancient religions, no.

The first claim is less problematic. That each of these human traditions *has* a general soteriological structure is uncontroversial. That these traditions just *are* this soteriological structure is a problematic contention. The traditions that we have come to call religions have been marked by a vast array of concerns and tasks that go far beyond what we have come to think of as religious—matters political and economic, for example, which we have now come to think of as secular. To become a religion is to be caught up in a process in which what traditions are is lost from view as they are reduced to religions, reduced among other things, to their soteriological elements. Insofar as Hick's work focuses on only the soteriological feature of these traditions, it can give the impression that this is what the religions essentially are. But he need not be so read.

Indeed, his claim about Marxism suggests that he is aware that religious traditions have always had broader commitments than soteriology narrowly construed. While it makes some sense to speak of Marxism as secularized soteriology, it may be truer to say that all traditions we now call religions have always contained visions of proper sociopolitical ordering. Marxism is not distinctive. What has been lost from view is just how secular—how worldly—all our traditions were prior to the inauguration of the modern divide between the religious and the secular— before, that is, our traditions were compelled to become religions.[18] Marxism differs from other religious traditions, not because it has a secularized soteriology; it is different because it has *only* a secular soteriology.

Far more problematic are Hick's central metaphors about religions insofar as these metaphors give the impression that religions are discrete entities. The Copernican language of planets orbiting around the same sun reinforces notions of religions as distinct self-existent entities. Even after religious traditions meet each other through interreligious dialogue, Hick imagines them as remaining largely unchanged. What would happen in the meeting and appreciation of religions is only that each tradition would, in time, leave aside claims to finality and superiority. Revising those claims will require considerable theological labor. But after that work, traditions would continue to carry out their independent soteriological projects as usual.

Finally, it is unclear how, on Hick's account, persons from one tradition could take the practices and insights of other traditions with religious interest. If each tradition operates according to its own settled logic, central metaphors, and conceptual structures, there is little reason for anyone to be religiously interested in the particularity of other practices and insights. They all make possible the same general transformation. The details vary, but the trajectory away from self-centeredness to reality-centeredness is the same. As the Real in itself remains refractory of our concepts and the practices bound up with those concepts, little hinges on the subtle textures of these differences. But then what are we to make of the deep interest in those who engage in multiple religious participation—namely, the sense that the divine is in the details, that those details point to facets of the divine life that are inaccessible without just those particular practices and ways of imagining and accessing divinity? This question is not easily answered from within Hick's frame.

## Mark Heim and the Step beyond (Identist) Pluralism

One critical step in thinking beyond Hick, while not leaving behind the merit of the questions he poses, comes with the work of S. Mark Heim. Heim's work is the crucial and decisive break beyond older models in thinking about TRD. Heim has emphatically argued that Hick's pluralism is not very pluralistic. In a provocative argument that opens up dramatically new possibilities, Heim argued that there is a profound point of agreement between the most conservative and most liberal of Christian theologians. Both agree that there is, at most, one worthwhile religious goal or end. The disagreement comes elsewhere: liberals assert that *many traditions* arrive at that single end, whereas conservatives believe that *only Christianity* provides access to that single end.

If two religions conflict, then at most one can be correct. Wishing to affirm Christianity, Christian exclusivists seek out conflicts and in each case affirm the error of the differing tradition. If your religion differs from mine, you must be wrong. Wishing not to attribute error to one religion against another, pluralists recognize difference but sever it from religious validity. They are convinced that where religions differ, the differences are only apparent . . . or are real but irrelevant in attaining the one true end of religion. If you think your religion is a real alternative to mine, you must be wrong.[19]

Neither camp takes difference seriously by entertaining the possibility that there might be multiple religious ends, many salvations.[20] Heim shows that exclusivists and pluralists do not consider the possibility that there might be more than one worthwhile religious end. Rather, it is a shared axiom for both camps that,

> there *could be* no more than one. The axiom challenges religious believers to recognize that those of other faiths actually are (in all truly important respects) seeking, being shaped by, and eventually realizing the same religious end. All paths lead to the same goal.[21]

After demonstrating that both exclusivists and pluralists are impoverished in their approach to difference, Heim offers a striking reformulation of the mountain climbing metaphor. He argues that there is no good reason to suppose that there is only one religious mountain worth climbing. He contends that we ought to understand the world religions as paths up very different mountains. The religious terrain is mountainous; traversing each of these mountains is a worthy quest as each leads to a different and legitimate destination. The different religions are not merely different ways to the same goal, but different ways to different goals.

It is difficult to overstate the extent to which Heim's position marks a creative breakthrough in the TRD conversation. He is right to wonder why pluralists have been so fixated on assuming that all religions are but various paths leading to the same destination. Surely, this cannot be. Heim is also right to insist that there must be intimate bonds between the religious practices/paths and the ends/goals to which they lead. Heim's breakthrough permits and authorizes a new measure of attention to the distinctive importance of religious practices. What is seen by way of Zen practice is unlikely to be exactly the same as what is seen by way of Eucharist.

Unfortunately and inevitably, metaphors not only open the mind to new possibilities—there really may be different and legitimate religious goods and different mountains worth climbing—but they can also constrain and forestall thought. Are "religions" accurately imagined as discrete mountains? Historically speaking, have religious traditions been discrete enough to sustain the metaphor? And do the various religions each possess only a single primary aim? And if so, who gets to make that call that one among the many ends on offer within the tradition is primary? Again, a promising option in TRD seems imperiled by too reified a notion of religion.

Heim, to his great credit, is not unaware of the problem of reification that constrains much reflection on the category religion. Hence, his writing is marked by the presence of both reifying and anti-reifying impulses. He is too careful a student of the history of religions to fall into the trap of characterizing religions as monolithic entities leading all their adherents in lockstep to their own discrete destinations, but he is too invested in the notion of multiple ends distributed across religions to altogether escape the propensity to reify.

Sometimes one can see both these impulses at work on a single page. Heim can speak of religious "traditions as ordinary and primary means of attaining to their own unique ends, in contrast with *the* Christian aim,"[22] while also recognizing that other religions are aware of and offer access to "various dimensions" of the divine life. The Christian aim? How is the definite article justifiable, as no creedal statement or doctrinal body has ever asserted that a particular Christian aim or construal thereof is or has to be mandatory for all Christians?[23] And "their own unique ends?" Which ends are those? Virtually any end on offer within a given religion is also on offer elsewhere. If communion with God by way of devotion is your preferred end or goal, that goal is legitimated and celebrated in a variety of traditions. If realization of nonduality or ecstatic union is your preferred goal, those options also are available in a variety of traditions, often the very same ones!

On the very same page, Heim advances a subtler claim:

> The interaction between traditions does not commonly present itself in flat and simple terms. . . . Christianity is not alone in registering the various dimensions we have outlined. Other religions have their own distinctive ways of interpreting this diversity, their own claims to unify it. Usually this involves an explanation that one of these dimensions is ultimately real and the others represent prefigurations or cruder approximations on the path from misunderstanding toward that truth. The

issues between the religions usually have to do with the manner in which the various dimensions are coordinated in theory and practice, how much basic reality is attributed to each dimension, and what the *means* of integration among them is to be. The religious traditions provide alternative normative ways of resolving this diversity of relation with the divine. Different configurations of the constellation of relations lead to different cumulative religious ends.[24]

Here, Heim recognizes that each religious tradition registers different dimensions of the divine life and hence has on offer a variety of distinctive religious ends conformed to those dimensions of this divine life. This is exactly right. On this fundamental contention (and much else besides), Heim and I agree. Religious ends are not distributed one per tradition, and "religions" are not unitary, tightly integrated systematic wholes. And he is not off the mark to say that what distinguishes religions is the way that they order and coordinate these various ends into some particular, integrated, and cumulative configuration.

The trouble is that the question of ordering and ranking religious ends is highly contested, not just *between* religious traditions but also *within* them. Any religious tradition is a community of disputation on just such questions rather than a community of consensus; understanding this feature of religious traditions is essential to any adequate theory of religion. Only at an extremely high level of generalization is it possible to speak of trends or tendencies that mark a given tradition. Closer to the ground, one discovers contestation: thinkers and communities within religious traditions are often engaged in heated contest about what the proper religious ends are and how those ends conform to different understandings of ultimate reality. I dare say that the minute one speaks of a characteristic or primary pattern of organizing religious ends within any tradition, a chorus of objections from *within* the tradition is sure to immediately arise.

Who gets to determine which is the more basic or cumulative *telos* in Hindu tradition: knowledge of nonduality of self and the Absolute or intimate communion but not nonduality? How do we determine whether Sankara or Ramanuja offers the definitive presentation of *the* Hindu end? Of the many meanings that the term "salvation" has had in Christian history, who gets to determine which understanding is the most adequate Christian naming? Beyond the minimal consensus that human beings are saved by the life, death, and resurrection of Jesus—and even which of those three is most important in the saving work of God in Christ is not a settled matter—Christians have agreed to very little else.

Once it is acknowledged that each "religion" has on offer a multiplicity of religious goals or ends, it becomes unsustainable to talk about religious traditions as ascending entirely different mountains. Any conception of religions as marked by such radical particularity as to lead to incommensurability, incompossibility, or outright contradiction is belied by the facts. It might be just as or even more difficult, in some cases, to try to live out faithfully two different conceptions of the Christian life as it might be to integrate a particular kind of Christian piety with a Hindu one. As Heim sometimes (but not always) recognizes these truths, his own position can be formulated in less reifying ways than he himself sometimes does.

Heim's reifying impulses are most evident when he suggests the possibility that commitment to different ends and to the distinctive paths that lead to those ends can lead persons to entirely different eschatological destinations even after death.[25] If what people seek in the divine life is truly distinctive, and if following the way to that distinctive end which accords with some feature of the divine life so profoundly shapes persons, then Heim argues that it follows that the trajectory one adopts may well extend beyond death. This hypothesis is the most striking extension of attention to particularity that may be available in the TRD literature.

While I am in profound sympathy with Heim's claim that the way and the goal to which that way leads ought not to be separated—the former is not extrinsic to the latter—I find the notion of entirely different eschatological destinations unlikely and unpersuasive. Given that multiple religious ends are available *within* any given historical tradition, it does not seem likely that persons might be shaped in such radically different ways as to lead to entirely different postmortem destinations across traditions. This possibility also seems unlikely because persons within and across traditions are often shaped by the practices and thought forms of the various strands of their own tradition as well as that of others. Even elite specialists routinely take up and so are formed by the practices of other strands of their own traditions and those of others. Such religious cross-training mitigates against the possibility of different postmortem destinations. If Hick runs the risk of flattening out the differences between and within traditions, Heim comes close to exaggerating them.

Still, I stand with Heim in his answer to the following crucial and decisive question: Does talk of different mountains and different legitimate soteriological ends imply that there are multiple ultimate realities? Deep pluralists, such as Cobb and Griffin, argue yes. There are many ultimate realities. Heim says no. In the end, he argues that affirming genuinely different religious ends or goods need not imply that there are many ultimate realities. All that is required is one multifaceted ultimate reality, which in his case is the trinity, understood within a creative theological interpretation of Heim's own. In this respect, I stand with Heim against Griffin in arguing for one ultimate reality understood in trinitarian fashion, although my theology of the trinity is rather different from Heim's.[26]

How can multiple ends be affirmed without affirming multiple discrete mountains or an ontology of multiple ultimate realities? In contrast to Heim's many mountains approach, I wish to note that there is another imaginative possibility housed within the one mountain metaphor, which was signaled quite some time ago by R. Panikkar: even if there is but one mountain to climb, that mountain itself is not homogeneous. It is multifaceted.

> The Way cannot be severed from the Goal. The spatial metaphor here may be misleading if taken superficially. It is not simply that there are different ways leading to the peak, but that the summit itself would collapse if all the paths disappeared. The peak is in a certain sense the result of the slopes leading to it.[27]

A truly striking formulation! Any way of ascending the mountain is not extrinsic to the summit to which it leads. My path and yours are borne up and made possible by the mountain and is itself inseparable from the goal. All climbing is grace throughout. We can climb only because of the footing the mountain affords us. Moreover, each way of ascending the mountain tells us something about the mountain itself, a knowledge made possible only by making just that particular ascent. So, to reduce the mountain to what I have come to (even truly) know of it by way of my particular path of ascent and to sanctify my path as the only one that makes ascent possible, even if it is a true and efficacious path, is woefully incomplete and so insufficient.

Paul Knitter, too, has noted that Panikkar is a special kind of pluralist. After calling attention to just this quotation above, Knitter rightly draws the conclusion that, for Panikkar, "God or the Divine is itself as diverse as are the religions! That's what Panikkar is announcing. The Divine delights in and includes and exists in diversity."[28] God is one—hence there is but one ultimate reality—but that one ultimate reality is marked by multiplicity.

Heim is right to suggest that some pluralisms are not very pluralistic at all. The various religious traditions teach nothing new or really different in Hick's version of pluralism. But what if each of the various religious traditions—or more accurately, the various strands of the various religious traditions—discover different dimensions of a complex reality as each makes its particular ascent? Furthermore, while multiplicity and genuine diversity must be affirmed, it is not at all clear to me why that multiplicity must mean that there are entirely different mountains (Heim) or, as some theologians have taken to affirming, multiple ultimate realities. Panikkar rightly takes a different tack. As for Heim, although he posits different mountains, different worthwhile religious ends, he ultimately affirms that each religion grants access only to different dimensions of one reality—namely, the trinity. For that reason, Panikkar's imagery of the multifaceted mountain is likely truer to Heim's own theological vision than the latter's many mountains metaphor.

Theologians of religious diversity have classified Heim's invitation to affirm robust difference between religions as a post-pluralist, postliberal position. Heim's position has been variously classified as an instance of a new model, "the acceptance model" in Knitter's new classificatory scheme, and as "the particularist model" in Paul Hedges's scheme.[29] A discussion of Heim's position is, therefore, in a part a discussion of the virtues of this newer model. Among theologians who work within this new model, Heim is the most sophisticated and most compelling. I see no way to a satisfactory theology of religious diversity that does not first pass through Heim.

As for Heim, he has variously characterized his own position as a version of inclusivism and, more recently, as a form of differential pluralism.[30] It's possible to see that both labels are accurate, albeit in different respects. The inclusivist label works because Heim maintains that each religion, by definition, is bound to believe that the end to which it aspires is the most desirable aim or the most comprehensive good. Paths and the ends to which they lead are intimately and inseparably connected. One must take the road to Rome to get to Rome. To reach nirvana, one must follow the Noble Eightfold Path. To be committed to one's tradition is to be committed to the distinctive excellence that one's own religion pursues and the means to that end that only one's own religion affords. To recognize that there are other mountains worth climbing does not mean that one wishes to climb them; still more, Heim appears to believe that one is bound to believe that one's own summit is the tallest and so supreme. As for Heim, he believes that communion with the life of the trinity, in any case, affords a summative good that contains and includes the partial goods that other traditions have on offer. Hence, his position can rightly be counted as a distinctive and novel version of inclusivism. Heim also recognizes and expects that persons from other religious traditions will make analogous claims. He believes that one is bound to hold that the good or end offered by one's own tradition is superior to the goods on offer elsewhere. Otherwise, why not convert?

With Heim, I see no reason whatsoever to deny a diversity of religious ends. Heim makes a distinctive and compelling contribution to TRD literature with this proposal. Also vital is his proper emphasis on the intimate connection between practices and the goods to which they lead. But there is no reason to suppose that these ends are distributed across religions, one per tradition, and as I have already noted, even Heim does not believe that to be the case. There is no single Christian end and no single practice or set of practices that leads to that end. Nor is it evident that I am required by my tradition to believe that the summative end that is on offer in my tradition is the most comprehensive or the most excellent. Interreligious learning may even supplement the goods that my tradition or strand thereof has to offer. My very understanding of the goods of my tradition may be deepened and enriched by the wisdom and practices of other traditions.

My own trinitarianism bears some similarities with Heim's, but it is nonetheless a form of pluralism because I do not believe that one is bound to believe that the goods on offer in one's own tradition are the best or the most encompassing. I reject both superiority and parity claims. Contra Heim, it would be more accurate to say that each tradition has on offer a variety of salvations and that crosscutting patterns of similarity and difference obtain *between and within* religious traditions. Even Heim's more nuanced contention that each tradition recognizes a diversity of claims but then settles on some way of ranking and integrating them into a summative goal is inadequate. History rarely gives us reason to believe that such enduring settlements are achieved within traditions. Heim is right to pluralize our imaginations, but he still remains captive to subtle reifications in his conception of religion that limit the promise of his extraordinary insights.[31]

## Deep Pluralism and the Question of Multiple Ultimate Realities

What, then, of the deep pluralists? What about their argument that there are multiple ultimate realities? As already noted, Heim could have taken this route, but he does not. David Ray Griffin, by contrast, does. Griffin traces deep pluralism to the work of John Cobb and points to Cobb's compelling claim that "alongside all the errors and distortions that can be found in all our traditions there are insights arising from profound thought and experience *that are diverse modes of apprehending diverse aspects of the totality of reality.*"[32] Appealing to a technical distinction between creativity and the God found in the metaphysics of process philosophy, Griffin argues that for Cobb there must be at least two religious ultimates. Creativity is the impersonal ultimate reality, and God, the personal ultimate.

The virtue of having at least two ultimate realities, Griffin notes, is that it permits us to recognize both the difference between and the validity of traditions that insist upon a personal and loving ultimate reality—God, Allah, Isvara, and Christ—and other traditions that insist that ultimate reality is an impersonal or transpersonal reality—*nirguna Brahman*, *dharmakaya* or *sunyata*/emptiness. Cobb's deep pluralism permits him to affirm that both are right because there are two ultimate realities, and neither can be reduced to the other. One doesn't have to be wrong for the other to be right. Hick, by contrast, must hold that both are mistaken insofar as God is finally neither personal nor impersonal but infinitely beyond both kinds of attribution.

As Griffin argues, ". . . the two types of experience can be taken to be equally veridical if we think of them as experiences of different ultimates."[33] Griffin goes on to show that there are three ultimates in Cobb's vision—creativity, God, and the world, each undergirding a different kind of religious experience or tradition; creativity can serve as the basis for nontheistic traditions, God serves as the basis for theistic traditions, and the world as the basis for cosmic religions.[34]

Cobb, Griffin, and other deep pluralists offer a profound pluralizing gift to the theological imagination. They invite us to take difference seriously and refuse the quick impulse to gather up a variety of religious data into one unified ultimate. In fact, there may be good reason to press further still beyond the work of deep pluralists. After all, there is no reason to suppose that every "religion" is oriented around one ultimate reality *or* many. Some among those traditions we have come to call religions may be uninterested in framing their projects as quests to understand the nature of one or many transcendent ultimate realities. The first task of the comparativist is to listen and to learn; comparative religionists must let the traditions speak on their own terms. And when such listening takes place, what presents itself is a diversity that dizzies the imagination, not a diversity that can be easily corralled into any unifying frame whatsoever. Cobb and Griffin point philosophers and theologians of religious diversity in this helpful direction.

The work of the comparative theologian must be a second step that proceeds with caution only after this first phenomenological hiatus, one that allows diversity to speak and speak fully. And yet, the comparative theologian who hopes to learn from diversity and who believes that such learning will only become *theological* learning—rather than an exercise in historical, anthropological, or phenomenological information gathering—when such information is integrated into extant theological frameworks, with modification as necessary, must undertake a further constructive step. My own approach as a comparative theologian, rooted primarily in the Christian tradition, is to gather up diversity into one ultimate reality, albeit with the following caveats: (1) the church fathers affirmed that what number means for the divine life cannot be the same as the meaning of number for finite entities; (2) Christian tradition has never affirmed a oneness that is at odds with multiplicity—hence trinity; and (3) the oneness of God is never other to the multiplicity of creation, not a one over against the many but a one that is, as Nicholas of Cusa would affirm, not-other than the many. I'll say more about these matters in Chapter 7 of this book. My central assertion for now is this: there are ways to think about divine unity that do not stand opposed to multiplicity. From this perspective, I hold that it is possible to affirm a *divine multiplicity* without falling into a discourse of *multiple divinities* or *multiple ultimate realities*.

My two-stop itinerary travels the following route. I hold that human cultures have routinely been motivated by truth-seeking activities that aspire to what I call *comprehensive qualitative orientation*—my definition of the religious (see Chapter 5). In that quest, diversely executed, traditions routinely identify certain *features or traits* of reality as sacred, fundamental, or even, in some cases, ultimate. When *beginning* comparison, it would be prudent to refrain from assuming that all traditions gather up these features or traits and posit them as grounded in a single transcendent ultimate reality. We must ask rather than assume that any given tradition posits a unifying ultimate connecting those traits or in which they reside. I myself argue that a variety of cultures recognize diverse traits of reality, experienced in moments of wonder, as ultimate. I then argue that these traits do, in fact, point to one multifaceted ultimate reality (see Chapter 7). For these reasons, I reject talk about many ultimate realities even as I affirm that there are many ultimate features of reality. In the final analysis, I affirm that those features of reality that are recognized as ultimate in the traditions that I study (Christianity, Buddhist, and Hinduism) all point to one ultimate reality that is nonetheless a multiplicity. But my case hinges and rests upon my particular data set: these three traditions. Whether a similar case can be made when working with other traditions cannot be stipulated in advance.

The upshot of this line of argument is that I see no need to posit multiple ultimates. The very idea of multiple ultimates appears self-contradictory and runs contrary to the very idea of ultimacy. The virtue of a position of the sort articulated by Cobb and Griffin is this: if traditions are oriented toward different ultimates and these ultimates are real, then when traditions find themselves in disagreement, this disagreement becomes a possible resource rather than a contradiction. The challenge is to find out how contradictory claims might turn out, upon further exploration, to be complementary rather than contradictory. We might be able to combine the insights of multiple religious traditions to generate a richer vision of reality than we are able to derive from one religion alone. With Cobb and Griffin, I agree that there is profound promise in the claim that the different religions enable us to get at "diverse aspects of the totality of reality."

However, against Cobb and Griffin, I would argue—as does Mark Heim and a host of other Christian theologians—that there is another way of affirming John Cobb's core claim that there are "diverse modes of apprehending diverse aspects of the totality of reality" without distributing that diversity over more than one ultimate. It suffices to posit one ultimate reality with a diversity of aspects, and that is what is entailed by any trinitarian conception of ultimate reality. That is precisely what Mark Heim, Raimon Panikkar, and I maintain. A variety of Christian theologians have argued that trinity is a natural framework that Christian theology can employ to take up the problem of religious diversity. We all affirm that distinctive soteriological trajectories engage different dimensions of the divine life. Because Christian doctrine does not regard

God as a homogeneous simplicity, we should expect that different traditions are rightly oriented to genuine distinctions internal to the divine life. Beyond homogeneous singularity and irreducible diversity, there lies an alternate possibility that Christian theology finds in the trinity. The divine life is neither an undifferentiated absolute nor a plurality of more or less loosely related ultimates.

In any case Cobb, Griffin, and Heim have performed an invaluable service in challenging pluralist positions to become genuinely pluralist—to admit more diversity into our thinking about religious diversity. My own approach, sketched in the penultimate chapter, affirms the positive gains advanced by Cobb, Griffin, and, most especially, Heim. With the latter, I proceed on trinitarian grounds. What is distinctive about my own approach is that I do not hold that affirming trinitarianism means that Christians have an inclusive or comprehensive knowledge of the divine life, nor do I hold, as Heim does, that the highest summative good on offer in all the world's religions is communion with the triune God. No tradition need posit that the good it has on offer is the highest good—a genuine and worthy good, yes, but the highest good or the most comprehensive good, no. Trinitarianism affords Christians with a framework for articulating how there can be a diversity within the divine life, but it may well be that some dimensions of the divine life are better understood and accessed by other traditions.

My own suspicion is that many Christians hold impoverished and distorted conceptions of the trinitarian life because of an overemphasis on conceptions of personality. Each of the "persons" of the trinity is too often understood in ways that church fathers and early theologians could not have imagined, as centers of will and consciousness, a gradual development as Western Christianity moved further away from the Greek *hypostases* and the Latin *persona* to the English "person." The result is a homogenization of distinctions (not separations) within the trinity. Each person in the trinity is like the other, and trinitarian distinctions come to seem meaningless. A personal God, trice repeated, leads to redundancy and thus gives rise to unitarian tendencies. The end result is an impoverished conception of how the divine life is encountered in Christian practice and piety.

Encountering the God who is the ground and abysmal depth of being (Father/Mother), the personal address of the Word (*logos*/Son), and the ecstatic and binding presence of the Spirit (*spiritus/pneuma*)—these are not identical experiences. Nor are the practices that disclose each face of divinity interchangeable. The distinctions made possible by a trinitarian conception of divine life, distinctions that are registered by the pieties and practices of other religious traditions, are lost in what passes for an enfeebled trinitarianism, both in contemporary ecclesial life and in much contemporary theology. Ironically, it may well be that the promise of Christian trinitarianism can best be recovered and deepened precisely as we come to see the trinity anew by way of the resources of other religious traditions. That such enrichment is possible by way of comparative theological learning is what I shall argue in Chapter 7. The promise of relational pluralism rests precisely in the way in which it offers a conceptual grounding for affirming that our traditions can be enriched by what they learn from each other.

Let us assess these moves in the direction of greater pluralism by appealing to the four criteria articulated earlier in this chapter: (1) the difference without incommensurability criterion; (2) the truth criterion; (3) the critical theory of religion criterion; and (4) the intrinsic religious interest criterion. Cobb and Griffin seem to meet all four criteria. There is real difference between traditions: so much so that various religions may have their own distinctive aims and goods, but, crucially, these differences do not lead to incommensurability. Traditions are capable of learning from each other and being transformed in the process. Cobb and Griffin also affirm that other religious traditions advance valid and distinctive truth claims that happen to be true and are not already in the possession of one's home tradition. Cobb likewise meets the critical theory of religion test. He was among the first to suggest that there are serious problems with prevalent understandings of religion, so much so that he now prefers to speak of wisdom traditions rather than religions. Cobb is a pioneer here, and we have yet to learn all that we can from him on this score.

Hick, by contrast, passes this test of difference without incommensurability but at great expense. Yes, traditions are different from one another, but they are not incommensurable. Why? Because no tradition can arrive at the truth of what ultimate reality is in itself. We need only worry about the possibility of incommensurability if we take difference seriously, but where difference is emptied of its meaning and significance, there can be no question of conflict or incommensurability. Hick affirms our first criterion at the expense of our second. Moreover, Hick's planetary metaphor—if not his formal theorizing about religion—appears to suggest that religions are reified entities like planets orbiting around the same sun. It does not seem to me that he adequately corrects for the distorting force of his basic metaphor. Finally, it's hard to see what can motivate genuine religious interest in other traditions if each tradition is but another way of accomplishing the very same good made available in one's own home tradition.

Cobb, Griffin, and Heim all avoid the limitations that come with Hick's vision. And yet it is here, if anywhere, that Cobb may be in need of supplementation, and likewise also Heim. Insofar as there is the suggestion that any particular religion or tradition is, as an entirety, oriented toward one primary religious good or one religious ultimate and that another "religion" or "wisdom tradition" is oriented toward another religious good or ultimate, the danger of reification presents itself. Traditions are multiplicities; they are polydox in character. They do not sing just one note. Nor is the whole of a tradition oriented toward a single ultimate or salvation. The internal complexity of any given tradition and its longstanding historical interaction with others mean that it is unlikely, if not impossible, that any given tradition speaks with just one voice on questions of either ultimacy or soteriology.

Cobb, Griffin, and Heim are all aware of these multiplicities but often sound like they entertain subtle forms of reification: Buddhists are oriented to a transpersonal ultimate, whereas Christians are oriented to a personal God (Cobb and Griffin); or Christians aim toward communion with the trinitarian God, whereas Buddhists seek nirvana and so are headed toward a different postmortem destination (Heim). If these reifications cannot and do not hold, might it not also be the case that the idea of multiple distinct ultimates is also a fruit of reifying imagination? Why not posit, contra Cobb and Griffin, that one complex ultimate reality might have personal and impersonal dimensions? Such a formulation would be closer to Heim than to Hick. The divine life would contain both personal and impersonal dimensions rather than neither.

## "Brahman Is My Womb": The *Bhagavad Gita* and Divine Multiplicity

The notion of a complex divine multiplicity, one that includes both personal and impersonal dimensions, is not novel; nor is it to be found within Christian quarters alone. On the contrary, we find this recognition of internal divine multiplicity in the *Bhagavad Gita* (*BG*). In the fourteenth chapter of the *Gita*, the Supreme Divine, Krishna, speaks of having both personal and impersonal aspects:

Son of Bharata,
the Great Brahman is my womb;
in this I place
the embryo.
From that emerges
the origin of all beings. (*BG* 14:3)

Son of Kunti
Brahman is
the great womb
of all forms
that exist;
I am the father
Who places the seeds. (14:4)

I am the support
of Brahman,
the immortal
and imperishable;
and the support
of everlasting *dharma*;
and the support
of absolute bliss. (14:27)[35]

In all three verses, the personal Lord, Krishna, claims to have a relationship of inclusion with Brahman. Krishna claims either to contain Brahman as His womb (*sic*) or claims that He is Brahman's support, basis, or foundation. Krishna, the personal absolute, holds that there is an impersonal dimension to His being—namely, Brahman, which is His womb. Krishna not only manages to combine the personal and the impersonal but, in a queer case of gender bending, articulates an intersex divinity. The grammatical cases here are wild: the *neuter* Brahman is the *male* Krishna's *female* womb (*yoni*). Hence the divine life can be rightly encountered as both personal and transpersonal—a term I prefer to impersonal. A playful outsider reading of these verses suggests that ultimate might be understood as male, female, neuter, and intersexed. Given the possibilities afforded by such a vision of divine multiplicity, why posit discrete ultimate realities and the reifying temptations that come with the idea that different "religions" are oriented toward different ultimates?

To affirm divine multiplicity, either in a trinitarian fashion or in the *Gita*'s style, does not resolve ongoing disputes within and across traditions about how best to understand that multiplicity. Hence, it is hardly surprising that commentarial glosses on these verses are marked by strident disagreement. It is especially unsurprising that *BG* 14:27, taken at face value, proves to be a problem for Sankara, the founding teacher of the nondualist Advaita Vedanta theological tradition. For Advaitins, although ultimate reality can be encountered and worshipped as God, only Divinity's transpersonal dimension is final. Devotion to a personal God, however important, is religiously penultimate. Devotion (*bhakti*) is a means to knowledge (*jnana*) and not the other way around. Understanding that one's true nature just is Brahman, the infinite ground of both world and self—that is what liberates. Naturally, for a theologian who stands within this tradition, a verse that appears to suggest that the personal God is the support or basis of Brahman rather than the other way around requires some exegetical finessing. Other theological traditions, like Ramanuja's Visistadvaita, are able to read the verse without subjecting it to a great deal of exegetical finessing.

Regardless of one's reading strategy or theological school, what is important to note here is that readers of *BG* 14:27 may quarrel about how rightly to prioritize divinity's personal nature as opposed to divinity's transpersonal nature, but the exegetical tradition does not attempt to resolve the issue by bifurcating the divine into two discrete ultimates—one of which is personal, and the other transpersonal—as deep pluralists like Griffin and Cobb seem to suggest. I propose that it would be more economical (Occam's razor) to adopt the *Gita*'s general strategy rather than posit more than one ultimate. For now, we can leave the question disputed by Ramanuja and Sankara open.[36] That particular dispute is not just an intra-Vedanta quarrel but one that takes place within many traditions. Cobb and Griffin are right to argue that such theological debates matter precisely because different depictions of ultimate reality point to genuine diversity. I agree. But with the *Gita*, I hold that such diversity is to be found within a single ultimate reality.

Hick resolves the problem by dissolving it; he argues that ultimate reality is beyond both concepts and is an inscrutable noumenal something. That strategy is dissatisfying because it dismisses the worth of such disputes. Why take them seriously if all our conceptual claims about ultimate reality are merely the result of our various cultural-linguistic modes of situatedness? All are inapplicable to divinity. A far more appealing solution is to engage in comparative theological investigation, across traditions, by reading thinkers like Sankara and Ramanuja as they struggle with scriptural texts that suggest ultimate reality can be both personal and transpersonal, albeit in different respects.

Now, our final criterion: Can the deep pluralists or Mark Heim support sustained religious interest in the claims, practices, and aims of other traditions? The matter is not easily settled, as there are differences between those who fall within this broad camp. Cobb is himself an interesting case in point. His thinking on this matter occurs within the context of his analysis of multiple religious belonging. Cobb quite rightly notes that multiple religious belonging has been a common feature of human history. It would then seem to follow that sustained religious interest in other traditions is not only possible but actual and even desirable, not least because these traditions are not in fact alien. A variety of traditions have flowed through most human communities of any notable size and historical depth.

Nonetheless, Cobb begins by articulating reservations:

> Christianity is a way of ordering the whole of life and society. For the serious Christian, being a Christian provides one's primary identity. One may also be an American, a lawyer, a father, and Rotarian, but one is not truly a Christian unless that identity is controlling. The real Christian decides what it means to be an American as a Christian, not the other way around. Hence, belonging to a Christian community is normatively a way of expressing one's primary identity. One may be a member of many other groups and organizations, but they must all be subordinated to this identity. If the other group understands itself in such a way that this subordinate role is possible, there need be no problem, but the term "multiple belonging" seems open to participation in more than one group claiming this primacy. That is highly problematic from a Christian point of view.[37]

Cobb's argument is intriguing, but it raises many questions. To what extent can our religious identities be disaggregated from our various other identities? Supposing it can, do all religious traditions insist that religious identity must be primary? But if they do not insist on being primary, does it then follow that they would be welcoming subordination? These questions aside, Cobb's concern is worth taking seriously.

But despite his apprehension, Cobb does not close the door to multiple religious belonging. Here again, we must cite his words at length:

Although the Christian ideal is that Christian faith order the whole of life, centuries of secularization have in fact relegated it for most adherents to particular areas of life. The recognition that there are other great religious paths has further relativized the meaning of faith for many of the most sensitive and perceptive Christians. It is unrealistic to oppose multiple belonging in the name of an ideal or norm that is largely inoperative. If there is to be a recovery of an effective religious vision, it is unlikely to come from any one religious community alone. It will have to grow out of the new situation of radical religious pluralism in which we now find ourselves. . . . Furthermore, we must recognize that today many of the most religiously sensitive and perceptive people find it impossible to identify themselves fully with any one of the competing traditions. To ask them to do so is to call for a surrender of their integrity that is alien to all of these traditions. The choice is between distancing themselves from all communities of faith, creating a new one, or multiple belonging.[38]

A sentiment of concession colors Cobb's reasoning. In the world as we now have it, wherein Christianity has become one religion among many—a religion occupying just one sphere of life—it is unrealistic to demand that Christianity must hold sway over all spheres of life. Besides, it is not just the religiously unmusical who are drawn to religious multiplicity; rather it is "the most religiously sensitive and perceptive people." We ought not to alienate them because a new and effective religious vision will have to be derived from the resources of more than one religious tradition. In all of these ways, which are neither half-hearted nor full-throated, Cobb allows multiple belonging and thereby opens the door to the notion that pluralists can take substantive interest in the claims, aims, and practices of other traditions.

Cobb cautiously opens the door to multiple religious participation but nonetheless maintains that "those of us deeply rooted in one tradition or another will not be attracted to this." How does that square with his recognition that it is the "most religiously sensitive" that are drawn toward taking up the claims, aims, and practices of other traditions? Must we suppose that the deeply rooted are not the "most religiously sensitive"? Might it be time for us to take our mark from the latter and not the former?

Might Cobb's notion that our traditions are oriented toward different ultimate realities constrain his sense of what is religiously possible with respect to serious engagement with multiplicity? That is a difficult question to answer. Cobb cannot see how multiple religious belonging is possible, given the comprehensive claims religions make. But if we supposed that, even in their comprehensiveness, at least some strands of some traditions are oriented to different faces/facets of one ultimate reality, the tensions between traditions might be reconcilable; such tensions might be productive rather than contradictory.

Cobb is engaged in a delicate balancing act between affirming the priority and normativity of singular belonging even as he also recognizes that faithful singular belongers "can be grateful that there are those who are" attracted to more than one tradition because "as they participate seriously in more than one community of faith, they will come to understand the contributions and limitations of these communities in ways that will otherwise remain invisible. They will also discover ways in which these communities can support one another and supplement one another. They can interpret us to one another. They may discover new forms of self-identity appropriate to a pluralistic age."[39] Cobb the visionary comes into full view in this last proposal: new "forms of self-identity" might emerge, ones that refuse the notion that human beings and ultimate reality must be marked by homogeneous simplicity. Might it be that our own multiplicity might in some way mirror the divine unity-in-multiplicity?

What about Mark Heim? Can he imagine a way of celebrating and even incorporating the claims, aims, and practices of other religious traditions? On what grounds? In a fertile recent essay, Heim defends the possibility of multiple religious participation and argues that it is possible precisely on trinitarian grounds. In making these arguments, Heim opens subtle theological possibilities that overcome the impression found in some of his writing that the various religious traditions are paths up fundamentally different mountains. As already noted, the trouble with that image is that it is impossible to see how persons might straddle two mountains. Or to use a slightly different metaphor, how can it be possible to simultaneously travel from New York to San Francisco and from New York to London? Thankfully, Heim's religious vision is far subtler than these metaphors.

A full treatment of Heim's position is not possible within the constraints of this already long chapter. For now, I note only that for Heim, multiple religious participation can only be a meaningful possibility precisely if there is real difference between religious paths—else why take up more than one practice—and those differences can be held together within a single, albeit internally diverse, ultimate reality. That, of course, is precisely what holds in the case of a trinitarian vision. In so doing, even though Heim's account of trinity is quite different from mine, we both affirm virtually identical accounts of multiple religious participation.[40] Heim and I both suggest that this is the only kind of pluralism that can prove to be satisfactory.

## Toward a Relational Pluralism

The most promising option now available in theologies of religious diversity is the "relational pluralism" of Roland Faber and Catherine Keller. It, too, operates within a process theological frame and is indebted to John Cobb, but unlike deep pluralism, as formulated by Cobb and Griffin, Faber and Keller do not deploy a metaphysical framework that posits discrete multiple ultimate realities. Theirs is a theopoetic discourse that embraces an apophatic reserve in naming ultimate reality and a cataphatic profusion of divine names: they speak of multiplicities, manifolds, and plurisingularities. God or ultimate reality is neither an undifferentiated one nor a set of unrelated or loosely related ones that constitute an assemblage of manys. The divine is a multi*pli*city—an enfolding of the one in the many, and the many in the one.

Relational pluralism is marked by a "taste for multiplicity" and its "delight in the gifts of other wisdoms."[41] Relational pluralism refuses reified accounts of religion and religions, accounts that erase multiplicity within and across traditions. Faber and Keller instead speak of "the inherent multiplicity of religion—and of the religious character of multiplicity."[42] Faber and Keller refuse a "separative pluralism" in which the various religions remain alongside each other in isolation even if out of a legitimate fear of (mis)appropriation, that some might make off with other wisdoms in an uncritical colonialist syncretism. Without bypassing these concerns, Faber and Keller realize that there can be no recourse to "a pristine sense of simple identity externally related."[43] Our wisdom traditions have always been porous to and shaped by encounters with each other well before they ever became religions.

Faber and Keller affirm that "contrasting Wisdoms produce an *infinity of categories*; complexity produces always new constellations of ways to connect."[44] The "unprecedented event of the sacred" will generate ever new divine disclosures—disclosures that are shaped, in part, by the meeting and growing together of religious traditions. They keep the future open to the mutual transformation of traditions. Their goal is not to re-place the various names of ultimate reality deployed by the religions, but they are convinced that divine disclosure is never finished and so can-not be contained by any fixed set of metaphysical categories. Contrary to Cobb and Griffin, Faber and Keller do not confine themselves to the three discrete ultimate realities of John Cobb's process theology (God, creativity, and world).

Most striking is their claim that relational pluralism must be a "poly-philic pluralism," a pluralism that cultivates a love for the manifold and a love for and between the many wisdom traditions. Theirs is both an erotic and an ethical project; each tradition is lured into a longing for the other and the wisdom of the other as necessary for its own unfolding. Animated by this *eros* for the religious other, Faber and Keller hope that there will emerge "sacred interactivity in, between, across, and beyond those very traditions." This interactivity resulting therefrom should di-minish "the war-ridden exclusivities of simple identities" that now per-sist between traditions.[45]

My own version of pluralism, to be sketched in Chapter 7, is most as-suredly a relational/polyphilic pluralism. It cherishes the differential plu-ralism of Cobb and Griffin but does not find compelling the notion that there are discrete multiple ultimate realities. Likewise, the notion that each religion has its own religious *telos* or salvation—as Heim sometimes appears to contend—is also untenable. Faber and Keller, by contrast, are cognizant of the internal diversities and porosities of traditions. They rec-ognize that we have always been multiple. Historical or phenomenologi-cal consideration of any wisdom tradition reveals ongoing contestation rooted in diverse conceptions of ultimate reality and soteriology. More-over, comparative consideration of traditions shows complex crosscut-ting patterns; for example, Christian ground of being theologians, like Eckhart or Tillich, are far closer to the nondualism of Sankara than they sometimes are to their theistic and dualistic coreligionists. Affiliations across religions and tensions within them should compel theologians of religious diversity to surrender TRDs that are captive to a reifying imag-ination that ignores internal diversities and external resonances.

Relational polyphilic pluralism recognizes these complexities and does still more: it proceeds to speak of a need and desire for the other. Even a theology of multiple religious ends can issue in a theology of mu-tual indifference. Buddhists can seek their own legitimate *telos* as Chris-tians pursue theirs, each convinced of the superiority of the goal they seek. Faber and Keller seek to move beyond such "separative pluralism." Far too many Christian theologians of religious diversity would feel no theological loss, no compulsion to mourn if, hypothetically speaking, religious diversity should pass away, as long as one's own religion abides. If my tradition affords the only or most adequate means of access to the *summum bonum* and other traditions seek valid but deficient goods that my tradition already contains, if everything of theological worth is available in my religion, then a world without religious diversity is no calamity. Polyphilic pluralism, by contrast, desires others in their very particularity. Such pluralism even dares to imagine that the unfolding of the divine life requires diverse wisdoms in relation. Even God needs a world marked by diversity if God is to be more fully known. That is the most radical affirmation of religious diversity imaginable. Therein lies the promise of relational pluralism.

## A Concluding Warning: The Trouble with Religion

Despite my argument for relational pluralism, I conclude with a note of warning about structural problems that complicate easy accommodation to any of these categories. Something is awry in our discourse about other religious traditions. Ponder a simple truth: it is possible to simultaneously be exclusivist, inclusivist, and pluralist at the same time, albeit in different respects, with respect to other traditions and even one's own. For example, although I am powerfully shaped by encounter with Hindu traditions, Sankara's Advaita Vedanta in particular, I am an exclusivist when it comes to the ideology of caste that is part of Sankara's Brahmanical imagination. Ongoing discrimination and horrific violence against Dalits, including lynching, remain at the heart of daily reality in India. Halfway measures on caste are insufficient; it will not do to affirm the qualified viability of caste while opposing untouchability. To put an end to the latter, one must put an end to the former. For these reasons, I am an exclusivist when it comes to certain features of Hindu traditions.

Likewise, one is necessarily exclusivist toward strands of *one's own* tradition that one finds problematic or repellant. My stance toward right-wing Christian fundamentalists, both theologically and politically, is negative. Notional assent that Jesus is Lord and acceptance of sacrificial theories of atonement which affirm a punitive divinity who has to impose his, always *his*, divine wrath onto someone do not save. I repudiate most atonement theories that some take to be essential to Christian life. The political convictions that often follow in the wake of these theologies are often toxic: anti-immigration, anti-queer, pro-death penalty, anti-science, anti-evolutionary theory, and anti-environmentalist entailments often seem inextricable from some fundamentalist theological positions.

Similarly, I am strongly inclusivist in my disposition toward other religious traditions or strands thereof. When it comes to Sankara's Advaita, I affirm his nondualist intentions but am wary about the unresolved dualism in his thought between the unchanging absolute and a changing world. Sankara resolves that dualism by downgrading the ontological standing of the world in order to privilege the ontological reality of the unchanging divine. But this dualism is problematic from the standpoint of Christian commitments that affirm creation. For these reasons, I make an inclusivist judgment that celebrates Sankara's nondualism but dismisses his claims regarding the status of the world.

With respect to nondualism, I remain resolutely pluralist in temper. Although Christian traditions rarely approach a full-blown nondualism— one finds nondualist moments in Marguerite Porete and Meister Eckhart— Sankara's Advaita affirms nondualism as both ontologically true and soteriologically vital. With Sankara, I affirm that there is a dimension of self that opens out into divinity. For this reason, I hold that Advaita Vedanta affords transformative access to the divine life.

If I am not confused but consistent in being exclusivist, inclusivist, and pluralist with respect to the same strand of the Hindu tradition, then what are we to make of these categories? Prevailing discourse, which measures entire "religions" on some scale to find out whether we find them inferior or equal to our own, is problematic. At best, such claims are shorthand for subtler claims: transforming truth and power exist in certain strands of other traditions because these traditions have access to dimensions of ultimate reality. The same must be said for our own: salvific power is present *in some strands* of our tradition whereas others continue to be toxic. Theologies of religious diversity venture constructive theological judgments; if such judgments are to have merit, they must be made in tandem with the painstaking work of comparative theology. Still more, the trajectory of theological assessment cannot be unidirectional. If theological judgments are to be marked by a spirit of mutuality and hospitality, we must be prepared to field similar critiques from our religious neighbors.

Neither TRD nor CT will succeed as long as theologians remain in thrall to problematic accounts of "religion" and "the religions." Hence, we must contest conventional accounts of religion that limit the promise of both theological projects. But deconstruction is not enough. Troubling extant notions of religion (Chapter 4) is only the first step; we must also offer a new constructive proposal for how we ought to think about the religious (Chapter 5). Despite multiple proposals to discard the category altogether, beginning with the work of W. C. Smith, religion remains a fixed feature of the intellectual furniture of the modern and now postmodern world. The category won't be discarded any time soon. Given that reality, before us lies the work of reformulating the notion of the religious and then religious traditions in such a way that their porosity, internal multiplicity, and the grounds for polyphilia in each of our traditions can be foregrounded. Only then can we imagine constructive theological work that truly learns from religious diversity.

# 4 Comparative Theology after Religion?

*The word "Aryan," which, for Max Müller and his generation, had a purely linguistic meaning, was now in the hands of less academic persons, poisoners, who were speaking of races of men, races of masters and races of servants and other races too, races whose fundamental impurity necessitated drastic measures, races who were not wanted on the voyage, who were surplus to requirements, races to be cut, blackballed and deposited in the bin of history.*

—SALMAN RUSHDIE, *The Ground beneath Her Feet*

## Denaturalizing "Religion" and "Religions"

The preceding two chapters show that within productive theologies of religious diversity, one finds viable intuitions about the category religion, even if those intuitions have not been rendered explicit. Conversely, when theologies of religious diversity fail, they often do so because they are in thrall to confused and errant assumptions about just what "religion" and "the religions" are.

Ironically, TRD and comparative theology emerged at the same time that a new literature arose that challenged the coherence and meaningfulness of the very categories "religion," "religions," and their regnant definitions. Although applying any single classificatory term to this sprawling literature is simplistic, I deploy "genealogy of religion" as a viable rubric. Among the most important voices in this literature include Wilfred Cantwell Smith, Talal Asad, and more recent voices such as Richard King, Tomoko Masuzawa, Arvind Mandair, Jason Ananda Josephson, and many others. These two bodies of literature—TRD and CT, on the one hand, and genealogy of religion, on the other—have proceeded along parallel rather than intersecting tracks, until recently.

What has genealogy of religion accomplished? It has, for all its tentativeness and ongoing contestations, served to denaturalize the category "religion." Taking this literature seriously makes it impossible to carry on in a reflective style that makes religion seem like part of the very fabric of the real. Historians and genealogists have demonstrated that human collectivities have not always thought about the world as bifurcated into the "religious" and "the secular." There have long been collective cultural-historical flows, or traditions, and these traditions include those we have come more recently to call "Hinduism," "Buddhism," "Confucianism," "Sikhism," and the like, but most of these traditions and their languages had no conceptual analogue to "religion" prior to modernity. We have long had traditions, but we have not long had religions.

Even in the West, the terms "religion" and "the secular" have had a shifting trajectory of meanings dating from Roman uses to Christian appropriations and redeployments. Telling the story of "religion" is no simple matter, and every available account is contested. Scholars argue fiercely about the provenance of contemporary meanings and uses of the term "religion." Is the term fundamentally a Western notion with Christianity serving as the ideal prototype for what counts as a religion? So says Daniel Dubuisson.[1] Is the category, as we have come to deploy it, of more recent vintage, perhaps a child of modernity? So says Talal Asad.[2] Is the category a product of cross-cultural encounter, a category that emerges when communities recognize that other human communities also traffic with the supernatural, with gods and demons, and have other ways of orienting themselves within some interpretive scheme that offers a map of the whole of things? Many others subscribe to just such an explanatory account.[3]

In what follows, I do not seek to resolve these ongoing disputes by offering my own master narrative. No such resolution will be forthcoming for the foreseeable future. I wish only to highlight some crucial implications of this literature for TRD and CT. Given the daunting scope of these interrogations, my account here will be selective. My goal is to point to some historical processes that have shaped our thinking about the categories of religion and religions, processes that theologians of religious diversity and comparative theologians are only now coming to fully appreciate. We tend to assume we know what these terms mean, how they came to bear those meanings, and how they function. Some even suggest that there is little noteworthy gain to be had by paying close and critical attention to category construction, a contention I reject.[4]

My hope is that, henceforth, should we elect to deploy these terms—I will argue in the next chapter that we must—we will do so strategically, self-consciously, and only after accounting for the emergence of category religion and the meanings it now bears. Failure to think through these categories will cause us to be oblivious to just what it is we do when we label the various traditions "religions" and thereby structure the very ground on which comparison takes place. Put otherwise, certain similarities and differences are imposed upon traditions when we configure them as religions, and this is done well before comparison begins. That process largely transpires beneath theoretical awareness. Comparison then risks discovering just what we have already imposed upon traditions when we rendered them into religions in the first place.

As for the now massive literature on TRD and CT, some writers have taken up the genealogical literature. Hugh Nicholson, Paul Hedges, and Jenny Daggers are among those who have done so, and they have done it well.[5] They have made an important beginning in arguing that neither comparative theology nor theology of religious diversity can begin by taking "religion" for granted. These important contributions notwithstanding, more remains to be done. Despite their groundbreaking work, theological imagination still remains captive to uninterrogated constructions of religion. My work in this chapter does not seek to supplant their contributions but rather to supplement them.

One problem in particular captures my attention: the notion that stark and immutable lines separate "the religions." Christian reflection has, from its inception, been situated in a world of fluid crosscutting differences. Indeed, it would be possible to craft a history of Christian thought and practice written as a series of interactions with and transmutations of movements and traditions that Christians have come to demarcate as non-Christian. Such a history would demonstrate not only that many of the central categories, practices, and symbols of Christian life are borrowed from Hellenistic philosophical schools, mystery religions, and, of course, most vitally from what we now call "Judaism," but that for long stretches of history, no clearly defined and rigid boundaries existed between "Christianity" and those traditions we now take to be Christianity's others. Alongside such a history, a companion work could be written that would take note of tremors within (especially Western) Christian self-awareness when such profound entanglements come to surface. I suspect that such a companion history would unearth moments of widespread anxiety among custodians of tradition at just those junctures when "the unbearable proximity"[6] of those whom Christians regard as other is most keenly felt.

What has been true for Christian traditions is demonstrably true for all traditions. Each has emerged in and through robust, sustained, and ongoing encounter with a variety of other traditions. Moreover, communal life is a rich tapestry of ongoing and fluid encounter; those traditions cleanly organized into "world religions" on the pages of textbooks are nowhere to be found in pristine form in real life. No Christian lives only a Christian life. No Hindu does either. Each human being and every human community is a site of ongoing historical flows and never sites of settled and singular habitation. To be is to be in relation—a truth not only for any general ontology but also for any adequate account of interreligious encounter. Our discourse about "religions" obscures this reality by generating a propensity toward reification. To think CT from the perspective of relational pluralism is to challenge such casts of mind.

Nevertheless, contemporary Christian theology largely operates as a discourse enamored of fixed boundaries. How are Christians to think about "other religions?" This way of framing Christian reflection seems natural and commonplace because it takes for granted the notion that we inhabit a world marked by entities called religions, entities possessing neat boundaries—boundaries that are, moreover, transhistorically and cross-culturally stable.

Of course, social and cultural worlds are never marked by clean boundaries. Every boundary—even (or rather especially) the boundaries of nation states—is constructed. So, too, with the boundaries between "religions" and the boundaries between "religion" and "the secular." Ironically, as Wendy Brown has demonstrated, the recent unrestrained global enthusiasm for wall building occurs at the very moment in which national sovereignty has been undercut by global flows of people, labor, technologies, capital, media, and terror. We build walls, she argues, precisely when their futility is most in evidence, thereby giving to these walls a kind of parodic character. Walls unmask themselves in their very construction.[7] Might we not wonder whether the global discourse of world religions emerges for the same reason, precisely at the moment when Western colonialism and globalization brought traditions into ever greater proximity?

How might we live with categories like religion and the religions in a spirit of critical freedom, thinking with and even against them without being bound and fettered by them? How can we hold in mind their constructed character so that we might be released from the temptation on the one hand to homogenize traditions (all are instances of some stable cross-cultural category called religion), and/or on the other to reify them into incompatible otherness (all are incommensurably different religions)? I hold that a powerful aid in gaining such conceptual freedom will come by casting an eye at another category that we have learned rather well to recognize as invented. "Religion" and "religions" are as real *and as imaginary* as another creation that bedevils American life: "race." Race, too, is a fiction—lacking a basis in biological fact—but once invented and institutionalized in social, economic, and political life, it exerts a distorting gravitational pull on all dimensions of life that should chance to enter into its orbit.

Consider what the notions "race" and "races" manage to accomplish. The generic notion of race functions to create homogeneity; innumerable kinds of human diversity are suppressed from view as one and only one kind of difference is selected, marked, and privileged as a primary and often definitive axis for establishing and stabilizing difference, often on the basis of some singular, arbitrary, and unstable epigenetic trait like skin pigmentation. In a peculiar way, race homogenizes by picking out for us the one kind of difference that should matter, the kind to which we shall attend when organizing social and political bodies and, in so doing, erasing from view other *kinds* of difference that are therefore left unseen.

Thereafter, in a second move, the plural "races" divide what "race" had first homogenized; now, the races are marked out as fundamentally different but along *only one axis*. The result is a peculiar essentialism that dismisses a host of striated and overlapping differences between and within groups so organized. *Reified difference* divides by ignoring a host of such diversities. In a counterintuitive way, attention to the dynamics of racialization demonstrates that expansive attention to difference leads to a richer sense of human kinship between communities in a way that essentialist single-factor modes of differentiation cannot. Not all differences divide; only some do, especially when the difference in question is invented for just that purpose!

So, too, with "religion" and "religions." What are the processes by which some aspects of cultural life are identified as religious and then assembled into the abstract noun "religion"? How are communities and traditions homogenized as they are compelled to take on the exemplary markers of religion through processes of religionization? And once religionized, how are these traditions then divided into reified and essentialized religions? How is difference then imposed onto communities whose fluid patterns of belonging defy the reifications that the notion of discrete religions seeks to impose?

In sum, the categories, religion and religions, are neither eternal nor innocent; they have been invented and institutionalized for specific and often questionable purposes. Therefore, theological reflection must pause, just as critical race theorists pause to bring thought to bear on the conditions under and the purposes for which "race" was invented. Theologians, especially those who call themselves theologians of "religion," must do likewise. Failing to do so will distort reflection just as the uninterrogated use of the category race manages to do.

Therein lies the promise of genealogy of religion—to serve as the doppelganger of critical race theory and accomplish for religion what critical race theory does for race. We must now ask, what functions and purposes do the categories religion and the religions serve? Asking this question does not make religionization disappear any more than critical race theory makes processes of racialization and their material consequences disappear. But both interrogations can serve the work of denaturalization—of reminding us that there is nothing natural, immutable, or eternal about race and religion. That critical interruption can generate the space in which we find a certain freedom to think and construct otherwise.

Failing to appreciate the way in which thought as such in the modern West has been molded by these unexamined categories, religion, and religions has had powerful distorting effects for theology of religious diversity and comparative theology and, indeed, for constructive theology as such. Most fundamentally, inventing religions has played a critical role in generating and naturalizing a conception of theology as intramural reflection, reflection about God, world, and human carried out by appeal to the resources of one religion alone. Other religions can be thought *about* but not thought *with*; theology just is thought as it operates within the (presumably) natural boundaries of one religion. It, therefore, must not be constructively shaped by the claims and aims of "other religions." This conceptual constellation is the strong headwind that attempts to prevent the flight of comparative theology.

## Interrogating "Religion" and "Race"

The consequences of the vast, indeed global, transformations generated by the category "religion" are difficult to grasp. Before dipping into the genealogical literature that tries to trace and map those transformations, let us turn, as promised, to another provincial category that has also come to be globalized—namely, the idea of race. Indeed, modern notions about race and religion emerged in roughly the same historical moment and were together deployed to manage, curtail, and contain the consequences of the Indological discovery of Proto-Indo-European.[8] Rather than turn to theory first to make this case, I turn to fiction, in particular Salman Rushdie's 1999 novel, *The Ground beneath Her Feet.*

Early in the novel, Rushdie depicts two characters—one British, William Methwold (who, it should be noted, had to bear the weight of actual existence before assuming the added, albeit posthumous burden, of becoming a character in a Rushdie novel), and the other an (entirely fictional but nonetheless compelling) Anglophile Bombay Parsi named Darius Xerxes Cama. Both are doing their very best to avoid, ignore, and altogether escape the unmaking of the colonial world, a world of which they are exceedingly fond and to which they are quite accustomed. For them, Gandhi and the nationalist movement of the 1930s and 1940s are nothing more than disturbers of the *Pax Britannica.* They choose as their avenue of scholarly escapism the deliberately arcane and far removed world of philology. Their heroes are Max Müller and Georges Dumézil. They pass their days examining parallels between the *Iliad* and the *Ramayana,* between Helen of Troy and Sita, relishing in the happy knowledge that Indological philology has demonstrated that British and Indian alike are all "barbarians," and that the East is not so far removed from the West. The discovery of the venerable antiquity of Sanskrit and its place within a shared Indo-European family of languages, languages that could be traced to a common "Aryan" racial stock, rendered colonizer and colonized alike into brethren.[9]

Their blissful sanctuary comes crashing down when news blows into their scholarly haven that the word "Aryan" and indeed the entire legacy of their escapist labors had been sullied by the Nazi use of the term. The temporal priority of Müller and Dumézil does not shield their heroes from the poison, which "works its way backward through time and sideways into the reputation of innocent men" and brings their own life passion to naught.[10] Their labors turn out to be far from safely arcane. A world in which all alike are barbarians is replaced by another populated by races, races everywhere, most of whom are impure, tainted, inferior, and dangerous. Rushdie powerfully demonstrates in fictional idiom how race discourse came to be deployed to reify and thereby to separate peoples and traditions whose complex and intertwined histories hardly permit of essentialist disjuncture. He points to a crucial historical moment in which our knowledge of the radical proximity of the other was not just managed but eventually contained and ultimately negated.

Rushdie's novelistic treatment can be enriched by nonfictional supplementation. Of particular importance is Thomas Trautmann's erudite historical analysis of the strong opposition mounted by "the race scientists" of Max Müller's own day against philological theories that posited common origins between people of various racial stocks. Central to Trautmann's account is the work of James Cowles Prichard and the role he played in the unfolding of Victorian anthropology. Trautmann's analysis of Prichard, and even more of those who followed in his wake, shows that there was no need to wait for the Nazis to institute walls of separation when common origin accounts threatened to undo hegemonic European claims to superiority. Trautmann shows that race scientists, Müller's own contemporaries, appealed to theories in which the various racial stocks emerge from the various sons of Noah. These theories, in which Ham is the father of the darker races, make appeal to "the claims of physical features" in order to "defeat the authority of the Indo-European doctrine and of Sanskritists for ethnological classifications."[11] Sharp attacks on Müller's work were at the center of this racial project.

"The fundamental idea" of Prichard's work, as rehearsed by Trautmann, is that "civilization and skin color covary, that the human race is descended from a single pair (Adam and Eve) who were black of skin, and that change of skin color was brought about not by climate (the more usual view) but by civilization, the effect of which, it is claimed, is to lighten the skin."[12] The remainder of Prichard's shifting argument need not be rehearsed here. It suffices to note that accounts of race and skin color attenuate any sense of kinship generated by shared philological ties. The argument goes as follows: while it may be true that the origins of early civilization can be traced to Egyptians and Indians, whose common origins are exhibited in their darkness, they themselves lightened over the course of time as they became civilized, a process that accelerates and reaches its culmination with European peoples.

Trautmann goes on to show that Prichard's successors were even more vociferous than he was in seeking to undo Müller's work and the so-called "tyranny of the Sanskritists." Important for our purposes is Trautmann's observation that,

> India was at the center of the growing quarrel between ethnology and philology . . . between race science and the Sanskritists. . . . At opposite extremes lay the light-skinned civilized European and the dark-skinned savage. The results of anatomical investigation of Europeans and Negroes were read not as parallel departures from simian forms (as under the tree paradigm) but as establishing the top and bottom of a progressive series of human races (as in the figure of a scale or staircase of human races). . . . [13]

India, he argued, "was the critical battleground for the claims of ethnology and philology exactly because of its intermediate location, both in the scale of civilization . . . and for its variety of complexions lying between the extremes of the scale of physical types defined by race science. The Indo-European concept established a kinship between Indians and Europeans that was increasingly at odds with the search for discrete races."[14]

By recourse to extraordinary measures and barely concealed motivations, race science sought to undo this kinship. To get a flavor for the tenor of race science, it suffices to hear the language of Robert Latham, writing in 1861, who rejected philological evidence by, among other means, rejecting the connections between Sanskrit and contemporary Indian languages in order to assert that there are no common ties between the English and contemporary Hindus.

> . . . I must come to the conclusion that the theory which makes all languages of Europe and Asia, from Bengal to the British Islands . . . to have sprung from the same stock, and hence, all the people speaking them, black, swarthy, and fair, to be of one and the same race of man, is utterly groundless. . . . I can by no means, then, agree with a very learned professor from Oxford, that the same blood ran in the veins of the soldiers of Alexander and Clive as in those of the Hindus whom, at the interval of two-and-twenty ages, they both scattered with the same facility . . . for that would amount to allowing that there was no difference in the faculties of the people that produced Homer and Shakespear [sic], and those that have produced nothing better than the authors of the Mahabharat

and Ramayana; no difference between the home-keeping Hindus, who never made a foreign conquest of any kind, and the nations who discovered, conquered, and peopled a new world.[15]

Race theory and imperial aggression are intertwined and blessed. Of course, where there are no discrete races, there can be no question of ranking them into an ordered hierarchy of superiors and inferiors possessed of different grades of cultural capacity and merit. Hence, such leveling must not be permitted. And that is why race science had to so aggressively counter "the very learned professor" Müller's enthusiastic affirmation that the Europeans and Indians were "brethren."

As we shall soon see, the work of stratification introduced by race scientists parallels Hegel's labor to stratify religions. In both cases, the same discovery of kinship had to be undone in order to sustain hegemonic claims to European superiority. Indeed, the connection between race and religion is hard to disentangle. After all, assertions of racial superiority are ventured in order to sustain claims to cultural and religious superiority; they are not as such ends in themselves. Racial reification, the invention of discrete races, and religious reification, the invention of separate boundaried religions, serve to advance the same basic agenda.[16] One must reify in order to rank.

At the conclusion of the second decade of the twenty-first century, we find ourselves in an analogous moment. Ours also is a time of persistent and multidirectional transnational flows of peoples, images, ideas, institutions, and practices; the world we inhabit admits of no neat cartographies that affix hard and fast boundaries between communities and traditions. And yet we see both in certain quarters of Christian theology and beyond ever more vehement arguments that insist upon the fundamental incommensurability of civilizations and their respective religions. Indeed, some contend that "the religion line" will replace W. E. B. Du Bois's "color line" as this century's primary site of contention. My sense is that both categories are deployed in analogous ways precisely to manage and contain proximity. In our time, these categories even seem to mutate into each other as certain religions—Islam most especially—are racialized. Hence, some are said to "look Muslim," an ascription randomly imposed on a wide range of those who are brown. In any case, it is difficult to imagine that "races" will somehow be replaced by "religions" even when the latter category functions similarly. Because both categories are made to serve analogously, it seems reasonable to examine the work of critical race theorists and their critique of the category "race" if similar moves are to be made in a critique of "religion."

The careful work of scholars of racialization has done much to displace long-standing conceptions of race as a biological or ontological given. Like Rushdie, we are more than ever aware that we can trace, if not date, the origins of notion of race and the idea of multiple, discrete races; understanding these contingent origins has helped us to appreciate that these categories are fictions, albeit dangerous and recalcitrant ones. The work of Robert Miles, in particular, has done much to cultivate a genealogical sensibility around the category of race. Miles's work has, I contend, special importance for theologians and religious studies scholars because of his stringent critique of the "race relations" paradigm in racism studies.[17] Perhaps the fundamental conviction that drives Miles's work is the following:

> If "races" are not naturally occurring populations, the reasons and conditions for the social process whereby the discourse of "race" is employed to label, constitute and exclude social collectivities requires explanation rather than be assumed to be a natural and universal process. In other words, the construction and reproduction of the idea of "race", is something that requires investigation. This task is circumvented by the transformation of the idea itself ("race") into an analytical concept. Thereby, what needs to be represented as a social process and explained is reconstructed as a social fact that can be used to explain other social facts.[18]

And that is precisely the problem with the race relations paradigm: race was treated as a *realis*. Of course, Miles and his colleague Malcolm Brown are not claiming that race does not have real and brutal social consequences; they mean only to insist that negating those social consequences will require undoing and unmasking the very idea of race by denaturalizing it. Miles and Brown stipulate that "the analytical task is not to explain 'race relations'; rather, it is the generation of concepts with which one can grasp and portray the historical processes by which notions of 'race' become accepted and/or used in a plurality of discourses."[19]

What are the implications of the deconstruction and historicizing of the category "race" for the work of religionists and theologians, especially for theologians whose work is dedicated to improving "interreligious relations?" How might religious studies and theology need to be reconfigured if, *mutatis mutandis*, the very claim advanced by Miles and Brown were to be applied to our disciplinary discourses about "religion?" To feel the full force of this question, let us, if a bit mechanically, substitute the term "religion" for "race" in the preceding quotation:

> If "religions" are not naturally occurring populations, the reasons and conditions for the social process whereby the discourse of "religion" is employed to label, constitute and exclude social collectivities requires explanation rather than be assumed to be a natural and universal process. In other words, the construction and reproduction of the idea of "religion", is something that requires investigation. This task is circumvented by the transformation of the idea itself ("religion") into an analytical concept. Thereby, what needs to be represented as a social process and explained is reconstructed as a social fact that can be used to explain other social facts.

This simple substitution calls for just the work that genealogy of religion hopes to accomplish. Rather than take "religion" and "religions" as natural kinds or simple "social facts"—what happens when religion is taken to be a straightforwardly "analytical concept"—genealogy of religion turns the table by calling attention to complex global processes by which we have come to think of the global population as belonging to a certain delimited number of nonporous religions. The substitution reminds us that religions are no more natural than are races. Genealogical treatments of religion show that persons had to be taught to believe that they belong to religions, that they can normatively belong to only one religion at a time, that to belong to a religion is to belong to a tightly knit and relatively unified community of belonging, that some aspects of their lives count as religious and others as secular. There is nothing natural or timeless about these assumptions. Moreover, once these distinctions are securely in place and taken for granted, particularly the religious versus secular divide, it is easy to characterize traditions that do not recognize and abide by such distinctions as "fundamentalist" in character.

By asking about the origins of regnant conceptions of religion and religions, genealogy denaturalizes and provincializes, both spatially and temporally, our ideas about religion. We come to recognize that religion, far from being a universal and timeless feature of human experience, is not only of Western provenance but perhaps one of the West's most successful exports. I have already observed at the outset of this chapter that although there is considerable agreement on the matter of geographical provenance within this literature, no such consensus exists on the question of temporality. Who should be awarded the patent for the discovery of religion—Lactantius or Herbert of Cherbury? A great deal hinges on these questions; answering them determines whether religion will be considered a product of the West as such or a product of modernity in particular.

But what matters most at this particular juncture is the more basic task of transmuting the question posed by Miles into religious studies and theology. What might it mean for theology to think beyond and after "religion"? Does the discourse of religion and interreligious dialogue already presume that others are constructed in our image before they are permitted and perhaps obligated to respond? Does not interreligious dialogue, as presently constituted, take for granted the universal translatability of the category *religio*? Just what are the operative politics of translation at stake in presuming that such translatability is even possible? These are the questions that arise for comparative theologians and theologians of religious diversity when genealogy of religion is juxtaposed with critical race theory.

## Who Can We Think About, Who Can We Think With?: On Policing Normativity

I am not the first to note the peculiar role that the invention of religion plays in constraining and limiting the role of normative reflection. Arvind Mandair argues that similar constraints also operate in philosophy of religion, or more precisely, in how the borders between philosophy of religion and history of religion are maintained and patrolled.[20] His work is motivated by a basic question: "Why is it that despite the recent proliferation of postcolonial critiques of Indology, its modern successors such as history of religions and area studies . . . continue to reconstitute past imperialisms, such as the hegemony of theory as specifically Western and/or the division of intellectual labor between universal and particular knowledge formations?"[21] Mandair is interested in interrogating the dichotomy between the normative/theoretical work of philosophy of religion (universal) and the history of religions (particular). This dichotomy reduces the religious traditions of Asia to data to be studied by history of religions. They are not permitted to furnish conceptual resources for the normative work of philosophy of religion. That work can operate only by appeal to and within the boundaries of Western religious traditions. The persistence of this divide, as Mandair notes, is all the more peculiar since "cultural theory has helped not only to dismantle well-worn dualisms such as religion/politics, theism/atheism, sacred/secular, but more importantly has helped to narrow the gap between academic practices and cultural practices such as religion that scholars seek to study."[22]

Mandair observes that the work of cultural and critical theory has been productive for Christian theology. Pointing to "a reversal of critical theory's atheistic roots in 'the masters of suspicion,'" Mandair notes that Christian theologians have not only managed to "dispute the atheistic presuppositions of modern secular thinking in the social sciences" but also to legitimize "the use of phenomena from these particular traditions as resources for critical thinking about religion per se."[23] Mandair cites as evidence a variety of texts including John Milbank's groundbreaking work on *Theology and Social Theory*.[24] In texts such as these, Christian theology is not merely the object of social theory but claims for itself the conceptual power and resources to engage in social analysis itself.

Despite such gains in the case of Western traditions, no comparable turn is evident in the case of Asian religions. There, the unmitigated divide between the universal and the particular, between theory and data persists. Asian religious traditions are to be thought *about*. They are not what we think *with*. Why? Ironically, one answer that Mandair advances is that postcolonial critics have been so anxious to protect Indian culture from the "religious effects" of imperialism—the configuration of Indian traditions as "religions" on the West's own terms, terms extrinsic and alien to Indian traditions—that the only form of anti-imperialist critique permitted is a secular one.[25] What Mandair wishes to interrogate is the peculiar way in which an exclusive commitment to secular critique repeats the long-standing depiction of the West as the scene of dynamic history over against South Asia, which remains bound to religion now characterized as static and even atavistic.[26] On such accounts, Indian religious traditions remain objects to be theorized and not subjects who are agential contributors to theorizing.

My own questions are akin to Mandair's: Why do Christian theologians, by and large, remain unwilling to enter into a substantive engagement with the normative claims and aims of other traditions? What conceptions of the theological task make it permissible for Christian theologians to pretend that the truth-seeking work of theology need not take account of the normative commitments of Hindus, Buddhists, and others?

Like Mandair, I seek to interrupt the duality between theory and data, between those traditions that are accorded the status of universality and others that remain merely particular. This challenge may well be greater within Christian theology than in philosophy of religion because Christian thinkers rarely recognize the practices and claims of other traditions *even as data* for theological reflection. Even apologetic encounters with other religious traditions would amount to recognition that such traditions are conversation partners who make normative claims. What prevails instead is a failure of engagement. Christian theologians proceed without feeling any compulsion to reckon with religious alternatives. They have largely contained the effects of religious diversity by arbitrarily delimiting their interlocutors. While Western philosophical traditions and secularity as such are worthy of interrogation and perhaps even refutation, traditions of the East are too often simply ignored.[27]

## Managing Proximity by Inventing Religions

Both philosophy of religion and Christian theology presume and presuppose a divide between the universal and the particular, between the West and the Rest. What are the roots of this dichotomy? Mandair believes that the roots of the divide between the universal and the particular can be traced back to a critical historical moment: the early Indological discovery of the antiquity of Sanskrit and the common origin of European and Indian languages in some form of Proto-Indo-European.[28] Mandair argues, as Trautmann does, that these discoveries threatened the ideological foundations of the colonial project by undermining European notions of civilizational separateness and superiority. Just as accounts that seek to depict human communities as divided into discrete biological groups marked by asymmetrical intellectual endowments are interrupted by Darwin's theory of evolution, so it is with the Indological discovery of common linguistic and cultural origins. Monogenetic accounts of origin, whether biological or cultural, prove inconvenient for theorists of racial or cultural superiority who seek to posit essentialist disjuncture as a precondition for claims of superiority.[29] The proximity of South Asia was especially threatening, Mandair argues, because the work of noted Indophiles like Schelling offered intellectually credible and appreciative engagements with Eastern pantheism, and in so doing, ventured alternative possibilities for the future of European Christianity.[30]

Mandair contends that it was Hegel, especially in his *Lectures on the Philosophy of Religion*, who managed most effectively the disruptive potential of the challenge posed by philology. Hence, Hegel does for religions what the race theorists do by appeal to races. Central to Mandair's reading of Hegel is the latter's claim that the origin of thought is coincident with the origins of religion. Therefore, if the historical evidence suggests that the origin of religion can be traced back to Indian antiquity, then a monogenetic account of history, religion, and thought would undercut claims to radical difference necessary to support the superiority claims of one culture over against all others.[31] Mandair argues that positing a typology of religion*s*—the plural is important—alleviated this threat to "Western man's" claim to be historically different from "the Rest" by serving both to reify and to map the religions and their respective civilizations over against each other. Mandair's argument is too rich to treat here without distortion.[32] It must suffice to note that Hegel is a critical figure because he generates a typology of religions that allows non-Western traditions to be fixed to more primitive evolutionary strata and hence no longer relevant to the ongoing unfolding of history. Their time has come and gone, and only Christianity remains a living religion for the present. Mandair contends that Hegel, in so doing, reduces these religions to the status of mere objects of the historian's gaze. Henceforth, these traditions can be studied by the history of religions, but they cannot figure into the normative work that constitutes philosophy of religion proper, which is grounded in and appeals only to more advanced Western religious materials.

## Universalizing Religion

Mandair is just one of many scholars who are now demonstrating that the categories "religion" and "religions" are neither innocent nor cross-cultural universals that refer to natural kinds or ontological givens. The literature on the Western origins of the notion, along with its subsequent export to and reconfiguration by communities beyond the West, is a tale now told by many. One cumulative conclusion of this literature is that much of the world not only lacked the word "religion" but also lacked any analogous concept prior to encounter with the West.

In this respect, Jason Ananda Josephson's work on Japan is convincing because he can specify the very date on which the Japanese first encountered and were compelled to tangle with the category religion: July 8, 1853. He writes of the arrival of American warships on the Japanese coast, in contravention of Japanese law, firing canons, and demanding that two letters be delivered to the Japanese emperor. The magistrate presented with those letters discovered that "'Religion' appears twice in the official communications brought by the Americans, both times to assure the Japanese that the United States had no interest in violating the country's centuries-old prohibition of Christianity. But on this point the Americans were not being truthful."[33] But more to the heart of our case is Josephson's compelling claim, a claim on behalf of which the whole of his book is a tight, forceful, and persuasive argument:

> When Japanese translators encountered the term "religion" they had no idea what it meant. They produced multiple versions of the American letters, rendering "religion" with a range of terms, each of which implied something radically different. No word then existed in the Japanese language equivalent to the English term or covering anything close to the same range of meanings. This book will explore the process by which Japanese officials, when confronted with the Western concept in a moment of political crisis, invented religion in Japan.[34]

That tale is an arresting one, and readers would do well to engage the whole of Josephson's nuanced argument. An intriguing feature of the argument is the way in which Japanese thinkers worked with a three-fold scheme of categories of "superstition," "religion," and "the secular" to do the work of segmenting Japanese life into different domains. Especially striking is the tale that Josephson tells about the conceptual work undertaken by the state in order to define certain aspects of Shinto as secular so that the "Shinto secular" could be required for all Japanese. Josephson shows that,

> Following the Meiji Restoration, Shinto gained power not as a relic of feudalism but as a product of the politics of a modern nation-state and it did so by being excluded from freedom of religion and the requirements of tolerance. Over the course of Japanese modernity, Shinto was located in the public sphere and its commitments and institutions gained, rather than lost, social significance. . . . The Shinto secular was distinguished from religion and served as the foundation of the outward form of Japanese politics and national identity. As such, it was made the duty of all Japanese subjects. The state was thereby able to promote its ideology and reduce Christianity (as well as Buddhism and Sect Shinto) to merely one option among others.[35]

Josephson shows how traditional forms of Shinto were reconfigured and redistributed so that some could be accounted as secular and hence public and compulsory and others merely private and optional and hence a religious part of Sect Shinto. This division, far from being natural, was a product of the exigencies generated by cross-cultural encounter.

Even this passing glimpse into Josephson's work gives a flavor of the power of historical and genealogical work. Josephson shows that, contrary to some scholarly accounts such as that of J. Z. Smith, religion is hardly a product of the scholar's study but often came to have the meanings it now bears through international diplomacy and the asymmetrical exercise of power. The force of the American letters, presented to the Japanese emperor, did not rest in their rhetorical or conceptual power but rested instead in the armed warships that delivered them.

But Josephson also shows that the Western thinkers did not operate alone in imposing concepts ad extra. Japanese thinkers, even if under the threat of force, took up on their own the work of inventing religion in Japan and its correlate the secular in surprising, distinctive, and unexpected ways for their own national purposes. He shows

> that the category of religion was not mere imposition. It was not simply a *mondialatinisation* in the Derridean sense. The asymmetries of power did give inordinate influence to Euro-American conceptual structures, but the Japanese were far from passive recipients or imitators. Instead Japanese intellectuals, leaders, policymakers, and diplomats were involved in a process of negotiation that *produced* religion in Japan.[36]

Imagine undertaking a comparative study of Christian and Shinto motifs that bypassed such processes of East-West encounter but instead operated on the assumption that Shinto is a religion in the same sense as Christianity is. For that matter, Josephson's work should trigger in the reader's mind recursive questions about the senses in which Christianity itself is a "religion" and the various national contexts in which Christianity has come to be configured differently. Josephson's work and the work of other genealogists alert us to the fact that religion-making is a complex multidirectional global process, albeit a process that is triggered by asymmetrical Western processes of aggressive expansion and encounter.

What do theologians of religious diversity presume they will find when they set out to look for religion in Japan, India, or South Africa? What provincial categorical schemes are subconsciously operative when the

comparative theologian sets out to engage in Hindu-Christian comparison? Do we assume that Hinduism and Christianity are religions in the
same sense before we begin comparison? Do traditions have to configure themselves as religions in order to be welcomed onto the stage of interreligious encounter and comparison? What themes count as "religious"
and are so subject to comparison, and what themes fail to be considered
because they are not religious? To bypass these questions, to operate by
appeal to notions of religion that are left implicit is sure to compromise the subtle labor of theology of religious diversity and comparative
theology.

## Religion and the Invention of Singular Religious Identities

A crucial challenge posed by the category religion, as we customarily employ it, is that it takes for granted singular belonging as the norm.
Learning to think by way of the category "religion" has given rise to the
idea and even the reality of singular religious identity. What is at stake is
not merely a matter of thought but of knowledge-power configurations.
When the category religion is employed to organize and govern, religiously multiple populations are constrained and corralled into singular modes of belonging.

Over the course of two important books, Peter Gottschalk has shown,
by appeal first to ethnography and then to historical studies, that British
modes of administration and governance first determined that (a) religion would be the governing category for representing Indian populations, and then (b) would be imposed upon those populations with
religion understood as an essentialist, singular, and exclusive category.
Those who brought the category to bear on Indian populations operated
*from the start* under the assumption that to be Hindu is not to be Muslim and conversely to be Muslim is not to be Hindu. This understanding
was baked into the operating assumptions that framed how the category
was used to understand and configure Indian life even when observers
recognized that sorting populations into mutually exclusive categories
was unworkable and untrue to experience.

In *Beyond Hindu and Muslim*, Gottschalk engages in the subtle ethnographic work of a town he has called "Arampur" to demonstrate that
although the categories "Hindu" and "Muslim" play an important and
even, at times, conflict-generating role in community life, a deeper descriptive dive discloses a more complex picture. Gottschalk makes sev-

eral kinds of arguments. He contests Western preoccupation with religion as *the* defining identity category for understanding Indian life. This preoccupation, he argues, fails to register the variety of categories that shape, often in more significant ways, individual and communal life. These include regional and village identities, caste and subcaste identities, and family identities. By privileging the category religion, the role and import of these other categories are diminished.[37]

Moreover, even when religious life is the focus of attention, religious identities turn out to be complex and fluid. Hindus and Muslims often participate in each other's rituals, visit and revere common sacred sites, and trace their identities to common ancestors despite formal religious identifications. These forms of fluidity are lost from view and even compromised when scholars bring singular categories to bear on the composite identities of persons and communities. There is, therefore, little empirical resonance between the way Western scholars imagine religion and the way religious identities are actually lived out on the ground.

Ignoring such lived multiplicity, Gottschalk argues, was central to "British epistemological imperialism."[38] The central problem of epistemological imperialism is captured in the title that he gives to his first chapter: "Multiple Identities, Singular Representation."[39] Imperial mapmakers brought with them an inadequate conceptual apparatus when they came to survey Indian territory. What becomes lost from view when an alien conceptual apparatus overwrites local realities? Among other things, one fails to notice the ways in which Muslims have absorbed elements from the larger Hindu milieu into their local practices, but also vice versa. The pattern of mutual ritual participation is a vital local reality, and the flows seem to go in every direction.[40]

I share Gottschalk's concerns about the complex and problematic relationship between representations (map) and the realities that those representations are meant to portray (territory). His work demonstrates not only that map rarely fits territory, but, in the context of colonial power, map *reconfigures* territory. The use of the categories religion and religions actually creates new realities on the ground. Moreover, Gottschalk notes that native communalists are all too ready to exploit these singular representations grounded in alien notions of what "religion" and "religions" are for their own interests, interests that then tear and fray the social fabric.[41] Hence, scholarly representations become complicit with divisive communal forces of the Hindu Right, which is all too eager to depict Muslims as discrete and alien others. Gottschalk shows that epistemological violence contributes toward real material violence and provides aid and comfort to those who wish to advance narratives which describe Muslims as foreign to Mother India, ignoring the innumerable ways in which, in the course of daily life, Indians routinely inhabit forms of multiplicity that go well beyond religious labels.

Gottschalk's second book adds the weight of historical evidence to the ethnographic work recounted in his first. In the second, he demonstrates the naive confidence that the British had in the categories that they brought to the putatively neutral mathematical work of the census, a confidence belied by the complexities of the actual work of counting. Gottschalk shows that these categories were hardly neutral or objective particularly because British census takers "presumed mutually exclusive categories that apply universally."[42] He shows, quite rightly, that the validity of enumeration hinges on the viability of the categories deployed in the first place. If the categories are contestable, then the meaningfulness of the counting falls into question. Gottschalk writes—and his words are quite striking—that census takers had "only a few short weeks as they compiled the literally millions of census slips from each of their provinces. An identity that did not fit obviously existing categories had to be either reconciled with a preexisting category, sloughed off into the 'other' category, or accorded its own. The mechanism of the census demanded specificity and unambiguity. Tabulation relied upon a slip of information for each individual that workers placed into slots: one per category. Census officials truly pigeonholed individuals, even those who had not pigeonholed themselves."[43]

But why select religion as the category for counting? That choice is anything but natural, as Gottschalk's telling observation about census taking in Britain makes clear:

> . . . Parliament would acquiesce to a question about religion once in the British census's first two centuries of operation. In that instance, outrage among Nonconformist parliamentary members torpedoed a proposal to enumerate church attendance in England as an unjustifiable intrusion into the liberties of religious conscience. In fact, *it was not until 2001* that a census would ask all residents of the United Kingdom about their religious preference. In contrast, religion serves as the primary category of difference in India.[44]

Decisions were made before the fact. India was seen as a peculiarly religious country and hence the selection of the category. And, then, baked into the category was the assumption already named, that each individual could only belong to one religion. These contestable a priori decisions give the lie to the putatively "scientific" character of census taking and the results generated therefrom. Reading Gottschalk's two books, one is struck time and again by the power of alien "descriptive" categories to materially reshape on the ground realities on the Indian subcontinent—a reshaping that continues to have massive ramifications in current Indian life, influencing the way in which even those unfamiliar with Indian life have come to think of India as wracked by irresolvable interreligious conflict.

For theologians of religious diversity and comparative theologians, Gottschalk's ethnographic and historical work offers further evidence that mandates caution about the central categories at play in both endeavors: religion and religions. As I have argued throughout, internal homogeneity and external reified difference are generated by the way in which these categories are put to use. Human communities and the religious traditions to which they belong are far more variegated and relationally co-constituted than the categories themselves suggest. Gottschalk, Josephson, Mandair, and others have generated a massive literature that demonstrates that we must proceed with great critical caution in how we deploy these categories should we elect to preserve them.

## Interreligious Dialogue and Comparative Theology after "Religion"

As a Christian comparative theologian, I am committed to theological reflection that seeks to learn from multiple religious traditions and to rethink my own theological commitments and those of the Christian tradition in light of these encounters. Comparative theology is constructive reflection that insists upon learning from and with—and here we immediately run into difficulties that we now know are more than merely terminological—"other religions." What this chapter's foray into genealogy of religions has demonstrated is that otherness is already folded into our conception of religions. Certainly, historical and genealogical studies show (1) that we have not always thought by recourse to the term, and (2) that the term has been neither neutral nor innocent even, or perhaps especially, when it is put to use in that most apparently objective of tasks: mere counting. Hence, the question arises: Might we imagine a comparative theology after religion or at least after the critical interrogation thereof? The work of Chapters 2 and 3 has made plain the urgent need for such an undertaking in theologies of religious diversity. In virtually every case in which the ship of TRD runs into rocky shoals, we have seen the enterprise founder on questionable assumptions about religion and religions. We have every reason to believe that comparative theology also runs such risks if it assumes the innocence of its fundamental categories.

As is the case with race, to fall under the uncritical spell of religion and religions is to become vulnerable to a host of essentialisms and reifications. Within a given religion, sameness reigns, and without, there is only difference. Comparison can hardly get off the ground if it is bound to such assumptions. Hence, the fact that most "religions" contain within them alternative and indeed sharply different salvations, to use Mark Heim's plural term, hardly registers in some conversations within TRD. As is the case with race, in religion, singular identity is normative and multiple identities are aberrant, abnormal, or at the very least, atypical. The coercive power of the category, by constituting traditions as spaces of homogeneity, erases what should be obvious to any clear-eyed observer: religious traditions are internally marked by the widest and wildest kinds of difference, even on central questions of soteriology and eschatology. There is no consensus within Christian communities or within Hindu communities about such central questions as the nature of postmortem existence, whether persons should aspire to union with divinity or, at best, communion. But perhaps the most subtle and consequential work accomplished by the category religion, particularly in its plural version, is the way in which the category generates, without anything so blatant as an assertion, the stark demarcation between the religions themselves, between internal and external, and between self and other.

Paulo Gonçalves's marvelous essay, "Religious 'Worlds' and their Alien Invaders," offers the shrewdest account both of religion's power to generate homogeneity within a tradition and why such homogeneity serves the interests of those who aspire to gain authoritative control over a tradition.[45] Gonçalves aims his laser-like critique at Christian theologians within the radical orthodoxy and postliberal theology movements. Theologians in both camps, he notes, are committed to rejecting the kind of homogenizing reflection about religion that drives the work of pluralists like John Hick. In the name of affirming genuine pluralism, both camps appeal to notions of narrativity to assert that religions are tightly woven, seamless, and integrated metanarratives or cultural-linguistic worlds. Each religion is, on such accounts, a world unto itself with its own, albeit nonfoundational, narrative integrity. About such positions, Gonçalves makes a telling observation, one that must be quoted at length:

> I am concerned that, precisely in their attempts to affirm the particularity, alterity and difference of various traditions, such approaches are not, as they claim, so much *describing*, but rather *generating, promoting and perpetuating* idealized or romanticized fantasms of quasi-autonomous and homogenous religious traditions—fantasms which are possibly far removed from their actual and historical forms, and which ignore the agonistic history of their constitution as "traditions" or "religions." In this manner, approaches which rightfully criticize the universalist notions of mysticism and essential religiosity which have dominated the discourse on religions are now seduced by what I will suggest is another chimera of strongly differentiated religious identities.[46]

Gonçalves's argument is powerful because it demonstrates that the category religion and the further idea of "religious worlds" disfigure not only Asian traditions—as has been rightly pointed out by scholars like Mandair and Richard King[47]—but also Christian traditions. He observes that "*the very same forms* of homogenization, and thus the very same problems, occur in the representation of Christian identity, theology and history, and that consequently these representations can and should be challenged by the same sort of critique."[48]

This contribution, alone, would be enough to establish the signal importance of Gonçalves's essay, but he proceeds to demonstrate that such homogenization serves the controlling interests of the postliberals and the radically orthodox. Their readings of tradition are rendered authoritative inasmuch as these theologians can insist that their proposal is not just one among many contested alternatives but instead represents "*the* biblical story."[49] Regarding the practice by radical orthodoxy thinkers of "the use of 'theology' without qualifiers, presenting it as a clear univocal practice, and the ascription to it of a '*fundamental nature*' and '*original form*,'" Gonçalves poses the following trenchant questions:

> Does theology have a "fundamental nature" and "original form"? Who decides what this "fundamental nature" is, and what interests does this serve? Is there a uniform and homogenous pre-modern Christian

theology? Can we speak "theology" in this abstract manner? Is it accurate to depict the Enlightenment as an alien invasion of theology . . . ?[50]

Gonçalves's argument demonstrates that the creation of homogeneous accounts of Christian theology not only serves to mask and privilege the interests of postliberal and radically orthodox theologians but also makes it entirely unnecessary for theologians to take account of those they deem to be external to *the* tradition. The creation of stark boundaries generates a neat duality between those who are inside and those who are on the outside. Accounts of Christian theology that regard theology as an exercise in faithfulness to the deep grammar of Christian practice or keeping faith with the singular biblical metanarrative inoculate theology from having to engage all those who stand outside the tradition. These others are to be repulsed as threats, and dissenters are but heretics.

Comparative theology becomes spurious when theology is so conceived. Because postliberals and the radically orthodox take persons to be situated within homogeneous matrices, and because there is no neutral arbiter—no generalized reason derived from Enlightenment sources—that might serve as mediator between these matrices, reflective engagement across religious boundaries is *ipso facto* impossible and ruled out of court. After all, religions in this view are impermeable worlds. The only traffic possible between these worlds is conversion or contest. One can understand a religious world only by taking up residence therein, which is to say by conversion. Persons can be driven to conversion only by way of contest that discloses *aporia* internal to the other's religious system. Driven by such discontent, one can jump ship and leave one religious world for another, but the reasons and claims of "other religions" cannot make a positive contribution to one's own tradition; there is no possibility of mutual transformation or of double inhabitation. Most peculiarly, theological movements that are enamored by the metaphor of language are unable to imagine that persons might become bilingual or multilingual.[51] The way to multiple religious identities or even to a serious vision of collaborative comparative theology is foreclosed.

If comparative theology is prohibited by postliberal theology and by radical orthodoxy, can we discover resources for comparative theology by engaging postcolonial theory? Postcolonial theory can indeed help to disrupt the reifications and homogeneities that come with a colonial deployment of the category "religion"—which suggests that comparative

theology can find in postcolonial theory a powerful resource and partner. However, poststructuralist and postcolonial theorists are unlikely to
offer their resources to comparative theology without contest and challenge. After all, there is reason to believe that the stern warning regarding the untranslatability of *religio* applies to "theology" as well. Engaging
the resources of other traditions in the work of Christian theology might
fall afoul of the danger that the very project—and naturally the object
too—of theology is taken to be universal. The theologian is duly warned
that neither religion nor theology can be taken as universals, and that
warning interrupts any unreflective movement to comparative theology
or interreligious dialogue.

We have already seen that extreme caution is warranted in the matter
of interreligious dialogue: the very idea of interreligious dialogue or interfaith conversation, while advanced in the name of peaceful coexis-
tence, might replicate the problems of race relations discourse. As
already noted, to speak of improving race relations is to endorse, at least
tacitly, the very idea that race is a biological or ontological reality and thus
writ into the very fabric of things—rather than writ into the fabric of
things by various acts and regimes of power. Likewise, much talk about
interreligious or interfaith dialogue seems to take for granted that the
world is naturally divided up into various impermeable world religions
inclined toward mutual suspicion and hostility along with some other
minor traditions that do not properly rise to the status of world religions.
Postcolonial theorists, Spivak in particular, would caution theologians
to take account of the very real material asymmetries of power between
traditions. Who represents whom? For whose interests? In what language?[52] The cumulative force of these queries prevents any quick turn
to comparative theology.

But is the way entirely barred? I think not. What is decisively foreclosed, and thankfully so, is any mode of religious reflection wedded,
either in theory or in practice, to purity of identity. Any theology that
knows beforehand—that is to say, before conversation and encounter—
what its proper agenda is and ought to be is bound to co-opt, assimilate,
and domesticate other traditions. Resistance is futile. But is it possible
to imagine that theology might proceed otherwise than by way of appeal to questions and criteria established before and apart from dialogue? Can one imagine the possibility of a theology that is aware from
the outset that no tradition is itself pure, singular, homogeneous, and
thus "uncontaminated?"

This possibility is suggested by Gonçalves. He proposes a turn to Derrida and poststructuralism in order to undermine the structuralist philosophical underpinnings of postliberal theology. Gonçalves rightly observes that postliberal theology's talk about "the internal logic or grammar of religions" is heavily indebted to the structuralism of Clifford Geertz and William Christian.[53] What theology needs to countermand structuralist fictions, he asserts, is "alternative modes of theorizing religious identity and its representation which are sensitive to blurred boundaries, variations of interpretation, marginalization by influential elites and the dynamics of innovation and transformation."[54] For Gonçalves, Derrida's work—especially his critique of the closure of metaphysics—offers invaluable resources. He cites Derrida:

> The closure of metaphysics, above all, is not a circle surrounding a homogenous field, a field homogenous with itself on its inside, whose outside then would be homogenous also. The limit has the form of always different faults, of fissures whose mark or scar is borne by all the texts of philosophy.[55]

What does Gonçalves hope will result from this turn to deconstruction? He expects that the infusion of deconstructive energies will demonstrate that religious identities are always already hybrid and polyphonic. If such a vision of religious identity is taken to heart, Gonçalves expects that the end result will be a vision of "both 'religious studies' and 'theology' as carnivalesque, messy, agonistic, creative, critical, multiple, transformative and unpredictable areas of study."[56]

As a comparative theologian, I can do no other than to endorse the carnivalesque vision of theology that Gonçalves advances, for such a vision can help to disrupt the idea that comparative theology is a special but marginal subdiscipline within theology proper. When we realize that theology has always been "messy, agonistic, creative and multiple," the term "comparative theology" begins to sound more like a redundancy rather an oxymoron. How could theology be anything other than comparative? The call for a robust comparative theology must be, on this account, understood as a call for reflection that lives into and thinks out of the inherent creative multiplicity of tradition(s), a multiplicity that already bears within it the mark of tradition's encounters with difference.

But for the comparative theologian, a turn to deconstruction alone is inadequate. Comparative theologians should insist that the theoretical resources for reconfiguring theology must be informed and enriched precisely by the traditions that they study. Comparative theology must remain faithful to doing theology in conversation with a variety of religious traditions by refusing to reduce the insights and aims of other traditions solely to the status of data for reflection. *Resources from other traditions must shape comparative theological method itself.*

I agree with Gonçalves that we need richer accounts of identity, but I am persuaded that some of those richer accounts will ultimately come from non-Western traditions. While I embrace Gonçalves's call for creative multiplicity, I am not entirely sanguine about turning to poststructuralist and postcolonial theory, not least because both streams of thought are, to my taste, much too enamored with the *tout autre*, with the wholly Other. I find the figure of the nondual more adequate to experience than recourse to talk about the wholly Other. Elsewhere, I argue, inspired by the work of the philosopher of relationality, Harold Oliver, that much Western theology has too often confused the Holy Other with the wholly Other.[57] The former bespeaks an encounter, a presence, a relation, and the latter suggests that which simply cannot enter into relation and, therefore, simply cannot be. The former points to that which exceeds my grasp, and the latter is merely a postulate, a sheer fiction on the order of the hare's horn in Indian philosophy—something that can be uttered but has no reality.

## Thinking Identity with a Little Help from Nagarjuna

No thinker has done more to problematize the idea of the wholly Other than Nagarjuna, the founder of the Madhyamaka philosophical tradition. For Nagarjuna and the Madhyamikas, more generally, such a refutation takes place by way of a rejection of *svabhava* (own-being or essence). Madhyamaka Buddhism is the anti-essentialist tradition par excellence. Indeed, the two central terms of Madhyamaka tradition, *pratityasamutpada*, dependent co-arising, and *sunyata*, emptiness, are understood to be different but complementary ways of dislodging the innate human habit of reification—of taking the world to be composed of unrelated entities, each with some essence entirely its own.

Dependent co-arising is an ancient notion rooted in the Buddha's own teaching. The idea, in the earliest stratum of Buddhist literature, refers to nexuses of factors that together perpetuate the cycle of transmigration. Nothing at all arises apart from some set of antecedent causes and conditions. In Nagarjuna, this idea of dependent co-arising can be understood, in Western philosophical terms, as a doctrine of universal internal relations. Nagarjuna's philosophical project can be read as a rigorous attempt to think through what is entailed by affirming dependent co-arising. What exactly does it mean to posit that nothing arises apart from causes and conditions? As it turns out, in Nagarjuna's hands, dependent co-arising can only be rigorously understood by appeal to and even as emptiness.

But first, a step back from metaphysics to soteriology: at the heart of Nagarjuna's religious vision is the conviction that human beings are driven by craving. That hardly counts as news for anyone acquainted with Buddhist traditions; it is but a restatement of the Second Noble Truth. Nagarjuna and the Madhyamaka tradition go further by insisting that the most subtle—and so also the most recalcitrant—manifestation of craving is evident in the cognitive habit of reification—of taking reality to be made up of things, of discrete entities. This point can be made by appeal to the double meaning of the English word "grasp" which signifies both taking a hold of something but also serves to signify the act of understanding. The cognitive activity of grasping can give rise to a distorted vision of reality that takes experience to be composed of graspable particulars, by entities that have own-being or essence.

Madhyamika thinkers are speaking here of innate cognitive patterns and not about formal philosophical position taking. Human beings pre-reflectively take reality to be composed of discrete entities, each with own-being. Under the force of such habituation, even the notion of dependent co-arising is misunderstood when it is formalized into a theory of causation. In any theory of causation, one inevitably asks about the relationship between cause and effect. When that question is posed, one quickly finds oneself in insoluble contradictions, because we revert to treating them as independent entities. When cause and effect are so imagined, no viable account of causation can be generated. Nagarjuna makes this point by way of a comprehensive critique of then extant theories of causation in the first chapter of his *Mulamadhyamakakarika*. His demonstration is too extensive to recount here; it suffices to note that if causes and effects have essences of their own, then it is impossible to get them back into relation. It will not do to attempt to argue either that effects, in some fashion, preexist in their causes or that an independently existing cause gives rise to an independently existent effect. If the effect exists independently of its cause, then it does not need to be caused. Demonstrating that absurdities follow from essentialization is the intention of the compressed first verse of chapter 1:

Neither from itself nor from another,
Nor from both,
Nor without a cause,
Does anything whatever, anywhere arise.[58]

If dependent co-arising is to be rightly understood, it turns out that one needs to be cured of one's innate disposition toward substantialist habits of mind, and that is just precisely why one needs to understand the meaning of *pratityasamutpada* by way of *sunyata*, or emptiness. Only when one understands that nothing whatsoever has essence or own-being—that everything is empty of self-existence—can one understand the deep intention of the Buddha's teaching.

But suppose, Nagarjuna asks, we assume a given reality has own-being, or *svabhava*. What would that mean? Well, first, if any being anywhere did enjoy own-being, then it would follow that such a reality would be changeless and eternal, terms much privileged in some classical accounts of divinity. Any such reality could never have come into being and would never cease to be. But, of course, no world composed of such entities is conceivable, as such a world would be changeless and static. What is changeless and static cannot enter in relation. We could not know it; nor could it make itself known. By means of extended *reductio ad absurdum* argumentation, Nagarjuna demonstrates that it is impossible to think the world in such fashion.

Nagarjuna then takes great care to see that emptiness itself is not reified and thereby treated as an absolute, on the order of Brahman. Emptiness, to quote the Heart Sutra, is not other than form, form not other than emptiness. Emptiness is not a substratum. It does not point to an absolute or ultimate reality that stands behind or beneath the world as experienced. To understand emptiness is to see the conventional, everyday world rightly, to see it on the far side of reification and essentialism, which amounts to saying that the world is the realm of dependent co-arising, a world of relation. The world without *svabhava* is wondrous, unthinkable, excessive, and mysterious but also profoundly ordinary. It is the world of quotidian experience seen rightly, seen outside the compulsive spell of reification. It is utterly refractory of the drive of thinking to grasp objects and essences, because there are no objects to be grasped anywhere.

This elementary sketch of Nagarjuna's thought, I suggest, is nonetheless a fecund theoretical resource for reflection that seeks to deconstruct notions of homogeneous and unrelated identity operative in world religions discourse. Turning to Nagarjuna and the Madhyamaka tradition is a compelling move for the comparative theologian whose aim is not merely to think about, theorize, or otherwise to explain religious others and their "beliefs." In turning to Nagarjuna as a resource for theory as well as a religious resource for addressing enduring afflictions that plague the human predicament, the comparative theologian hopes to challenge those within religious studies and secularist area studies who remain perfectly content to theorize about the religious other, to let the other serve as native informant, but not as a normative thinker whose claims and arguments require us to rethink and reformulate our own. Indeed, the very idea of *sunyata* reminds us that all talk of self and other must be handled with extreme care. As a mode of ordinary language, as a way of negotiating day-to-day interactions, such language is both useful and unavoidable. But when such discourse leads us into essentializing patterns of reflection and behavior, we fall prey to ignorance, an ignorance that has ethical consequence because it overlooks the fundamental nonduality of self and other. To reify is to break communion and to violate compassion.

It goes without saying that at least some Christian theologians are likely to be unsettled by a thoroughgoing encounter with the Madhyamaka affirmation of emptiness understood as the rejection of *svabhava*. Not only will Christian theologians encounter therein a mode of religious reflection that is not determined by divinity, but they will encounter a tradition that rejects the very idea that any reality whatsoever, whether mundane or transcendent, can be eternal and changeless—the instantiation par excellence of *svabhava*, of essence. To engage Madhyamaka seriously will require a substantive and difficult transformation of Christian theology.

On the other hand, classical Christian theology has also been, from the first, determined by two motifs that are through and through relational: the motif of incarnation and the motif of Trinity. The latter figure understands the divine life as perichoretic: each member of the Trinity is distinct but not separate. The former figure, incarnation, is basis for the ancient but often forgotten theme that divinity is fundamentally communicable, a communicable wellness if you will. God became human so that the human might become divine. A deep encounter with emptiness might well allow theologians to reframe and revivify elements at the very heart of tradition that have remained muted or submerged for far too long. These are questions to which we shall return in Chapter 7. Here, I want to delimit thinking about emptiness to questions about the nature of identity and, most importantly, to the question of religion.

Comparative theology has a complex and ambivalent relationship with "religion." On the one hand, comparative theology is driven by the desire not just to take account of religious difference but to learn from it. Nonetheless, the way to comparative theology can be barred by the entrenched weight of the category "religion." The force of the category can authorize a conception of theology as determined wholly by past construals of revelatory sources and motifs. Consequently, it comes as no surprise that theology is customarily taken to be thinking from and for a particular religious tradition that engages "other religions," if at all, solely for apologetic contest.

Theology pays a devastating price when it buys into such conservative configurations of its own work. If, as radical orthodoxy theologians have argued, Christian faith is driven by the quest for a peaceable kingdom, it will hardly do for theology to serve as the ideological handmaiden for the clash of civilizations discourse that now pervades and structures so much of our public life. Ironically and even tragically, theologians who aspire to give to faith countercultural power by forming Christian communities in sectarian fashion have proven to be accommodationists par excellence. Their vision of fundamentally incommensurable religions that ground and animate fundamentally different civilizations serves the interests of those who wish to insist upon the inevitability of conflict. A comparative theology that works against the reifying power of identity configurations, sanctified in the name of religion, is a powerful and desperately needed counterforce to those agonistic energies.

## But Were There No Boundaries before "Religion"?

My argument risks generating the impression that prior to the invention of religions, we lived in a world without boundaries. Then, sadly, after religion, the world suddenly acquired rigid and inflexible boundaries. Have not religious communities always sought to distinguish and differentiate themselves from each other? Aren't processes of differentiation integral to all group formation? Answering these questions is no simple matter. What would it mean to imagine religions as opposing each other before they were (made out to be) religions?

What is at stake here is a question of kinds. Just as human groups distinguish themselves in a multiplicity of ways before the invention of "race" or "nation," so, too, before "religion." Nonetheless, these *particular* categories are novel and have a peculiar logic that can be traced through a contingent narrative unfolding. There is something new about the logic of race and nation even if that novelty is not, in every respect, unprecedented. So likewise with the logic of religion. Nevertheless, it must be allowed that Chinese traditions have long recognized that there are a variety of ways—patterns of living for the formation of proper human comportment to nature, divine beings, other humans, and animals. Cross-cultural encounter and transmission—for example, the arrival of Buddhism in China—also triggers "recognition" that Buddhism, too, is a way, as in the Way of the Buddha (*fo dao*) that is formally comparable with East Asian traditions even if materially different in content.[59] Robert Ford Campany's indispensable essay on the category religion lists the following Chinese categories for "what-we-would-call-religion" including *dao, fa*, and more recently, *jiao*.[60] Each of these terms is deployed in distinctive ways and emerges in a variety of contexts. About *fa*, Campany writes, "In translations of imported scriptures this term was (like *dao*) often employed as a technical equivalent of the Sanskrit *dharma*, but in contexts such as the ones collected here its use is clearly more generalizing than that, referring to the sum total of teachings, communities, institutions, and practices associated with the Indian sage."[61]

The third term, Campany shows, emerges in the modern period as "writers of Japanese and Chinese began to use expressions of the form 'X *jiao*' to denote what Euro-Americans were calling 'religions.'"[62] Not only does the term emerge as a result of encounter with the West, but it takes on characteristics that Campany, appealing to Smith, argues are unprecedented. He holds that "in the Chinese Buddhist canon, for example, one finds over four thousand instances of the juxtaposition of the terms *fo* and *jiao*, but more than ninety-nine percent of these simply mean something like 'the Buddha taught' or 'the Buddha's teaching [that].' Only with extreme rarity do such compounds seem to gather up and nominalize everything that one might mean in Euro-American discourse by a term such as 'Buddhism,' and even when one does find such cases, the ambiguity of the syntax usually permits other, nonreifying readings."[63] Campany's article should be mandatory reading for those who care about the distinctive logics embedded in the metaphors used in various languages for what Westerners have lately taken to calling religion. These snippets suffice to show that even when Chinese and Japanese thinkers recognized and named traditions, the imaginaries in operation were markedly different from Western understandings of religions and their interaction.

Similar observations can be made with respect to the South Asian context with respect to the multiplicity of *dharma*s: a variety of ways of configuring duty and obligation with respect to some comprehensive interpretation of the order of things taught by competing teachers and schools has long been part of South Asian life. Communal self-definition has always required contrast along some axis of difference, some way of distinguishing between "us" and "them."⁶⁴ But none of these modes of differentiation operates along the novel logic imposed by the categories "religion" and "religions."

We have already taken note of one way in which difference itself is configured differently: in South and East Asia, categories of "religious" differentiation permit multiple religious belonging. As I have demonstrated earlier, non-exclusivity along religious axes is far more the norm than the exception, particularly in premodern South and East Asia. One needn't be exclusively Buddhist, Taoist, or Confucian in East Asia. By contrast, built into Western constructions of religion is precisely such exclusivity. Furthermore, the notion that some parts of life are religious and others secular is largely without precedent even in the premodern West. The invention of religion in its modern sense is novel in these respects.

Boundaries are not new, but these particular ones are. To be mindful about these innovations entails constant vigilance about how the lines are drawn between traditions. Are the boundaries between human communities, whether religious or not, more like the membranes between cells and living tissues—vital and flexible precisely because they are porous and fluid—or like the fixed, impermeable, and unbreachable walls that xenophobes everywhere love so well? Who has the power to construct those boundaries, and how well do they work? On whom are those boundaries imposed and under what circumstances? What are the terms, the oppositions, for the construction of these boundaries?

Hugh Nicholson has taken particular care to investigate the question of boundaries with extraordinary rigor and subtlety. Nicholson notes that those who hold that there is a fundamental consensus between traditions on all core concerns tend to be dismissive about tensions between religious traditions. The result is a homogenizing utopian naivete, one in which an emphasis on "the pristine unity of a transcendental experience of faith" leads to inattention to the oppositional elements of religious commitment, elements that include "parochialism, chauvinism, intolerance, and polemics."[65] Nicholson has in mind pluralist theologians, most especially Wilfred Cantwell Smith and John Hick, but also, to a lesser degree, Paul Knitter.[66] Particularly problematic is the claim of Smith and Hick that religious diversity is merely phenomenal and superficial. On such accounts, faith is universally one, and variable are only its extrinsic embodiments. The stubborn persistence of difference, and even of disagreement, is wished away. The result is a hegemonic imposition of sameness upon divergent religious communities. Hence pluralism stands accused of imposing sameness and requiring consensus before interreligious encounter even begins.

Nicholson is not alone in making this claim about the imposition of sameness, a sameness that takes itself to be neutral, but proves, upon closer examination, to be anything but. Among those who have made much the same claim are Kathryn Tanner and Tomoko Masuzawa, to whom Nicholson is indebted.[67] Nicholson joins them in arguing that certain forms of pluralism impose on other traditions theistic and Christian conceptions of religion. However, the problem is not confined to contemporary pluralists. They are but a manifestation of the much larger problem this chapter has been exploring: the category of religion itself, and hence the field of religious studies as such, despite its pretense to objective neutrality, is anything but. As Masuzawa shows, the very idea of a certain privatized and universally present domain of the religious is a recent invention, and moreover one in which Christian theologians played a constitutive role. As Masuzawa states, "Christian liberals . . . paved the royal road to today's predominance of the world religions discourse," a discourse in which the various religions are all to be regarded with an equalizing sympathy grounded in a fundamentally theological premise that religious diversity is "divinely ordained."[68] Such liberal Christian discourse was meant to replace an older spirit of exclusivism, intolerance, and superiority perpetuated by confessional Christians. Ironically, what comes to be imposed universally is still a hegemonic European universalism with far more than a tinge of Christianity.

I insist, however, that what was imposed on other traditions was first imposed on Western Christianity. Christianity was compelled to configure itself as a religion, a process whose roots go further back in history to European colonial encounter with other cultures but only reaches its culmination in and even as modernity. The invention of world religions is simultaneous with secularization, which requires the depoliticization of Christianity. Christianity has to become a "religion" before it can provide the template for the creation of the other "world religions." This late arrival of religion and the religions is why accounts of "religion" and "Christianity" as coeval concepts—that Christianity has *always* been a religion and that religion is a Christian notion—are unconvincing. The larger point stands—a hegemonic sameness embedded in the idea of religion, invented in the name of tolerance largely by Christian scholars, has come to be imposed on other traditions so that they, too, become religions. Contemporary pluralists render explicit what was already implicitly operational in the very construction of the category religion—that all are divinely ordained ways to one and the same ultimate reality.[69]

What is the root of this predilection for sameness? Nicholson argues that the core pluralist mistake is a refusal to recognize the stubborn intractability of the political, which, in turn, leads pluralists to imagine religious traditions as so many various responses to the selfsame transcendent. He puts this point forcefully when he argues that "a major, if not the dominant, trajectory in modern religious thought can be understood in terms of an effort to isolate a putative core of religious conviction and experience from relations of social antagonism."[70] The scale of the problem as identified by Nicholson is striking; pluralists are in good company with much of "modern religious thought" as such. When moderns seek to identify religion or the religious by contrasting it with what is not religion (namely, the domain of the secular), the political is quarantined outside the latter space. Religion may subsequently have political effects but is not itself intrinsically political.

But what exactly does Nicholson mean by "relations of social antagonism," and why do modern liberals avoid recognizing the way in which such antagonism shapes religious traditions? For Nicholson, drawing from the work of Chantal Mouffe, politics just is by definition these "relations of social antagonism." So, in seeking to isolate religion from the political, Nicholson argues that pluralists fail to acknowledge just how much religious identity is shaped by the logic of rivalry. To correct for this pluralist error, one must (a) restore the unavoidable labor of the political into our accounts of religious identity constitution and (b) formulate a viable account of the political to correct for and revise pluralist errors. In the service of advancing these two tasks, Nicholson writes,

According to a relational conception of social identity, all forms of collective identity are constituted by difference; a group's sense of identity
is constituted by the other against which it defines itself. Social identity
therefore has an "us" versus "them" structure; it presupposes, in other
words, a political moment of exclusion. In contrast to Schmitt's conception of the political, however, this [Chantal Mouffe's] conception does
not imply the inevitability of violent conflict. . . . [A] relational conception of the political recognizes that a sense of political identity is constituted by its adversarial "other," and not, as in Schmitt's theory, by the
possibility of their destruction. This revised conception of the political
will allow us to make a critical distinction between, as Mouffe puts it,
an adversary to be tolerated, even respected on the one hand, and enemy
to be destroyed, on the other.[71]

First, Nicholson is on the mark that pluralist styles of theology have
ignored the role of the political in identity constitution. Second, he
is also right to commend a relational account of the political; group
identity is not pregiven in essentialist isolation but formed through
relational encounter. Third, he is right to urge us to step away from
Schmitt's antagonistic account of the political and move to modes of
imagining the political in which respectful struggle, agonism, replaces
antagonism.

But I have reservations about this third step; I suspect that the many
modes of encounter mark the political, agonism being but one. I propose
the following compressed axiom. There can be no thinking about the political *without* agonism; there must be no thinking of the political only
*as* agonism.

I begin with a confession: I recognize in myself some of the impulses
that Nicholson ascribes to liberal pluralist theologians. I worry more
about the dangers of reification between communities than I do about
the dangers posed by hegemonic homogenization. Given that propensity,
I receive Nicholson's admonition about agonism seriously. Nonetheless,
I wish to argue that there is no single mode of the political. The political
can be defined *neither* by appeal to Schmitt's friend-enemy distinction
*nor* by the modified agonism that Nicholson borrows from Chantal
Mouffe. Agonism is one form taken by political, but only one. Any genuine pluralism must recognize the sustained presence of difference and
hence the inevitability of groups organized around competing visions of

the good. But boundary construction between religious communities and their others is a complex and unpredictable process.

Take any group to which I belong as opposed to any other. There will be a sense in which to say that I belong to Group A is most definitely to say that I do not belong to Group B. But rarely, if ever, will my no to Group B amount to a total negation in every respect of what it means to belong to Group B. Moreover, the most important and relevant site of no-saying— of establishing that "we" are not (like) "them"—in the case of religious communities may not be with another religious community but with other communities of practice within the culture at large. For example, it may be more important for Christians to contrast themselves with regnant capitalist practices than with Buddhist practices. Any given Christian may have to say no far more often to the predations of con- temporary turbo-capitalism than to what any given Buddhist happens to hold. The risk of the captive power of the category "religion" is that we might fall into imagining that religious communities engage in agonis- tic self-constitution primarily over against other religions. Any complex social body is striated by multiple kinds of group belonging. I am myself a Christian who seeks to learn from Hindu and Buddhist traditions, but I am also a member of the academy, an American citizen, but one who is an immigrant from India who feels a powerful love for his country of ori- gin, a Democrat, an NPR contributor, an Episcopalian—this list could go on virtually ad infinitum.

Hence, the political represents a multiplicity of scenes of encounter whose possible forms include agnostic struggle, even enmity, but also friendship and love. There is no reason to define the normative nature of the political as defined by *any one* of these modes. Nicholson has identi- fied the apolitical and thus covertly hegemonic impulses buried within some pluralist theologies. In so doing, he offers comparative theology a profound service. Particularly compelling is the way in which he recog- nizes that the category religion functions in just this obscuring fashion. I depart from his work only inasmuch as he takes rivalry to be *constitu- tive* of the political and so also constitutive of relationships between re- ligious communities.

The site(s) of political engagement between communities and tradi- tions are too numerous, too complex, and too varied to admit of any es- sential form. What religion-making does is to sharply curtail this variety by delimiting the legitimate political actors within religions to certain authoritative figures and bodies—elites, clerics, scriptures, text scholars, theologians, ecumenical councils, interfaith dialogue tables, and the like—thereby removing from view the numerous other non-sovereign sites of meeting and encounter often navigated by voices from the margin, women in particular, as elite sites of the political are almost without fail in the hands of men.[72]

By lifting up the logic of us-them rivalry as definitive of the political and hence of the shape taken by interreligious encounter, Nicholson risks foregrounding official organs and authorities of self-definition which do tilt toward rivalry for the sake of exercising authority. In so doing, Nicholson risks privileging the very voices that his astute genealogical sensibility helps to contest. What is undone by remembering the construction of "religion" may be reinstituted by privileging politics as rivalry.

Popular religious practice, for example, is marked by modes of syncretism and hybridity that would make elites blush, if not apoplectic. But here, I am in deeper agreement with the larger goal of Nicholson's work: to demonstrate that comparison has the power to show that every us-them distinction is inevitably troubled by comparison itself. Comparison shows that every religious community is marked by robust internal variation; every community is striated by patterns of similarity and difference that makes any facile opposition between us and them unsustainable. Comparison interrupts reification.

Comparison can interrupt the reification of communal boundaries generated by the political constitution of communal identity. Nicholson summarizes the goals of comparison with lucidity when he writes, "Inasmuch as comparison serves as a technique for "thawing out" reified notions of identity, it forms an integral part of a Christian theology embodying the change in strategy I propose with respect to the problems of the political in religion—namely, from the "depoliticization" to the "denaturalization" of religious self-understanding."[73]

To this vision of the comparative project, a hearty amen! My own contention in this chapter is that genealogy of religion can supplement Nicholson's work of denaturalization by launching the labor of denaturalization *even before* comparison begins, lest comparison be left to undo gratuitous forms of reification that we build into our very idea of religion. The boundaries between traditions are always already more "permeable and flexible" than partisans and official boundary keepers like to imagine!

## Race and Religion Redux: Learning to Live with Categories We Do Not Love

There is, however, a question that we cannot defer. Does thinking with Nagarjuna, does the comparative theologian's desire to undo reification, entail dismissing categories such as race and religion? What about caste? Here, we face complex questions that demand context-specific responses. Dalit thinkers like Ambedkar have argued vigorously that caste must go. The caste system produces the outcaste; there is no way to contest the latter without undoing the former. Must the same be said about race and religion? Must we now join with John Lennon and "imagine no religion"?[74] Despite deconstruction and denaturalization, despite rupturing the apparent ontological naturalness of categories like race and religion, they persist in cultural imagination and political life. Moreover, they continue to generate powerful material consequences that do not disappear once their provincial and invented character is disclosed. To know that there is no biological basis for "race," to know that that the invention of race is, in part, a product of now discredited pseudoscience does not make racialization disappear. Neither do the categories or their effects disappear once we have denaturalized them.

What is triggered instead is a debate. What should we do with these invented categories? Should we keep them in play or discard them? Must categories like race and religion be eliminated in order to give rise to new forms of human solidarity that the categories were invented to suppress? If so, at what cost? What about extant forms of solidarity generated by these admittedly ambiguous categories? While race may be a fiction and invented for invidious purposes, it has nonetheless also served to generate a sense of community, for example, among Black people across the African diaspora. Is it possible to preserve social solidarity but not the category, or are the two impossible to disentangle?

That debate persists among philosophers of race. So it ought not to surprise that a similar debate is also now under way among philosophers of religion and theologians with respect to the category religion. Having appealed to critical race theorists to help us think about religion, we would do well to return to theorists of race to see what comparative theologians might have to learn from the ongoing argument about "race" regarding what to do about "religion."

With respect to race, on one side stand eliminationists such as Kwame Anthony Appiah who believe that we must think against and after race.[75]

On the other stands a host of thinkers, Lucius Outlaw and Thomas Shelby among them, who, despite calling for critical awareness of the disfiguring powers of race, nonetheless believe that race must, in some fashion, be retained. They argue that the category is not entirely invidious and can offer possibilities for social solidarity and so cannot be discarded. I cannot hope to present herein an expansive account of this closely argued philosophical conflict. I wish to argue that although we have much to learn from both camps, in the end, I stand with the retentionists on the question of religion. As to the question of retentionism and race, I remain more skeptical. What is important to remember is that retentionist philosophers and theologians have argued that both categories, *once denaturalized*, can be preserved and put to positive use. It is, at any rate, impossible to think and live our way into the foreseeable future without them. We must learn to live with categories we do not love, categories we regard with justifiable suspicion.

Among those who have learned from both camps, few excel Victor Anderson, who seeks a middle way between those who hold weak and strong accounts of race. In the end, he holds for a cautious preservation of the category and offers what he calls a relational account of race inspired by Charles Long. The trajectory of his work over the course of two books, *Beyond Ontological Blackness* and *Creative Exchange*, demonstrates that the rigorous work of disrupting ontological conceptions of blackness need not entail dismissal of the category. Genealogists and theorists of religion have much to learn from his creative via media.

Ontological conceptions of blackness have to go. What does ontological blackness mean? Anderson writes: "The disclosure of the ways in which race is reified—i.e., treated as if it objectively exists independent of historically contingent factors and subjective intentions . . . I describe this tendency toward racial reification as ontological blackness."[76] Ontological blackness names habits of thought marked by totalizing essentialization and a wholesale entanglement with "the blackness that whiteness created."[77] When race is ontologized, a constructed category is naturalized and taken to be part of the fabric of the real. Race is thereby granted a power that must be named as "idolatrous."[78] Under such conditions, racial identity exercises a comprehensive sway over who we take ourselves to be.

Thus far, Anderson stands in continuity with the critical race theorists. An invented category must not be granted totalizing power even if the quest to speak of blackness is motivated by liberative aspirations. And yet, even as he critiques reification, Anderson acknowledges that "postmodern blackness recognizes the *permanency* of race as an effective category in identity formation."[79] The use of the word "permanency" is striking; it acknowledges the intransigence of categories even after they have been denaturalized. Are we in the same situation with respect to religion?

Anderson acknowledges that race continues to constitute the "embodied relations" that constitute the thick specificities of life. So, too, with religion: critiquing the category's distorting powers does not grant us a religionless world. Our traditions may not have always been religions, but they are now, albeit to different degrees. Religionization, like racialization, is a process that operates in distinctive fashion in diverse locales. These differences notwithstanding, it is difficult to imagine any proximate future in which the effects of religionization can be called back.

Anderson's strategy, drawing on the work of Edward Farley, is to treat race as a deep symbol. The central point Anderson wishes to make is that when race is so construed, it can be used to generate new modes of ever expanding solidarity, what he calls "enlargement." Rather than divide, race as deep symbol can generate "sympathetic filiations" across lines of difference.[80] The point is not *whether* to deploy the category race; it's not going anywhere. The question instead is a matter of *how*.

Can we speak of religion in like fashion? Can we imagine religion and religions beyond reification, beyond essentialization and totalization, and against rigid and impermeable boundaries? Can we find skillful uses for the category that do not erase particularities within religious traditions thereby lending credence to homogenizing discourses about monolithic Hindu or Christian identity? Can we recognize that religious traditions are more accurately characterized as communities of argumentation rather than as communities of agreement? Can we do all that without appearing to describe away the thick sense of co-belonging generated by the category?

We can and we must. The quest to leave "religion" aside is quixotic. What I seek is a comparative theology *after the reification and essentialization of religion* and not a comparative theology that discards the category. With Anderson on race, I find attempts to think after religion altogether "a cognitive feat near unimaginable."[81] Smith, it must be remembered, long ago proposed substitutions—"faith" and "cumulative tradition" in place of the term "religion"—only to gain no traction whatsoever.[82] More recent thinkers have also suggested substitutions; they are likely to meet the same fate.[83]

I commend a different strategy. I offer a new stipulative definition of the religious, but one that does not arise ex nihilo. It carries forward elements from the work of past theorists, most especially Peter Berger and Robert Neville. But my definition neither repeats nor reinforces commonsense intuitions. It challenges the reifying essentialisms that genealogical studies of category formation have identified, essentialisms that lead to epistemological and material violence. I propose a definition of "the religious"—and I chose the adjectival formation precisely to interrupt the power of reification—which seeks to render the notion malleable and to locate it within the pulse and flow of human life rather than quarantine it within a private domain. Religious traditions, too, are described beyond reification and homogenization.

Anderson's relational terms like "sympathetic filiations" and "enlargement" are suggestive and applicable also with respect to the religious traditions, but I would like to introduce, along with Nicholson, a note of contestation, albeit at a different site, not *between* traditions but *within* them. Religious traditions are not communities of consensus so much as they are sites of internal contestation. One knows that one belongs to tradition X if one is claimed by the arguments that consume tradition X and not by some supposed agreement shared by all.

Comparison shows that religious traditions are marked by neither simple difference nor flat sameness. Precisely because traditions are marked by internal contestation, comparison can show surprising lines of affiliation across traditions. As David Tracy long ago wrote, comparison discloses similarity-in-difference and difference-in-similarity.[84] Indeed comparative theology in both its tasks, comparison and construction, could not operate otherwise. If simple sameness obtained across traditions, comparison would prove uninteresting and unproductive. If simple difference obtained, comparison would be impossible and learning forestalled. Hence, any definition of the religious that is empirically credible and normatively fecund must interrupt reifications of religious traditions as bounded homogeneities.

In striking fashion, genealogy resonates well with the core ontological vision of Nagarjuna's Madhyamaka tradition, specifically in its affirmation of two-truth theory. Conventional truth is the truth of things as they appear. Ultimate truth is the truth of things as they really are beyond appearances. The surprising turn in Madhyamaka thought is that these two truths are seen ultimately to be one and indivisible.

In Nagarjuna's Madhyamaka, the conventional world is the only world there is. The trouble is that we see the world wrongly as composed of reified entities possessed of self-existence or own-being. Subtract the illusion of self-existence and nothing happens to the world. The world, after all, was never characterized by such reification. Nowhere has there ever been a thing that possessed existence apart from relation. To see the world rightly, the world does not have to change. Nor do you have to see beyond the world of appearance to another truer realm behind it. One just has to see the one world that there is rightly—without self-existent essences.

So it is likewise with categories such as race and religion; these categories do not name fixed essences that exist in the world apart from the on-going flux of historical experience. Race and religion are not ontological givens. Like the world of conventional reality in Nagarjuna's thought—a world which is neither real in the sense of composed of unchanging substances nor unreal in the sense of being illusory—so, too, with race and religion. They are neither real nor unreal. To rupture race and religion as ultimate ontological truths opens up the possibility of putting these notions to novel conventional uses. Learning to see them as relative configurations, not timeless and eternal, not writ into the very fabric of things, is to recognize that they admit of reconfiguration. How, then, do we wish race and religion to function? What concrete work do we want these categories to accomplish? If they are unlikely to disappear by wishing it to be so, might we think of new definitions that come with a measure of instability built into them? That is precisely what I venture in the chapter to come—a definition of the religious that seeks, from the first, to work against the reifications that plague most extant understandings of "religion" and the "religions." To be religious is not to belong to a timeless cultural-linguistic framework with a deep and stable transhistorical grammar but to seek comprehensive qualitative orientation by the creative use of contested and porous traditions that are always composed of what they are and what they are not. To that labor we now turn.

# 5 Defining the Religious

## COMPREHENSIVE QUALITATIVE
## ORIENTATION

Religiousness *seems easier to exploit. Marketing agencies avidly make use of the remains of beliefs that were formerly violently opposed as superstitions. Advertising is becoming evangelical. Many managers in the economic and social sphere are disturbed by the slow breaking of the Churches in which lie the remains of "values" which the managers want to recuperate and make use of by rebaptizing them as "up-to-date." Before these beliefs go down with the ships that carried them, they are hurriedly taken off and put into businesses and administrations. The people who use these relics no longer believe in them. They nevertheless form, along with all sorts of "fundamentalists," ideological and financial associations in order to refit these shipwrecks of history and make Churches museums of beliefs without believers, put there in reserve so that they can be exploited by laissez-faire capitalism.*

—MICHEL DE CERTEAU, *The Practice of Everyday Life*

## Toward a New Definition of the Religious

I propose to you, dear reader, a minor experiment. Turn on your TV and watch a favorite show, but this time, pay attention to the ads. See how long it is before you find yourself watching a commercial in which an attractive, fit woman is depicted in a yoga asana while a narrator praises the virtue of some product. The products can vary wildly: yogurt, a breakfast cereal, or even pet food. The presence of the asana is never a matter of comment; the message is so transparent that it feels banal to spell it out. "Buy this product because it will be a perfect part of your healthy and balanced lifestyle." If it's pet food, the voiceover will say in dulcet tones, "You take good care of yourself, but what about your cat?" In either case, the claim is clear. Buying this product is an important part of your spiritual life; it will give you and perhaps your cat—if I can mix religious idioms here—a taste of the peace that passes all understanding.

De Certeau is right. Advertising culture is interested in appropriating whatever power remains in religious idioms for an alternative religiousness, in this case the religion of the market. The disturbing inversion here is that the Yoga tradition, which rejects self-seeking desire, is now mobilized for the sake of the capitalist practice of generating ever new desires for au courant products that you did not know you wanted. The spirituality on offer in these commercials is capitalism as a therapeutic regimen that trains persons to buy and to spend in order to perpetuate the proper functioning of the market. The result is a capitalism that makes you feel good, even spiritual. What could be better?

This recurrent, almost clichéd, visual trope is fascinating, nonetheless, because now advertisers are deploying "Eastern" symbols and practices and not Christian ones. Christian symbols no longer have sufficient power or resonance to be appropriated for commercial ends. The fact that yoga, by contrast, does have the power to generate associations of spiritual calm, balance, and poise speaks to the now pervasive presence of yoga practice in American life. But under the influence of De Certeau's evangelical advertisers, the yoga in question is utterly denatured of its grounding in Hindu wisdom and made to serve another religiosity.

If everyday immersion in the practices of market capitalism constitutes a form of religiosity, does that mean that most Americans who call themselves Christian but remain engaged in the market are routinely engaged in syncretism if not multiple religious belonging?[1] The answer to that question depends on how the religious is defined. If genealogical inquiry of the sort undertaken in the previous chapter leads to an interrogation and then redefinition of what one takes religion to be, it may become possible to regard life lived in service to economic goods as a form of religious life. That discovery, in turn, can provoke a critical question: If capitalist Christianity is indeed a syncretistic religiosity that has become common for most professing Christians in America, why is such syncretism regarded as harmless and unworthy of interrogation whereas those who engage in Buddhist-Christian life are called out as unfaithful?[2] Moreover, what then becomes of the assumption that multiple religious belonging is an esoteric Eastern phenomenon and largely absent in the West?

These questions are provocations meant to open up a more encompassing line of investigation: What possibilities open up for theologies of religious diversity and comparative theology once certain idées fixes about the nature of religions are disturbed? Might it be the case that certain possibilities like multiple religious belonging and deep interreligious learning seem foreclosed to us not because they are unchristian but because of rigid ideas about the nature of religion?

This chapter takes on the following tasks. First, it contends that genealogy of religions does not dispel the possibility of advancing new theories of the religious. Genealogical inquiry can provide a clearing in which new critically self-conscious definitions of the religious can be deployed. Second, I offer a definition of the religious that attempts to avoid the kinds of reifications that have plagued theories that have not passed through the turbulent waters of the genealogical project.

But what is the point of venturing any definition of religion or the religions whatsoever? Might we learn to live without them or adopt alternatives as Wilfred Cantwell Smith suggested decades ago? Given their ambiguous legacy, why bother keeping them in circulation? A first punchy answer is that the terms are going to remain in circulation regardless of scholarly intentions. Our powers are limited. So any attempt to do without some working definitions of religion and the religions is unrealistic. The structure of Western societies, political philosophies, and even basic categories of thought will continue to be organized around these terms. A prudent alternative is to give the old terms new content by way of new definitions.

Genealogy compels scholars to articulate the purposes that such definitions are meant to serve and to be alert to the effects that such definitions generate. Such intentionality is required even for those scholars (such as myself) who believe that there are cross-culturally stable functions present across human cultures that can meaningfully be designated as "religious." Even if you believe that such functions exist, those functions have been, throughout history, diversely dispersed throughout human cultures. We have only recently learned to collect a variety of cultural projects into the province of the religious, thereby opening up the space of the secular.

The work of this chapter amounts to a deep Amen to Wilfred Cantwell Smith, who, as Talal Asad and others have noted, stands as among the first to alert us to the troubling inadequacies of most operative assumptions about reified religion. Nonetheless, this chapter also marks a refusal of his proposed solution—namely, to replace the singular "religion" with two substitute terms: "faith" and "cumulative traditions." I am tutored by his account of "traditions," but not as a replacement for religion. Nor do I speak of "faith," given the Protestant and privatistic readings of that term. Rather than seek to banish the term as Smith did, better to redefine it by stipulating what the term should mean.

Proposing a stipulative definition also amounts to a divergence from Talal Asad. For Asad, the upshot of genealogy of religion is that the genealogist stops asking about what "religion" really means and is instead committed to the work of tracking the effects generated by any particular configuration of "religion." He has no interest in generating new accounts of religion.

That might be well and good for the anthropologist of religion, but the constructive theologian, with normative goals in mind, aspires to more. Mindful of Asad's labors, the theologian as normative culture worker aspires to generate new effects, new uses, new disruptions, and new generative articulations of the religious. Embracing this additional work is not so much a no to Asad but a yes to the distinctive obligations that fall to the theologian, the theologian who strives to release healing energies into cultural life and shape them to just and creative purposes. In what follows, I propose to thread a needle, inspired by both Asad and Smith, the patron saints for these peculiar theoretical labors. From Asad, I learn to be mindful that every account of religion is an intervention in and a reconfiguration of culture. From Smith, I learn that there is no doing without some guiding concepts to discuss certain features of the human condition.

## Defining the "Religious"

It might seem awkward to propose a theory of the religious after calling, in the previous chapter, for a comparative theology after religion.[3] Not so. The task at hand is to propose a theory of the religious free of the theoretical naivete that afflicts those who have not passed through the fiery brook of genealogy of religion. Theologians who advance theory after genealogy do so self-consciously, knowing that they engage in a cultural intervention—a reconfiguration of cultural tropes around religion for constructive purposes. Theologians who propose new accounts of the religious can do so in either of two modes: a severely abstemious mode or a more realist mode. In the abstemious mode, the theologian may dispense with every attempt to posit an intrinsically religious dimension of life, having concluded that genealogy undoes the very possibility. Henceforth, every proposal for a theory of the religious is offered for merely strategic and functional reasons, preserving the category without positing universals.

I contend, however, that neither knowledge of the wide variety of ways in which human societies have configured cultural space nor knowledge of the material consequences of Western constructions of religion rules out the possibility that there is a cross-culturally available dimension of human experience that can be recognized as religious. I will argue that all known human societies do engage in a kind of cultural labor that can be called religious. That labor, however, is cordoned off into a distinct province of "religion" as opposed to the "secular" only in some modern societies. That practice is anything but universal.

There is no better way to demonstrate that a more flexible and counter-modern definition of the religious is possible than by offering one. I contend that whether a society has a religion—several, or none—is a contingent matter. Much depends on how religions are defined. What is not contingent is the following: every enduring human society takes up the project of *comprehensive qualitative orientation*. The cultural work of providing comprehensive qualitative orientation is what I take the term "religious" to mean. This particular cultural labor takes place in every human community of any historical depth regardless of whether those communities have religions or not. Native American communities, at least prior to contact with the West, did not demarcate religions as some special set of material and discursive processes over against the rest of communal life, but they did take up the work of comprehensive qualitative orientation. Even in societies that do have religions—societies that have created a division between the secular sphere and the religious sphere—the work of comprehensive qualitative orientation cannot be confined to the sphere designated for religious work. Economic and political institutions also perform this work even when they pretend to abstain from or remain neutral on religious matters. Religiousness is a leaky business that refuses to be quarantined.

In what follows, I will define what I mean by comprehensive qualitative orientation beginning with the term "orientation." I will then turn to the structures and processes in which this project of qualitative orientation is customarily performed. In brief, I will argue that the work of orientation in a religious key, although dispersed throughout culture and housed in a variety of institutions, is not free floating but finds instantiation in *interpretative schemes* and *therapeutic regimes*. Cognitive and performative dimensions intertwine in complex ways in generating comprehensive qualitative orientations. Those traditions that we have come to think of as religions house a variety of interpretative schemes and therapeutic regimes that are created by selective improvisation which draws upon a shared *repertoire* of rituals, myths, symbols, narratives of various sorts, and scriptures. No religion is an interpretive scheme. What binds a religious tradition together is an argument about how to use a repertoire (which includes arguments about what should even be in that repertoire) that is at the tradition's disposal and not a shared interpretative scheme.[4]

In addition to this traditional assemblage of materials that we associate with religious repertoires, it is vital to remain alert to the religious functions of other cultural practices. Political structures, media, advertising, economic practices, configurations of gender and sexuality, and even discoveries in the natural sciences—very nearly anything and everything has been recruited for the work of generating comprehensive qualitative orientation.

Societies are not oriented around a singular interpretative scheme. Cultural space, within any society, is characterized by contestation and improvisation. This is not to deny the vast disciplinary power of institutions, ideologies, and elites to impose particular interpretative schemes and therapeutic regimes upon a given populace thereby generating shared convictions, bodily comportments, authoritative definitions of sex and gender roles, and the like. But the disciplinary power of cultural and economic elites is never total. Resistance, far from being futile, is inevitable.

Furthermore, no society is an island. Although particular societies have been, for certain historical periods, isolated from routine intercultural contact, such periods of isolation cannot be taken as normative. Far too much is made of global flows as peculiarly modern phenomena. Though unprecedented in its contemporary sweep, intercultural contact and exchange are not peculiar to our time and hence by no means novel.

## Orientation

Robert Neville has aptly defined the technical term "orientation." For Neville, orientation

> is how a self comports itself or takes up a stance toward some level or dimension of reality. All specific actions take place within the habits formed by our orientations. . . . Orientations are made up of learned ritual conventions. Most are picked up unconsciously as we are socialized into our culture's rituals. . . . The point of an orientation is to discern the important or humanly relevant nature of its object and to comport human life appropriately toward it. The ritual structure of an orientation includes both the discernment and the comportment. Accurate discernment is itself a problem for finding adequate orientations, and appropriate comportment is another.[5]

Several features of this definition of orientation merit close attention. First, orientation is double-sided; it is both a matter of discernment—that is to say, truth-seeking—and a matter of comportment, of seeing to it that persons and communities are rightly disposed toward whatever the relevant object of orientation happens to be. Second, the work of orientation is performed through *ritual* and is not in the first instance a matter of explicit self-conscious reflection. Human beings are acculturated into such rituals and thereby come to assume orientations toward those dimensions of reality that a society recognizes as important.

Given the concrete specificity of ritual practices, members of a given society might orient themselves to some dimensions of reality that are not valorized or even recognized by persons in other societies that employ other rituals. Different cultures might also be oriented toward the same reality but register it in only those respects that are recognizable, given the rituals and symbol systems available to the culture in question. Inasmuch as these ramifications are built into Neville's account of orientation, his theory is crafted with an eye toward cross-cultural comparison. On Neville's account of orientation, comparison can serve a normative function by allowing us to ask whether a given society might recognize dimensions of reality not available in others.

Given that definition of orientation, what, then, is *comprehensive qualitative* orientation? A *comprehensive orientation* is one that asks about the *nature of reality as such*. Such orientation aims to be encompassing and seeks to transcend regional projects such as orientation to topogra-

phy, climate, the shifting seasons, and the historical, political, or economic dimensions of life. Comprehensive orientation requires giving
some account of *the world* and its fundamental structures. As such, the
quest for comprehensive orientation is metaphysical in character even if
the language utilized for such work is not the vocabulary of any particular philosophical program.

Sociology of the religion provides ample reason to believe that the
human quest for comprehensive orientation is a genuine cross-cultural
constant rooted ultimately in biology. Peter Berger has argued that human
beings are creatures, who, by virtue of a distinctive biology, are driven
to ask questions about the character of the world as such:

> ... man [sic] is curiously "unfinished" at birth. . . . The "unfin-
> ished" character of the human organism at birth is closely related to
> the relatively unspecialized character of its instinctual structure.
> The non-human animal enters the world with highly specialized and
> firmly directed drives. As a result, it lives in a world that is more or
> less completely determined by its instinctual structure. . . . By contrast,
> man's instinctual structure at birth is both underspecialized and un-
> directed toward a species-specific environment. There is no man-
> world in the above sense. Man's world is imperfectly programmed by
> his own constitution. It is an open world. That is, it is a world that
> must be fashioned by man's own activity. . . . Biologically deprived of
> a man-world, he constructs a human world. This world, of course, is
> culture.[6]

Contemporary theory, inside and outside sociology, would take issue with
Berger's neat distinctions between nature and culture, between human
and animal. Animal studies have found ample signs of cultural activities among animals, making stark distinctions between the human and
the animal no longer tenable. The climate crisis also troubles every notion of the human world as free floating from ecological dependencies.
For these reasons, Berger's account must be rectified.[7]

Nonetheless, one feature of Berger's analysis remains persuasive.
Because of our distinctive evolutionary emergence as a species—no ex-
ceptionalism there—human beings have a natural need for culture, a
need for some account of the world. Human experience is driven toward
extension or comprehensiveness in imaginative scope. It may even be that
the underspecialized nature of human biology is a primal cause for our
capacity to generate the very concept of infinity. About any conception

of the world whatsoever, the human being can ask, "What extends beyond that limit?"

Berger and Neville share a sense that orientation aims at proper comportment, of congruence between human beings and the world as they take it to be. Human communities seek to generate this fit between world as imagined and persons by way of rituals. Rituals are culturally particular ways by which societies distribute tasks, responsibilities, roles, and functions as well as stipulate norms and styles for regulating bodily comportment (who can make eye contact with whom, for how long, and for what reason, for example), emotional display, and even language use to persons according to some usually implicit account of the world such that persons can be rightly comported to that world.[8]

Religious rituals are a subset of life which is pervasively ritualized, that subset which is intimately involved in the work of generating, maintaining and, if necessary, reforming the cultural work of comprehensive qualitative orientation. Rituals, religious or otherwise, cannot be understood as merely installing persons in a static world that would work well enough without rituals, but should instead be understood as creating/performing the world as imagined and forming persons so as to fit within that world. Thus, religious traditions often assert that a failure to perform requisite rituals threatens the stability and proper functioning of the world. Religious life is thus a matter of practice and not just claim-making. Qualitative orientation is both a matter of knowing *and doing*, of truth-seeking interpretation *and performance*.

Thus far, I have argued that human beings collectively engage in the work of orientation. Moreover, by appeal to Berger, in particular, I have argued that human beings need *comprehensive orientation*. But are all efforts at comprehensive orientation religious? Is religiosity really determined by scale alone? I would argue not. Not every cultural activity that generates worldviews ought to be construed as religious because on such a definition, every worldview would count as religious. Scientific work—cosmology in particular—aims at orientation that is in scope as comprehensive as any of the classical cosmogonic accounts proposed by religious thinkers or traditions. Even Mahayana Buddhist visions of multiple universes have met their match in contemporary scientific multiverse speculation.[9]

Might such scientific exercises also be regarded as religious? They might, but the question must be posed: *Under what conditions?* I contend that religious orientation differs from scientific orientation just to the extent that the former aims at *qualitative* orientation, whereas the latter does not. The comprehensiveness of a scheme, alone, does not mark it as religious. Only those projects that seek comprehensive orientation of a *qualitative* sort count as religious.

Let me offer an illustration before venturing an abstract definition. Einstein's groundbreaking theories of general and special relativity plainly offer new knowledge about our cosmic milieu and, in so doing, serve an orienting function. That work might have religious ramifications—I would argue that it does—but it is not meant to be religious. By contrast, Einstein's oft-cited objection to quantum mechanics, "God does not play dice with the universe!," is religious. Einstein's objection was triggered by visceral displeasure with a vision of the universe as unpredictable and probabilistic rather than orderly. Einstein's assertion is religious rather than scientific *not* because he appealed to God but because he advanced a comprehensive *and explicitly qualitative* confession that the universe is marked by order, regularity, and predictability. Scientific work, at least in principle, can be neutral about whether universe is or is not orderly, but Einstein, in this case, was not.

It might be argued that all scientists are likely to make the low-grade qualitative assumption that the universe is characterized by patterns of regularity sufficient to sustain repeatable scientific experimentation. So minimalist an assertion about the character of experience does not, in my judgment, merit the designation religious. However, the term does seem appropriate with reference to the broader conviction that cooperative scientific labor is the only enterprise that can yield genuine knowledge capable of securing a prosperous human future. Such faith in science and its prospects—and I do not use the term "faith" loosely—counts as religious because it amounts to a comprehensive and qualitative stance or attitude about how human beings ought to best comport themselves in the universe as we know it.

William Connolly's notion of "existential faith" aptly characterizes this particular kind of conviction:

> An existential faith is a committed view of the world layered into affective dispositions, habits, loyalties, and institutional injunctions. The intensity of commitment to it typically exceeds the power of the arguments and evidence advanced on its behalf. . . . Existential faith is ubiquitous. To be human is to be invested by faith before you reach the age of critical reflection, even if these investments are laden with ambivalence,

periodically marked by crisis, and occasionally susceptible to reconfiguration. An existential faith is lodged on the visceral register of being as well as the more refined intellectual register to which the visceral is linked by multiple circuits. It infiltrates habits of desire, conscience and perception as well as the presumptions of reflective judgment.[10]

Connolly makes appeal to the notion of existential faith because he finds it an important tool for interrupting the stark dualism between the secular and the religious. He contends that no one is free of some committed view of the world that is rooted in and motivated by existential faith. Because existential faith is hardly confined to those who call themselves "religious," secularists are in no position to banish religious voices from the public sphere. Let she who is without existential faith exit first! In this way, the pervasiveness of existential faith dismantles a secularist conception of political life that would segregate and exile the religious from public deliberation. My conception of the religious as a quest for qualitative orientation serves the same function. Either way of speaking of faith or the religious gives the lie to the notion that religious convictions can be neatly privatized and set off from matters of public deliberation about the nature and purposes of civic life.

For many a modernist, faith in the scientific method, at least implicitly and often explicitly, reaches the status of existential faith. John Dewey is an exemplary case of explicit faith in science. Dewey is forthright in his advocacy of mobilizing religious faith on behalf of scientific intelligence: "The whole story of man shows that there are no objects that may not deeply stir engrossing emotion. One of the few experiments in the attachment of emotion to ends that mankind has not tried is that of devotion, so intense as to be religious, to intelligence as a force in social action."[11] Dewey commends faith in intelligence—so much so that it would be appropriate to characterize Dewey as an ardent evangelist for scientific faith. But Dewey does not call for such a faith as a hypothetical and technocratic venture in human improvement. By no means! He is committed to the faith he commends; he is a sincere devotee of a faith for which he recruits postulants. That his faith can be regarded as a venture in comprehensive qualitative orientation is impossible to deny. His words glow and gleam with zealous ardor:

> The community of causes and consequences in which we, together with those not born, are enmeshed is the widest and deepest symbol of the mysterious totality of being the imagination calls the universe. It is the

embodiment for sense and thought of that encompassing scope of existence the intellect cannot grasp. It is the matrix within which our ideal
aspirations are born and bred. It is the source of the values that the moral
imagination projects as directive criteria and as shaping purposes. . . . A
"creed" founded on this material will change and grow, but it cannot be
shaken.[12]

Dewey's work is striking because of his candor in commending scientific
faith. In this respect, he is unlike the latter-day modernists of our time
who deny that their deepest world-orienting convictions are, in any sense,
religious. What he does share with his contemporary successors—I am
thinking of Dawkins, Dennett, and their like—is the conviction that his
faith is empirically verifiable rather than entirely contestable, as Connolly
argues. Faith in the power of falsifiable science as the most promising
method available to the human community for improving our collective
lot is not itself falsifiable.

 Despite this performative contradiction on the part of Dewey and his
inferiors, the pursuit of scientific inquiry, insofar as it remains neutral
to questions about the qualitative character of experience, cannot be
characterized as religious by appeal to the criterion of comprehensiveness alone. Only when the scientific enterprise becomes for us a source
for comprehensive *qualitative* orientation does it become religious. Put
otherwise, the difference between scientific inquiry as a method of aug-
menting our knowledge about the world and a commitment to science
that becomes religious should not be understood, at least initially, as a
matter of seriousness, as a shift from science as but one penultimate concern to science now become an ultimate concern, to use Tillich's categories. Rather, the shift is best understood as a matter of function. To
determine whether your interest and investment in science have become
religious, you must ask yourself whether you have come to believe that
science is a reliable way of answering qualitative questions about the character of the universe and so has come to determine your stance or attitude toward the world as such.

 A critical question: Can something rise to the status of the religious if
it serves merely as "*a* reliable way" of answering fundamental questions
rather than "the final source of appeal" for answering qualitative questions? I employ the indefinite article rather than the definite because
human beings remain promiscuous and polycentric in the sources to
which they appeal in the work of orientation and comportment. The quest

to secure qualitative orientation by appeal to a stable and comprehensive interpretation of the world that orients human activity does drive toward singularity and ultimacy. Tillich is not wrong to argue that a drive toward ultimate concern is present within religious life. Persons committed to a particular religious vision, who find that vision disrupted by trauma, violence, or even startlingly new scientific information, are likely to experience such disruptions as world shaking or even world shattering. It is quite natural to be deeply and even ultimately invested in interpretative schemes and practices that offer comprehensive qualitative orientation. Nonetheless, because human life as it is actually lived is a polycentric affair that is funded by multiple data streams and symbols from which we take our bearings, it is important not to build into one's definition of the religious an exaggerated emphasis on the singular.

*Any qualitative interpretation of the felt character of the universe— that the universe is homelike or hostile, elegant and orderly, or absurd and random—I take to be religious when such an interpretation is accompanied by a commitment to practices that shape communal and personal comportment in the universe as so interpreted. Conversely, commitment to practices that so shape communal and personal comportment, such that they imply and generate a qualitative interpretation of the felt character of the universe—as, for example, worthy of human trust or as inimical to human habitation—is also religious.* If I have come to believe that the universe is characterized by constant flux such that attempts to cling to anything whatsoever is sure to eventuate in suffering and disappointment and so have committed myself to practices meant to give rise in me an attitude of detachment that will lead to calm and serenity, then I am engaged in the project of comprehensive qualitative orientation. Alternatively, if I spend my waking life in a competitive and individualistic acquisition of wealth and consumer goods, driven by feelings of isolation and pervasive vulnerability to forces beyond my control, and so come to believe that the human being stands alone in an unpredictable world that is fundamentally driven by self-seeking, such a life, too, must be accounted as religious. That is why I argue that the practices of market capitalism, structured so as to shape human desiring within an account of what makes human life and collective flourishing possible, most certainly count as religious.

There is something profoundly ordinary about the quest for qualitative orientation. In a sense, the work of cosmic qualitative orientation is not very different from the sort of thing people do when they move into a new house. The questions are the same, although the scale is vastly different. Is the place safe? Will it keep my family and me safe? Are there structural problems endemic to the house that will compromise our health or our safety? What is the neighborhood like? Am I invested in taking care of the place? Or perhaps a more painful and searching question, Am I the sort of person who can responsibly care for the place so that it won't fall down on me? What differentiates comprehensive qualitative orientation from its domestic analog is that the former project is driven by the anthropological drive for world building. The question, "What is the neighborhood like?" becomes encompassing indeed.

What makes the work of qualitative orientation inevitable for human beings is that all human projects, indeed the human project itself—raising families, buying and trading goods, the construction of various kinds of political regimes, artistic and creative ventures of all sorts, and the widest sorts of meaning-making activities that come under the general rubric of culture—require that human beings assume some basic *attitude* toward the whole of things rooted in a (perhaps only implicit) conviction that such an attitude is realistic and worthy.[13] It is impossible to live human life without making a decision about what sort of existential investment can be risked or ventured under some evaluation of what the world itself is like. The work of qualitative orientation is driven by the following kinds of properly basic questions: What can and should human beings hope for? What stance or attitude toward the whole of things is commensurate with the prospects afforded by the universe for the project of meaningful living? How should human lives be organized such that human *desiring* is in accord with the felt character of the universe?

*Qualitative* orientation can be distinguished from other kinds of orienting projects precisely because qualitative orientation is a matter of erotics. What ought to command my attention and desire? What is worth desiring and what is reasonable and appropriate for me to desire? Human beings need qualitative orientation precisely in order to organize and prioritize the wide range of human desires, desires that include but go well beyond the instinctual and the biological. Hindu traditions contend that human desires are basically fourfold in nature: *kama, artha, dharma,* and *moksa.* Human beings desire pleasure (*kama*), wealth (*artha*), dharma (ethical goods, duty), and liberation (*moksa*). These desires and their objects are legitimate and good, and a time in life is given over for the pursuit of each within traditional Hindu conceptions of the life cycle. However, Hindu traditions—and I am thinking in particular of Advaita

Vedanta—teach that the first three of these goods are finally flawed because they are impermanent. The only good that is permanent is liberation. Liberation is therefore the *summum bonum*, the ultimate human good (*paramapurusartha*). By stipulating that the desire for liberation is the one truly worthy object of human longing and then prescribing a *therapeutic regime* for redirecting desire away from other genuine, albeit flawed, objects of desire, Advaita Vedanta offers human beings comprehensive qualitative orientation. Advaita Vedanta is, therefore, a pedagogy for desire and seeks to so form human beings that they give themselves over only to those desires recognized as worthy under its particular conception of the universe.

A vision of the sort offered by Advaita Vedanta raises a difficult question about the use of the term religious. Should the term be reserved for the pursuit of the ultimate human good alone? Under such a restriction, only the pursuit of liberation would be recognized as religious. Or should the term be used with reference to the entire scheme which, taken as a whole, serves to organize human desiring? Any attempt to restrict the term religious to the quest for liberation alone risks generating a division that too closely approximates the Western dichotomy between secular pursuits as opposed to the pursuit of a transworldly goal which alone is taken to be religious. This dichotomy does not seem true to the character of Hindu life as classically conceived or the way in which life is imagined and lived in any of the religious traditions, particularly in nonsecularized societies. The pursuit of pleasure and wealth under the criterion of ethical duty is as integral to Hindu cosmology as is the pursuit of liberation, especially because the latter quest is, on some accounts, largely illegitimate for most and reserved only for a few elite male Brahmins who are capable of radical renunciation. Likewise, the pursuit of righteous rule on the part of the soldier/ruler (*ksatriyas*) is surely as religious as the Brahmin's quest for liberation. The *ksatriya* is rightly attuned to reality when his life is dedicated to the pursuit of duty which, in his case, may require fighting and dying in a just war as in the *Bhagavad Gita*.

On the other hand, insofar as the term religious points to comprehensive frameworks for *organizing* human valuation and desiring such that the question "What is the character of the universe and what mode of human living best integrates selves and communities such that they are rightly oriented to the universe as so understood?" can be answered, the religious is inevitably tied to figurations of *ultimacy*. Beyond a variety of legitimate goods that are desirable, is there an ultimate good that transcends all others? Religious texts and thinkers routinely ask and answer this question and then seek to persuade and compel persons to pursue what they deem to be the ultimate good. In the work of qualitative orientation, traditions routinely articulate and defend the finality of some end or goal that orders and integrates (and subsumes) all others, some *paramapurusartha*. That goal or end, as is the case with Advaita, is correlated with some fundamental feature or aspect of reality that is taken to be ultimate.

This vague notion of ultimacy cannot be given thick content in a general theory of the religious without running the risk of importing into that theory some particular ontology derived from one tradition or another. Better to begin (and this is only a beginning) by treating ultimacy as a function of the quest for comprehensive qualitative orientation. In such an approach, ultimacy can be recognized, at least initially, as a formal feature of the project of qualitative orientation. Without specifying in advance the nature of any such ultimate—God, the Tao, Buddha-nature, *sunyata*, the Market—it will suffice to venture a working hypothesis that seems empirically well grounded: any tradition's *value ultimate* will necessarily be correlated, if not identified, with some *ontological ultimate*. The latter either renders the value ultimate realizable or is taken to be itself the value ultimate.

The effort to orient human life around the pursuit of a single ultimate goal or reality is a central feature of many religious traditions. As already noted, orientation toward ultimacy serves to coordinate and integrate human desires so that human beings can assume a proper comportment toward reality as such. Ultimacy, at the very least, seems a structural feature of religious life understood as the quest for comprehensive qualitative orientation. Even in colloquial usage, to pursue something religiously is to be invested single-mindedly in the object of one's pursuit as determinative of one's life trajectory. In more formal usage, a venture is often taken to be religious insofar as its *telos* or goal promises access to the supreme good that organizes and integrates human desire according to some overall conception of human flourishing. One might even argue that a life given over to the scattered pursuit of penultimate goods can be fairly described as disorientation.

Two possible objections can be ventured against linking ultimacy to the project of organizing human desire. First, do we not trivialize and domesticate religious ultimates by linking them so proximately to human fulfillment? Perhaps ultimacy is indifferent to, or better, utterly transcendent to the human project of qualitative orientation. Is such radical transcendence possible when ultimacy is so closely tied to human goals? This objection is valid but only as long as human orientation is construed narrowly. Right orientation might well be more radical and disruptive. To be rightly oriented to ultimacy might mean recognizing that the God who can capture Leviathan on his hook exceeds all human grasping. Just as the author of Job refuses a covenant theology that suggests that God will order the universe such that the righteous will always find due recompense and the wicked will face divine wrath, right orientation may amount to a radical recognition of mystery and the inevitable failure of any effort to secure knowledge either of God or God's universe.

A second possible objection may be ventured from the perspective of the various polytheisms. Is orientation toward a singular and unifying supreme good the mark of a monotheistic fondness for the one over the many? Might not a fulfilling human life be imagined that is given over to multiple goods rather than some singular *summum bonum*? This objection cannot be dismissed lightly. Indeed, the question has force even for monotheistic traditions. Religious norms notwithstanding, it must be acknowledged that even in monotheistic and nondualistic traditions a high degree of integration is rarely accomplished save perhaps in the lives of ascetics, mystics, and monastics. Religious leaders may invite and even cajole human beings to give themselves over to the single-minded pursuit of an ultimate good, but religious life remains intractably diffuse, eclectic, and multiple. Moreover, even the most demanding of religious traditions valorize a variety of legitimate goods. The movement toward ultimacy is motivated not by a rejection of penultimate goods but instead by a drive to see that these goods are recognized as good but nonetheless penultimate. The terrain here is too luxuriant to venture sweeping judgments without detailed comparative projects. Surely, ascetical and monastic traditions seek to cultivate a rigorous and single-minded attention to a singular ultimate good but, even in these traditions, the attainment of union with the ultimate eventuates in "a return to the market with open hands," a sacralizing of the ordinary and the mundane which is often seen as pervaded by the presence of the ultimate. In light of the wild efflorescence of diversity within religious traditions, the rhetoric of ultimacy should not mislead theoreticians into generating definitions that unduly privilege the singular.

What reason do we have to believe that the project of qualitative orientation is a fundamental anthropological task? Here, too, Berger has much to offer—though, this time, as a theologian. In an early collection of theological meditations, Berger suggests that theologians would do well to begin with the human and venture an inductive argument for faith rather than begin with a Barthian move from above. His proposal is to look for "signals of transcendence" in the world that might point beyond it. One such signal, Berger contends, is "the argument from order." In pursuit of such an argument, Berger weaves with his customary economy and linguistic verve a scene of ordinary domesticity, but one that is nonetheless fraught with significance. He invites us to reflect upon a scene familiar to every parent. A child wakes up at night frightened by an unknown something and finds himself "beset by nameless threats." In the solitary darkness, "the contours of trusted reality are blurred or invisible." Facing "the terror of the incipient chaos the child cries out for his mother." So far, the scene is utterly quotidian. What provokes Berger's attention is what mothers tend to say when they arrive to comfort their children in such everyday situations: "Don't be afraid—everything is in order, everything is all right." Berger poses a critical question:

> All this, of course, belongs to the most routine experiences of life and does not depend upon any religious preconceptions. Yet this common scene raises a far from ordinary question, which immediately introduces a religious dimension: *Is the mother lying to the child?* The answer, in the most profound sense, can be "no" only if there is some truth in the religious interpretation of human existence.[14]

Beyond questions about the overall efficacy of Berger's brief on behalf of religious truth, what is important in his domestic vignette is its power in showing that the search for qualitative orientation is motivated by a visceral human need for order—a need that seems anchored in the human constitution and even appears to play a vital role in normal child development. Berger's question is haunting because it evokes in readers awareness that something like this basic question is omnipresent in human experience.

But Berger's appeal to this household scene is part of a much larger argument that is macroscopic in nature. Drawing upon his work as a sociologist, Berger argues that human history has been throughout a venture in creating order. His summary argument is forceful: "In the observable propensity to order reality there is an intrinsic impulse to give cosmic scope to this order, an impulse that implies not only that human order in some way corresponds to an order that transcends it, but that this transcendent order is of such a character that man can trust himself and his destiny to it."[15] For my purposes, however, what Berger offers is a broad sociological and anthropological argument grounded in the vast sweep of human history and the intimate detail of individual psychology that shows just why something like qualitative orientation is an inevitable and necessary human task. Berger shows that human history is a long series of attempts to ask and answer questions about whether reality itself is orderly and ultimately trustworthy. Asking and answering that question is plainly a venture in *comprehensive qualitative orientation.*

But contrary to Berger, I contend that any comprehensive qualitative reading of experience can be called religious in character, even an account that is skeptical about human prospects for fulfilling living. To decide that the universe is disorderly and so unfriendly to the human quest for fulfillment is also a religious judgment, albeit in a negative key. Of course, it hardly seems possible that any religious tradition can hope to sustain itself if it advances so bleak a vision. Hence, it is not surprising that religious traditions customarily assert that affirmation is the final word. All manner of things shall be well. Nonetheless, against readers who may be skeptical of religious traditions and inclined to think of them as Pollyannaish in character, I argue that the quest for religious orientation is *truth-seeking* in character. If the project of qualitative orientation is to be efficacious and enduring, it cannot be driven by wishful thinking and naivete. Religious institutions and traditions cannot long endure if they are willfully inattentive to the complexities and ambiguities of life in the world. Religious thinkers cannot propound reasons for hope that neglect the tragic, random, and even malevolent dimensions of life in the world.

Skeptics who are unwilling to affirm that the religious traditions are driven by a truth-seeking impulse may wish to assert that *religion is the quest to affirm that things are as they ought to be despite evidence to the contrary.* As definitions of religion go, this is not a bad one. It is a valid specification of my larger account to the religious. This contrarian characterization of religiousness identifies well a tension intrinsic to the project of qualitative orientation: religious texts and thinkers strive for radical affirmation and hope even as they seek to acknowledge that life is marked by fragility, lack, fault, and suffering. To orient persons and communities rightly requires an attempt to reconcile these two competing and apparently irreconcilable intuitions about the character of life in the world. It may well be that one criterion for determining the power of a religious vision is the degree to which the vision in question is able maximally to affirm both intuitions: that things are as they ought to be while simultaneously offering the most clear-eyed assessment of life as marked by suffering and tragedy.

While Berger most certainly has considerable empirical grounding for his claims regarding the order-seeking impulse of religious traditions— it is impossible to deny that religious institutions often play a profoundly conservative role—it is nonetheless important to recognize that religious traditions also interrogate and interrupt contingent social orders. The history of religions includes many moments when religious voices call into question not only given social orders but also the very project of sacralizing those orders as inadequate or even idolatrous. The history of religion is also a history of religion's self-critique. Religious traditions also challenge, both in theory and practice, not just earlier sacralizing ventures but also overweening confidence in the human capacity to secure any order against the deep and chaotic mystery that assails every human effort to domesticate the universe into a securely habitable and knowable dwelling. The reminder that the universe is not built to human scale is one of the functions of religious visions and traditions.[16] But these dimensions of religious traditions are rarely on display in Berger's account of religion.

The quest for qualitative orientation is by no means an intrinsically conservative venture that seeks to sacralize contingent social orders and, in so doing, reassure human beings that things are as they ought to be. Religious traditions may offer consolation, but such consolation may well be disruptive and sobering. No project in comprehensive qualitative orientation can long endure without a rigorous and honest commitment to truth-seeking that recognizes that the real remains irreducibly mysterious and even indifferent to the human order. If cosmic security is not the final word—erecting and preserving a sacred canopy is not the sole and final end of religion—then we can fairly suppose that religious thinkers and communities are engaged in the *work* of comprehensive qualitative orientation. Such work demands wrestling with the tension between yes and no, between trust that all manner of things shall be well and the clear-eyed recognition that things most definitely are not so, at least not now. Religious traditions are conversations and *contestations* about such matters and never merely efforts at generating and maintaining sacred canopies.

## On the Religious and Religion

In much of this chapter, I have spoken largely of the religious rather than of religion or the religions. Why this preference for the adjective? I begin with the adjective in order to signal that human cultures engage in religious work even when they do not organize cultural space into those formations that contemporaries might recognize as "religion" or "religions."[17] In societies that are not organized such that a distinctively religious realm is set off against a secular realm, the religious work of comprehensive qualitative orientation is broadly diffused throughout every domain or province of human life. Borrowing from the work of Timothy Fitzgerald, we may call this "encompassing religion."[18] The labor of seeking comprehensive and qualitative orientation is woven into the very fabric of human habitation, of the distinctly human work of world-making.

Moreover, even when a given society does configure its sociopolitical terrain so as to demarcate a religious sphere over against a secular sphere as in modern Western societies that aim to separate church and state, *putatively secular institutions and activities continue to perform religious work.* The religious, as I understand it, refuses to be confined to the sphere of religion or the religions even though moderns have come to think of comprehensive qualitative orientation as the special prerogative of what we now call religions. The assumption that such qualitative orientation can be so segregated has resulted in ignorance of the ways in which this cultural labor is performed by "secular" philosophies and institutions. More will be said about these matters shortly. For now, I wish only to highlight that the stipulative definition of the religious that I offer here is meant explicitly to contest the notion that religious work can be safely distilled out of and subsequently cordoned away from politics, economics, and culture at large. With Tillich—although under a different definition of the religious—I am convinced that the religious is not a separate province or domain of life.

As long as we are clear that the religious is never confined solely to the religions, it is then possible to turn to the religious traditions themselves with a measure of clarity. Turning to religious traditions as moderns have come to know them is unavoidable if we are to answer the following basic question: In what material and ideational formations does religious work typically transpire or take place? Even though religious work is ubiquitous and refuses to be confined to one province or domain of culture, how is such labor typically accomplished in our time? Although institutional forms vary wildly, I suggest that the work of comprehensive qualitative orientation typically requires *interpretative schemes linked to therapeutic regimes*. I will begin by defining the latter term before taking up the former.

Earlier in this chapter, I spoke of theoretical and ritual dimensions of world creation and world maintenance. Among the ritual formations that serve to comport persons and communities to the world as such are *therapeutic regimes*. Therapeutic regimes are ways of disciplining the bodies and minds of persons and communities so that they might become rightly disposed toward the world as rightly understood. Religious traditions house such therapeutic regimes, in particular those religious traditions that contend that human capacities for right orientation are fundamentally compromised. Questions about the extent to which human capacities are compromised are contested matters within as well as across those traditions we have come to think of as religions. The importance of such debates for comparative theology and theologies of religious diversity will become clearer in due course. What is important to recognize at this juncture is that the labor of comprehensive qualitative orientation is not just theoretical but *therapeutic*: something *must be done* to heal the ailments responsible for the chronic human failure to be rightly oriented whether such failure is understood as a matter of sin or ignorance (*avidya*). Therapeutic regimes are necessary if right orientation and proper comportment are to become genuine human possibilities. Right orientation is thus a work of *transformation*, not merely *information*; in modernity, we have come to impute such work to the religions even if such work also routinely takes place elsewhere in culture.

Those traditions which stipulate that human beings are congenitally incapable of proper comportment without healing and so stand in need of a concrete therapeutic regime can be understood, and even compared, according to what I have elsewhere called the medical model. Such traditions routinely posit that human beings suffer because of some underlying disease (*diagnosis*) generated by some fundamental cause like ignorance or sin (*etiology*). This root cause can be alleviated or perhaps even totally eradicated (*prognosis*)—there is no unanimity even within a single religious tradition on this matter—if the appropriate course of treatment (*therapy*) is followed. In truth, every aspect of this medical model is a source of considerable debate within and across traditions. Indeed, even the contention that human beings are fundamentally broken or ill is itself a matter that divides religious traditions from each other. Appealing to the medical model is likely to be of limited value when studying or comparing traditions that refuse to posit that there is any congenital ailment that prevents human beings from right orientation to the world as such.

Because not all traditions posit the existence of a fundamental fault, rupture, or ailment, not all ritual activity within religious traditions ought to be classified under the rubric of "therapeutic regimes." Ritual life takes on other vital forms in traditions that posit no impairment in the human capacity for right orientation. Even in these traditions, right comportment still requires bringing about a certain fit between human beings and the world as rightly understood. In a *secondary and derivative sense*, any work that brings about such a fit can be regarded as a therapeutic regime. At any rate, such congruence is never merely given but is instead a task to be performed.

Orientation is a matter of seeing that persons and communities are rightly comported to the world either as it is or as it ought to be. Therefore, comprehensive qualitative orientation is a matter of disciplining individual and communal bodies such that those bodies come into right alignment or congruence with the world rightly understood. Just as persons who are lost in a forest need a compass that accurately points them in the right direction (a function of knowing narrowly understood) but then must also dispose their bodies to follow the path so indicated, the cultural work of qualitative orientation is a matter of practice and performance. To extend this analogy still further, wilderness hikers must possess the requisite strength, endurance, and know-how cultivated over time to be capable of navigating the rigors of the path indicated by the compass even if they are in perfect health. The reference to "know-how" is meant to indicate that qualitative orientation is only, in part, a matter of "knowing that." Any adequate conception of the religious must not overstate the extent to which the orientation is a matter of explicit theorizing and debate even if it is the case that theologians find precisely these theoretical dimensions most intriguing. Qualitative orientation is customarily not accomplished by formulating propositions and debating doctrines or worldviews. Bodies are comported to socially constructed worlds through processes of habituation that are accomplished by practices of socialization that operate at registers that are more basic and elemental than explicit cogitation. Persons come to be rightly comported to reality as habits, dispositions, inclinations, moods, and motivations come to be shaped by social matrices that we inhabit.

However, it is also possible to *understate* the reflective dimensions of orientation, and this may well be the characteristic error in much contemporary theology. On the one hand, it seems accurate to say that theoretical figurations about the character of the universe as implied by religious practices only become a matter of explicit reflection under special circumstances. Even theologians manage their everyday lives largely without resorting to theorizing and worldview formation! The problem with such general claims is that the "special circumstances" that give rise to thought—the disruptions caused by chaos and evil, religious diversity that prevents any given religious tradition from seeming to be the sole natural and inevitable option, new knowledge generated by the sciences, internal diversity and conflict within a religious tradition and the like—are fairly commonplace. The prudent middle claim—between overstating and understating the explicitly theoretical dimensions of orientation—is to affirm that the reflection and revision required for qualitative orientation are, at the very least, a matter of constant upkeep rather than radical reconstruction. The latter work may well be rare and is customarily the special province of theologians and their analogues; the former is everyday work that is by no means restricted to the cognoscenti.[19] In sum, although large-scale revision and reconstruction of interpretative schemes may be the work of theologians, interpretative schemes are embodied, performed, refined, and even transformed to some extent by all participants in a culture just as all users of a language transform it in some measure, not just its poets or novelists.

The labor of comprehensive qualitative orientation, however widely dispersed throughout culture, finds expression in *interpretive schemes*. An interpretive scheme is some more or less systematic representation for taking or construing the world as such so that persons and communities can assume a place in the world as so construed. Comprehensive interpretative schemes include representations not just of the world but also of persons as part of that world. Human beings as self-conscious creatures are capable of and burdened by the task of having to comport themselves so as to be rightly oriented to the world as construed by an interpretative scheme. That such comportment is a task to be accomplished and is not something preprogrammed by instinct or evolutionary biology accounts for the sense in which the human beings experience themselves to be distinct from the world. Human beings know themselves to be creatures who must give an account of themselves, of the kind of creatures they are. But every comprehensive scheme must situate human beings within some larger horizon to which they belong.

To be clear from the very beginning, let me stipulate explicitly that *none of the traditions that moderns recognize as "religions" is itself an interpretive scheme*. It must be emphatically stated that religions are not interpretative schemes, paradigms, or worldviews; no error has generated more confusion and misguided thinking in theologies of religious diversity and comparative theology than the assertion that any particular religion is, as such, an interpretative scheme or paradigm. Such claims occlude the profound diversities within any historically deep religious tradition and obscure the striking similarities that can obtain across them. Almost always, those traditions that we have now come to designate as religious offer multiple interpretive schemes which are often in considerable tension with each other even if these interpretive schemes are, within a given tradition, formulated by drawing from a shared *repertoire* of myths, symbols, founding narratives, motifs, practices, scriptures, and histories.

Robert Campany has advanced the most compelling argument that I know of for understanding religions as repertoires. Drawing upon the work of the sociologist Ann Swidler, Campany contends that religions ought not to be thought of as "as fully integrated systems and as containers into which persons, ideas, practices, and texts may be fit without remainder"; rather he suggests that they ought to be imagined "as repertoires of resources."[20] Swidler's own work on repertoires is motivated by an attempt to understand the ways in which Americans think about love. Her argument is that people draw on different strands of culture and the traditions found therein in trying to make sense of what they mean by love. In service of this project, she believes that we need "new metaphors" to think about the way culture works: "We must think of culture less as a great stream in which we are all immersed, and more as a bag of tricks or an oddly assorted tool kit containing implements of varying shapes that fit the hand more or less well, are not always easy to use, and only sometimes do the job."[21]

With Campany, I want to reimagine religion in a Swidlerian key. Suppose we take up Campany's recommendation and substitute the word "religion" for "culture" in the following argument: "Perhaps we do best to think of culture [religion] as a repertoire, like that of an actor, a musician or a dancer. This image suggests that culture [religion] cultivates skills and habits in its users, so that one can be more or less good at the cultural [religious] repertoire one performs, and that such cultured [religious] capacities may exist both as discrete skills, habits, and orientations and, in larger assemblages, like the pieces a musician has mastered or the plays an actor has performed. It is in this sense that people have an array of cultural [religious] resources upon which they can draw."[22]

Swidler's proposal still leaves ample room to talk about the ways in which cultures and religions are formative milieu that shape persons and communities in incalculable ways, but her argument also opens up dramatic possibilities for thinking of cultural and religious life as creative rather than scripted performance. Swidler offers her take on culture as an explicit alternative to Clifford Geertz, who treats culture—and of course religion too—as a unified system. Although Swidler is appreciative of the power of Geertz's approach to culture and the way in which he is able to show how "cultural systems both teach and express general orientations" to the world, she quite rightly finds that Geertz's "analysis does not take us very far in understanding the varying ways people appropriate and use cultural meanings."[23] The view of culture that results from Geertz's theoretical perspective is one in which attention to agency is muted and in which cultures tend to be viewed as "unified wholes." Swidler makes the keen observation that in a Geertzian analysis, a Balinese cockfight or art in Yoruba society are so read that they are taken to be integral moments within a seamless and coherent web or network. Hence, in a typical thick description, one moves from any discrete element within a culture to inferences about the sensibility of the culture as a whole. Swidler notes that such an approach "makes sense only if we imagine cultures as unified around a shared sensibility. If cultures are more discordant than this, with competing perspectives and clashing sensibilities, he can say little about how these modes of understanding interest, interact, or compete."[24]

On the matter of agency, Swidler wants to know what people concretely "do with the different ways of framing meaning they have available." When this question is moved to the foreground, Swidler shows that investigators are in a better position to understand cultural variety, "the variable ways people hold or use culture," and cultural change itself.[25]

Swidler and Campany can help us to understand religious traditions as historically deep *conversations and contestations* about just how to employ the resources of a given repertoire. *Persons and communities recognize themselves to be part of a common tradition because they engage in the work of comprehensive qualitative orientation by drawing upon, broadly speaking, the same repertoire.* However, agreement about shared repertoire does not eventuate in agreement about how that repertoire should be employed. No historically deep tradition is marked by such agreement. Even the claim that the unity of a given tradition is constituted by agreement about a shared repertoire is true only to a limited extent. Catholics and Protestants might agree about the importance of the Bible as the central resource in the Christian repertoire, but they don't agree about just what the Bible is, as there are different books in their respective Bibles. Nor do they agree about how those Bibles are to be read. The status of tradition as an element in a theological repertoire is a source of even deeper contestation.

Persons within any given tradition thus find themselves compelled to generate rules for drawing upon a shared repertoire precisely because they are aware that any tradition's repertoire is usually so internally variegated and of such breadth that wildly different interpretative schemes can be generated from the same common stock. Appeal to authoritative texts like scriptures rarely settle such arguments because the scriptures are themselves a collection of authoritative arguments rather than authoritative agreements. The creation of rules for the use of shared repertoires rarely, if ever, settles arguments about what kinds of interpretative schemes are permissible because the rules themselves become the subject of debate. Arguments about the shape and interpretation of those rules also then become part of tradition. Within any given tradition, some rules about how a shared repertoire ought to be employed in the construction of interpretative schemes attain to the status of doctrine. George Lindbeck and the postliberal theological school are quite right to argue that doctrines are broadly recognized authoritative rules—a regulative grammar—for the generation of what I am herein calling interpretative schemes. But even doctrines are meant to offer broad and open-ended constraints on theological reflection and not to stifle it. The trouble is that appeals to such doctrines to rule out certain interpretative schemes as impermissible rarely work except in highly particular circumstances wherein those responsible for the enforcement of doctrines have the requisite power to regulate communities with sufficient rigor. After all, there is no consensus about the meaning of core doctrines.

The relationship between interpretative schemes and the repertoires from which they are created can be fruitfully compared with dishes and the stock of spices that a given regional or national cuisine typically has available. As a middling cook of South Indian or, specifically, Kerala dishes, I draw on recipes that employ a fairly prescribed though still extensive range of spices including cumin, coriander, garlic, ginger, turmeric, cloves, cinnamon, fennel, mustard seeds, curry leaves, and cardamom among other spices. Even when drawing upon this determinate repertoire of spices, the recipes and the dishes eventually prepared from those recipes can and do vary immensely. When one gets down to the particularity of individual cooks and then compares, for example, how my dishes resemble my mother's or that of my brother-in law's, the variations even in the case of "the same dish" like a basic Kerala chicken curry can be striking!

Are recipes that specify just which spices to use and in what proportion in order to generate a specific curry analogous to doctrines? Perhaps. A given cuisine is a tradition constituted by practical agreement about the stock of spices and foodstuffs employed in cooking. The agreed upon stock of available spices is the repertoire, the dishes prepared can be compared to interpretative schemes generated out of a shared common stock, and the recipes can be fruitfully compared to the broad and relatively open-ended constraints that guide the generation of an interpretative scheme. Of course, the analogy breaks down at just this juncture because there are no culturally sanctioned institutions or authorities that generate and enforce recipes. Moreover, few expert cooks operate with or from recipes even if they can generate such recipes in retrospect should it prove to be necessary.

The relationship between a distinct regional cuisine and the larger category of Indian cooking is still more complex. In principle, South Indian cuisine across states has more in common than does South Indian cooking with North Indian cooking. But the patterns are complex and crosscutting. Geographical proximity, history, migration, and the culinary equivalent of multiple religious belonging complicate matters immensely. Goan cooking, featuring such dishes as vindaloos, for example, bears the distinctive imprint of Portuguese colonial influence. Whether such blending can be characterized as hybridity is debatable, as the use of the term implies some original purity that has subsequently been rendered multiple; it would, of course, be impossible to isolate some such moment of original purity.

Moreover, spices like garlic and ginger are used extensively in other national cuisines. The foodstuffs that are so spiced are also often shared. As is well known, pasta is important to both Italians and the Chinese, and historians can give an account of why this is so. The long-term presence of Indians in African countries has given rise to hybrid cuisines that are both like and importantly unlike what Indians serve up in India.

To move from analogy to the topic at hand, religious traditions are likewise not rigidly bounded and impermeable entities. Material objects like rosaries, symbols like halos, spiritual practices like meditation, and praxis-idea complexes like *satyagraha*/nonviolent resistance move across societies and varied cultural landscapes. Most historically deep human societies are shaped by a variety of religious traditions. Individuals and communities within these societies operate within and often construct interpretative schemes that draw from a variety of religious repertoires just as most reasonably competent cooks in America, regardless of ethnicity or national origin, can put together a reasonable spaghetti sauce or a Chinese stir-fry. Any given repertoire—a Christian repertoire in America, Europe, or India—is always already a sedimented composite of resources accumulated from a variety of tributaries.

Moreover, just as garlic is not just an Italian spice, neither is the rosary Catholic alone. Given the internal complexities of human societies, a shared biological and evolutionary heritage, the common task of having to be world-making creatures, complex patterns of local innovation and creativity, and translocal cultural flows, it is hard to predict how interpretive schemes within and across religions will sort themselves out in terms of similarity and difference. Only intrareligious and interreligious comparison can determine how similar or dissimilar interpretative schemes within and across religions are likely to be. The category religion has, to date, constrained and compelled theologians of religious diversity to believe that religions are marked by internal homogeneity and external diversity when there is ample reason to believe that so simplistic a picture cannot be true. This fundamental error is, in no small measure, due to the fact that religions have simply been equated with interpretive schemes, metanarratives, or paradigms as such.

It would be far more accurate to stipulate that *religious traditions are (arguments about) shared repertoires for performing the work of comprehensive qualitative orientation*. Every religious tradition houses a variety of therapeutic regimes and a host of interpretative schemes that are always under construction. Religious thinkers and communities are never finished with the work of qualitative orientation, as new knowledge that bears upon the project is always emerging. Such new knowledge may be dramatic—for example, Darwin's theory of evolution—which generates profound questions about the character of the universe and compels religious thinkers to rethink fundamental conceptions of divine creation. Even after radical theological transformation, the need for substantive reconsideration continues. Liberal Christians who seek to hold together some account of divine creation with evolutionary theory gradually realize that there are new problems to be solved. For example, just what does it mean to affirm that God creates through evolution when the evolutionary process entails boundless animal suffering? The question of animal suffering then proves to be a daunting problem to those who wish to advance an affirmative account of qualitative orientation. In the process of accounting for new knowledge and problems as they arise, religious thinkers and communities constantly create, evaluate, and reform interpretative schemes as needed.

In pluralistic societies, the generation of such interpretative schemes is never done in isolation from analogous work that persons in other traditions are also doing. Maintaining the plausibility of the interpretative schemes generated in one's own tradition requires conversation, engagement, and even debate. Moreover, in pluralistic societies, persons routinely draw upon resources from more than one repertoire in doing the work of comprehensive qualitative orientation. Indeed, over the course of time, elements in these repertoires move and float across boundaries. Or, to be more accurate still, the boundaries between traditions are themselves always under construction and revision.

One reason for the malleability of the boundaries between traditions is that core practices that form the therapeutic regimes by which persons and communities are transformed for proper comportment are portable. Meditative practices in South Asian traditions, for example, move about but are infused with radically different theoretical content. Virtually the "same" practices can be called upon to aid practitioners who realize that there is no abiding self or that there is such a self indeed. The content given to therapeutic regimes varies according to the purposes for which they are deployed. Similar mobility of practices is evident in the way that the therapeutic regimes from Hellenistic philosophical schools were incorporated into Christian traditions during their formation.

Therapeutic regimes and the disciplines they prescribe are intended to shape and mold *desire* such that human beings learn to want what is taken to be worthy and attainable in a world taken to be of the texture and character described by an interpretive scheme. Hence, the import of these regimes changes as they come be inscribed into different meaning-making interpretative schemes. But because these practices have always been floating like dandelion petals in a strong breeze, one can never assume that the "boundaries" between traditions are stable and clearly demarcated.

Religious thinkers, texts, and traditions are marked by considerable internal debate precisely because traditions draw from variegated repertoires and must integrate an enormous variety of data as they seek to settle evaluative questions about the character of experience. Once we come to see that religious traditions are engaged in the work of comprehensive qualitative orientation, we can appreciate why such religious traditions are unlikely to be marked by strong and stable internal consensus. The questions at the heart of qualitative orientation allow for multiple responses—and debate about these responses is never settled. Christian traditions, for example, are marked by core debates about the kind of transformation that might legitimately be expected from human beings. Can we expect that persons are capable of entire sanctification, or must we be soberer about human sinfulness and thus refuse a maximally optimistic interpretative scheme for qualitative orientation and so reject as well a vision of religious life in which therapeutic practice is commended as integral to human life?

We may conclude this conversation about the religions with yet another reminder that a focus on the religions can obscure from collective view the fact that such questions are never asked and answered solely within the religions. The religious work of comprehensive qualitative orientation is not restricted to the "religions." It is a diffuse cultural labor performed at a variety of sites and by a host of practitioners. In doing such work, these other "secular" traditions also assert that human efforts to orient themselves truly in the cosmos go awry. They also prescribe redemptive and healing practices for transforming persons and communities such that they might be brought into right comportment with the universe as they understand it. I bring this chapter to conclusion by arguing that capitalism is itself a religious tradition—that is to say, an extensive repertoire that offers a variety of therapeutic regimes for organizing human desires such that human beings are rightly comported within the universe as understood by a variety of interpretative schemes generated by economists, who are the high priests and theologians of their traditions. They, too, seek to answer the fundamental question: What does it mean that self-conscious creatures like human beings exist, and what are our prospects given the world as we "know" it to be?

## Economics as Religion

Throughout this chapter, I have argued that dimensions of human life other than those conventionally encompassed by the term "religion" perform religious work—namely, comprehensive qualitative orientation. Of course, that thesis depends on rethinking the meaning of the term "religious." Once the term is redefined, it becomes evident that the modern attempt to cordon off religion into a private sphere so as to open up the public sphere to scientific rationality has never succeeded. The religious has always been and remains today a pervasive feature of every dimension of human life including most especially the political and the economic.

In what follows, I argue that theologians of religious diversity and comparative theologians ignore the religious nature and function of neo-liberal capitalism at great peril.[26] If a case can be made that the dominant religiosity of our time is constructed by economic practices and the neoliberal ideologies that undergird them, then theologians of religious diversity become complicit in marginalizing their own work should they restrict their attention to religious traditions as conventionally defined. By choosing to delimit arbitrarily the scope of their inquiries, theologians of religious diversity miss what is perhaps the most encompassing frame for meaning-making available in our time. Such inattention not only serves to leave in place Enlightenment configurations of religion but also ignores the fundamental economic principles that have long been and still remain at the very heart of religious traditions themselves. By ignoring economic life, theologians of religious diversity perpetuate distorted notions of the religious as given over to the pursuit of private or transcendental goods when every religious tradition has claimed for itself a larger mandate—one that includes visions of the good life in the here and now.

Given the remarkable proliferation of theologians who have taken up the question of theology and economics, what do theologians of religious diversity have to offer to this ongoing conversation? The difficulty of making the case that theologians of religious diversity have a role to play in this conversation is not inconsiderable because, to date, comparative theologians have paid little attention to questions of economy, although some theologians of religious diversity are beginning to engage political practice and theory. Constructive and systematic theologians have been quite articulate about why it matters to unearth the religious underpinnings of economic practices and philosophies: if material theological claims are embedded in political and economic theories that are depicted as empirical and scientific, such claims are thereby insulated from theological critique.[27] To fail to excavate the concealed theological premises of economic systems and ideologies is to acquiesce to forms of life that often run counter to core Christian convictions about theological anthropology, soteriology, and eschatology. Theological critique that uncovers religious or quasi-religious claims embedded within economic schemes is thus a vital prophetic practice and a responsible exercise of the theological vocation.

But why should such labor matter for theologians of religious diversity and comparative theologians in particular? What have they to contribute to the project of interrogating the secular? I argue that the general unwillingness and failure to recognize the religious character of economic structures and philosophies has had profound consequences for our thinking about religious diversity. In essence, inattentiveness to the religious work performed by economic practices and ideologies has led theologians of religious diversity to cultivate the impression that privatized religion, as configured within modernity, is normative for what we take religion to be. The consequences of this assumption for interreligious dialogue, TRD, and comparative theology are so extensive that they are difficult to enumerate with any comprehensiveness. Comparative theologians will need more time to diagnose how thinking about religious diversity has been constrained and compromised by prevailing habits of mind.

For now, I would like highlight just two of these consequences. The first and perhaps most worrisome is that many in the West tend to characterize those who refuse to draw a hard and fast line of separation between religion and economics (or politics) as "fundamentalist." Islam has been particularly vulnerable to such characterizations because Muslim thinkers customarily refuse to admit that economic practices and systems are religiously neutral. The Western engagement with Islam is therefore a paradigmatic case of failed recognition that falls over into stereotype and distortion. Such caricatures of Islam are tragic in two ways. Most obviously, such caricatures prevent us from appreciating the meaning and intention behind Muslim unwillingness to treat economics as a religiously neutral matter. What is less obvious is that religious voices that advocate for privatized conceptions of religion participate in neutering their own traditions. By accepting the notion that religion ought to be privatized, they undercut the plenitude of resources available to the religious traditions for profound socioeconomic critique.

By assuming that "religion" just means privatized religion, we have, at the very least, narrowed the topics and conversation partners for comparative theology. A more capacious conception of the religious would generate a variety of comparative projects that have thus far been overlooked. For example, it is easy to imagine a comparative theological project that might compare and contrast religious rationales against usury as developed across a variety of traditions. How is usury defined by the various traditions? What are normative criteria to which traditions appeal in rejecting usury as a legitimate practice? What might Christians learn by approaching how other traditions have taken up this question? Might such learning lead Christians to rethink how they approach economic life? As in all comparative theology, such work would not only unearth similarity and difference but would also be a constructive offering that combines resources from multiple traditions for socioeconomic criticism.

Second, a failure to recognize the religious work performed by economic regimes prevents theologians of religious diversity and comparative theologians from clear thinking about the categories of multiple religious belonging and syncretism. To use Paul Tillich's language here, if capitalism is, at the very least, a quasi-religion, then it seems incontestable that virtually all American Christians are engaged in a complex and arguably idolatrous form of syncretism if not multiple religious belonging. If capitalism can be understood as a complex therapeutic regime that so forms human desires such that human beings come to be embedded within a complex comprehensive qualitative vision with its own theological anthropology and eschatology, then few American Christians are in a position to deny that their customary mode of religious life is other than syncretistic. Coming to recognize that such syncretism or multiple belonging does in fact obtain has far-reaching implications for theologians who think about religious diversity. The widely shared assumption (rather than argument) that multiple religious belonging is a rare phenomenon in the Global North, one that is confined to the South and East Asia, is shown to be problematic.

The claim that living as an American capitalist Christian—the matter is made still more complicated by adding nationalism as a quasi-religion into the mix—counts as a form of syncretistic living is one that inevitably elicits questions about normative judgment. Are all forms of syncretistic living problematic? If so, how does one attain to a purity of Christian living that refuses any and all forms of admixture? Is such purity possible or even desirable? Short of adopting forms of Christian sectarianism in which the whole of life is brought under conformity to an integrated Christian vision or, by contrast, setting out on a quest for a new Christendom in which pluralistic societies are constrained to conform to a Christian order, the quest for purity of religious vision and practice seems doomed to fail. Nonetheless, it is worth noting that among Christian theologians who have done some of the most probing work in bringing theological critique to bear against prevailing forms of economic and political life, temptations to either sectarianism, on the one hand, or a nostalgic recovery of Christendom on the other, are strong indeed.[28]

By contrast, I argue that comparative theologians can offer a robust alternative to naive visions of homogeneity and purity. Comparative theologians can and must learn from the remarkable and rigorous work of theologians and political philosophers who refuse narrowly secularist visions because they have seen through to the core religious convictions that inform and undergird forms of secular practice.[29] But comparative theologians can help Christians—whose lives are always intertwined with several secular and religious traditions—to refuse both the quixotic attempt to withdraw into sectarian modes of religious life and the aggressive quest to colonize pluralistic public space under a singular Christian vision. One, perhaps the only, viable alternative to this dichotomy is to set out on a comparative theological conversation in which traditions meet to engage in pluralistic collaboration to determine criteria for economic well-being derived from the resources of more than one tradition. In this way, comparative theology—once it has been purified of the temptation to take privatized religion to be normative of religiosity—can itself become a pluralistic practice for religiously diverse polities.

Part of the work taken up in any such practice will have to be critical reflection about what forms of syncretism or multiple religious belonging are problematic and which are not only permissible but life-giving. Theologians will have to ask the following critical question: By what criteria are we to adjudge that some forms of syncretism are problematic whereas others escape the charge? The fundamental question cannot be whether or not to live lives marked by unadulterated adherence to an exclusively Christian vision of human life—knowing that every Christianity is already shaped by millennia of interreligious encounter—but rather one of determining whether the tangled lives we live can be clarified by generating norms and criteria for determining what modes of living are genuinely life-giving rather than death-dealing.

As I noted at the beginning of this chapter, many assume that any attempt to integrate Buddhist and Christian forms of wisdom is syncretistic whereas a fusion of Christianity and capitalism is not. Why does the latter practice escape critical scrutiny? Presumably, because capitalism is not a religion! But the persuasiveness of such a strategy depends on how one defines "religion." The comparative theologian, by contrast, finds it difficult to argue that Christians formed by the study and practice of Buddhism—both traditions skeptical of modes of life fixated upon creating novel forms of desire in order to generate demand for new consumer goods—are engaged in impermissible syncretism, especially when Christians who venture such argumentation are themselves engaged in a fusion of "capitalism and Christianity, American style."[30]

## Capitalism as Religion

Of late a variety of arguments have been advanced by both theologians and economists that together amount to a persuasive case that capitalism—especially as theorized by neoliberal economists—is a religious phenomenon. Several overlapping strands of argument have been deployed in support of this remarkable proposition. Economists such as Robert H. Nelson, theologians like Marion Grau, Stephen Long, John Milbank, and Kathryn Tanner, theorists of religion like Jeremy Carrette and Richard King, and political theorists such as William Connolly have each advanced their version of this argument. Given their extensive and expert work in this terrain, I confine myself to a brief rehearsal of some shared emphases present throughout this literature.

One recurring thematic in the literature is the questionable faith among economists in the market mechanism as the sole and scientific method for determining value. Regarding the whole question of interest and usury, Robert H. Nelson challenges Samuelson's contention that only the market ought to determine what interest rates ought to be charged and not extrinsic moral considerations derived from philosophical or theological sources. Against Samuelson's charge that only appeal to the market is permissible, Nelson writes,

If I determine my attitudes toward interest from reading Aristotle, or from the condemnation of usury by a twelfth-century Lateran Council ... or from Christian theology as developed by Thomas Aquinas, and consequently have an aversion to high bank-interest rates, who is Samuelson to tell me that my strong feelings should not count? In ruling out my negative reactions as a valid economic cost, Samuelson is here again asserting a powerful value system of his own. He is rejecting my values in favor of a set of powerful convictions automatically incorporated into the standard belief system of professional economics.[31]

Nelson demonstrates that the fundamental assumptions of Samuelson's economic theory are neither value neutral nor scientific. They represent a system of values contrary to those offered by traditional religious worldviews and so are no more neutral than they are. Here then is a recurring theme in virtually all of the aforementioned literature: there is nothing natural nor inevitable, let alone scientific, about the fundamental assumptions made by economists, new and old. Whether it is Adam Smith's classical assumption that the invisible hand of the market will somehow generate a hidden harmony for all from out of the self-interested pursuit of each or some newer capitalist utopian version of the same or the theological anthropology at the heart of capitalist philosophies—that human beings are motivated by self-interest—the core assumptions of capitalist economy theory are unverifiable and counter-theological if not heretical.

Beyond the contentions regarding the theoretical underpinnings of classical and neoliberal versions of capitalist theory, there is also the important work of Carrette and King who attend not just to theory but also to the practices of market capitalism. Carrette and King demonstrate in vivid detail the ways in which religious traditions and their practices are being commodified, bought, and sold on the market. They show that religious traditions are being individualized, privatized, and co-opted by corporate culture. Their social-ethical dimensions are eviscerated in the process, and the capacity for these traditions to resist the rapaciousness of corporate capitalism is compromised. The picture they paint is bleak.

Especially sobering is their depiction of the market as the all-encompassing structuring social fact of our time: "No longer held in check by other countervailing forces in society (such as ideals of individual restraint, a social conscience and the promotion of a community-oriented ethic by traditional religious institutions), Capitalism has become the new religion of the contemporary (postmodern) world."[32] For Carrette and King, the use of religion is no mere trope because they show that there is both a formal and material analogy between religious ideologies and the ideology of the market. It is worth citing them at some length on this point:

> As with the rise of religious ideologies in previous historical eras, "the Market" is being presented to us as "natural" and inevitable. . . . It is gradually infiltrating all other dimensions of human life, translating and transforming everything in its wake into the language and philosophy of consumerism—a world of competitiveness, economically driven motivation and de-regulated market forces. Rather than setting out to convert the heathen to the gospel, as generations of European Christians did, or bring civilisation to the primitive . . . the explicit goal in this new phase of missionary activity is to convert the people of the world into consumers and all human societies into deregulated markets.[33]

In terms of the definition of the religious offered in this chapter, capitalism fits the bill. Human beings are asked to adopt a posture of fundamental trust in the market as the most assured means by which collective human prosperity can be won. We are asked, or better still, compelled to believe that market will reward those who put their trust in it, and punish those who violate its dictates. Left without interference, the market is omnipotent and will secure an *eschaton* in which consumption is increased and wealth generated.

The neoliberal theology of capitalism may be abstruse and understood only by economists-priests, but such understanding is not required for participation. The therapeutic regime of consumerism beguiles even those who do not have access to resources to sustain a consumerist lifestyle. Working to gain resources in order to consume—this therapeutic regime binds the mind-heart of devotees more completely than perhaps any therapeutic regime instituted and imposed by the world's religious traditions if not in human history, then certainly in our historical moment.

The work of naming capitalism as religion is an act of resistance against neoliberal ideology that wears the mask of mathematical objectivity. Carrette and King invite traditions to work collaboratively to resist the power of the market to commodify their traditions and their practices. They are altogether sober about the daunting work required for such resistance but do not believe that resistance is futile. For my purposes, the work of Nelson, Carrette and King, and countless others to name capitalism as religion is of vital importance because it breaks up encrusted notions about just what a religion is. Most importantly, it gives the lie to Western Christian assumptions that multiple religious belonging is just a marginal phenomenon.

Careful analysis demonstrates to the contrary that the practice of consumerism is the dominant therapeutic regime that bears on the lives of most Western Christians, and even God is recruited to sanctify the market. As Linda Kintz demonstrates with considerable subtlety, that is the work to which theologians like Michael Novak are committed. As she demonstrates, for Novak, "The corporation is fundamentally connected to the very soul of this nation, liberty. But this is not liberty conceptualized by anticapitalist intellectuals and theologians . . . but the liberty to create wealth, and even more, the moral obligation to do so."[34] The creation of wealth by means of market capitalism is commended as precisely the remedy for poverty and hence the amelioration of the human predicament. There is a deep soteriology at work in Novak's theology, and, as Kintz shows, he is able to articulate that theology winningly. Again, for our purposes, the details of Novak's theology are not of first importance. What is compelling is the cumulative evidence for the case that market capitalism is a project that seeks to afford human beings with comprehensive qualitative orientation and the attendant therapeutic regime to live in and out of that orientation.

## Interreligious Collaboration and Assessment of Multiple Religious Belonging

In an era of multiple religious belonging, it seems reasonable to hypothesize that theologians must engage in interreligious conversation and comparative theology in order to launch and sustain a collective conversation about criteria for determining which forms of religious multiplicity are salutary and which self-contradictory and potentially troubling. There is no reason to imagine that such conversation will be free from tension and debate; as already noted, any given tradition is best characterized as a community of argumentation rather than agreement. There is no reason to expect that conversation across traditions will be any simpler.

What might Buddhist theologians like David Loy have to offer to our thinking about economics that Christian theologians do not?[35] How can

Christian, Buddhist, and Muslim theologians, among others, together collaborate and critique the ways in which capitalist therapeutic regimes and interpretive schemes impinge on the lives of adherents of their religious communities? If every one of our traditions is a porous multiplicity, then appeals to religious purity and homogeneity must be recognized as fictive and unhelpful. The question is not about whether multiple religious belonging is desirable but rather which forms are likely to be life-giving.

What is difficult to imagine is that theologians in a multireligious age can think well about these questions in isolation, apart from collaborative conversation. If every community is shot through with multiple forms of religiousness, derived from secular sources and the various religious traditions, and if human beings engage in the labor of comprehensive qualitative orientation by appeal to data from any number of sources—religious traditions, economic theories, market practices, quantum theory, and evolutionary theory to name a few—then theologians of religious diversity and comparative theologians also have a role to play in these conversations. If, as Paul Knitter has argued, there is no way to be religious without being interreligious, then there is no way to think religiously save by thinking interreligiously.

The account of religiousness presented herein intimates that we are being interreligious well before any Christian elects to take up yoga or vipassana. Multiple varieties of religiousness shape every body, for good and for ill. Discernment is needed and collaboration indispensable to sort out which is which. Interreligious reflection is necessary if we are to field questions such as the following: What forms of qualitative orientation are likely to be persuasive and adequate? Are some therapeutic regimes derived from various religious and secular sources compatible, or might they be contraindicated? After all, not every medication can be combined with any other; just because my neighbor's medications work well for her does not mean that I would be well advised to raid her medicine cabinet. Can one simultaneously take up desire as tutored by the disciplining practices of kenotic Christianity and Buddhism even as one is also being formed by the desire as configured by the multiplying powers of market capitalism? To what ultimate or ultimates are religious and secular modes of religiousness seeking to attune their adherents?

Having surrendered conceptions of religion and religions that privilege singularity and homogeneity for accounts of religiousness that valorize multiplicity and porosity, the calling before us is to think well about giving and receiving across religious traditions. What do our traditions have to give each other? Even more important, especially for Christians, given our overeagerness to give—a giving with no expectation of receiving and learning—how can we learn to receive hospitably? How can we learn to think of religious diversity as promise rather than peril? One way to begin answering those questions is to study exemplary moments of interreligious hospitality when learning across religious traditions transpired to enormous good. The chapter to come traces one such moment, namely the encounter between Martin Luther King, Jr., and Mohandas Gandhi. We turn to this moment of transformative interreligious encounter to appreciate that there is nothing new about what comparative theologians seek to do in learning from and with other religious traditions. Gandhi openheartedly receives wisdom from Tolstoy's distinctive reading of the Sermon on the Mount, and King and his mentors before him receive from Gandhi's distinctively Hindu reading of Christ's teachings and Christ as the exemplary *satyagrahi* back into Christian tradition. All are transformed in the process of interreligious encounter. Careful study of such moments of exemplary transformative encounter can be a crucial testing and learning ground for the work of comparative theology.

# 6 The Hospitality of Receiving

## MOHANDAS GANDHI, MARTIN LUTHER KING, JR., AND INTERRELIGIOUS LEARNING

*You are here to find out the distress of the people of India and remove it. But I hope you are here also in a receptive mood, and if there is anything that India has to give, you will not stop your ears, you will not close your eyes, and steel your hearts, but open up your ears, eyes, and most of all your hearts to receive all that may be good in this land. . . . I therefore ask you to approach the problem before you with open heartedness and humility.*

—MOHANDAS GANDHI, *Gandhi on Christianity*

## Interreligious Receptivity: Welcoming Wisdom from Other Traditions

Thus far in this book, I have argued against reified conceptions of "religion" and "religions" that have contributed to an orientation in which interreligious learning seems aberrant and even incoherent. If religious traditions are imagined as tightly bounded, impermeable, and integrated conceptual schemes tied to transhistorically stable deep grammars, interreligious learning comes to seem impossible. To learn from and incorporate wisdom from other traditions would make about as much sense as incorporating elements of soccer into a game of chess. Both are games, but that is no reason to believe that elements from one can be incorporated into the other.

Having disrupted such counterfactual conceptions of religion and having argued for relational pluralism as the most compelling TRD, the time has come to actually generate a theology that takes up interreligious learning and makes it central to the labor of integrating theology of religious diversity, comparative theology, and constructive theology. That is the task I take up in the next chapter of this book.

In this chapter, I would like to take up one further task. I wish to demonstrate that interreligious learning is not just a desirable project to be pursued by academics. I wish to show that interreligious learning has taken place prominently in public life and with world-transforming significance. I hold that the circuit of learning between M. K. Gandhi and the black leaders of the American Civil Rights Movement is an exemplary instance of interreligious learning and the virtue of interreligious receptivity. By taking a brief look at this momentous engagement across religious traditions and the profound transformations generated by this auspicious instance of interreligious learning, I wish to show that what I have been calling for—constructive theology through interreligious learning—has already transpired to great public good.

I focus in particular on the work of learning in Martin Luther King, Jr.'s thought. A more extended argument would (1) demonstrate the degree to which Gandhi's own formulation of nonviolent resistance was itself the result of his deep interreligious learning and (2) show also just how much King's own teachers learned from Gandhi, often through direct personal conversation, and, in so doing, laid the groundwork for King's learning. Thankfully, others have undertaken both of those tasks.[1] Rather than replicate their work, my ruminations supplement and build on these other projects. The point of the argument in this chapter is to offer a proof of argument: interreligious learning is neither impossible nor incoherent because it has already taken place. In this instance of interreligious learning, we see exactly what I call for, the integration of a theology of religious diversity—King's particular form of open inclusivism—with comparative theology, and a new constructive theology of the Christ as *satyagrahi*.

Before I explore these processes of interreligious learning and my argument that they are instantiations of the hospitality of receiving, I venture a note of caution. In this historical moment, uncritically eulogistic writing about Gandhi is no longer permissible.[2] Far too much careful work has been done to demonstrate Gandhi's shortcomings on questions of race, gender, and, most especially, caste and untouchability.[3] The literature is now voluminous. Dalit critics in particular, from B. R. Ambedkar forward, have called into question Gandhi's status as Mahatma.[4] A grave sense of betrayal characterizes Dalit engagements with and remembrance of Gandhi. In faithfulness to Dalit communities, it is important to remember rather than repress the harms Gandhi wrought in his attempts to defend elements of Hindu orthodoxy, most especially the validity of caste.

And yet, despite the moral ambiguity of Gandhi's witness, we cannot afford to dismiss Gandhi's prodigious labors on behalf of theorizing and performing nonviolence. As Sarah Azaransky has brilliantly demonstrated, King's teachers were acutely aware of Gandhi's shortcomings but were nonetheless indebted to and transformed by what they learned from him. The give and take of interreligious learning does not transpire between saintly souls, nor need it be free from challenge and mutual critique. Nonetheless, it is possible to engage in the demanding work of interreligious learning in a spirit of hospitality. It is difficult to imagine what the world would look like now if Benjamin Mays, Howard Thurman, James Lawson, and others refused to learn from or sidelined Gandhi because of what they knew about his failings and inconsistencies.

## Gandhi's Demanding Invitation

Christian fascination with the life and work of Mohandas Gandhi is an enduring and ongoing phenomenon. This attraction is likely rooted in Gandhi's deep love for the life and teachings of Jesus, in particular the Sermon on the Mount, and the sense that Gandhi's self-sacrificial life had to it a Christ-like character. He, too, like Martin Luther King, Jr., a generation later, is one who gave his life for his friends and even his enemies.

Christian curiosity about Gandhi long predated his death, and Gandhi enjoyed many friendships with Christians, including missionaries. An abiding fruit of his encounters with missionaries is the many addresses that Gandhi delivered at their request. One senses in these invitations and missionary writings about him puzzlement about this ardent lover of Jesus who took no interest in conversion. Conversation *yes*, but conversion *no*.

Christian theologians have access to a number of Gandhi's addresses to missionaries. Sadly, they are rarely read despite the treasures they contain. In these addresses, a striking theme is repeatedly sounded—namely, an earnest call for receptivity. Gandhi pleads with his interlocutors to demonstrate a spirit of openness, openness to receiving from India. However commendable it may be that missionaries come to give—to remove "the distress of the people of India"—something is missing in the posture of missionaries, and that is a willingness to receive.

In what follows, I suggest that the African American community, under the leadership of Dr. King, answered this poignant invitation to learn from India in their openhearted reception of the theory and practice of nonviolent resistance from Gandhi himself.[5] It would behoove us to think of this reception of *satyagraha*—Gandhi's name for the power and practice of nonviolent resistance—as an exemplary act of *interreligious learning and receptivity*, indeed one of world historical significance.

In what follows, I will present the urgency and power of Gandhi's call for what I call "the hospitality of receiving." I shall then suggest that we must look to the African American reception and performance of nonviolence as itself a moment of interreligious receptivity. I conclude with a preliminary investigation of the theological convictions and resources that enabled Martin Luther King, Jr., to answer Gandhi's call and so to become a hospitable recipient of Gandhian wisdom. What should be clear throughout these reflections is the global horizon of King's deliberative life, a life marked by his readiness to learn from and be transformed by a Hindu reading of Jesus.

For the moment, let us stipulate that interreligious receptivity is the capacity for and the practice of receiving resources from the interpretive schemes and therapeutic regimes of a tradition other than one's own. Such receptivity is an ethical and religious virtue that accords to one's neighbors and their tradition's genuine respect. Other traditions are not celebrated as variations of one's own but are instead appreciated for the richness of their concrete claims, aims, and practices. Such receptivity is also rooted in a theological humility about one's own tradition. Even if maximal claims are made about the salvific power of what is disclosed in one's own tradition, the hospitable recipient believes that genuine learning is possible through encounter and conversation with religious neighbors. Others know what I do not yet know; other traditions and their adherents have access to practical disciplines that can deepen my own spiritual life.

Paying attention to critical moments of interreligious receptivity matters, especially in this historical moment, when, far too often, religious traditions and the civilizations that they fund are taken to be impermeable and reified entities that are bound to clash and predestined to undying hostility. Attention to moments of interreligious receptivity can give the lie to this dominant narrative and even problematize the idea of syncretism as the illegitimate conflation of ideas and practices from across religious traditions. What if our traditions have always been porous to each other? What if traditions are often enriched and transfigured by what they receive from external sources? Might our very understanding of tradition undergo modification as we observe critical moments of interreligious receptivity?

We cannot look to King himself for a vigorous argument in defense of interreligious receptivity. He performs such receptivity but does not theorize it. But an explicit appreciation of the virtue of interreligious receptivity, however, is present in many of his key teachers and mentors. They read Gandhi and traced the provenance of his core ideas about nonviolence to Indic traditions, most especially to Jainism and Hinduism. Sarah Azaransky has shown that, in their academic and public writings, figures such as Benjamin Mays and William Stuart Nelson were attentive to the synthetic interreligious character of Gandhi's understanding of nonviolence. Azaransky has even argued that these figures displayed patterns of thinking that would merit granting to these figures the status of comparative theologians *avant la lettre*.[6]

The kind of deliberate scholarly, interpersonal, and interreligious learning accomplished by King's mentors provided the foundation for King's work in the thick of the Civil Rights battle. That battle and its grueling demands on King's schedule and energies made it difficult, if not impossible, to do the kinds of detailed scholarship accomplished in the generation just preceding his. Even still, one can see King's sermons, books, and, above all, his public performance of nonviolent resistance, as a moment of interreligious receptivity and learning.

If it is right to think of the Civil Rights Movement as interreligious in nature, then it is time to broach the following questions: (1) Although it is widely known that King marched alongside and worked with Rabbi Abraham Joshua Heschel and admired the work of Thich Naht Hanh— so much so that he nominated him for the Nobel Peace Prize—why haven't we named this moment as interreligious? (2) What enabled King, his teachers, and his colleagues to learn from, be transformed by, and hold in reverence a non-Christian figure like Mahatma Gandhi? King's devotion to Gandhi was hardly uncontroversial in his own time. King was chastised for his dedication to Gandhi and his Christian faith called into question by prominent figures because of that very public devotion. Given such opposition, it is worth asking about the animating sources of King's own theological openness. Why was King able to engage so readily in the hospitality of receiving?

As I have argued in earlier chapters, comparative theology is the work of learning from the wisdom and practices of one's religious neighbors so that a more encompassing knowledge of ultimate reality and the world's relation to ultimate reality might be gained. Although King did not theorize his own study of Gandhi as a moment of interreligious learning and hence as a kind of comparative theology, insofar as he and others before him learned from Gandhi and therefore from Hindu and Jain traditions which inspired him, genuine interreligious learning, nonetheless, took place. It must also be borne in mind that Gandhi himself learned extensively from his study of Christian texts and traditions. When King and others subsequently studied Gandhi, they learned from a Hindu reading of Christian traditions that is not a reduplication of what Christians *already knew* about their own traditions. These Christians learned to receive their own tradition back again but afresh as it had been interpreted, performed, and transformed by a Hindu.

## Gandhi's Urgent Call for the Hospitality of Receiving

We can be helped in appreciating the importance of receptivity by turning to Mohandas Gandhi's many conversations with Christian missionaries in India. But first, a foundational query: Why should Christians adopt a posture of receptivity toward persons from other religious traditions? Gandhi's words, as presented in this chapter's epigraph, go a long way toward answering this question: "You are here to find out the distress of the people of India and remove it. But I hope you are here also in a receptive mood, and if there is anything that India has to give, you will not stop your ears, you will not close your eyes, and steel your hearts, but open up your ears, eyes, and most of all your hearts to receive all that may be good in this land."[7] One hears in Gandhi's plaintive appeal a profound pain that bespeaks injury. Time and again, Gandhi argues that Christian missionaries are present in India with an orientation that lacks mutuality. They seek to give but without receiving. But this posture is an unsustainable contradiction.

Here is Gandhi, again addressing missionaries: "To you who have come to teach India, I therefore say, you cannot give without taking. If you have come to give rich treasures of experiences, open your hearts out to receive the treasures of this land, and you will not be disappointed, neither will you have misread the message of the Bible."[8]

You cannot give without taking, without receiving. Here, Gandhi speaks a fundamental human truth: the one who seeks to give without receiving does neither. Authentic giving requires receptivity. Those who seek to give must stand prepared to receive, as any giving that comes from on high, from an attitude of asymmetrical condescension demeans and does not enrich. If you give in such a way that suggests that you have nothing to receive, then you do not, in truth, give. Instead, you violate.

Consider the gesture of holding the hand of someone whom you wish to console. In the very act of extending your hand, you render yourself vulnerable, as the lives of both Gandhi and King suggest. Will the one who is in need grasp your extended hand? Will your desire to give be accepted? And there is more—when you grasp the other's hand, you receive also the touch of the other. Here it becomes impossible to tell who comforts and who is comforted. In the mutuality of the embracing hands, both give and both receive. In touch and in life, it is impossible that one alone should give and the other alone receive.

Is such mutuality possible in interfaith relations? Gandhi, like King, asserts that it is not only possible but mandatory. The missionary cannot truly give without receiving. Gandhi suggests that any reading of the Bible that disposes one toward an attitude of nonreciprocal giving is sure to be a misreading. One cannot simply appeal to John 14:6 and assert that the "I am" saying—"I am the way, the truth and the life, no one comes to the Father but by me"—forecloses on the possibility of receiving healing wisdom from religious neighbors. In the same address to Christian missionaries, the Mahatma says, "You want to find men in India, and if you want to do that, you will have to go to the lowly cottages—not to give them something, but maybe to take something from them. A true friend as I claim to be of the missionaries of India and of the Europeans, I speak to you from the bottom of my heart. I miss receptiveness, humility, willingness on your part to identify yourself with the masses of India."[9] Gandhi invites Christian missionaries to give themselves in solidarity to India's poorest and serve them in love but also in expectancy, with an open heart that looks to receive as well as to give. Interestingly, Gandhi does not presume to tell Christians just what we might receive from Hindus when we so open our hearts. That is our work and not his. Gandhi believes that without the virtues of receptivity, humility, and solidarity, the missionary enterprise is compromised because it violates the dignity of those whom it seeks to serve.[10]

One cautionary note must be sounded about Gandhi's discourses to missionaries. Despite the importance of taking seriously Gandhi's challenge to missionaries, Gandhi's stance against conversion must be recognized as limited. For a variety of marginalized lower caste and Dalit communities, conversion out of Hindu traditions in pursuit of human dignity offered by Christian ecclesial communities proved to be lifesaving. In the contemporary context, in which the Hindu right dismisses and caricatures Christian converts as "rice Christians," Christians who are motivated only by material inducements, it will not do to present Gandhi's remarks in a way that suggests that the Hindu right may have in Gandhi support against missionizing activity and conversion. Every caution must be taken to ensure that the Indian decision at the constitutional level to include the freedom to propagate religion as part of the very fabric of freedom of religion is not compromised by an unsubtle appeal to Gandhi's ideas.

## King, Nonviolence, and Interreligious Receiving

The power of Gandhi's call might be felt with clarity if we come to appreciate the tremendous promise of interreligious receptivity as manifest in the life of King and in the Civil Rights Movement. There is no better argument for receptivity than a demonstration of its power in action. To assert that King's reception of Gandhian praxis and reflection is a case of interreligious learning hardly seems controversial, but that case has largely not been made. King famously asserted that he had learned to see Jesus differently as a result of his encounter with Gandhi. He learned from Gandhi what he did not already know about Jesus. King received his own tradition anew as mediated back to him by a Hindu. The primary question to be explored herein is this: "What features of King's own theology made such learning possible?" Ultimately, that is a question about King's theology of religious diversity.

As we have dedicated two chapters to exploring current options in theologies of religious diversity, we need not revisit that material. It must only be recognized that academic and ecclesial engagement with TRD was just beginning in King's time. If we take the promulgation of the Vatican II document *Nostra Aetate* as a founding event in the creation of theologies of religious diversity, we quickly realize that asking from King a formal TRD risks anachronism. That kind of theological labor was just getting under way. Therefore, we must bring to King's writings questions that have only now become central to the field and discern how King might have answered them. We must ask, Does King take religious diversity to be a positive good? Is it a promise to be received or a problem to be solved? What can we tell about whether he affirms the possibility of salvation outside of Christianity and the degree to which non-Christians have access to God's saving power?

In this book, we have shown that, over the course of the last fifty years, there has been a steady shift on the part of Christian theologians away from rigorous forms of exclusivism, which maintain that "outside of the church there is no salvation" toward inclusivist and even pluralist positions. We have shown that inclusivists have often appealed to part-whole logic which maintains that the fullness of God's saving presence and power is revealed in Jesus the Christ but that partial and even salvific disclosures of God are available in other religious traditions. Pluralists have gone further and argued that religious traditions must be regarded as on par in bringing about ultimate transformation from self-centeredness to reality-centeredness, with no tradition exceeding the other in decisive fashion. Repudiating a part-whole logic that would rank-order traditions, they insist that each tradition affords equal and independent access to saving truth and power. Beyond this threefold rubric, we have also traced a variety of positions that pressure, push beyond, or at very least call for revisions to the threefold model.

Where does Martin King stand on these questions? Fruitful and productive work remains to be done to survey King's writings on the relationship between Christianity and other religious traditions, to elicit therefrom his nascent theology of religious diversity. Here, I broach that question but in a distinctive key by asking, "What features of King's theology made it possible for him to function as a hospitable recipient of religious wisdom from other traditions?" This way of framing the question is more exigent than rank-ordering traditions on a soteriological scale because the capacity to receive marks a more decisive repudiation of religious isolationism and self-sufficiency than an abstract, fair-minded, and charitable assertion of the relative parity of religious traditions. After all, one might well posit the equality of traditions while remaining indifferent to or uninterested in the distinctive goods of those traditions. Indeed, a form of pluralism that asserts that religious traditions are mere variations on a theme and so different paths to the same destination may impede appreciation of enriching difference.

Despite the presence of pluralist elements in King's theology, I argue that King's TRD most closely approximates "open inclusivism." By open inclusivism, I mean that King confessed that God's revelation in Jesus the Christ represents the fullest disclosure of divinity available in the world's religions while remaining open to learning from other traditions. Put otherwise, his is an inclusivism that actually *includes new insights and practices* from other religious traditions and so materially learns from them. King's version of inclusivism does not hold that because the fullness of divine disclosure takes place in Jesus the Christ, Christians have nothing new to learn. His inclusivism is, therefore, qualitatively different from a hierarchical or self-sufficient version in which one's own tradition is said already to contain all that can be known of religious truth.

As I have argued (in Chapters 2 and 3), one criterion for measuring the adequacy of any TRD is the capacity to demonstrate deep interreligious receptivity marked by learning from a tradition other than one's own. To any TRD, the following question might be posed: Does this theology enable its advocates to receive wisdom from another tradition and be transformed thereby? I have already argued that some form of relational pluralism is the most adequate position in this regard. However, my concern here is not to argue that King is a relational pluralist. He is not. Rather my intention is to ask about the theological grounds for hospitable reception of wisdom from traditions other than one's own.

When thinking about the relationship between Gandhi, King, and the Civil Rights Movement at large, one oft-repeated phrase comes to mind: "Nonviolent resistance had emerged as the technique of the movement, while love stood as the regulating ideal. In other words, *Christ furnished the spirit and motivation, while Gandhi furnished the method.*"[11] King's assertion might be taken to imply that Gandhi's contribution was merely instrumental rather than substantive—a means rather than an end. On this account, the most important spiritual resources for nonviolent resistance come from the Christian tradition rather than from Gandhi's own religious milieu.

We see also in some discourse of the time a tendency to read Gandhi entirely in Christian terms and to depict him as the greatest Christian of the twentieth century. Without a doubt, calling Gandhi a Christian was meant as a blessing—and the epigraph of this chapter suggests that Gandhi would have received it as such. He intimates that Christ would receive as his own those who are not Christian. Gandhi, an avid reader of the Gospels, is likely to have had in mind John 10:16: "And other sheep I have, which are not of this fold: them also I must bring, and they shall hear my voice" (KJV). Hence, Gandhi is prepared to assert about others what some, particularly King, explicitly asserted of him. In his famous Palm Sunday Sermon about Gandhi, King cites this very verse, claiming that Jesus ". . . is saying in substance that 'I have people dedicated and following my ways who have not become attached to the institution surrounding my name. . . . And my influence is not limited to the institutional Christian church.'"[12] The import of King's claim is that among the followers of Jesus must be included his non-Christian disciples.

But these two propositions taken together hardly support the case that King and other leaders of the Civil Rights Movement were engaged in interreligious learning. If Gandhi offers only a method to implement what Jesus called for, and if Gandhi himself is among the greatest of Christians, how can learning from him be characterized as interreligious? To respond effectively to this problematizing query, one must show that King moved beyond these formulaic assertions and came to understand that in Gandhi we have a non-Christian who was nonetheless illumined by the presence of God while remaining self-avowedly non-Christian, and also that King learned with and from Gandhi that satyagraha was no mere method. Both of these propositions are readily demonstrable.

That King's understanding of Gandhi is not reductionist becomes evident in the preacher's preparedness to impute to him another more remarkable verse: "Verily, verily, I say unto you, he that believeth on me, the works that I do, shall he do also. And greater works than these shall he do because I go unto my Father" (John 14:12). King prepares a foundation for claiming that Christians have much to learn from Gandhi because the latter's works *exceed* the works of the Christ, a bold claim indeed, most especially for a Christian pastor. Perhaps readers would do well not to read uncharitably King's famous assertion about Gandhi as a great Christian. There is reason to believe that there is more going on in such claims than is apparent at first glance:

> And I believe these two passages of scripture apply more uniquely to the life and work of Mahatma Gandhi than to any other individual in the history of the world. For here was a man who was not a Christian in terms of being a member of the Christian church but who was a Christian. And it is one of the strange ironies of the modern world that the greatest Christian of the twentieth century was not a member of the Christian

church. And the second thing is, that this man took the message of Jesus Christ and was able to do even greater works than Jesus did in his lifetime.[13]

King makes clear that Gandhi is no son of the church; he does not intend surreptitiously to baptize the Mahatma. Secondly, he directs and prepares his Christian listeners to learn from Gandhi what they do not already know from following the Christ. He argues compellingly that the power of nonviolent resistance, as taught by Jesus, was enacted and vindicated on an unprecedented social scale by Gandhi. Gandhi dramatically demonstrates the wide social applicability of nonviolence by leading millions to freedom in a way that Jesus never did.

What, then, are we to make of King's apparent claim that Gandhi offers only a method for putting into practice what Jesus taught? Readers of King's language about nonviolent resistance as a method miss the genuine import of King's claim. To begin with, Civil Rights leaders like King and James Lawson knew with absolute clarity that it was inadequate to speak of nonviolent resistance as a means to an end. When one reads the writings of King, a common pattern presents itself: almost immediately after sentences in which King will speak of nonviolent resistance as a method, a corrective note is proffered cautioning readers that nonviolence must not be understood instrumentally. In Gandhi's thinking, means and ends can never be separated. One cannot use nonviolence as a means to some other extrinsic end. Nonviolence is both the means and the desired end.

King and Lawson fully appreciated this truth. And hence, soon after the above passage in which Gandhi is said to offer a method, King writes, "Nonviolence in the truest sense is not a strategy that one uses simply because it is expedient at the moment; nonviolence is ultimately a way of life that men live by because of the sheer morality of its claim."[14] Elsewhere in speaking of his "pilgrimage to nonviolence," he writes, "The experience in Montgomery did more to clarify my thinking on the question of nonviolence than all of the books that I had read. As the days unfolded I became more and more convinced of the power of nonviolence. Living through the actual experience of the protest, nonviolence became more than a method to which I gave intellectual assent; it became a commitment to a way of life."[15]

If it is true then that Gandhi offers more than a means but instead a way of life, more than an instrumental method to implement Jesus's teaching, how then are we to understand the relationship between Gandhi and Jesus? Here, it is critical to let King speak in his own voice and at length:

> As I delved deeper into the philosophy of Gandhi my skepticism concerning the power of love gradually diminished, and I came to see for the first time its potency in the area of social reform. Prior to reading Gandhi, I had about concluded that the ethics of Jesus were only effective in individual relationship. The "turn the other cheek" philosophy and the "love your enemies" philosophy were only valid, I felt, when individuals were in conflict with other individuals; when racial groups and nations were in conflict a more realistic approach seemed necessary. But after reading Gandhi, I saw how utterly mistaken I was. Gandhi was probably the first person in history to lift the love ethic of Jesus above mere interaction between individuals to a powerful and effective social force on a large scale. Love for Gandhi was a potent instrument for social and collective transformation.[16]

The deep significance of this familiar proclamation has yet to be fully appreciated for the lessons it can teach about interreligious giving and receiving. I contend that King must be read as asserting that Christians receive from Gandhi not merely a new method, but a new understanding of Jesus and so, perhaps, even a new Christology. The Christ who is made known to Christians by Gandhi's work is Jesus, the ideal *satyagrahi*, the ideal practitioner of nonviolent resistance understood as the power of truth—*satya* understood as truth, and *agraha* understood as firmness and force. King asserts that Christians did not have this Jesus prior to Gandhi's creative reading and enactment of his teachings. Prior to Gandhi, Jesus's Sermon on the Mount was understood largely as advancing a limited ethic applicable only to person-to-person encounter.

There is also a shared resonance in the way both Gandhi and King understand the meaning of Jesus's death; both move away from a focus on substitutionary atonement—the teaching that Jesus dies as a substitute sacrifice for human sin—a doctrine that both King and Gandhi found unappealing and unpersuasive.[17] The cross is understood instead as an act of nonviolent political resistance to the powers of violence and ultimately a sign that those principalities can never triumph over the power of love.

What matters here is not whether King is correct in asserting that no political account of Jesus as engaged in collective nonviolent resistance was available before Gandhi. What is incontestable is King's claim that Gandhi was the first to demonstrate and embody that vision on a mass sociopolitical scale and so vindicate any political reading of Jesus that might have been available prior to Gandhi. That a Hindu should be the first to accomplish this revolutionary work is what strikes King as remarkable. To assert the Christianness of Gandhi then is not so much an attempt to baptize him but is instead an act of affirmation that a Hindu understood and performed the true meaning of Jesus's life and teachings more deeply than any Christian had heretofore done.

How Gandhi generated his own Christology would take yet another chapter or indeed a book to lay out. That story would also be a tale of interreligious giving and receiving. Rather simplistically, one would have to say that Gandhi wedded the Jain notion of *ahimsa*, non-injury, together with the idea of *karma yoga* which he derived from his reading of the *Bhagavad Gita*, and added to both these ingredients a creative reading of the Sermon on the Mount as a program for nonviolent resistance. For Gandhi, Jesus's life and death on the cross perfectly exemplify suffering love lived both as means and end. In Jesus's life, as interpreted by Gandhi, nonviolent love is the way that births a new social order marked by nonviolent love.

In King's considered estimation, "Gandhi was probably the first person in history to lift the love ethic of Jesus above mere interaction between individuals to a powerful and effective social force on a large scale." This remarkable claim suggests that King recognized that Gandhi gives Christians more than a new method but a *new Jesus* whose redemptive work lies not just in the private atonement of individual persons from personal sin but in the collective redemption of the social order itself. What I am arguing here is that's King's recognition of Gandhi as offering a new understanding of Jesus's life and work is a historically profound instance of interreligious learning, a moment of hospitable receptivity.

At this juncture, a critical question must be posed: What features of King's theological orientation made it possible for him to receive what Gandhi had to teach him? Why was he prepared to assert that Gandhi performed greater deeds than Jesus himself? Any attempt to answer these questions must begin by noting that King's preparedness to learn from Gandhi was a source of controversy. The most telling evidence of this friction is discernible in the public criticism that King received for being involved in the founding of a Gandhi society in America. For taking this step, he was publically chastised by no less a figure than Dr. Harold Fey, editor of *The Christian Century*. In fact, Fey went so far as to call into question the sincerity of King's Christian faith because of his devotion to Gandhi. King's public interest in and love for the life and teachings of Gandhi did not come without cost. That is why King's (unpublished) response to Dr. Fey is noteworthy and worth citing here at length:

> As far as my Christology goes, I believe as firmly now as ever that God revealed himself uniquely and completely through Jesus Christ. . . . One's commitment to Jesus Christ as Lord and Savior, however, should not mean that one cannot be inspired by another great personality that enters the stage of history. . . . While I firmly believe that God reveals himself more completely and uniquely in Christianity than any other religion, I cannot make myself believe that God did not reveal himself in other religions. I believe that in some marvelous way, God worked through Gandhi, and the spirit of Jesus saturated his life. It is ironic, yet inescapably true that the greatest Christian of the modern world was a man who never embraced Christianity. This is not an indictment on Christ but a tribute to Him—a tribute to his universality and His Lordship. When I think of Gandhi, I think of the Master's way in the words of the fourth gospel: "I have other sheep that are not of this fold."[18]

Many features of King's response are noteworthy because we see in them the stirrings of theological resources for receptivity. First, King's openness to Gandhi was not impeded by nor did it require King to surrender his conviction that "God revealed himself uniquely and completely in Jesus." He is unwilling to relinquish this evangelical axiom. But crucially, King does not believe that God has revealed himself *only* in Jesus. Here King's discourse is inclusivist in character. It is "the spirit of Jesus" that "saturated" Gandhi's life.

Martin Luther King, Jr., makes a decisive step that many mainline Christian theologians and church bodies have since taken, though largely only after his passing.[19] Well before it was theologically popular to do so, King affirmed that divine revelation is available in other religions: "I cannot make myself believe that God did not reveal himself *in other religions*."[20] King asserts herein the power of spirit in Gandhi's individual life and also beyond the lives of exceptional persons. Other religions as such are repositories of revelation. Hence it seems reasonable to suppose that King would hold that Gandhi, and presumably other non-Christians, are not inspired *despite* the religious traditions to which they belong but precisely *because* of them. Affirming *both* these propositions entails that Gandhi's religious life would have to be understood from within its own context and as inspired by indigenous resources and not just the spirit of Jesus. King did not insist on this point but would, it seems, be open to such a claim.

To begin with, King is quite clear that Gandhi is not a Christian. He is prepared to recognize Gandhi as a *Hindu follower of Jesus*. While contemporary theologians may not hold this to be an especially noteworthy valorization of religious difference, King's openness to the possibility and indeed the reality of non-Christian Jesus followers is a theological advance with important ramifications, especially for any viable future theology of mission. King's openness to non-Christian Jesus followers suggests that the goal of mission need not be the conversion of persons from other traditions to one's own. Instead, all persons might understand themselves as invited to share membership in what King called "the beloved community." King's body of writing and preaching shows that he understood the beloved community, from the first and throughout his public career, as an *interreligious community* and not just an interracial community. In the beloved community, differences, including religious ones, are not erased but are no longer a cause for suspicion, rancor, or enmity.

King was prepared to recognize Gandhi's discipleship as an authentic way of following Jesus Christ. Indeed, King says far more; he speaks of Gandhi as "the greatest Christian of the modern world." If that is true, if Christ can be followed to the full, even unto death, without entering the church, then several convictions that have traditionally prevented Christians from adopting a posture of hospitality toward other religious traditions can also be called into question. These include the claims of the following sort: "True reception of Jesus the Christ requires becoming a member of the church, which is the body of the Christ." In any case, King is prepared to move toward an encompassing posture of hospitality and receptivity precisely because he sees nothing deficient or problematic in Gandhi's desire to follow the Christ *as a Hindu*! King seems prepared to reject the notion that faithful discipleship requires conversion wherein conversion is understood to be leaving the religion of one's birth and embracing another.

Intriguingly, this kind of openness toward non-Christians seems precisely to echo Gandhi's own stance toward and advice to missionaries. In Gandhi's recounting of an encounter with a South African chaplain, he reports that he appealed to the Gospels and argued, "It is not he who says 'Lord, Lord,' . . . who enters the Kingdom of Heaven, but he that do-eth his will. I reminded him, 'I am conscious of my weakness, and try to fight them—not in my own strength but in the strength of God. Is that enough or do you wish me to repeat parrot-like that Jesus has cleansed me from all sin?' He stopped me and said, 'I understand what you mean.' So I say that instead of wanting to find out how many heads you count as Christian, work away . . . silently among the people and let your work be the silent testimony of your worth. What do you want to convert them for?"[21] Gandhi advises his Christian interlocutor to adopt toward non-Christians the very position that King seems to have adopted toward Gandhi. Conversion to Christianity is not the goal but rather a faithful following of the divine will in discipleship to the call of Christ. King's focus on creating an interreligious beloved community is argu-ably a fulfillment of Gandhi's own desires and aspirations.

Perhaps King was able to focus resolutely on creating "a world-wide fellowship," one which did not seek to erase religious difference by way of conversion because of his conviction that the world's religious tradi-tions were oriented toward the selfsame reality best understood as love.

> This call for a world-wide fellowship that lifts neighborly concern beyond one's tribe, race, class, and nation is in reality a call for an all-embracing and unconditional love for all men. . . . When I speak of love I am not speaking of some sentimental and weak response. I am speaking of that force which all of the great religions have seen as the supreme unifying principle of life. Love is somehow the key that unlocks the door which leads to ultimate reality. This Hindu-Moslem-Christian-Jewish-Buddhist belief about ultimate reality is beautifully summed up in the first epistle of Saint John: "Let us love one another; for love is God and everyone that loveth is born of God and knoweth God. He that loveth not knoweth not God; for God is love. . . ."[22]

Here, King articulates a theological perspective that seems most akin to pluralism. The heart of the pluralist position, as noted earlier, is that the world's religious traditions are diverse ways of accessing ultimate real-ity. Most importantly, pluralists customarily insist that no tradition af-fords more complete or efficacious access to ultimate reality than any other.

In this particular statement, King does not claim that any tradition affords richer access to ultimate reality than any other. Hence, it might be read as indicative of a certain pluralist leaning. However, there is insufficient information to determine that King has moved beyond his earlier claim in which the completeness of divine disclosure takes place within Christianity. After all, he does not explicitly state that all traditions offer equally efficacious access to ultimate reality. He stipulates only that all alike are oriented to ultimate reality understood as love, and all alike insist that love can be accessed by love alone. No more can be said. What is distinctive to King's approach is his performative emphasis; not doctrinal correctness but only fidelity in love affords access to Love itself.

Given the lack of a fulsome and explicit statement from King, it may be impossible to ascertain whether this latter position marks a departure from his earlier inclusivist position. King *may* have shifted away from the inclusivist position he held in 1962 to the more pluralist position articulated here. Further investigation of King's papers is required before a claim of transition can be sustained. Moreover, he may have held both convictions together. It is possible to hold without contradiction both the pluralist conviction that all religious traditions are rightly oriented to ultimate reality while maintaining that ultimate reality is disclosed most completely in Jesus the Christ. One can be pluralist on the question of theological ontology while being an inclusivist on questions of revelation and epistemology.

What is clear, at any rate, is that by some combination of inclusivist and pluralist intuitions, King arrived at a theological posture of hospitable receiving. King was confident that God is at work in the lives of neighbors of other faiths. His conviction that revelation takes place outside the church justifies the hope that others possess riches from which Christians have much to learn. What is striking about King's stance is his capacity to be a hospitable receiver even when he maintained that the fullness of God's disclosure was available in Jesus the Christ. If Martin Luther King, Jr., is right that it is only in the twentieth century that Christians have come fully to appreciate Jesus as an embodiment of nonviolent love, and if furthermore, Christians learned that lesson most capaciously from a Hindu, then even Christians who confess the finality and unsurpassability of God's revelation in Jesus Christ need not adopt a posture of self-sufficiency toward other religious traditions. It may be that Christians will only know what it means to confess the Christ when the Christ is given away and received anew from persons of other religious traditions.

King's openness to learning from Gandhi, at personal cost, remains striking today. Even on the contemporary theological scene, few Christian leaders defend the possibility that non-Christians might receive something precious, transformative, and even salvific from Christian quarters *while remaining non-Christian*. Fewer still suggest that non-Christians have much to teach Christians, even about Christianity, because the resources of other traditions may illumine one's home tradition precisely in their very difference. On the contrary, the standard posture remains that those who receive from the Christian tradition must, if the work of reception is genuine and complete, cease to be non-Christian. The normative posture is that you, the non-Christian, not only need to receive this or that vital Christian good, but you must relinquish your religious identity in the very act of receiving. But how can giving that seeks to erase the otherness of the other be characterized as hospitable? King's openness to the reality of non-Christian followers of Jesus opens up the possibility of a giving that does not require that others cease to be who they are. Thus, a close reading of King has the promise to unfold new conceptions of mission and conversion. Conversion can be understood not as movement into a new religious tradition but as entrance into the beloved community.

The exchange between Gandhi and King is a profound and multidirectional movement marked by the hospitality of receiving. First, Gandhi received generously from Henry David Thoreau, Leo Tolstoy, and others from within the Christian tradition. In turn, King received a great deal from Gandhi perhaps because he was able to see Gandhi as a fellow disciple of Christ, *albeit a Hindu disciple*. Were King himself a scholar of Indian religious traditions, he would have recognized that what he received from Gandhi was a transformed understanding of Jesus as the ideal *satyagrahi*. He might see that that Christology includes and is enriched by fundamental Jain and Hindu notions and practices. Therefore, it is possible credibly to hold that King received from Gandhi a new Christology that was shaped, in part, by religious riches alien to the Christian tradition, riches that enlivened Christian reflection and practice. Furthermore, King's work of hospitality demonstrates that even Christians who are wholeheartedly committed to affirming the plenitude of God's self-disclosure in Christ can be open to hospitable receiving. He shows that there need be no conflict between searching faith and interreligious learning. Even traditionalist Christians can confess that God has disclosed God's self most fully in the Christ and yet also believe that one's Hindu neighbor may see dimensions of that fullness that Christians have not yet appreciated.

Depth of piety need never become an obstacle to the hospitality of receiving. How could it as authentic faith demand the work of welcoming wisdom whatever its source? These lessons offered by King remain very much ours to learn.

In the next chapter, I propose to engage in just such hospitable receptivity but now on the distinctive theme of the trinity. Can theological resources from other traditions deepen Christian thinking, even about the trinity? My answer is an emphatic *yes*. My appeal to Hindu and Buddhist resources to deepen and revivify Christian reflection on the trinity demonstrates what I have been calling for: the integration of theology of religious diversity, comparative theology, and constructive theology. The integration of what we say *about* others, what we have learned *from* others, and what we proceed to say *about* ultimate reality witnesses to what the hospitality of receiving can bring to pass.

# 7 God as Ground, Singularity, and Relation

## TRINITY AND RELIGIOUS DIVERSITY

> ... the one First Cause is not split and cut up into differing Godships, neither does the statement harmonize with the Jewish dogma, but the truth passes in the mean *between these two conceptions, destroying each heresy, and yet accepting what is useful to it from each. . . . For it is as if the number of the triad were a remedy in the case of those who are in error as to the One, and the assertion of the unity for those whose beliefs are dispersed among a number of divinities.*
>
> —GREGORY OF NYSSA

## Trinitarianism and Christianity's Others

We have traveled a complex theoretical journey to arrive now at this chapter in which I hope to render actual what I have argued is possible—namely, a theology of religious diversity (TRD) that builds on and draws from comparative theology and, in turn, contributes to a new constructive theology of the trinity. In fact, it will be impossible to separate these three projects in what follows as each contributes to the other in interdependent fashion. A theology of the trinity that is worked out with the help of Hindus and Buddhists will, I hope, exemplify the hospitality of receiving spoken of in the previous chapter. Such a theology would be simultaneously a way to think about religious neighbors, a way of learning from those neighbors, and a way to reimagine the divine life. The result is a new kind of intellectual project—namely, a comparative theology of religious diversity.

But why trinity? Why select trinity as the site for thinking about and learning from religious diversity? The answer to that question should be relatively clear from what I have argued in previous chapters, particularly Chapter 3: the trinity is a natural Christian way to speak about diversity in the divine life. On the basis of this diversity within the divine life, a variety of recent Christian theologians, most notably Mark Heim, have argued that the genuine diversity to be found within religious traditions is likely to find some footing within the very nature of God, a God who is many without ceasing to be one.[1]

Christian naming of divinity, even in the community's oldest baptismal formula, begins by affirming the threefold character of divine disclosure without abjuring divine unity. God is one, but not a one in whom there is no distinction. God is thus a multiplicity. The one God who created the world saves that very world by way of God's Word and Breath which two cannot be collapsed into an undifferentiated simplicity of the one Father. The logic of Christian reflection which led eventually to Nicene trinitarianism was also driven by a commitment to safeguarding divine unity and transcendence while affirming God's real and gracious self-giving. To assert that God gives something other or less than Godself in giving Word and Spirit imperils salvation, which can come about only as human beings are taken into the divine life and thereby deified. Hence, divine differentiation cannot fall into a gradation of many divine or semi-divine beings.

What is striking about early Christian reflection about divine accessibility is that trinitarian considerations were never far removed from reflection on religious diversity. No less a theologian than Gregory of Nyssa characterized the trinitarian conception of divinity as a mean between as well as a double refutation of the excesses of Jewish commitment to the One and a pagan commitment to the many. As the epigraph to this chapter demonstrates, Gregory did not separate the work of formulating and defending Christian trinitarianism from reflection about Christianity's others. To love the one alone is to err in a Jewish direction. To love the many without the one is to fall into paganism. Or so Gregory argued. In the work of crafting this argument, Gregory's theological labor illustrates the inseparability of self-constitution from the work of dialogue. We see in Gregory what I call for in this book: the seamless integration of comparison, a theological account of religious diversity, and constructive theology.

Contemporary conversations about trinity and religious diversity need not be confined to apologetics of Gregory's sort but now hold promise for an affirmative embrace of religious difference. My intention in evoking Gregory is not to commend him as an unambiguous model for contemporary comparative theology. Gregory matters, nonetheless, because he encapsulates a moment in which Christian theology maintained a unity we now seek to recover—the unity between constructive theology, comparative theology, and TRD.

In the contemporary moment, a variety of Christian theologians assert that trinitarianism is the distinctively Christian way of offering a *positive* resolution to the problem of religious diversity: by acknowledging distinction within the divine life, Christians can account for substantial differences among the world's religions as varying but nonetheless legitimate expressions of an encounter with God who will be experienced diversely just because God is not an undifferentiated singularity. The abiding differences between the world religions are neither illusory nor indicative of error. Religious diversity is a natural expression of human encounter with divine multiplicity.

Of course, a trinitarian approach to religious diversity cannot be a universal solution to questions of religious diversity. How, after all, are Christian theologians to honor the Jewish commitment to divine unity and Muslim affirmations that God is without associates? Moreover, trinitarian theologians of religious diversity must labor to resist a problematic apologetic temptation, the temptation to assert that whereas other traditions offer a monolithic account of divine life, Christian trinitarianism, by contrast, is encompassing and polyphonic. Christians see the whole whereas others see only in part. Such an error would return us once more to the territory of hierarchical inclusivism in which Christian traditions have little to learn from dialogue with other religious traditions.[2] Self-sufficiency trumps the possibility of mutual transformation.

Might it be possible for Christian theologians to envision a trinitarian engagement with religious diversity that is marked by a sense of *anticipation* that other traditions may have something to teach us about how to think even about trinity? Can we imagine the trinity as a site for interreligious exchange rather than as a prefabricated solution to the problem of religious diversity? My sense is that the trinity can indeed be an open site for interreligious dialogue and exchange but not as long as Christians bring to dialogue a completed and therefore closed conception of the trinity that can in no way be enriched by way of comparative theology.

Theology has been in the midst of a trinitarian efflorescence since the work of Karl Barth and Karl Rahner. This return of trinitarianism, however, is not marked by happy harmony but is instead characterized by

considerable dissensus. One conviction that drives the resurgence of trinitarianism is the notion in some quarters that trinity affords a promising resource for social ontology; social trinitarians argue that if to be is
to be in relation, then there is no clearer paradigm for that contention
than the trinity itself.[3] But about the nature of relationality within the
divine life, there is no consensus. On the one side stand the social trinitarians and, on the other, stand those who are persuaded that social trinitarianism is a fundamental distortion of the intentions of the ancients.[4]
Given the vigorous internal debate between Christian theologians, it is
natural to ask how engagements with religious diversity might bear on
such controversies.

The ongoing intra-Christian trinitarian debate reminds us that trinity is better understood as a question and a problem rather than as a
transparent dogmatic dictum. Rather than treat some ready-made account of the trinity as a final Christian answer to questions about theology and ontology or the problem of religious difference, an alternative
open-ended strategy would treat the trinity as itself a locus for interreligious conversation and exchange. Before any particular trinitarian formulation derived from intra-Christian resources alone is made to serve
as the normative basis for a Christian TRD, we might consider treating
trinity as a question for comparative theology.

What might it mean to consider trinity as a question and resource for
comparative theology? There are several possibilities. A first possibility
is to consider that the trinitarian divinity might be discernable in the creation of that trinitarian God. If so, Christians are unlikely to be the only
ones to have discerned certain dimensions of the divine life in the world
and in religious experience. Here, of course, we speak in a kind of rough
continuity with the great Augustinian *vestigio trinitatis* tradition. God's
nature and presence are discernible in a variety of sites within creation
including but not limited to the human person. That is just the kind of
claim that I advance in this chapter.[5]

A second implication of wedding comparative theology and trinitarian reflection is that, in doing so, we return trinitarian reflection to one
of the scenes of its initial formulation. If Gregory imagines trinity both
as a way to interpret the Christian experience of the multiplicity of divine self-giving and also as a means to interpret the religious insights and
experiences of other traditions, albeit critically, surely contemporary
Christian theologians can do likewise. Why not permit "trinity" to function again as something more than a token in intra-Christian discourse

alone? The very insularity of our in-house talk about trinity may be contributing to its marginalization and obscurity. Christian worship and reflection, outside of specialist circles, have surrendered recourse to the term save when preachers are compelled to say something on "Trinity Sunday." Perhaps thinking the trinity with the help of other traditions can revivify Christian and non-Christian interest in category.[6]

A third and related implication of engaging trinity by way of comparative theology is that by bringing a cherished notion like trinity to comparative encounter, Christians can practice theological vulnerability. We signal willingness to entertain the possibility that others may be able to shed more light even on our most precious categories than we can manage when left to our own devices. Perhaps we need Buddhists and Hindus if we are to be fully and truly Christian. Indeed, such vulnerability may itself be an enactment at the level of thought of what Christians are called to enact with our lives—to serve and to be served by others regardless of whether they belong to our in-group, our church, or our "religion."

In what follows, I advance a trinitarian formulation that draws from a comparative reading of Hindu, Christian, and Buddhist traditions. From Advaita Vedanta, I draw an account of ultimate reality as ground, from Christian resources, I offer an account of ultimate reality as singularity,[7] and from Buddhist traditions (specifically Madhyamaka), I draw an account of ultimate reality as relation. The result is a trinitarianism of God as ground, singularity, and relation derived by way of comparative theology. Although each of these concepts can be correlated with accounts of God as Father, Son, and Spirit, the task at hand is not to defend the orthodoxy of my formulation but to launch an experiment in formulating Christian doctrine in conversation with other traditions. A glance at Gregory suffices to show that something like this process of construction in conversation has long been a part of Christian theology. Only now such construction can take on the character of collaboration rather than apologetic contestation.

What about the number three? Does this venture hinge on positing a threefold structure to reality and the divine life? Is three too few for those who love the many? Is the multiplicity of the divine life constricted to the number three? In what follows, trinitarianism is meant to serve as a kind of Nyssan middle between the one and the many, albeit with a difference. I appeal to trinity as a refutation of any privileging of the One that would dismiss the exuberant diversity of creation and divinity as merely epiphenomenal or otherwise unreal—as some varieties of monism do—and likewise hold to trinity against any vision of the many as sheer, arbitrary difference without relation. The number three is neither arbitrary nor absolute. This speculative trinitarianism is committed to a vision of God as ground, singularity, and relation. However, theologians would do well to remember the warning of the Fathers that number cannot mean in the divine life what it means in quotidian experience. Only finite realities can be enumerated; the infinite cannot. Neither one nor three can mean for the divine life what numbers mean in conventional experience. Nonetheless, I say three.

A final word before venturing into the details: what is ventured here is a speculative and philosophical trinitarianism. Such a venture is uncommon in Christian theology but not unprecedented. It is a way of thinking with and about the trinity that seeks to revivify Christian thinking about divinity but in a speculative key that stands at some distance from standard dogmatic disputations and creedal tests. Speculative trinitarian thinkers—I follow in the Tillichian line—stand at an angle to dogmatic affirmations seeking neither to contest them nor to insure that one stands in good orthodox standing. That posture of relative freedom from doctrinal testing is likely to be felt as unnerving to some and freeing to others. My hope is that what is ventured here will be marked by a thinking that is free but also faith-full. I do take note in what follows of my indebtedness to crucial possibilities opened up by Tillich, but that is not the central goal of this chapter, which is to think trinitarian formulations afresh from insights gained by encounter with other traditions.

## God as Ground

In what follows, I propose a provisional, speculative trinitarianism derived not just from Christian resources but also from Buddhist-Christian-Hindu trialogue. With other trinitarian theologians of religious diversity, I hold that if ultimate reality is trinity, then we should expect to see trinitarian disclosures in human experience and the structure of reality as such. Therefore, these other religious traditions might deepen and augment what Christians have come to know about God's trinitarian life in and through the incarnation and the dispensation of the Holy Spirit.

I would like to argue for a theological threefold of *ground, (source of) singularity, and relation*. This threefold names three dimensions of the divine life that I correlate with three dimensions of experience rooted in an ontological threefold. This ontological threefold is *being, singular and contingent being, and being in relation*; these three are fundamental mysteries that are intraworldly signals of transcendence pointing to the divine life. We receive these intraworldly signals through experiences of ontological wonder, wonder that opens onto the divine life.

First, there is the awareness of the wonder and mystery that there is anything at all. The sheer "isness" of every existent thing—that there is something rather than nothing—is a primordial source of wonderment. The theological conclusions that religious traditions draw from this wonderment are many and often incommensurable, but wonder about *the fact that there is anything at all* is an intraworldly signal of transcendence that points to divinity. A second and primordial source of wonderment is singularity. Singularity speaks both to the non-necessary character of each and every item of experience but also to the fact that everything whatsoever—from atoms, to leaves, to persons, and galaxies—is utterly singular. To exist is to exist as an inimitable this, a particular haecceity. A third and fundamental source of worldly astonishment is that nothing whatsoever exists in isolation. Not one of the concrete particulars found in experience exists in splendid isolation. It both is what it is and no other, but it is what it is precisely by being in relation with every other. To be is to be in relation.

Each of these mysteries points to a dimension of the divine life. The fact that there is anything at all rather than nothing, the sheer fact of being, points to God's character as ground, as being itself. All that is exists because of its participation in God who is the ground and source of being. Singular being points to God's character as (source of) singularity. God is the creator of every particular in its absolutely distinctive concreteness. There is something in the divine life that gives rise to a world of inexhaustible particularity and diversity. Finally, the fact that creation is characterized throughout as marked by relation—that nothing whatsoever exists apart from relation—points to God as relation and the power of relation. God does not give rise to a world of isolated particulars but rather gives rise to a world that is through and through relational. That the world is like this discloses a face of ultimate reality as itself relation and the power of relation.

This double threefold, worldly and divine, is resonant with traditional trinitarian discourse. God as Father is the ultimate ground of divinity itself and the world, God as Son/Logos is the principle of distinction within the divine life and the source of particularity in the world. To speak is to speak not language in general but to say something concrete and singular. The world is the Word's utterance, an utterance marked by a rich profusion of diversity, a play of infinite variation, an inexhaustible fecundity of difference. But the world is not the domain of sheer monadic difference wherein each contingent particular is locked away in splendid isolation from every other particular. Nothing whatsoever exists apart from relation, least of all divinity. Spirit in the divine life is that which animates and binds the world together as a world of relation and secures the flourishing of beings.

Although the connections between this double threefold and traditional trinitarian formulations are not hard to miss, my focus here is not to establish their proper Christian credentials but to show how this double threefold both captures something integral about the nature of the Real and points to core themes and motifs to be found within a variety of religious traditions. Although for the sake of simplicity, I will associate each of these notions with particular strands from Hindu, Christian, and Buddhist traditions, these three traditions, in some fashion, register all dimensions of this threefold although not in equal and emphatic balance. Religious thinkers and their communities are most often committed to one of these three concept-intuitions and so are unlikely to appreciate in equal measure what is celebrated in the remaining pair. Indeed, sharp theological tensions arise across and even within traditions because strands of tradition fail to register or even deny the equal importance of all elements in this threefold.

This summary presentation of a double threefold, worldly and divine, might be read as a general ontology derived by means of phenomenological reflection which is subsequently correlated with a speculative trinitarianism. Such a project might well be ventured, but that is not what follows. What I am offering is a trinitarianism derived from an unavoidably selective reading of some strands from Hindu, Christian, and Buddhist traditions. The trouble with such a survey is that traditions never present ideal types. Families within a given religious tradition articulate highly particular accounts of being and divinity grounded in distinctive religious experiences, readings of scriptures, and traditions of practice. Given this robust particularity, no comparative theological reading— including the one I offer—can stake a claim to neutrality. Hence, what I offer is one fallible reconstruction, one moreover, reflective of my own theological commitments and tradition of origin. This is just one Christian theologian's venture at redescribing the elephant after a series of forays into Buddhist and Hindu traditions.

I begin with the first conceptual pair: being or being as such and God as ground of being. Speech about being or being as such is likely to strike at least some readers as unbearably abstract, but not if one takes the thought of being to begin with the sense of wonder. The philosophical question "Why is there something rather than nothing?" is a conceptual articulation of a more fundamental and primary existential intuition of being that is prompted by wonder. By "wonder" I do not mean a sunny intuition, although it does sometimes find positive affective expression. The range of affective moods which might elicit wonder about being find rich and varied expression in the opening of Heidegger's *Introduction to Metaphysics*. There, Heidegger writes,

> . . . we are touched once, maybe even now and then, by the concealed power of this question, without properly grasping what is happening to us. In great *despair*, for example, when all weight tends to dwindle away from things and the sense of things grows dark, the question looms. Perhaps it strikes only once, like the muffled tolling of a bell that resounds into Dasein and gradually fades away. The question is there in heartfelt *joy*, for then all things are transformed and surround us as if for the first time, as if it were easier to grasp that they were not, rather than that they are, and are as they are. The question is there in a spell of *boredom*, when we are equally distant from despair and joy, but when the stubborn ordinariness of beings lays open a wasteland in which it makes no difference to us whether beings are or are not—and then, in a distinctive form, the question resonates once again: Why are there beings at all instead of nothing?[8]

Despair, joy, and even boredom might prompt the question of why there are beings at all. But the question is one that haunts us even if only implicitly so as a kind of nagging. And once the question is posed, the question of ground presents itself. We would do well to remain with Heidegger a while longer even if we must soon part and enter into terrain that he himself urges the philosopher to shun:

> The scope of our question is *so* broad that we can never exceed it. We are not interrogating this being or that being, nor all beings, each in turn; instead, we are asking from the start about the whole of what is . . . beings as a whole and as such.
>
> Just as it is the broadest question, the question is also the deepest: Why are there beings at all . . . ? Why—that is, what is the ground? From

what ground do beings come? To what ground do beings go? The question does not ask this or that about beings—what they are in each case, here and there, how they are put together how they can be changed, what they can be used for, and so on. . . . But, because we are questioning, it remains an open question whether the ground is truly a grounding, foundation-effecting, originary ground; whether the ground refuses to provide a foundation, and so is an abyss; whether the ground is neither one nor the other, but merely offers the perhaps necessary illusion of a foundation and is thus an un-ground.[9]

We see here a shift from a beginning with moods that precipitate a wondering, a querying, to the metaphysical turn, an asking after ground. That turn is marked by a striking negation generated by the depth—and depth is the appropriate metaphor—of the query itself. What is the character of the negation? The turn away from particulars qua particulars. Particularity is registered but is not the focus of attention. Instead, the question is, What ground must there be for beings to be at all regardless of their particularity, beings as a whole and as such? This is significant for our project of naming three kinds of ontological attention or wondering. In other kinds of ontological querying, particularity is most emphatically the focus of attention, but not here, not now, not when the question is about being as such. In the question about what can be said to ground every being as such, the focus turns instead to what grounds every particular. In a powerful speculation in which Heidegger's indebtedness to medieval theology is evident, Heidegger notes that the foundation may prove to be an abyss, not a ground but an unground, evoking resonances with Meister Eckhart and Jacob Boehme.

"Why is there something rather than nothing" is the question to which Jim Holt's gripping *Why Does the World Exist? An Existential Detective Story* is dedicated. Holt observes that both Heidegger and Wittgenstein are taken with the question. With respect to Wittgenstein, Holt points to his war notebooks wherein Wittgenstein writes, "Aesthetically, the miracle is that the world exists."[10] Holt pairs that snippet from the war notebook with another brief apothegm from the *Tractatus Logico-Philosophicus* wherein Wittgenstein writes, "It is not *how* things are in the world that is mystical, but *that* it exists."[11]

Both Heidegger and Wittgenstein offer compelling testimony that it is possible to register the "thatness" of beings apart from their "whatness." What each makes of that recognition is a tale of utter contrast. Heidegger is prompted by wonder into an interrogation of the being of beings. Wittgenstein, however, does not believe that sheer mysterious thatness can lead to philosophical interrogation. It can be recognized as a matter of phenomenological witness but, given the limits of language, nothing further can be said. As Holt summarizes Wittgenstein's take on the matter: "attempting to explain the 'aesthetic miracle' of the world's existence was futile; it took one beyond the limits of language, Wittgenstein held, into the realm of the unsayable. While he 'deeply respected' the urge to ask *Why is there something rather than nothing?* he ultimately believed the question to be senseless. As he starkly put it in Tractatus proposition 6.5, 'The riddle does not exist.'"[12]

For Heidegger, by contrast, the philosopher can meaningfully ask about the ground of being, but one proposed answer is rejected: the theological turn to God. In what follows, I depart from both Heidegger and Wittgenstein by making just that theological turn, albeit in a key that Heidegger may not find distasteful, not least because I am guided by a theologian who was tutored, in part, by conversations with Heidegger and Heidegger's medieval sources. I have in mind Paul Tillich who ventured an account of God, not as a being among beings, not even Leibniz's necessary being, but rather God as ground (and abyss) of being.

In any case, for Heidegger, the theological turn is a refusal to ask the question—to genuinely endure the question itself—because the question is cut off before it is ventured by God as answer: ". . . anyone for whom the Bible is divine revelation and truth already has the answer to the question . . . before it is even asked: beings, with the exception of God Himself, are created by Him. God Himself 'is' as the uncreated Creator. One who holds on to such faith as a basis can, perhaps, emulate and participate in the asking of our question in a certain way, but he cannot authentically question without giving himself up as a believer, with all the consequences of this step."[13] With this Heideggerian argument that theology is a foreclosure of the question of being, a foolishness that refuses to engage the question, we take our leave from philosophical consideration of the deliverance of wonder about the reality of thatness.

We take from both Heidegger and Wittgenstein, as we leave, their shared wonder about the sheer givenness of things, not in their singular particularity, but in the very isness of whatever there is, of all there is. We then inaugurate an interreligious turn to ponder those traditions in which this recognition becomes a matter for theological attention and elaboration. We observe that in a variety of traditions under consideration, the sheer being of beings comes into relief by way of contrast elicited by the possible nonbeing of everything that is—hence the contrast, Why is there something rather than *nothing*? In other traditions, the sense of possible nonbeing seems less in the foreground than the overwhelming presence of, well, presence. Wherever one turns, one sees being, an underlying something that is sometimes imagined as substance. How isness/ thatness is treated leads to diverse strands of theological reflection. The moods under which the intuition of thatness is recognized also bear on the theological proposals that follow.

The turn to ultimacy, diversely named and understood, is a common interreligious turn, though not all strands of traditions make the turn to postulating the necessary being that Heidegger rejects. The character of the turn—from recognition of being to ultimacy—takes historically particular tradition-determined trajectories. Theologians call isness/thatness by many names even when there is a shared appeal to ultimacy. Hence, we now turn not only to particular religious traditions but to specific strands thereof.

Two affirmations though are made, at least in Hindu and Buddhist traditions, and in a different key also in the Christian West. The first is that sense of presence called being just is divine and is a name for divinity. Anything that is, exists because either it has a share in being-itself or because it just is being itself, which is divine. This notion finds expression in Buddhist, Hindu, and Christian traditions. Somewhat subtler and more complex is a second claim—that our awareness of being, indeed awareness itself, is itself also divine. The light by which we behold being is itself also divine. Hence, ultimate reality is both ground of being as well as the ground of knowing.

By ground, I refer to what Christians have typically referred to as the first person of the trinity. I derive the term from Paul Tillich's language of God as ground of being while remembering his added proviso that the ground is also as an unfathomable abyss. But rather than begin by characterizing God as ground by appeal to Christian resources, I turn to the Upanishads and the Advaita Vedanta commentarial tradition as exemplified in writing of the master teacher of that tradition, Sankara. In his commentary on the famous passage from the Chandogya Upanishad, "In the beginning all this was being (*sat*), One only, without a second," Sankara argues that all reality is but a transformation of Brahman, understood as being.[14] Just as clay pots, jars, cups, and the like are ultimately nothing but modifications of one lump of clay, so the world is ultimately nothing but Brahman. The world emerges from undifferentiated being-itself, and that is Brahman. Elsewhere, the Upanishads and Sankara also employ the image of sparks and flame to designate the nonduality of the world (sparks) and Brahman (flame).

Ultimately, Sankara pulls back from the language of the world as a transformation of Brahman in order to assert the unchangeable immutability of Brahman as world ground. Sankara invites readers to distinguish between two intuitions that are given in any experience—namely, the particular item of experience, on the one hand, and the intuition of being on the other. So if one sees a pot and affirms that "the pot is," Sankara would point out that whereas the pot comes and goes, the sense of being persists. One is never without the sense of being. That sense of being which is given everywhere points to the world ground that abides whereas particulars come and go. To return to the metaphor of clay and pots, jars, and the like, the clay is real and enduring in a way that its modifications are not. The encounter with being in and through and, ultimately, underneath particulars points to an abiding and infinite world ground—namely, Brahman—that upholds but is not equivalent to those particulars.

In his commentary on the Great Utterance (*mahavakya*) found in the Brhadaranyaka Upanishad, "In the beginning, all this was Brahman indeed. It knew itself as, 'I am Brahman, (*ahambrahmasmi*).'" Sankara argues that this world ground is not merely being but also the true and innermost Self (*atman*).[15] The self is understood as eternal luminous consciousness and not merely as the contingent psychophysical formations that make up quotidian identity. The latter formations are, just like the pot, too passing to be mistaken for the true abiding Self. When one sees that the light of consciousness (*cit*) that shines in the mind is the true Self and not the finite threatened egoistic person, then one stops living a life driven by compulsions. The result of understanding one's true identity is liberation from the cycle of rebirth. The transethical consequence of such knowledge is compassion rooted in knowledge of the nonduality of Brahman and self as well as nonduality between self and other. The true Self is one in all.

The discourse of ground then applies not just to the presentation of ultimate reality as being but also to consciousness as the ground of all experiencing. What makes experience possible is not itself one of the evanescent items to be experienced. Rather, consciousness (*cit*) is the ever present condition for the possibility of experiencing. Hence ground language is applicable to the true Self. The striking move that the Advaita tradition makes is that the ground of being and the ground of experiencing are the same. Brahman is both the world's ground as being-itself and the ground of the Self (*atman*) as consciousness. These two are not-two. Hence being-itself is consciousness.

There is no way to appreciate this abbreviated articulation of the Advaita Vedanta interpretive scheme independently of the therapeutic regimen and the diagnosis implied by that therapeutic regimen. What ails us, the human predicament as understood by Sankara's reading of the Upanishads, is bondage to the fundamental ignorance (*avidya*) of this nonduality. When human beings take themselves to be exhausted by their finite conventional identities as composed of caste, gender, stage of life, and the like, they inevitably feel themselves to be vulnerable. Out of that vulnerability, human beings become captive to craving, hatred, and delusion, the three great poisons in the Advaita tradition. They crave and are addicted to what promises to complete them, and they are averse to what threatens them. The cumulative force of this competing push and pull generates the profound disorientation called delusion. Captive to these forces, human beings perpetuate incalculable personal and social harm and are captive to the cycle of transmigration. Liberation from this cycle comes from knowledge provided by the scripture that the Self (*atman*) is the ultimate (Brahman). That is the point made in the *Brhadaranyaka* Upanishad: *Ahambrahmasmi*. I am Brahman.

Ultimately, the Upanishads, as read by Sankara, contend that Brahman is ineffable and beyond language and thought. It is immanent as ground but transcendent as mystery. One can know that one is Brahman, but Brahman itself cannot be known. Though designated provisionally as being, it exceeds all name and form. It is the ground for all that has name and form, but it exceeds all name and form even as it grounds them. Human beings are thus understood to be the ultimate luminous and unknowable mystery that no words can reach—not even the words "ground" or "being" or even "consciousness." Crucial here for the Advaitin is that the sheer being of the world is mystery, but what draws the Advaitin's attention is not the particular being of things qua particular. What captivates is that the world of name and form—though name and form are themselves utterly evanescent—nevertheless points to and speaks of being as such. Being which shines in everything whatsoever—actually for the Advaitin *underneath* everything—is holy mystery.

And here then is a crucial observation: at least in Sankara's Advaita, there is little intrinsic interest in the particularities of conventional worldly experience, let alone any feeling for the mystery of singularity. What captures attention—what captures religious sensibility, and what persons are then encouraged to cultivate—is attention to the intuition of being as such. In terms of the categories of the theory of the religious articulated in Chapter 5, Sankara trains his readers to a mode of comprehensive qualitative orientation in which attention is directed away from the particulars of experience to the ground of those particulars and the ground of experiencing as such, which is Brahman. The result of being stabilized in the knowledge that one is Brahman returns the wise knower to the world of particulars in a spirit of care and compassion, but attention to those particulars in their singularity is not a disposition that the therapeutic regimen of Advaita Vedanta seeks to foster in its practitioners.

Even the term "ground" is not quite on the mark. To speak of Brahman as ground is already to see Brahman from the standpoint of singularity. Brahman is ground when it serves as ground for something other than itself. Hence to name Brahman as ground or, in the vocabulary of the tradition itself, as Lord (*Isvara*) is already to see Brahman from the standpoint of otherness, of secondness, to use Peircean vocabulary. While Sankara is open to seeing Brahman from this perspective—we must begin from the world of singularity after all—that is not the final truth about Brahman. Hence, his desire to move beyond discourses of origin and source to a discourse of being as such, one only without a second. At this point, language inevitably breaks down because even a discourse of Brahman as being is rooted in the character of Brahman as source of being to beings. That is why Sankara's discourse takes, in the final analysis, an apophatic turn. The itinerary is complete: from Brahman as world source and creator, the source of being for every singular being, to being itself (*sat*) and finally to the truth that what one truly is exceeds language as such.

What one sees in Sankara is an exquisite and increasingly rigorous focus of attention. To teach the truth that one just is Brahman—and that this identity underlies all contingent and evanescent identities—attention is redirected away from singularity. For this reason—the selectivity of attention and its further disciplined cultivation—we can see why it may prove to be difficult to hold with equal reverence the three intuitions of being and their place within ultimate reality. This selectivity of religious attention is no mark of failure. Grounded in a primary religious intuition regarding the wonder that there is anything at all, that specific intuition is further molded through a reading of the Upanishads in which this mode of religious knowing finds explicit warrant.

However, other strands of the Vedanta tradition differ in that to which they attend. Ramanuja and his tradition of qualified nondualism (Visistadvaita) seek to balance attention to the oneness of Brahman and world while attending also to the singularities of the world. Qualified nondualism still holds that Brahman is all, but it does so by positing that the world itself is also affirmed as real. There is no turn of attention away from singularity, and, therefore, notions of Brahman as Lord are never held to be penultimate to some other truer encounter with Brahman. Indeed, Visistadvaita theologians worry about Advaita's turn away from singularity and find therein a temptation toward treating the world as illusory. This attention to and reverence for difference is even more emphatically affirmed by Madhva's thoroughgoing dualism. Even Ramanuja does not go far enough for Madhva's satisfaction. Attention to what I am calling singularity leads him to affirm several sharp dualisms, between God and world, and between souls and inert matter. These differences can never be sublated or reduced to some more basic underlying unity.

Each strand of tradition finds warrants for its position within the expansive scriptural and devotional repertoire of Hindu traditions and then formulates interpretive schemes and therapeutic regimen to cultivate in practitioners the appropriate mode of comportment called for by their respective readings. Might it be the case that the tensions and debates within strands of a single tradition, in this case Brahmanical Vedanta, strands that otherwise share so much in common, suggest that these strands and the communities to which they belong are claimed primarily by distinct intuitions of being which then lead to different theologies of ultimate reality? That is my claim. Should reverence to singularity become the all-encompassing focus of religious attention, difference reigns over all. God is then envisioned as other to the world, and the world other than God, and everything in the world different from every other thing. Should reverence to relation claim attention, what rises to focus as final and holy are readings of the ultimate as relation itself, what Buber calls "the between." And, as we have seen with Sankara, when attention rests on the sheer being of all things, that there is being at all, the surpassing name of ultimate reality becomes being-itself. My argument is that each of these ways of encountering ultimate reality cannot be reduced to mere projection; each has a secure foothold in both in the structure of the world, hence the structure of experience, as well as in ultimate reality itself.

Knowledge of being and ultimate reality as ground of being or being-itself are not an exclusive features of Advaita Vedanta. Ontological attention to ultimate reality as disclosed in being, and being-itself as ultimate is a feature of many traditions including Christian and even Buddhist traditions. That ground discourse is to be found in Buddhist traditions is not as well known as it should be. In the case of Tibetan Buddhist traditions, this lacuna may be due to a focus on the Dalai Lama's own Geluk tradition as opposed to, for example, reading the Nyingma tradition. Thankfully, that omission is now steadily being rectified. Particularly helpful in this regard is Douglas Duckworth's lucid work on Mipam's (1846–1912) understanding of Buddha-nature. Duckworth carefully shows that Mipam is not just willing to speak of Buddha-nature as a positive ground but argues that there must be such a ground for awakening to be possible. Duckworth writes, "The primordial endowment of the qualities of Buddha in sentient beings is a central part of the Mipam's presentation of Buddha-nature. . . . In contrast, exegetes in the Geluk tradition argue that scriptural statements that depict a Buddha-nature that is a permanent exalted body, with the qualities of the Buddha existing in sentient beings, are the provisional meaning."[16]

Duckworth offers a rich presentation of the interpretative debates among Tibetan Buddhists about the meaning of emptiness (*sunyata*). Is emptiness to be understood as negative or as a positive empty ground? More on the negative reading later, but I will telegraph here that I read this debate as one about whether ultimate reality is to be understood as *ground* or *relation*. After all, the negative reading of emptiness offered by Gelukpa thinkers is negative for a reason. As I note below, all things are said to be empty of self-existence or essence precisely in order to affirm that to be is to be in relation. Negation clears the ground for affirmation. But Mipam and his tradition posit the need for a deeper affirmation. There must be a positive ground for the qualities to be found in the Buddha and those who are awakened. Here, we see at work an argument internal to Tibetan Buddhist traditions about whether to construe ultimate reality as ground or as relation. The debates between Buddhist traditions express a keenly felt tension that it may not be possible to affirm both. Posit a positive ground beneath and within experience, and there is a fear that attention to the between will be missed. The world of the between is diminished in value when compared with value placed on ground. By contrast, speak only of emptiness as negative and there is the fear that a too thoroughgoing negation will lead to nihilism.

To avoid that negative possibility, Mipam posits a ground that makes possible both wisdom and compassion—the two cardinal qualities of awakened beings.

> In terms of the essence of the abiding reality itself, all phenomena are encompassed within the expanse of suchness and the essence of suchness itself abides, without arising or ceasing, as equality; without temporal distinctions such as the past or future, or aspects such as the good or bad, here or there, self or other, greater and lesser, in samsara or nirvana, etc.—the expanse of phenomena is the unchanging single sphere (*thig le nyag gcig*). Although the abiding reality is as such, in accord with the perspective of the appearances of adventitious delusion, even when bodies, minds, and domains of the three realms of samsara appear in this way and the nature of suchness is not seen, it is not that suchness does not exist; it exists without deviating in the slightest from its own nature. Therefore, although the suchness of mind is as such, it is not actualized due to being enclosed by adventitious defilements. Even so, it abides in the manner of an extract or an essential core in the center and is called "heritage" or the "essential nature".... [17]

The vocabulary is distinctively Buddhist (suchness is here Buddha-nature), but the general ontological thrust—and this might distress some Buddhists to affirm—is resonant with discourses about Brahman as ontological ground not only of beings but also of knowing because it is luminous consciousness itself.

What is distinctive in Mipam's Buddhism is that phenomena, all phenomena, are "encompassed within the expanse of suchness" whereas, in many moments, Sankara seeks to install a greater distance between Brahman and phenomenal beings. This difference is noteworthy as it gives rise to the possibility that phenomenal beings, in their very singularity, can be prized in Mipam's ground discourse in ways that Sankara's language makes challenging. True, both traditions seek to peer behind the singularity of beings to their unchanging ground, but in Mipam there appears to be a greater and more positive intimacy between phenomena and their ground. Hence Mipam writes, "From the beginning all phenomena are—as equality—the actual Buddha, primordially nirvana, naturally luminous and clear...." Duckworth states, "In actual reality, all phenomena are primordially Buddha in the essence of the Truth Body, which is the suchness of all phenomena."[18]

This primordial nature is explicitly called *ground* of all phenomena; ground discourse is not an extraneous importation into Buddhist materials from Christian or Hindu sources. Duckworth cites the work of Dolpopa (1292–1361), who asserts, "Moreover, this which is thusness, the Buddha-nature—having many synonyms such as suchness and so forth—is the ground of all phenomena."[19] We have, therefore, solid warrants to claim that ground—*gzhi* in Tibetan—has some interreligious generalizability.

In Christian traditions, the most prominent recent thinker of God as being-itself and ground of being is, of course, Paul Tillich. For Tillich, all beings have their being by way of participation from being-itself, which he also calls the ground of being. Tillich's discourse about divinity hinges itself on stringently asserting that God is not a being among beings so much so that Tillich is willing to assert that it is truer to say that God does not exist than to say that God does. Only beings exist. That which grounds all beings does not. The source of existence does not itself exist. What, then, is the relation between being-itself and beings? This question is a matter of great subtlety in Tillich's theology. Tillich is reluctant to use the language of causality as Tillich believes that none of the basic categories of thought is applicable to divinity. If God is imagined as cause of the world, Tillich believes that it becomes inevitable that God becomes the first in a chain of causation and is thereby rendered into the first and necessary being—an account which he wishes to reject.

Tillich also operates with another perhaps peculiarly Christian theological constraint. He holds that "the relation of the ground of revelation to those who receive revelation can be conceived *only* in personal categories; for that which is the ultimate concern of a person cannot be less than a person although it can be and must be more than personality."[20] While it is true that personal language for ultimate reality is nearly universal across religious traditions, having just encountered strands of Hindu and Buddhist traditions that tend to downgrade personal discourse and prioritize transpersonal accounts of ultimacy—traditions that have no particular difficulty in downgrading the relative significance of personal discourse—Tillich's "only" assertion is difficult to affirm. His comparative generalization is empirically unsustainable. What is important here is that Tillich perceives a double threat posed by the combination of symbolic exigencies and categorical temptations: both impel believers to slip into discourse that imagines ultimate reality as a being among beings, as a cause among causes, albeit the first cause, as a being among beings, even if the necessary or supreme being. Here, the language of "ground" has special utility and appeal for Tillich:

> Under these circumstances, the theologian must emphasize the symbolic character of all concepts which are used to describe the divine act of self-revelation, and he must try to use terms which indicate that their meaning is not categorical. "Ground" is such a term. It oscillates between cause and substance and transcends both of them. It indicates that the ground of revelation is neither a cause which keeps itself at a distance from revelatory effect nor a substance which effuses itself into the effect, but rather the mystery which appears in revelation and which remains a mystery in its appearance.[21]

What Tillich says here about God as revelation, he says elsewhere about God as ground of being. God is neither the cause of beings nor the substance of beings. As cause, God stands at too great a remove from beings. As substance, creatures have no independence from God. The singularity of creatures is lost. Ground discourse avoids dangers that come with both "cause" and "substance," while preserving both divine intimacy and creaturely distinctiveness and freedom.

So intimate is God as ground that Tillich's discourse comes into deep proximity to the nondualistic features of both Buddhist and Hindu ground discourse. Tillich's radicalness on this score has insufficiently been recognized. After all, Tillich stands prepared to say that God has no "external relations" with creatures! He writes,

> God as being-itself is the ground of every relation. In his life all relations are present beyond the distinctions between potentiality and actuality. But they are not the relations of the divine life with something else. They are the inner relations of the divine life. The internal relations are, of course, not conditioned by the actualization of finite freedom. But the question is whether there are external relations between God and the creature. The doctrine of creation affirms that God is the creative ground of everything in every moment. In this sense there is no creaturely independence from which an external relation between God and the creature could be derived.[22]

The doctrine of creation from the standpoint of a ground of being theology posits that creatures are inseparably bound to the divine life because

God "keeps" the creature in being in every moment. God is the creature's ground, and hence the relationship between God and creature must be called internal. Our Advaitin and Nyingma friends would, of course, prefer the term "nonduality." There is no ontological "outside" to the divine life. In a sense, then, Tillich's ground of being theology stands in considerable proximity to explicitly nondual ground traditions.

And there is no reason to wonder that this is the case. Tillich scholars know that more than virtually any other theologian of his time—surely any other Protestant theologian—Tillich was steeped in medieval theologians like Meister Eckhart and Nicholas Cusanus who explicitly, and to their great peril, embraced nondual convictions. His transtheistic theology of God as ground signals how even in dominantly theistic traditions, being-itself finds compelling articulation.

## God as Singularity

And yet, Tillich might be said to have a love-hate relationship with medieval forebears who are often classified as belonging to the mystical tradition; on the one hand, his theological labors evince a love for a certain "mystical element" and yet, in the final analysis, he refuses mysticism as such. Why? Because of what I am here calling singularity. Already in the previous quote, Tillich is cautious with his language. For Tillich, the creature is not, in every sense, identical to the divine life. Insofar as creatures are (not just possess) "finite freedom," they are not, in Tillich's language, "kept within the divine life." Insofar as creatures can engage in self-contradiction and hence act against the divine, they must be free because creatures bear individuality. In fact, for Tillich, a thinker of polarities, no thinking about either human beings or about divinity is adequate that ignores that all reality is marked by this polarity of individualization and participation. Emphasize one pole over the other in how we think about creatures or creator, and distortion is sure to result.

Every creature bears the marks of both individualization and participation, and both polarities are themselves part of the divine life. And, yet, it is in human beings—in persons that individuation finds for Tillich fullest expression:

> Although the individualization of a plant or an animal is expressed even in the smallest part of its centered whole, it is significant only in unity with individual persons or unique historical events. The individuality of

a nonhuman being gains significance if it is drawn into the processes of human life. But only then. Man [*sic*] is different. Even in collectivistic societies the individual as the bearer and, in the last analysis, the aim of the collective is significant rather than the species.[23]

Much here is contestable, from a variety of viewpoints. What is worth noting is Tillich's positive affirmation that individualization marks everything that is, not just humans. But it is in human beings, who are historical creatures, in which individualization arrives at fullest expression. There may be repeating patterns in history, but by definition, the events of history are fundamentally and ineradicably singular. Still, Tillich is emphatic: "Without individualization nothing would exist to be related. Without participation the category of relation would have no basis in reality. Every relation includes a kind of participation."[24] Within this snippet, all three terms of my threefold find expression, ground, singularity, and relation. But let us remain with singularity a while longer.

By singularity, I have in mind most especially theistic traditions and their appreciation not just for the wonder that anything is at all but rather the *irreducibly distinctive* character of all that is. I focus herein primarily on Christian theological readings of singularity wherein accounts of creation tend to be so dominant as to drown out other intuitions of being and divinity to the point that they are regarded as heretical. Here again, we see how attention to just one ontological intuition runs the risk that other modes of encounter with divinity are dismissed or are cordoned off into a tradition's esoteric strands. That is certainly what has transpired within mainstream Christian reflection. Tillich's primary influences, Nicholas and Eckhart, certainly met this fate. One of Eckhart's primary inspirations—namely, Marguerite Porete—was not merely marginalized but was burned at the stake for her nondualistic intuitions.

For Christian traditions, the doctrine of creation is the feature of its interpretive schemes that warrants such razor-like focus on questions of singularity. "God saw everything that he had made, and indeed, it was very good." Contrary to the Advaita impulse to look underneath name and form, singularity speaks to the conviction that each and every particular is what it is and has an intensity and singularity of value: just this arch of an eyebrow, just this particular curve of the face, just this chin and no other, just this Jewish carpenter who makes all the difference. Contingency also names the Jewish and Christian conviction that God plus world is more than God alone. As we have seen in our discussion of creaturely freedom in Tillich, God gives rise to what is not in every sense identical to himself or precontained in the divine plenitude.

The link between creation and singularity comes to limpid expression in Mary Oliver's poem "The Summer Day." In it, the poet asks,

> Who made the world?
> Who made the swan, and the black bear?
> Who made the grasshopper?
> *This grasshopper, I mean*—
> the one who has flung herself out of the grass,
> the one who is eating sugar out of my hand,
> who is moving her jaws back and forth instead of up and down—
> who is gazing around with her enormous and complicated eyes.
> Now she lifts her pale forearms and thoroughly washes her face.
> Now she snaps her wings open, and floats away.[25]

The theme of singularity is to be found in the poet's exquisite act of focused attention, one that leaves aside questions about the world as such or even the swan and the black bear as species but turns instead to her ode to *just this grasshopper*, the one who sits in Oliver's hand eating sugar and whose jaws move in just this back and forth fashion rather than up and down. It is the precious, albeit evanescent grasshopper, the one who "floats away," who teaches Oliver something about the nature of God's creative activity. God gives rise to singularity.

To celebrate singularity is to assert the worth and value of every element in creation as intrinsically good, good just in its very fragility and transience. And transient, indeed, is every singular. Oliver names the truth: "Doesn't everything die at last, and too soon?" Her grasshopper and now she herself have passed. To see each singular qua singular is to see both the loveliness and inimitable distinctiveness of every particular, but also to be haunted by what Whitehead and process theologians call "perpetual perishing." Each singular is here today and gone tomorrow. Hence, singularity and the truth of contingency are inseparable. And yet, these two sides of one coin are hard to hold together in mind. Some traditions that recognize the impermanence of singulars are haunted by a sense of their unreality. Hence, the turn to a ground or an unchanging real that is more real than fading singulars. Also possible is an invitation to look unwaveringly at impermanence in order to cultivate a sense of detachment so as to eliminate the pain that is inevitable for those who seek to hold on to what cannot be grasped.

Traditions in which singularity is prized, however, are not undone by the recognition of perpetual perishing. To be is to be fleeting *and to be precious*, precious precisely because we are fleeting.

Theistic traditions can affirm that by creating the world, God generates concrete instantiations of value. To insist on the distinction between world and God is to celebrate the irreducible worth of creaturely life. The worth of singular beings cannot be well affirmed in philosophical or theological accounts in which creaturely lives are said to be already (pre) contained in the divine life and only made manifest in creation, with no gain or loss to the divine life. In such traditions, the attempt to praise the glory of divine plenitude, at the expense of the rich world of concrete particulars, misses the meaning of the doctrine of creation. The doctrine of *creatio ex nihilo* is not so much meant to stipulate that God, by way of an exercise of sheer unilateral power, makes creatures to be out of sheer absolute nothingness (*ouk on*) as it is meant to affirm that the divine life is enriched by the life of the world in a way that some Neoplatonic accounts of creation as overflowing of the divine life cannot do. The world is more than the diminished exteriorization of what is already contained in the perfection of the divine life.

Speaking as a father of a lovely and utterly singular daughter, I want to affirm that the meaning of the doctrine of creation is that her particular being enriches God's very life—that my Katie adds a measure of richness to the divine life by virtue of her singular and lovely being, however contingent and evanescent. It seems entirely right to say, as a host of theologians have, that the divine life is not diminished by creation, but what is needed also is a robust affirmation that divine life is enriched by creaturely life precisely because the latter is not a mere manifestation of the former.

The contemporary strand of the Christian tradition that has best given expression to this affirmation is process theology. Alfred North Whitehead's account of God's consequent nature posits that God prehends each and every singular being. What a thing is, most fundamentally, is actualized value. To be is to be precious. When God's consequent nature prehends creatures, that value enriches the divine life itself. Indeed, Whitehead and process theologians insist that God's primordial nature is pure ideality and, as such, is deficient. In the primordial nature there is only potentiality but no actuality. The divine plenitude, apart from creation, is therefore on a plenitude of possibility. Actualized value requires creation.

In popular theological writing, the Franciscan contemplative, Richard Rohr, channels his lineage to make comparable points by drawing on his medieval predecessor, the Subtle Doctor, John Duns Scotus on haecceity. Rohr writes,

> . . . Blessed John Duns Scotus (1266–1308) taught extensively on the absolute uniqueness of each act of creation. His doctrine of *haecceity* is derived from *haec*, the Latin word for "this." Duns Scotus said the absolute freedom of God allows God to create, or *not* to create, each creature. Its existence means God has positively chosen to create that creature, precisely as it is. Each creature is thus not merely one member of a genus and species, but a unique aspect of the infinite Mystery of God. *God is continuously choosing each created thing specifically to exist, moment by moment.* This teaching alone made Duns Scotus a favorite of mystics and poets like Gerard Manley Hopkins and Thomas Merton, who both considered themselves "Scotists"—as do I.

Without formally committing myself to Scotus's distinctive notion of *haecceitas*—the metaphysical implications of this notion are tangled and may prove to be unnecessary in a non-substantialist metaphysics—I share in Fr. Rohr's affirmation of what I am calling singularity. Rohr is right to argue, alongside Scotus, that,

> you cannot know something spiritually by saying it is a *not-that*, by negation or distinguishing it from something else. You can only know anything by meeting it in its precise and irreplaceable *thisness* and honoring it there. Each individual act of creation is a once-in-eternity choice on God's part. The direct implication of this truth is that *love must precede all true knowledge,* which was at the heart of all Franciscan-based philosophy.[26]

To affirm singularity in either the process theological key or by way of the Scotist heritage is unlikely to lead theologians to equate beings with being itself or to ontologize away the distinction between divinity and world. On the contrary, the impulse will be to affirm that there is something in divinity that serves as source of singularity. For Christian theologians, that is precisely the nature and work of the Logos through whom all things come into being. There is in the divine life a *fundamentum in re* for a world replete with singularities.

By contrast, as already noted, those who orient themselves to the mystery of being qua being, and hence to the mystery of ultimate reality as ground and abyss, run the risk of dismissing singularity because each and every singular is contingent and fleeting. No singular is enduringly real in the way that their ground is. Hence, their focus shifts to the sheer fact of being and not singular being.

Those who celebrate singularity insist that every particular is a communicative expression of a good beyond being. Creation comes about through the Logos of God and is itself an expression of that Logos. The God whose Logos gives rise to the lovely world can be experienced as a lover who loves the lovely world into being. To acknowledge and celebrate singularity is to experience the ground not just as an impersonal or transpersonal absolute but as a personal, creative, and communicative source—as the Father and Mother of the Logos. God speaks the world into being and sustains the world in being. The world itself is a logos of God, the speech of God, and the gift of God. God gives Godself to the world by speaking the world into being and giving to the world concrete, lovely, and contingent (need not have been but now is) being. The world's being is not simply and without remainder the same as God's being.

The human predicament when seen in light of singularity is the failure of particular persons and communities to love God's lovely world and cherish the giver of that world. Whereas ignorance of the nonduality of self and absolute ground is the shape of the human predicament in Advaita, the human predicament under the sign of singularity is a failure to love widely as well as particularly. The shape of this failure can be variegated, but we can speak of a constricted selfhood that does not love widely and with passionate intensity. Love is of insufficient breadth should it love only what is one's own—one's family alone, one's nation alone. Even the hypocrites do that. Nevertheless, under the sign of singularity, there can be no mandate to renounce particular loves. Apart from singularity, there is no possibility of the erotic, of a genuine, inexhaustible, and generous desire for the other in all his, her, or their concrete loveliness. Where there is no otherness, divine or human, there can be no eros for the other.

Sankara and the Advaita tradition urge human beings to renounce particular and contingent loves for the sake of realizing nonduality. The focus of our attention is called away from our particular and contingent being to the sheer fact of being. When one has realized the nonduality of self and Brahman and so is no longer captive to the narrow and constricted ego, a universal compassion takes its place. The calling of singularity is otherwise. True, it is also a calling to move beyond constricted and egoistic selfhood, but the calling of singularity is for a deeper and, yes, erotic appreciation for the loveliness of the world and loveliness of the world's giver. The vocation is not to give up on particular loves but to expand the range of particular loves without surrendering the call toward intensity which can only be fulfilled when we limit ourselves for the sake of reverence and piety to loving just this particular person or partner.

But is singularity also rooted in the divine life? Is the divine life itself marked by singularity, and if so, in what sense? On the one hand, the very idea of singularity as presented herein is meant to affirm the real ontological status of the world and the world's particulars as irreducible to divinity. The world both is the scene of difference and is itself a difference that makes it *not God* or at least not reducible to God. God gives rise to what is not merely Godself. That said, further questions remain: Is the divine life enriched by the world God creates? Is there something in the divine life that impels and receives the luxuriant prolixity of worldly particularity? Is God changed by the loving labor of creativity? Does the world birthed by divine labor remain merely ad extra, outside the divine life?

A Christian scriptural resource for thinking these questions can be found in Colossians wherein the writer describes the Christ as

> . . . the image of the invisible God, the firstborn of all creation; for in him all things were created in heaven and on earth, visible and invisible, whether thrones or dominions or principalities or authorities—all things were created through him and *for him*. He is before all things and in him all things hold together. (Col 1:15–17; NRSV; emphasis added)

The author portrays the Christ as the principle of singularity within the divine life. The Christ is the one in and through whom the world is created. Still more, the world is created *for him*.

What is the meaning of this *for him*? Perhaps it means that the reality within the divine life which gives rise to singularity is also enriched by that very singularity. The world is made *for* the Christ and it is sustained *in* the Christ who holds the world together. The divine life is enriched by the worldly life to which it gives rise. The principle of singularity within the divine life is "before all things" and is not itself one of those things. Those things, however, can enrich the Christ precisely because they are not what He is, and He is not what they are. He is enriched by

what He is not—at least not at first. Insofar as the Christ holds them together, they now become part of his very life. In this sense, the divine
life is enriched by the distinct but not separate life of the world.[27]

## God as Relation

Let us now turn to the third in our trinity—namely relation, a third that
has already been broached both here and also in our discussion of Nagarjuna in Chapter 4. Relation names the truth that nothing *whatsoever* is
what it is apart from its relation. To be is to be in relation. This truth finds
exemplary expression in the Madhyamaka truth of emptiness. To be more
specific still, it is the Gelukpa reading of emptiness that is most resolutely
insistent on the truth of relationality. Gelukpa Madhyamikas insist that
to speak of emptiness is not to posit some impersonal world ground or
ground of consciousness that is empty. To say that everything is empty
is to say that no thing whatsoever has self-existence or own-being. Indeed, to be is to be no thing at all, if to be a thing is to have some own-
being or self-existence (*svabhava*) that an entity possesses apart from
relationship. Nothing whatsoever exists outside of relation. More rigorously still, no being whatsoever has an essence or core that it is non-
relationally derived, not even God. On this reading, emptiness is just
another way of designating that all of reality is *pratityasamutpada*, dependent co-arising.[28]

The human predicament is understood under the sign of relation as
craving, craving generated by the false idea that one is a disconnected
and non-relational self. The ignorant notion that one is a self apart from
relation generates a constricted ego that imagines the world to be made
up of things that the self can then grasp. There is something tragicomic
about the human predicament so understood: when human beings take
themselves to be disconnected and reified entities and take the world to
be likewise composed of such things, they are impelled toward grasping
just those realities with which they are already intimately bound in and
through relation. I seek to own you as a thing when I could discover that
you and I are already bound up in utter intimacy if I come to see that
neither I nor you are a thing that grasps or a thing to be grasped. Madhyamaka Buddhists share with Advaitins the sense that the ego is driven
by craving, hatred, and delusion, but they differ radically about the cure
to this ailment. The cure is not to discover the true Self that is the world's
ground, but to discover that there is no self whatsoever apart from rela-

tion. There is no transworldly absolute according to the Madhyamikas.[29] Posting such an absolute behind the world is to risk losing the manifest world of relation. After all, the absolute is by definition that which withdraws from relation—that which is without relation.

Speaking here in my own stead rather than as a Madhyamika thinker, I would argue that when the truth of relationality is obscured, then the coherence of reality is lost. Nothing holds together. Even our theologies are radically compromised. As a consequence, we risk accounts of God as an unrelated and immutable ultimate, a God who is being God when there is no world for which God can be God for. We make the mistake of supposing that the world is other than God in some non-relational sense and so suppose that God and world are marked not by internal relation but external relation. God is understood to be what the world is not and the world what God is not. As a result, an irresolvable dualism emerges. The profound temptation that lies within every theology that forgets relation is that it might so personalize God that God becomes a being, a person who loves us from without. Against this dualistic vision stands a depiction of God as Spirit-relation who is the Love with which I love God, the one who prays within me with sighs and groans too deep for words.

Here, I stand with Tillich who argues that the temptation to claim that God is a person arises from a failure—in his language to hold individualization and participation (or relation)—in harmony. When God is seen solely from the standpoint of individualization, error results. Tillich insists that this error is rather recent in theology. He writes, "It should not be forgotten that classical theology employed the term 'persona' for the trinitarian hypostases but not for God himself. God became 'a person' only in the nineteenth century. . . . Ordinary theism has made God a heavenly, completely perfect person who resides above the world and mankind." This is the theological error that emerges when individualization so thoroughly trumps accounts of God as participation or relation that theology gives rise to a flat and reified theism. Hence, Tillich's appropriate insistence that, "God is not God without universal participation."[30] Hence, it would be wiser to say that God is the ground of personality, or even that, in God, there is something that warrants our encounter with God as personal—it is not merely a matter of projection— but not to reduce God to a person, let alone three.

The fundamental tension between a theological account that resolutely insists on relation and one that insists with equal vigor on singularity-contingency is hard to miss. Speak only of relation and one risks losing a world of value that is, *in some sense*, other than and irreducible to the divine life. Without positing such otherness, it is hard to know how worldly existents can have a particularity that is distinct enough *from* the divine life to *enrich* the divine life. But to speak only of otherness is to fall into dualism in which God becomes a being among beings—an infinite being which, as Tillich and others have demonstrated, is a contradiction in terms.

To speak of God as contingency and relation without affirming God as ground/abyss is to run still other risks. Against the Gelukpa Madyamikas stand Nyingma Buddhists who want to preserve some account of Buddha-nature as non-reified ground. As we have seen, these Buddhists rightly fear that an account of ultimate reality as emptiness read only negatively might risk a nihilism that denies the very ground of the human capacity for transformation and awakening. To affirm that there is in the real an infinite fund for wisdom and compassion—that is the reason for insisting that emptiness is not merely a negation of own-being or self-existence (*svabhava*). Of course, such Buddhists are (too) anxious to affirm that to posit such a ground is in no way tantamount to advancing a vision of ultimate reality as non-relational Being-Itself, the putative sin of Advaita.[31]

## A Comparative Theology of Religious Diversity

This brief treatment of the tensions between depictions of ultimate reality as ground, singularity, and relation demonstrates that a trinitarian problem remains: How does one formulate a theological vision that does not privilege one of these dimensions at the expense of others? The answer lies in interreligious learning, a constructive theology that emerges through comparative theology. Comparative theology is a necessary discipline for constructive theology precisely because particular traditions tend to settle questions about ultimate reality in a dominant inflection leaving other options inadequately considered. At worst, minority voices are dismissed as heretical for refusing the dominant account. Christian traditions in their logos-centrism offer rich resources for celebrating singularity, but under the dominance of singularity, God is often reduced to personhood, the sovereign person, or, worse still, in social trinitarianism, three persons who are somehow also one. Driven by a singular focus on singularity, some go so far as to subscribe to a vision of each person in the trinity as a center of will and consciousness. Personal otherness is inscribed into the heart of the divine life but in a way that erases the character of God as ground and relation. This trinitarianism without difference might as well be a unitarianism trice repeated.

Comparative theology, by contrast, can shed rich light on these questions even as they continue to play out in intra-Christian debates about the character of the divine life. How are we rightly to speak of God as inexhaustible ground and abyss, God as one who speaks and so gives rise to a world that is not in every sense identical to the divine life, and speak also about ultimate reality as relation? That Spirit has throughout the history of Christian theology shaken off personal attributions—that, from the first, Christian theology was unable to fix the character of the Spirit—speaks to the nature of ultimate reality as relation, as the energy of the between and so not itself reducible either to abyssal depth or source of personal address.

By contrast, some schools of Hinduism and Buddhism described herein were formulated by male renunciants who posit visions of ultimate reality that call for detachment from singularity. The shape of these particular strands of Buddhism and Hinduism are suspicious of the erotic, if by the erotic we mean not just sexual love but intense attunement to the loveliness of singular realities. The male monastic dismissal of the female body is but an extreme instance of a larger turn away from particularity. This is not to say that these strands disregard singularity altogether. I have already observed that both Visistadvaita and Dvaita Vedanta celebrate the importance of singularity.

Attention to singularity rests squarely at the beating heart of Zen and is disclosed in the exquisite attention paid to particularity, especially in the natural world. In Japanese Zen Buddhist tradition, perhaps most especially in Haiku and other poetic forms, equal and hallowed attention is paid both to singularity and impermanence, beauty and its contingent fleetingness. Roshi Robert Aitken, while writing about Zen and Basho's Haiku in particular, observes: "It becomes clear that the universe and its beings are a complementarity of empty infinity, intimate interrelationships, and *total uniqueness of each and every being*. This fundamental complementarity is the theme of Zen, and masters have played with its facets and interactions in dialogues and sermons down through the ages."[32] In Aitken, one hears a threefold that resonates richly with the one articulated here. Aitken affirms that Zen attempts to affirm infinity, singularity, and relation, and in equal measure at that, a goal that I most deeply affirm.

Within any particular strand of a given religious tradition, distinctions in emphasis shape the work of orientation. Hence, the texture and fruits of healing transformation in these different traditions will differ and may generate tensions in persons who take up the practices of more than one tradition. But tension need not amount to contradiction. Theological differences between ground, singularity, and relation and the way in which human beings are oriented distinctively to these dimensions of ultimate reality can generate positive resources for interreligious collaboration and multiple religious participation. Given the focused ways in which religious schools seek to shape comportment, there is likely no way of seeing what a given tradition wishes adherents to see without taking up the particular therapeutic regimen that is prescribed in order to render such seeing possible. Hence, at least some comparative theologians will have to take up multiple religious participation.

I do not wish to downplay the tensions between these various spiritual trajectories. Those dedicated to the mystery of relation worry that orientation to the mystery of ground might lead to world loss. Spiritual practitioners who are dedicated to a vision of the world of name and form as unreal and so become caught up in a sense of the hyperreality of the transpersonal ground-abyss may deny the realm of relation and encounter and so fall prey to world negation.

This danger is one that those oriented toward singularity can appreciate, albeit in a different key. Those who celebrate the mystery of singularity worry that lovers of relation can miss the inexhaustible singularity of lovely particulars because the latter are so intent on denying that particulars can come to be apart from relation. Might not an exclusive orientation toward relationality jeopardize attention to the particular and hence the possibility of the erotic, of love for the particular not because I am incomplete without it but because the loveliness of the singular has its own claim and inviolable beauty to which I owe the piety of desire?

The tension between these three mysteries notwithstanding, spiritual life lived in relation to these three mysteries need not result in contradiction or incommensurability. This assertion is made in the key of faith and not ratiocination, which must come later. By way of that latter work of reflection, theologians can and must give an account of the *perichoresis* of these three mysteries. If both world and divinity bear this trinitarian structure, if ground, singularity, and relation are distinct but not separate, then one would expect that any historically deep tradition can find resources to orient persons to all three dimensions of the Real even if any given strand typically tends to focus in one direction.

So, as already noted, we find, in a variety of Tibetan Buddhist traditions, thinkers who are worried that the Gelukpa understanding of emptiness is too negative and cannot give an adequate account of our innate Buddha-nature as a positive reality. These traditions argue that while it is true that Buddha-nature cannot be a non-relational entity, Buddha-nature must be understood also as a positive and luminous ground of wisdom and compassion. This internal difference *within Tibetan Buddhism* accounts for the long-standing debates between proponents of "self-emptiness" and proponents of "other-emptiness." In the tension, debate, and ultimately in efforts to synthesize these different commitments, one can find in Buddhist traditions the motifs of ground and relation together with an appreciation for the suchness of each particular.

Christian traditions are, by and large, deeply committed to a vision of singularity and so tend to configure the ground not just as creativity but as a personal creator who loves. Under the pressure of singularity, the ground is personalized and is experienced as Lover. But there are many Christian theologians, mystics in particular, who desire a unitive or nondual experience of God. In such thinkers, the experience of God as ground and relation complements a vision of God as loving creator of a contingent and lovely world. Figures like Marguerite Porete and Meister Eckhart come readily to mind.

In both Jewish and Christian thinkers, we also find theologians of the Spirit who encounter God primarily not as ground or even as singularity but under the sign of relation. The modern Jewish philosopher of relation, par excellence, is Martin Buber, the thinker of I-Thou relation, the thinker of the event of meeting. Many contemporary Christian theologians, most especially process and feminist thinkers, are attempting to articulate a theology of God as relation and reality as relatedness in order to correct for excessively individualistic visions in which relatedness has been obscured.[33]

In sum, this account of ultimate reality as ground, singularity, and relation suggests that religious traditions—and even strands and thinkers within them—are likely to be oriented toward one or the other of these mysteries at the expense of others. Rare is the theologian who manages to see how these three are one and yet also three. Thinkers and traditions have their particular genius and will customarily resonate with one of these mysteries at the expense of the others. Christians can take no consolation in or assert religious superiority by appealing to trinity. Despite that commitment, Christian traditions have a long history of erring on the side of personalism under the weight of singularity, so much so that they have burned mystics like Porete who have given voice to a unitive experience of divinity best captured in visions of God as ground and relation. For those who hold to such personalist visions, the radical quest for an abyssal experience of nonduality in which the self discovers that her true depth just is the divine ground or that the self can plunge directly into that abyss is verboten.

By appealing to a trinitarianism of ground, singularity, and relation, I argue that differences between *and within* religious traditions are vital and not merely phenomenal cultural variations. Religious differences are rooted in genuine distinctions within the divine life. The work of comparative theology is religiously important because it is a way of gathering up differences for the sake of integral vision. If we are to understand how these mysteries might be marked by mutual interpenetration, we must take up interreligious dialogue here in the key of comparative theology. Interreligious dialogue cannot be motivated by the proximate work of peacemaking alone, a worthy endeavor no doubt, but must be seen as vital to the quest for comprehensive qualitative orientation. To paraphrase Paul Knitter, there is no way to be deeply religious without being interreligious. We cannot move fully into the life of the trinitarian God apart from a deeper movement into communion with our non-Christian neighbors.

As we have seen, John Hick argues that the Real is ultimately neither personal nor impersonal and that all ways of experiencing the Real fail to tell us anything about what Ultimate Reality is in itself. There is a sharp and irrevocable dualism between the One Real and its various manifestations. All are equally true and equally false, which can mean that they are equally a matter of indifference. For Hick, the texture of human lives as they move from self-centeredness to reality-centeredness is not a matter of deep interest. What matters is that all traditions make a generic turn to reality-centeredness possible.

By contrast, in this trinitarian vision, the particular texture of soteriological transformation matters. Christian *agape* is not the same as Buddhist *karuna*, which is not to say that one is superior to the other. We may need both. If this trinitarian account is on the mark, then there are specific forms of healing and virtue that can come about only by engaging in the concrete practices of particular traditions. But these differences need not lead to mutual indifference, let alone hostility. This trinitarian vision provides grounds for a certain holy envy for the special excellences accomplished by Buddhist and Hindu forms of practice.

Also ruled out is any eschatological vision in which different religious communities arrive at entirely different post-mortem destinations, some of which are more encompassing. Such a vision is problematic not least because traditions are marked by deep internal variegations. Religious goods do not sort themselves out one per tradition. Moreover, any theological vision risks incompleteness, if not outright error, if it fails to become properly attuned to each of these three dimensions of the divine life. The religious quest of our time cannot be imagined as one in which each religious community engages in the work of climbing its own mountain in relative isolation from other religious communities. Only by more deeply appreciating the distinctive goods of other religious traditions can we move more deeply into the divine life. There is no movement into depth of divine life without a movement toward our neighbors, and that is why religious diversity is not a problem but is instead a source of profound promise for our collective well-being. It is for that reason that I issue the call to combine what has too long been sundered, the work of learning *about* our neighbors, the work of learning *from* our neighbors so that we might ourselves learn *more* about God.

One further word: this trinitarianism of God or ultimate reality as ground, singularity, and relation is simultaneously a constructive theology formulated through comparative theology *and* the basis of a theology of religious diversity. That is why this trinitarian account also constitutes a comparative theology of religious diversity; two projects, often set at odds, are integrated herein. As a TRD, this account does not posit three ultimates as Cobb and Griffin do, one transpersonal ultimate (creativity), one personal ultimate (God), and the world, for naturalistic religious traditions. In Cobb, all impersonal or transpersonal religious traditions are gathered up into one basket, theisms into another, and indigenous traditions that venerate the sacrality of the world into a third. By contrast, I posit one threefold ultimate.

Ultimate reality as *ground* recognizes those traditions that posit a transpersonal world ground. Under the sign of *singularity*, I gather those traditions that celebrate singular creatures who address and are addressed by a "personal" dimension of the divine life. In feeling so addressed, theistic traditions figure ultimate reality as a singularity or source of singularity; within ultimate reality, they affirm that there is that which can truly be encountered as One who loves the world into its singular and distinctive being. Ultimate reality as *relation*, by contrast, cannot be figured either as personal or impersonal. Relation is not "substantial" enough to be figured as transpersonal ground, on the one hand, or personal being on the other. The holiness of relation seems to slip through these alternatives. It is recognized in *kensho* when our reifying dispositions are dissolved through zazen, it is recognized when we enter into the space of the between, and it is recognized when we are claimed by that which inspirits us into the holiness of encounter and meeting. It is a third that exceeds and refuses being conveniently named as either transpersonal or personal. It cannot be grasped.

The distinction between ultimate reality as ground and ultimate reality as relation is especially noteworthy because it refuses the questionable propensity among philosophers and theologians to conflate all transpersonal accounts of ultimacy into one as happens, for example, when Brahman and *sunyata* are identified. But given the long insistence on the part of Madhyamikas that *sunyata* is most decidedly not Brahman, not a world ground, equating the two is misguided. By contrast, there are in Buddhist traditions, as we have seen, discourses of Buddha-nature as world ground. The kinship between those forms of Buddhism and other ground traditions is genuine. Introducing a distinction between ground and relation adds nuance and makes it possible to take religious traditions at their word when they assert that they are at odds with each other in certain respects.

What, then, of naturalist traditions? Recall that each three of these figurations of the ultimate begins in intraworldly wonder, the wonder that there is anything at all, the wonder that whatever exists is singularly and inimitably what it is, and the wonder that whatever exists does so only in relation. These features are writ into the fabric of the world and experience. At least some religious persons, whether they be contemporary naturalists or indigenous animists, may choose not to posit any figures of ultimate reality as distinct from the world. This threefold can acknowledge and valorize such sacred this-worldliness as well.

Ground, singularity, and relation—they are distinct but not separate, three yet one. Articulating just how that might be so will require further investigations in comparative theology, further adventures in circling the elephant.

# 8 This Is Not a Conclusion

*Not a many but a manifold, not one set of ones, but a multiplicity, this collection of creatures is folding in and out of each other, forming collectivities that may dissipate or organize. These are not the dissociative quantities of a numbing relativism but the ecologies of an unbounded relationalism. In relation to doctrine, it has been called polydoxy, enfolding the disarmed honesties of theological orthodoxy.*

—CATHERINE KELLER, *Cloud of the Impossible: Negative Theology and Planetary Entanglement*

This book is not finished. Nor is the itinerary it traces. If its central figure is that of circumnavigating an elephant, and if the elephant itself stands in for the infinite, how could we ever complete the circle, that circle whose center is everywhere and whose circumference is nowhere?

Still more, imagine that our very capacity to know the infinite requires its self-disclosure, one that stands in interdependence with our searching, the seeker and the sought so bound together that we might even imagine that not just knowledge of the elephant but the elephant herself grows as we seek and know her. Against all charges leveled against this allegory, contemporary readers need not imagine omniscience as its sought-for goal; interreligious learning is an endless process because there is always more to be known.

This book has been a sustained argument against religious insularity, against postures of life and thought that presume, "I can understand God without help from you. In the quest for religious truth, I don't need you if you aren't part of my tradition." Such claims are rarely, if ever, flatly asserted, but they are routinely presupposed. Even when articulated with bracing clarity, such insularity might be recognized as limiting but not invidious. Unfortunately, insularity often brings in its train a further presumption: "I can also understand the meaning of *your* faith, your tradition, even without speaking with you. Because my religious categories help me to understand God and the world better than yours can, I am also able to understand your religion better than you can yourself. I am in a better position to discern what is legitimate in your faith than you are."

Those convictions sound crude and violating. Unfortunately, they are not uncommon in Christian writing about religious diversity. The commandment "Love thy neighbor" has not been taken to entail that we must cherish our neighbor's wisdom. The default assumption instead is that we can love our neighbors well enough without learning to love what our neighbor loves. I might embrace my neighbor but not my neighbor's wisdom. Far from regarding religious diversity as a gift, some Christians find it natural and unproblematic to wonder why the Christian God even bothers to let non-Christians exist.

How does such dismissive thinking come to seem natural? I have offered one answer in this book: we have come to think of our traditions as isolated "religious worlds" surrounded by impermeable Trumpian walls. Each religion has its own seamless narrative and conceptual integrity. To grant allegiance to a given tradition is taken to require that one believes that one's tradition is not only distinctive but uniquely superior. If not, why remain rather than convert? If you believe that your tradition is truer to the nature of the Real and hence soteriologically more efficacious than other traditions, it comes to seem natural also to maintain that your tradition offers the interpretive keys both to what is good and true in other traditions and how they remain deficient.

Between these incommensurable narrative worlds, there can be no mediation, no neutral terrain. When from within one of these worlds you try to understand someone from another, understanding can only take place by the categories of your own home world. At best, I can see from my perspective how your categories, deficient though they are, allow you to see a ray, a glimmer of that light that has come to be known fully in my tradition.

But just where do these religious worlds come from? With Madhyamika thinkers, suppose we ask, "Is our religious world self-arisen? Does it have self-existence (*svabhava*)? The answer must obviously be no.

As Thich Naht Hanh eloquently puts it, "We are not separate. We are inextricably interrelated. The rose is the garbage, and the non-prostitute is the prostitute. The rich man is the very poor woman, and the Buddhist is the non-Buddhist. The non-Buddhist cannot help but be a Buddhist, because we inter-are."[1] Our traditions are not exempt from metaphysical rules that govern reality as such; nothing is what it is apart from relation. If so, then religions cannot be walled communities. "Something there is that doesn't love a wall."

In a robustly relational world, zero-sum thinking makes little sense, whether in trade policy or in interreligious exchange.[2] My gain does not have to come at your loss nor yours at my expense. We need not close borders or build a wall. Our traditions came to be only through relationship, and they remain alive and vital only through ongoing relationship. Where there is permeability, there is life; where there is impermeability, only death.

Even when this point is begrudgingly admitted, there are those who insist that when our tradition borrows from yours, its impurities, corruptions, and idolatries are filtered out. In an allegorical reading of scripture favored by some evangelicals, they remind us that when we, the chosen people, plunder the treasures of Egypt, those treasures are purified and transformed through subjugation to the pristine categorical logic of our tradition. In this way, even if I must grant that my tradition interexists with yours, I can do so without rendering myself genuinely vulnerable to learning and transformation. Plundering indeed! Taking without asking—the very antithesis of the hospitality of receiving.

*Circling the Elephant* repudiates religious isolationism and calls for thoroughgoing vulnerability. If I am truly to be open to the mystery of the infinite, I must be vulnerable to the mystery of my neighbor. If I am to move ever more fully into the divine life, I must move toward my neighbor in receptivity and love. No pilgrimage to God apart from a pilgrimage toward the holiness of my neighbor. I must entertain the possibility that you know what I do not know precisely because your vocabulary and practices are not identical to mine. A minor marginalized note in my tradition is sometimes a symphony in yours. Even the line between what is yours and what is mine is provisional and remains ever in flux. We negotiate those lines together and cross them routinely in life and learning. Inside and outside, yours and mine, are relative not absolute categories. Our "religions" are not ontologically reified and isolated; they are distinct but not separate.

To contest religious insularity and to cultivate interreligious conviviality, we must interrogate racialized understandings of religions as reified entities that can be hierarchically ordered. Genealogy of religion dismantles the notion that there has always existed a fixed set of world religions together with some other local or indigenous religions, all of which can be rank-ordered on a scale of truth and soteriological power. It also disrupts the notion that each religion is governed by a static transhistorical grammar that persists even when surface details change. Claims for the existence of such grammars are essential to theological strategies that suggest that the mixing of ingredients from more than one religion is a recipe for nonsense and incoherent gibberish.

Neither is it credible to argue that each religion possesses but a single worldview or interpretive scheme. There is neither a single Christian worldview nor a single Buddhist worldview. A key plank in that critical argument is the claim that religious traditions are enduring arguments about a historically fluid repertoire. What should be in our repertoire, and how should we employ that repertoire to arrive at comprehensive qualitative orientation? What interpretive schemes can be generated by means of our repertoire, and how can those schemes be installed in individual and social bodies for the sake of right comportment to reality rightly understood? Traditions are arguments about these questions. This way of imagining religious traditions allows for both distinctiveness and relation. Not everything in my repertoire is in yours or yours in mine. The cross is in my Christian repertoire not in your Hindu repertoire. Ahimsa is in your Hindu repertoire but not my Christian repertoire.

Except, of course, matters are never so neat. As we saw from our study of Martin Luther King, Jr., and Mohandas Gandhi, elements from our repertoires float across boundary lines. Leo Tolstoy writes about the Sermon on the Mount, American abolitionists and pacifists read him and send him their writings. He is struck by the ongoing and undiminished vitality of nonviolent readings of the Sermon within certain American communities. He includes extended excerpts from those writings in his treatise, *The Kingdom of God Is Within You*. A young Indian lawyer in South Africa reads those writings and incorporates a reading of the Sermon and its preacher into his experiments in satyagraha. His reading and performance of the Sermon generate a new Christology of Jesus as the exemplary satyagrahi.

The lines between Christian and Hindu repertoires are muddied. Gandhi's reading of Jesus as satyagrahi and his glad Hindu discipleship to that Jesus and his construction of new therapeutic regimes for cultivating the capacity for nonviolent resistance are expressions of genuine interreligious creativity. Novel insight is birthed by the open-handed giving and receiving of religious gifts. Then, Gandhi's new reading and performance of The Sermon on the Mount are received back again in the US context by King's teachers and then by King himself. As a result, Christians know more about Christ with Hindu help than they did before. Here, the central allegory is, if not disrupted, then complicated: we can no longer think of religious traditions as isolated blindfolded persons, each focused on one aspect of the elephant because each tradition, in its spiraling around ultimate reality, begins to interpenetrate each other. Relational pluralism acknowledges this reality: relation entangles. What enters into relation is transformed.

What are we to make of such processes of transmission and transformation? The cross has now become an ingredient within the repertoire of some Hindus, and nonviolent readings of the *Bhagavad Gita* part of the repertoire of some Christians. A Black Baptist preacher gives a Palm Sunday Sermon, which explicitly argues that a twentieth-century Hindu is the greatest Christian who ever lived, one who did greater things than the Christ himself. In the process, both traditions are transformed. On the Hindu side, ahimsa, non-injury, can no longer be understood solely as a means for avoiding negative personal karma; now it is also understood as a sociopolitical process of remediating colonial violence and structural injustice.

On the Christian side, Jesus's death on the cross cannot be severed from his preaching and teaching of enemy love. The Proclaimer (Jesus) and the proclaimed (the Kingdom of God) are reintegrated. The cross is no longer reducible to a transcendental operation for metaphysical debt satisfaction, one that can permit Christians to ignore calls to enemy love and beloved community, or even to dismiss them as the peculiar unrealistic fulminations of an apocalyptic perfectionist. Christians are now called to follow Jesus the satyagrahi.

As we study these transformations, circling, circling, we might find ourselves wondering how we ever came to think that we could truly understand the religious treasures of our own traditions until we gave them away and received them back again, enriched and transformed. Just where again exactly is the line between what is mine and what is yours? How did we persuade ourselves that we could claim to love you without learning to cherish and appreciate what you treasure? I cannot claim to love my neighbor if I disregard and dismiss my neighbor's wisdom. I can know neither God nor even myself apart from you. If no religion is an island, then postures of religious insularity and isolationism must be surrendered. It follows then that what I say about you and your tradition (theology of religious diversity), my knowledge and appreciation for what you know of ultimate reality (comparative theology), and the work of coming to new intimacy with ultimate reality (constructive theology) cannot and must not be severed. I need you if I am to understand myself. I need you if I am to understand God. Reality seems so structured that these operations are inseparable.

That interdependence between knowledge of God and knowledge of neighbor is the deep meaning of relational pluralism. Relational pluralism affirms that our traditions grow as they learn from each other; that has always been the case. What God or reality has joined together, let no human being put asunder. There's nothing new in relational pluralism; relational pluralism merely refuses to arrest processes of mutual transformation by which our traditions came to be in the first place. Such mutual transformation not only deepens our knowledge of each other but also leads to deeper knowledge of ultimate reality. Knowledge about each other is enriched by our conversation with each other; conversation with each other deepens our knowledge of the divine life.

We must circle the elephant together if we are to understand each other, let alone the elephant. If I am to know why you name the elephant as you do, I must strive to know *as* you do. That requires that I attempt to, insofar as possible, walk over to your side of the elephant.

In truth, this means I must become multiple. Without forsaking fidelity to what I have come to know through my tradition, I must risk being transformed by coming to know what you know. I must strive to see how it might be that both of us might be right, how both of our interpretive schemes and our therapeutic regimes may together teach me more than I could have known alone. But if I am to know *what* you know, then I must strive to know *as* you know. At least some comparative theologians will have to venture into multiple religious participation. We can only know ultimate reality by means of the particular practices that are meant to grant access to just those dimensions or features of ultimate reality.

We need not fear becoming multiple. As this book has argued, we have always been multiple. Not multiplicity as such but the wrong kind of multiplicity—such as the inclusion of neoliberalism's ubiquitous therapeutic regime—should be worrisome. Buddhist disciplines for crafting and regulating desire are likely to be of immense help to Christians who seek to constrain late capitalist soulcraft and its toxic account of the good life. There is plenty of religiousness at play in our lives, well before we decide to become multiple belongers, and much of it comes from purportedly secular space, a truth that most definitions of religion obscure from recognition.

So, what have we learned by way of engagement with selected strands of Hindu, Christian, and Buddhist traditions? We have learned that reality itself is trinitarian. (1) Why is there something rather than nothing? There is a ground/abyss in which all things participate. (2) Reality is marked throughout by radical, singular, and inimitable thisness. Singularity is a law of life. A variety of traditions hold that there is something in ultimate reality that generates radical particularity. There is, they affirm, a principle of singularity in ultimate reality. Those traditions and religious thinkers tend to read ultimate realty as One who births unending differences. (3) But singularity cannot take place apart from relation. There is no singular that arises apart from relation. Mindful relation sets human beings free from egoistic craving and opens my eyes to the truth that I am what I am only in and through relation. So relation itself, along with the power to restore persons to relation, is also a dimension of ultimate reality. Sheer being, singular being, and relational being are irreducible features of reality that point to a trifold ultimate of ground, singularity, and relation.

To affirm that ultimate reality, or God, for Christians, is ground, singularity, and relation is by no means to arrive at a fully formulated doctrine of God or even to maintain that this account of ultimacy neatly maps onto some particular classical account of the trinity. Considerable further work, well beyond the constraints of this book, will be needed to compare and contrast this philosophical trinitarianism with confessional trinitarianisms of various stripes. This particular trinity is plainly closer to some varieties of anti-social trinitarianism than it is to social trinitarianism. For instance, I fear recent attempts to depict trinity as community risk diminishing the promise of trinitarian discourse because they fail to register transpersonal dimensions of divinity, at least not without positing a further distinction between the three persons and something beneath, beyond, or between the persons that might be regarded as transpersonal.

However such questions are resolved, *Circling the Elephant* issues a call for reflective collaboration across religious traditions. Disrupting the boundaries between "religions" entails dislodging convictions about Christian theology as in-house domestic labor to be kept separate from alien reflection about "other religions," which is consigned to the history and philosophy of religions. Relational pluralism affirms that God has not left Godself without witness in creation and in the wisdom of our religious neighbors. That witness is irreducible to pale imitations of what we already know about divinity prior to encounter and dialogue.

Nor will our own categories survive interreligious encounter unchanged. To meet, truly meet, religious accounts of ultimacy as Atman/Brahman or as *sunyata* will call Christian theologians to searching transformation. What can it mean for Christians to hear Advaita affirmations that the true self and ultimate reality are one? How might such testimony help us to hear again and afresh Augustine's contention that God is nearer to me than I am to myself? What might it mean truly to hear Madhyamaka affirmations that to be is to be-in-relation?

Receiving such wisdom hospitably will entail rethinking Christian trinitarianism. Every genuine act of receiving elicits and drives transformation. Strands of Christian tradition historically repressed—some violently—will receive renewed attention. What has been heretofore marginalized receives fresh hearing. How might we hear Marguerite Porete anew, she whom the Church burned at the stake, if nondualist wisdom from Hindu neighbors becomes familiar among Christians? How might the relational theologies of feminist theologians such as Ivone Gebara be heard afresh in light of Buddhist testimony regarding emptiness (*sunyata*) as dependent co-arising (*pratityasamutpada*)?

Consider, for example, the promise of what might emerge from a sustained conversation between Madhyamika thinkers and Gebara. She writes,

> As I see it, relatedness is the primary and the ultimate ground of all that exists. Relatedness, as expressed in human language, means "experience" as a condition and a value. However, it goes beyond the human world and beyond all we can articulate. Both the world we see around us and humanity within it are expressions of the relatedness that characterizes

all things. It is on the basis of this experience, and on going beyond it, that we can thus affirm that God is relatedness.[3]

Save for the single word, God, Shantideva would find nothing to deny here. Imagine also how Buddhist friends might hear relatedness as inflected through the vision of an ecofeminist theologian who mobilizes relatedness for ecojustice. These are the kinds of conversations that await us when the reifying walls between our traditions are recognized for the illusions that they are, when we come to see that human beings, our traditions, and even ultimate reality itself might all be described as multiplicity in relation.[4]

And need we declare once more the exigency of such conversations on a wounded planet, a planet in which hundreds of species are driven toward extinction each day by the recklessness of just one? Among those threatened species happens to be the elephant whose wondrous multiplicity has been for us a stand-in and symbol for divine multiplicity. Curiously, the survival of the elephant may depend, in part, on the gift that elephant as allegory has offered us—namely, to serve as a doorway to understanding our theological interdependence with religious neighbors. Might that interreligious *theological* interdependence serve also as a gateway to understanding *ecological* interdependence in a time of peril, the promise of religious diversity offering one desperately needed antidote for the poisons of insularity and greed, poisons that reduce others to the instrumental use we can make of them?

Here, we are haunted by an unthought because it is largely unknown fact—that the word "elephant" itself is derived from the Greek, "*elephas*," which, "when first used by the ancient Greeks themselves primarily referred to ivory, not the animal."[5] Our very name for the species bears the marring trace of instrumentality, a propensity to diminish the mystery of our animal kin to monetizable use. Naming under the impress of instrumentality wounds and desecrates.

What if our naming of divine things runs the risk of becoming likewise reductive? What if, ensconced within the taken-for-granted vocabulary of a given tradition, we feel as though we *know* the mystery, laboring under the illusion that our all too familiar idioms capture what they seek to name? What if our names for the mystery also come to bear the imprint of control or even mastery—the illusion that we securely know what words like "God" or "Trinity" mean? Surely such idolatrous instrumentality is unmasked when we begin to think of other religious traditions as inferior to our own, traditions that contain only a spark of what we already know in full.

What if the calling of our time, a calling from the Holy Herself, is to adventure and sojourn into new religious terrain, not now to convert and to conquer as Western Christians once did, but to humbly and hospitably receive other wisdoms? Mitigating the threat of planetary gloom will require cultivating a love for interreligious wisdom that will lead us forward into intimacy with unknown depths of the divine. Only as we learn other vocabularies and apprentice ourselves to other disciplines that also and otherwise mediate the mystery, will we more fully enter into the healing darkness where God dwells.

# ACKNOWLEDGMENTS

Any book that has taken some time to make its way into the world accumulates considerable debts. This book is no exception. I stand indebted to a multiplicity of persons and communities who have helped me think and live into what is written herein. A comprehensive list is impossible and unintended omissions inevitable.

A great deal of thinking about central themes in this book took place in conversations made possible by a grant from the Luce Foundation. The AAR/Luce Summer Seminars in Theologies of Religious Pluralism and Comparative Theology offered a fertile community of inquiry for test-driving ideas. I directed those seminars along with Francis X. Clooney, S.J., Mark Heim, Marcia Hermansen, Steven Kepnes, John Makransky, Peter Ochs, Anantanand Rambachan, Devorah Schoenfeld, and Najeeba Syeed. The three Cohorts of AAR/Luce Fellows have also enriched my life and writing immeasurably. Their number comes close to sixty and so cannot be named here, but their influence is significant nonetheless. I am still pondering questions they posed some years ago.

In my former institution, Vanderbilt Divinity School, I am indebted to Ellen Armour and Paul Lim, who were not just intellectual partners but treasured companions. At Vanderbilt, I overlapped for a time with Richard King. My interest in genealogy of religion is due, in no small measure, to his work. Other colleagues whose work is present in these pages include Victor Anderson, Lewis Baldwin, and Robert Campany.

I am immensely indebted to my colleagues at Union Theological Seminary. I owe to all considerable debts, most especially to Sarah Azaransky, Mary Boys, Claudio Carvalhaes, Pamela Cooper-White, Gary Dorrien, Roger Haight, Serene Jones, Aliou Niang, Jerusha Rhodes, Greg Synder, and the late James Cone, whose warm welcome to Union was a source of great encouragement. I wish also to name David Carr and Andrea White in particular because they read several chapters with great care. David Carr has been a steadfast friend and writing coach throughout the process. Paul Knitter is a spiritual and theological pioneer in the work of theologies of religious diversity and comparative theology; he also welcomed me warmly to the Union community. Chapters of this book were read and discussed in the classes we taught together. I owe to Paul an immeasurable debt of gratitude.

Two Episcopal communities kept me grounded in Christian Eucharistic life even as I immersed myself ever more deeply in Buddhist practice. In St. Augustine's Episcopal Chapel in Nashville, Tennessee, led by Rev. Becca Stevens, several members of the congregation also participated in vipassana with Insight Nashville, a Buddhist practice community led by Gordon Peerman and his late wife, Kathy Woods. Gordon and Kathy were invaluable in moving my practice into a communal key. In New York, I am grateful for St. Mark's Church-in-the-Bowery and its Rector, Rev. Anne Sawyer, for welcoming me as a teaching and preaching Christian theologian. On the Buddhist front, I practice within the Foundation for Active Compassion community led by Lama John Makransky.

Students in many classes have read and offered feedback on these chapters, particularly Chapters 4 and 5. Their excitement proved an encouragement for the journey. I am indebted to my doctoral students, former and current, especially Joshua Samuel, Jamall Calloway, Christopher Fici, Esther Parajuli, and Poonam Rai. Poonam Rai edited and formatted these chapters with great care. Jamall Calloway also offered important help on Chapter 4.

My friends in the Workgroup for Constructive Theology have been a constant and enduring source of support. I am grateful to Stephen Ray, Laurel Schneider, and to many others in the Workgroup. Other friends and colleagues who must be named include Duane Bidwell, James Bowley, Wendy Farley, Marion Grau, Todd Green, Peter Heltzel, Mari Kim, Jerry Martin, Darby Ray, Steven G. Smith, Michelle Voss Roberts, and Charles Jobe. My thanks also go to my new son, Mo Dryden, who keeps me young and marginally less nerdy.

I owe special thanks to my coeditor for the series in which this book appears, Dr. Loye Ashton. Ashton has long been my intellectual companion, particularly in a metaphysical key. This book could not have been written without the inspiration of my doktorvater, Robert Neville. His imprint can be found on virtually every page. A special thanks to my editor, Richard Morrison, who not only supported me during the emergence of this book but is also an enthusiastic supporter of the entire "Comparative Theology: Thinking Across Traditions" series. I would also like to thank the entire team at Fordham University Press, most especially Mildred Sanchez, whose meticulous and attentive copy-editing has made this book much the better.

The two anonymous readers of this book offered priceless advice. I have attempted to take as much of it as humanly possible within available time constraints.

My father, John T. John; my mother, Leelamma John; my sister, Rachel Cherian; my brother-in-law, Dennis Cherian; and my niece, Priya Cherian, have also fed me and kept me in good health as I wrote.

This book is dedicated to Catherine Keller, theologian of the impossible, who always and without fail believed in the possibility and actuality of this book, well before its birth. The book is also dedicated to two Kates, my daughter, Kate Fulton-John, and my wife, Kate Newman. Kate FJ has never known a day of her life in which her Papa was not working on a book. She has generously shared me with readers, real and imagined, for the whole of her life. Kate Newman and the joy of our new life together served as the crucial final impetus for pushing this text out into the world. Words fail.

# NOTES

*Preface*

1. For more on this matter, see Catherine Cornille's illuminating essay, "The Problem of Choice in Comparative Theology," in Francis X. Clooney, S.J., and Klaus Von Stosch, eds., *How to Do Comparative Theology* (New York: Fordham University Press, 2018), 19–36.

2. For a brief but illuminating history of the St. Thomas Christian communities within an ethnographical study of these communities in the United States, see Raymond Brady Williams's *Christian Pluralism in the United States: The Indian Immigrant Experience* (New York: Cambridge University Press, 1996). Also, see my co-edited volume of interviews with the former Mar Thoma Metropolitan Philipose Mar Chrysostom in Jesudas M. Athyal and John J. Thatamanil, eds., *Metropolitan Chrysostom on Mission in the Market Place* (Tiruvalla, Kerala: Christava Sahitya Samithy, 2002).

3. For M. M. Thomas's constructive approach to theologies of religious diversity, see his book *Risking Christ for Christ's Sake: Towards an Ecumenical Theology of Pluralism* (Geneva: World Council of Churches, 1987).

4. Advaita Vedanta's core claim is that Brahman, the ultimate reality and ground of the world, is not-other than Atman, the essence of the self. Advaita—the term literally means "not-two"—is thus a nondualism grounded in the scriptures that make up the end (*anta*) of the Vedas—hence Vedanta. Those scriptures are the Upanishads.

5. See Paul F. Knitter, *Without the Buddha, I Could Not Be a Christian.* (London: Oneworld, 2009).

6. I have written in autobiographical terms about this period in my life in "Managing Multiple Religious and Scholarly Identities: An Argument for a Theological Study of Hinduism," *Journal of the American Academy of Religion* 68, no. 4 (December 2000): 791–803.

7. Gordon Peerman, *Blessed Relief: What Christians Can Learn from Buddhists about Suffering* (Woodstock, VT: Skylight Paths, 2008).

8. For a preliminary treatment of multiple religious participation and multiple belonging and related notions, see my "Eucharist Upstairs, Yoga Downstairs: On Multiple Religious Participation," in *Many Yet One? Multiple Religious Belonging*, ed. Peniel

Jesudason Rufus Rajkumar and Joseph Prabhakar Dayam (Geneva: World Council of Churches, 2016).

## Introduction: Revisiting an Old Tale

In the epigraph, Heschel's words are from his inaugural lecture for his appointment as the Harry Emerson Fosdick Visiting Professor at Union Theological Seminary on November 10, 1965. *Union Theological Quarterly* XXI:2 (1966), 126. The lecture is also available in Abraham Joshua Heschel, *No Religion Is an Island: Abraham Joshua Heschel and Interreligious Dialogue*, ed. Harold Kasimow and Byron L. Sherwin (Eugene, OR: Wipf and Stock, 1991), 3–22.

1. There are some noteworthy exceptions to this rule. See, for example, Terrence W. Tilley with Ernest W. Durbin II, "Is Religious Diversity a Problem To Be Solved? Not Particularly," in *Religious Diversity and the American Experience: A Theological Approach*, ed. Terrence W. Tilley (New York: Continuum, 2007), 110–124. See also Rita M. Gross, "Excuse Me, but What's the Question? Isn't Religious Diversity Normal?," in *The Myth of Religious Superiority: A Multifaith Exploration*, ed. Paul Knitter (Maryknoll, NY: Orbis Books, 2005), 75–87. See also her expanded argument in her book, *Religious Diversity—What's the Problem?: Buddhist Advice for Flourishing with Religious Diversity* (Eugene, OR: Cascade Books, 2014).
2. Roland Faber and Catherine Keller, "A Taste for Multiplicity: The Skillful Means of Religious Pluralism," in *Religions in the Making: Whitehead and the Wisdom Traditions of the World*, ed. John Cobb, Jr. (Eugene, OR: Cascade Books, 2012), 182.
3. On the SBNRs, see Linda A. Mercadante, *Belief without Borders: Inside the Minds of the Spiritual but Not Religious* (New York: Oxford University Press, 2014).
4. On the theme of holy envy, see Barbara Brown Taylor, *Holy Envy: Finding God in the Faith of Others* (New York: HarperOne, 2019).
5. I am indebted here to Robert Cummings Neville who notes that things can only be compared in some respect or the other. Much of the labor of comparison hinges on precisely identifying the respect in which two or more things are to be compared. See his *Normative Cultures* (Albany: SUNY Press, 1995), 79–81. The respect in which two or more things can be compared can be precisely formulated as a comparative category. For his work on comparative categories, see idem, 62–68.
6. On the secular concerns of the traditions we call "religions," see John Cobb's vital book, *Spiritual Bankruptcy: A Prophetic Call to Action* (Nashville: Abingdon Press, 2010).
7. For a taste of what such arguments look like, see Parimal G. Patil's fine book on Buddhist arguments against Hindu notions of divinity in, *Against a Hindu God: Buddhist Philosophy of Religion in India* (New York: Columbia University Press, 2009).
8. Dating this narrative would be a complex undertaking given the uncertainties generated by oral transmission. Early Buddhist traditions state that Buddhist scriptures came to be written down only in the first century BCE. However, the tale is ascribed to the Buddha himself (fifth century BCE). What is quite clear is that this ancient tale has become an Indic staple and is variously deployed in ancient, medieval, and modern thinking by Buddhists, Jains, and Hindus.

9. Hull made his remarks as part of an untitled lecture for a conference on "Anglican Lutheran Relations with Diaspora Hindus" sponsored by the Anglican Council's Network for Inter Faith Concerns (NIFCON). The Queen's Foundation for Ecumenical Theological Education, Birmingham, UK, October 30, 2014.

10. For more on tactile knowing, see John M. Hull, *The Tactile Heart: Blindness and Faith* (London: SCM Press, 2013).

11. For a recent important rehabilitation of apophatic theology, see Catherine Keller, *The Cloud of the Impossible: Negative Theology and Planetary Entanglement* (New York: Columbia University Press, 2014).

12. Jeffery D. Long, *A Vision for Hinduism: Beyond Hindu Nationalism* (New York: I.B. Tauris, 2007), front matter. Long notes that the tale is both a Buddhist and Jain allegory and based on Udana 6.4: 66–69. Interestingly, I use this allegory in a different way than Long does. I employ the allegory to suggest that a single complex ultimate reality can have multiple dimensions whereas Long appeals to process theology's deep pluralism, which posits that there are multiple ultimate realities. Nevertheless, Long and I share many common convictions. More on this matter follows immediately.

13. Jeffery Long observes that what the elephant stands for, in various retellings, must obviously vary. For some traditions, the elephant must stand in for reality as such but not God, as Buddhist traditions are not interested in the existence of God. In Sri Ramakrishna's version, the elephant does stand for God. See Swami Nikhilananda, *The Gospel of Sri Ramakrishna* (New York: Ramakrishna-Vivekananda Center, 1942), 191. I'm indebted to Long for this observation about divergent significations of the elephant. Personal e-mail conversation with Long. January 24, 2019.

14. Lesslie Newbigin, *The Gospel in a Pluralist Society* (Grand Rapids, MI: Wm. B. Eerdmans, 1989), 9–10.

15. I am indebted herein to John Cobb's notion of "mutual transformation." For an important collection of his seminal essays, see John B. Cobb, Jr., *Transforming Christianity and the World: A Way Beyond Absolutism and Relativism*, ed. Paul F. Knitter (Maryknoll, NY: Orbis Books, 1999).

16. Perry Schmidt-Leukel argues that pluralists need not affirm that *all* religious traditions are true or salvific. He defines pluralism as the affirmation that, "Salvific knowledge of a transcendent reality is mediated by more than one religion (not necessarily by all of them), and there is none among them whose mediation of that knowledge is superior to all the rest." See Perry Schmidt-Leukel, "Exclusivism, Inclusivism, Pluralism: The Tripolar Typology—Clarified and Reaffirmed," in *The Myth of Religious Superiority*, ed. Paul F. Knitter (Maryknoll, NY: Orbis Books, 2005), p. 20.

17. Newbigin, *Pluralist Society*, 10.

18. On the centrality of the virtue of humility for interreligious engagement, see the first chapter of Catherine Cornille's indispensable work, *The Im-possibility of Interreligious Dialogue* (New York: Crossroad Publishing, 2008), 9–58. On the connection between apophasis and "doctrinal humility," see Cornille, *Interreligious Dialogue*, 40–42. I am also indebted to her work on the virtue of hospitality (see Cornille, 177–210).

19. I owe this point to oral conversations with my colleague, Dr. Jerusha Rhodes, who, like me, is intrigued by the pedagogical promise and limitations of this elephantine image.

20. Paul Tillich, *Systematic Theology, Vol. I* (Chicago: University of Chicago Press, 1951), 109. Tillich writes, "Whatever is essentially mysterious cannot lose its mysteriousness even when it is revealed. Otherwise something which only seemed to be mysterious would be revealed, and not that which is essentially mysterious. But is it not a contradiction in terms to speak of the revelation of something which remains a mystery in its very revelation? It is just this seeming paradox which is asserted by religion and theology."

21. On the notion of polydoxy—a position that seeks to find a way around the limiting and rigid binary between orthodoxy and heterodoxy, see Catherine Keller and Laurel Schneider, eds., *Polydoxy: Theology of Multiplicity and Relation* (New York: Routledge Press, 2010).

22. Heschel, *No Religion Is an Island*, 119.

23. Hugh Nicholson has made this point well in his book, *Comparative Theology and the Logic of Religious Rivalry* (New York: Oxford University Press, 2011). The resonances between Nicholson's work and mine are many, although they were derived independently.

24. I explain the reasons for my preference for the term "theology of religious diversity" in a moment. I note only that I am not alone. See Terrence W. Tilley, "Theologies of Religious Diversity: Toward a Catholic and a Catholic Assessment," in *Can Only One Religion Be True? Paul Knitter and Harold Netland in Dialogue*, ed. Robert B. Stewart (Minneapolis, MN: Fortress Press, 2013), 55–77.

25. See John Hick, *An Interpretation of Religion* (New Haven, CT: Yale University Press, 1989), 245.

26. I borrow the phrase, "relational pluralism" from Roland Faber and Catherine Keller. See their essay, "A Taste for Multiplicity: The Skillfull [*sic*] Means of Religious Pluralism," in *Religions in the Making: Whitehead and the Wisdom Traditions of the World*, ed. John B. Cobb, Jr. (Eugene, OR: Cascade Books, 2012), 180–207.

## *1. Religious Difference and Christian Theology: Thinking About, Thinking With, and Thinking Through*

1. I refer here to the work of Peter Berger on "plausibility structures" and the effect of diversity on them. See Peter Berger, *The Sacred Canopy: Elements of a Sociological Theory of Religion* (New York: Anchor Press, 1969), 45–51.

2. Gerald R. McDermott, *God's Rivals: Why Has God Allowed Different Religions? Insights from the Bible and the Early Church* (Downers Grove, IL: Intervarsity Press Academic, 2007).

3. McDermott concludes his book with an appendix that offers a tangled defense of the masculine pronoun for God, even though McDermott insists that God is not male. McDermott, *God's Rivals*, 169–173.

4. W. E. B. DuBois, *The Souls of Black Folk* (New York: Simon and Schuster, 2005), 6.

5. For a first such collection of essays, see Michelle Voss Roberts, ed., *Comparing Faithfully: Insights for Systematic Theological Reflection* (New York: Fordham University Press, 2016).

6. I borrow the language of "normal science" and "paradigm" from Thomas Kuhn, *The Structure of Scientific Revolutions* (Chicago: University of Chicago Press, 1970).

7. On the necessarily hybrid nature of Christian tradition and theological reflection, see the compelling work of Kathryn Tanner, *Theories of Culture: A New Agenda for Theology* (Minneapolis, MN: Fortress Press, 1997). She writes, "... while there are boundaries between Christian and non-Christian ways of life, those boundaries are fluid and permeable. Claims and values that are outside are brought inside (or, much the same thing, what is inside is brought outside) in processes of transformation at the boundary. Christian identity is therefore no longer a matter of unmixed purity, but a hybrid affair established through unusual uses of materials found elsewhere." (152).

8. See Paul Tillich, *Systematic Theology, Vol. I* (Chicago: University of Chicago Press, 1951), 139.

9. On the gradual process by which such lines came to be drawn, see Daniel Boyarin, *Border Lines: The Partition of Judaeo-Christianity* (Philadelphia: University of Pennsylvania Press, 2006).

10. The use of the term "pagan" is, of course, fraught both historically and theologically. In these early pages, I use the term in keeping with early Christian usage to name all those who were neither Christian nor Jews. Thus, the term served to designate almost all non-Christian communities until the modern "invention of the world religions."

11. Pierre Hadot, *Philosophy as a Way of Life: Spiritual Exercises from Socrates to Foucault* (Malden, MA: Wiley-Blackwell, 1995).

12. On the matter of polydoxy, see Catherine Keller and Laurel Schneider, *Polydoxy: Theology of Multiplicity and Relation* (New York: Routledge, 2010).

13. On the production of world religions discourse, see Tomoko Masuzawa, *The Invention of World Religions: Or, How European Universalism Was Preserved in the Language of Pluralism* (Chicago: University of Chicago Press, 2005). Roger Johnson has argued that the birth of the category "religion" is far from modern and can be traced to the sixteenth-century work of Nicholas of Cusa. See Roger A. Johnson, *Peacemaking and Religious Violence: From Thomas Aquinas to Thomas Jefferson* (Eugene, OR: Pickwick Publications, 2009), 107–158.

14. See Jenny Daggers, *Postcolonial Theology of Religions: Particularity and Pluralism in World Christianity* (New York: Routledge, 2013), 13–35; and Paul Hedges, *Controversies in Interreligious Dialogue and the Theology of Religions* (London: SCM Press, 2010), 64–87.

15. On the notion of "religion-making," see the work of Arvind Mandair and his colleagues in Markus Dressler and Arvind-Pal S. Mandair, *Secularism and Religion-Making* (New York: Oxford University Press, 2011).

16. Christian scholarship about other traditions has a significantly longer history. Christian missionary writing about religious diversity and scholarship by Indologists, Sinologists, and their analogs have been with us for several centuries. For a brief discussion on missionary scholarship as a precursor to contemporary comparative theology, see Francis X. Clooney, *Comparative Theology: Deep Learning Across Religious Borders* (Malden, MA: Wiley-Blackwell, 2010), 27–30.

17. On Hegel's critical role in this work of imagining the West in contradistinction to the East, see Arvind-Pal S. Mandair's, *Religion and the Specter of the West: Sikhism, India, Postcoloniality, and the Politics of Translation*, chap. 2 (New York: Columbia University Press, 2009).

18. Samuel P. Huntington, *The Clash of Civilizations and the Remaking of World Order* (New York: Simon and Schuster, 2011); and John Milbank, Catherine Pickstock, and Graham Ward, eds., *Radical Orthodoxy: A New Theology* (New York: Routledge, 1999).

19. The peculiar ongoing identification between the Christian Right and American empire suggests that it would be premature to speak of this historical moment as one in which Christian traditions in the West are finished with Constantinianism. Nonetheless, the diminished cultural capital of Christianity is hard to miss. On the connection between the Christian Right and empire see Mark Lewis Taylor, *Religion, Politics, and the Christian Right: Post-9/11 Powers and American Empire* (Minneapolis, MN: Fortress Press, 2005).

20. There is also a larger and somewhat amorphous body of literature on interreligious dialogue, both as a popular movement and as an academic venture. That literature, though quite important, is not the focus of this book.

21. Persons from other religious traditions have begun to advance their own theologies of religious diversity. For Buddhist examples of TRD, see Perry Schmidt-Leukel's edited collection, *Buddhist Attitudes to Other Religions* (St. Ottilien, Germany: EOS Editions, 2008). See also Kristin Beise Kiblinger, *Buddhist Inclusivism: Attitudes Toward Religious Others* (Burlington, VT: Ashgate, 2005). Hence, we now have well-articulated Buddhist TRDs. Must comparative theology also take a tradition-specific prefix? To date, our most prominent comparative theologians have remained rooted in a primary home tradition even as they learn from and draw upon the resources of another tradition. I would contend that nothing prohibits a person who embraces multiple religious belonging from venturing a hyphenated or hybrid comparative theological project. We have just such a venture in Paul Knitter's book, *Without Buddha I Could Not Be a Christian* (Oxford: One World Publications, 2009). It is also possible to imagine a hybrid comparative theology—one informed by the resources of more than one tradition—that does not require the theologian to be himself formally committed to multiple religious participation or belonging. This book is itself an example of such comparative theology.

22. On this point, see James Fredericks, *Buddhists and Christians: Through Comparative Theology to Solidarity* (Maryknoll, NY: Orbis Books, 2004), 15–16. See also Fredericks's earlier book, *Faith Among Faiths: Christian Theology and Non-Christian Religions* (Mahwah, NJ: Paulist Press, 1999). For a recent example of the kind of patient and focused comparative theological reflection that Clooney commends, see his *Beyond Compare: St. Francis de Sales and Sri Vedanta Desika on Loving Surrender to God* (Washington, DC: Georgetown University Press, 2008).

23. Kristin Biese Kiblinger, "Relating Theology of Religions and Comparative Theology," in *The New Comparative Theology: Interreligious Insights from the Next Generation*, ed. Francis X. Clooney, S.J. (New York: T and T Clark, 2010), 21–42.

24. I prefer the term "theology of religious diversity" to "theology of religions" precisely because I find the adjectival form viable whereas the nouns "religion" or "religions" seem fraught with the temptation to reify and so mislead. For my theory of the religious, see Chapters 3 and 4.

25. I owe the notion that TRD is inadequate if it cannot account for why I stand to learn and gain from my neighbor's faith to conversations with Anantanand Rambachan.

26. See especially Stephen Duffy's essay, "A Theology of the Religions and/or a Comparative Theology" in *Horizons* 26.1 (2001): 105–115. S. Mark Heim's *The Depth of the Riches: A Trinitarian Theology of Religious Ends* (Grand Rapids, MI: Wm. B. Eerdmans, 2000) formulates a Trinitarian theology of religious diversity that includes substantive engagements with a variety of religious traditions. Heim thus makes an important step toward the kind of integration that I call for. Stephen Kaplan's *Different Paths, Different Summits: A Model for Religious Pluralism* (Lanham, MD: Rowman and Littlefield, 2002) engages in comparison across traditions and also proposes a general philosophy of religious pluralism.

27. The situation is changing as a younger generation of comparative theologians seems willing to make explicitly normative proposals. See, in particular, the work of Michelle Voss Roberts and Jon Paul Sydnor. Roberts, *Dualities: A Theology of Difference* (Louisville, KY: Westminster John Knox Press, 2010). Sydnor, *Ramanuja and Schleiermacher: Toward a Constructive Comparative Theology* (Eugene, OR: Wipf and Stock Publishers, 2011).

28. Gavin D'Costa is exactly right that the boundaries between theologies of religious diversity and comparative theology are "porous." He maintains that "in doing comparative theology, one's theology of religion might change and vice versa." Quite so. Like him, "I would prefer to see theology of religions and comparative theology as complementary, as aspects of dogma on the one hand, and missiology and inculturation on the other," although our understandings of dogma, missiology, and inculturation are sure to be marked by major differences. See his fine book, *Christianity and World Religions: Disputed Questions in the Theology of Religions* (Malden, MA: Wiley-Blackwell, 2009), 44–45.

29. Robert Miles and Malcolm Brown, *Racism* (New York: Routledge, 2003). See also Robert Miles, *Racism after "Race Relations"* (New York: Routledge, 1993).

30. For more on Islamophobia, see Todd H. Green, *The Fear of Islam: An Introduction to Islamophobia in the West*, 2nd ed. (Minneapolis, MN: Fortress Press, 2019).

## 2. The Limits and Promise of Exclusivism and Inclusivism: Assessing Major Options in Theologies of Religious Diversity

1. Paul Hedges, *Controversies in Interreligious Dialogue and the Theology of Religions* (London: SCM Press, 2010); and Paul F. Knitter, *Introducing Theologies of Religion* (Maryknoll, NY: Orbis Press, 2014).

2. Hedges, *Introducing Theologies of Religion*, 112.

3. Roland Faber and Catherine Keller, "A Taste for Multiplicity: The Skillful Means of Religious Pluralism," *Religions in the Making: Whitehead and the Wisdom Traditions of the World*, ed. John B. Cobb, Jr. (Eugene, OR: Cascade Books), 180–207.

4. Any discussion about taking seriously the aims of other traditions raises questions whether those aims are compatible with Christian aims and aspirations. That question inevitably leads to the topic of multiple religious participation and even belonging. On these matters, see Chapters 2–4. To anticipate, I hold that any theory of religion that holds that persons can belong to only one "religion" at a time runs roughshod over the historical reality of human religious practice in much of the globe. Worse still

are definitions of religion that build in exclusive singular religious belonging as normative. No theory of religion can be viable if it rules out as impossible what historical and ethnographic study show to be common.

5. See Knitter, *Introducing Theologies of Religions*, 19–60.

6. Given what I have just said about the importance of intrinsic religious interest, I worry about where Griffiths's distinction might lead. Nonetheless, it is a distinction that, at least, provisionally, clarifies and advances thought. It is, after all, possible to be interested in what a tradition has to say about the world without wanting to take up the transformative practices and aspirations of that tradition. I believe that such a piecemeal interest limits learning, but limited learning is still better than no learning at all. On Griffiths's fine work on the question of religious truth, see Chapter 2 of his still invaluable book, *Problems of Religious Diversity* (Malden, MA: Blackwell Publishing), 21–65.

7. Gavin D'Costa, *Christianity and World Religions: Disputed Questions in the Theology of Religions* (Malden, MA: Wiley-Blackwell, 2009).

8. Indeed, so much so that one wonders about whether one ought to accept D'Costa's characterization of himself as an exclusivist. If exclusivists there must be, then would there be more exclusivists of his stripe! For more, see the discussion of his work that follows.

9. It must be noted that Strange displays ambivalence about the standard typology in theologies of religion. He has described himself as an exclusivist, and other times he shies away from the label. Despite his reservations, I think the term is an apt fit for his position. About his reasons for ambivalence, see Daniel Strange, "Perilous Exchange, Precious Good News: A Reformed 'Subversive Fulfilment'[sic] Interpretation of Other Religions," in *Only One Way? Three Christian Responses on the Uniqueness of Christ in a Religiously Plural World*, ed. Gavin D'Costa, Paul Knitter, and Daniel Strange (London: SCM Press, 2011), 95–96.

10. Daniel Strange, "Exclusivisms: 'Indeed Their Rock Is Not Like Our Rock,'" in *Christian Approaches to Other Faiths*, ed. Alan Race and Paul M. Hedges (London: SCM Press, 2008), 49.

11. Strange, "Perilous Exchange," 134.

12. J. H. Bavinck, quoted in Strange, "Perilous Exchange," 134.

13. Bavinck, 134–135.

14. Bavinck, 91–92.

15. Bavinck, 117.

16. Bavinck, 117.

17. Gavin D'Costa, "Christianity and the World Religions: A Theological Appraisal," in *Only One Way? Three Christian Responses on the Uniqueness of Christ in a Religiously Plural World*, ed. Gavin D'Costa, Paul Knitter, and Daniel Strange, (London: SCM Press), 9–10.

18. Gavin D'Costa, *The Meeting of Religions and the Trinity* (Maryknoll, NY: Orbis Books, 2000), 111. Emphasis in original.

19. D'Costa, *Meeting of Religions*, 111.

20. D'Costa, 112.

21. D'Costa, 112.

22. D'Costa, 113.

23. D'Costa, 113.

24. D'Costa, 113; emphasis added.

25. D'Costa, 114.

26. For his arguments against the *de jure* validity of other religions, see his response to and exchange with Terence Tilley. The conversation begins with Tilley's, "Christian Orthodoxy and Religious Pluralism," *Modern Theology*, Vol. 22, no. 1 (January 2006), to which D'Costa responds with, "Christian Orthodoxy and Religious Pluralism: A Response to Terrence W. Tilley," *Modern Theology*, Vol. 23, no. 3 (July 2007).

27. D'Costa, *Christianity and World Religions*, 51.

28. D'Costa, 52.

29. The question of whether his interpretation of the magisterium as prohibiting *de jure* acceptance of other traditions is not something I can take up here. I leave that question to others, in particular, Paul Knitter and Terence Tilley.

30. Wayne Morris, *Salvation as Praxis: A Practical Theology of Salvation for a Multi-Faith World* (New York: Bloomsbury, 2014), 73.

31. Gerald R. McDermott, *God's Rivals: Why Has God Allowed Different Religions? Insights from the Bible and the Early Church* (Madison, WI: InterVarsity Press, 2007)157–158.

32. McDermott, *God's Rivals*, 158.

33. McDermott, 166–167; emphasis added.

34. McDermott, 167; emphasis added.

35. McDermott, 167.

36. Griffiths, *Problems of Religious Diversity*, 59. By this definition, it would seem that some features of McDermott's position can be classified as a form of "open inclusivism," as he plainly does not believe that all possible religious truth is already *explicitly* found in Biblical revelation.

37. Griffiths, *Problems of Religious Diversity*, 59

38. Griffiths, 63.

39. Griffiths, 21–65.

40. More on this matter in the discussion of John Hick found in the next chapter.

41. Griffiths, 12.

42. Griffiths, 34; emphasis added.

43. Paul J. Griffiths, *An Apology for Apologetics: A Study in the Logic of Interreligious Dialogue* (Maryknoll, NY: Orbis Books, 1991).

44. In Chapter 4, I offer a genealogy of the category "religion," which is, in part, meant to critique many received accounts of what "religion" and "the religions" are. Chapter 5 is meant to be a constructive vision of the religious that escapes the problems with prevailing accounts. But a thorough critique of postliberal accounts of religion as tightly integrated forms of life is already available in Kathryn Tanner's fine book, *Theories of Culture: A New Agenda for Theology* (Minneapolis, MN: Fortress Press, 1997). I refer readers to that book rather than rehearse those particular arguments here.

45. For an argument analogous to mine made by another pluralist (Paul Knitter) writing to and for another open inclusivist (Catherine Cornille), see Knitter, "Virtuous

Comparativists Are Practicing Pluralists," in *Religious Pluralism and the Modern World: An Ongoing Engagement with John Hick*, ed. Sharada Sugirtharajah (New York: Palgrave Macmillan, 2012), 46–57.

## 3. *No One Ascends Alone: Toward a Relational Pluralism*

1. Paul Hedges, *Controversies in Interreligious Dialogue and the Theology of Religions*, 109–145, 228–253.
2. See, for example, Knitter's important offering, "Is the Pluralist Model a Western Imposition? A Response in Five Voices," in *The Myth of Religious Superiority: A Multifaith Exploration*, ed. Paul F. Knitter (Maryknoll, NY: Orbis Books, 2005), 28–42.
3. To be precise, the elective affinity that Heim recognizes is between trinitarian theologies of religious pluralism in general and deep pluralism, not just with his trinitarian theology alone. See S. Mark Heim, "The Shifting Significance of Theologies of Religious Pluralism," in *Understanding Religious Pluralism: Perspectives from Religious Studies and Theology*, ed. Peter C. Phan and Jonathan S. Ray (Eugene, OR: Wipf and Stock, 2014), 254.
4. Here, I echo a point made by Griffin. See David Ray Griffin, "Religious Pluralism: Generic, Identist, and Deep," in *Deep Religious Pluralism*, ed. David Ray Griffin (Louisville, KY: Westminster John Knox Press, 2005), 21–38.
5. Griffin, "Religious Pluralism," 3–38.
6. The literature treating John Hick, both critical and appreciative, is extensive. For an important recent review essay of four books surveying contemporary engagements with pluralism and Hick's version in particular, see Kevin Schilbrack, "Religious Pluralism: A Checkup," *Religious Studies Review* 40, no. 1 (March 2014): 1–7. I am in material engagement with Schilbrack's assessment of Hick: "However, the third assumption (Hick's Kantian-inspired 'transcendental agnosticism') leads to a host of contradictions internal to Hick's own project. As Nah, Eddy, Yandell, and Adams show, the intellectual costs to the coherence of his version of religious pluralism are deep and significant. Considering these internal wounds, I do not see any way to save the patient" (4).
7. I borrow this idea from Raimundo Panikkar. See note 27.
8. This point is made superbly by K. P. Aleaz, "Pluralism Calls for Pluralistic Inclusivism: An Indian Christian Experience," in *The Myth of Religious Superiority: A Multifaith Exploration* (Maryknoll, NY: Orbis Books, 2005), 162–175.
9. The most comprehensive articulation of J. Hick's philosophy of religion can be found in the published version of his Gifford Lectures, *An Interpretation of Religion: Human Responses to the Transcendent* (New Haven, CT: Yale University Press, 1989).
10. John Hick, *A Christian Theology of Religions: The Rainbow of Faiths* (Louisville, KY: Westminster John Knox Press, 1995), 61–63. I highlight the word "neither" here because I will argue later in this chapter that it may be more compelling to argue that the divine is *both* personal and transpersonal, albeit in different dimensions. See the section titled "Brahman Is My Womb" later in this chapter.
11. Paul Knitter has made this claim to me on numerous occasions in personal conversation. The core of Knitter's contention is that Hick's Kantianism is vastly overstated. I am not so sure.

12. Hick writes, "The truthfulness of a myth is thus practical truthfulness, consisting in its capacity to orient us rightly in our lives." Hick, *Christian Theology of Religions*, 51.
13. Hick, 68.
14. Hick, 69.
15. Perry Schmidt-Leukel, "Religious Pluralism and the Need for an Interreligious Theology," in *Religious Pluralism and the Modern World: An Ongoing Engagement with John Hick*, ed. Sharada Sugirtharajah (New York: Palgrave Macmillan, 2012), 28–29.
16. John Hick, *Interpretation of Religion*, 32.
17. Leora Batnitzky, *How Judaism Became a Religion* (Princeton, NJ: Princeton University Press, 2013).
18. This recognition of the worldly and secular character of all our traditions is particularly clear in the work of John Cobb. See his book *Spiritual Bankruptcy: A Prophetic Call to Action* (Nashville: Abingdon Press, 2010).
19. S. Mark Heim, *The Depth of the Riches: A Trinitarian Theology of Religious Ends* (Grand Rapids, MI: Wm. B. Eerdmans, 2001), 2–3.
20. Hence, the title of his book, *Salvations: Truth and Difference in Religion* (Maryknoll, NY: Orbis Books, 1995).
21. Heim, *Depth of the Riches*, 3.
22. Heim, 216; emphasis added.
23. I once more commend Wayne Morris's book to the reader. It is a book-length argument that (1) there are many salvations on offer within the Christian tradition, and (2) that a liberationist reading of salvation as liberating praxis is the most praiseworthy and compelling option for Christians to adopt in a multi-faith world. See Wayne Morris, *Salvation as Praxis: A Practical Theology of Salvation for a Multi-Faith World* (New York: Bloomsbury, 2014).
24. Morris, *Salvation as Praxis*.
25. Writing about the virtues of his theology of religious ends, Heim writes that in such a theology, "Focus falls on their *positive* self-descriptions. They can be taken with full seriousness as alternatives, both here and now and eschatologically." Heim's commitment to valorizing difference all the way into postmortem existence is truly striking and provocative of thought. Heim, *Depth of the Riches*, 291.
26. Heim's theology falls back into a kind of particularistic inclusivism. Although there are many different soteriological goods, only one summit is the *summum bonum* because it includes all other partial goods—namely, communion with the trinity. One mountain reaches a higher elevation. I do not take that position. While time does not permit me to offer a complete accounting of the differences between our positions, I note that his account presupposes a social trinity; mine does not. My differences with him do not in any way diminish my profound appreciation for Heim's groundbreaking work. And, as noted, we share dissatisfaction with the notion of multiple ultimate realities. For Heim's generous account of the differences between his position and mine, see his "Differential Pluralism and Trinitarian Theologies of Religion," in *Divine Multiplicity: Trinities, Diversities, and the Nature of Relation*, ed. Chris Boesel and S. Wesley Ariarajah (New York: Fordham University Press, 2014), 119–136.
27. Raimundo Panikkar, *The Unknown Christ of Hinduism* (Bangalore: Asian Trading Corporation, 1981), 24.

28. Paul F. Knitter, *Introducing Theologies of Religions* (Maryknoll, NY: Orbis Books, 2002), 129.

29. Knitter, *Introducing Theologies of Religions*, 192–202. For Paul Hedges, see *Controversies in Interreligious Dialogue and Theology of Religions* (London: SCM Press, 2010), 163–164.

30. On this newer way of characterizing his own work, see Heim, "Differential Pluralism." Here, he notes that David Ray Griffin has characterized John Cobb and Heim himself as deep or differential pluralists—that is to say, as persons who believe that religions have distinct ends or religious goals, what Heim in his earlier work spoke of as "salvations" (126). But Heim is quick to nuance this point as follows: "It is my contention that rich trinitarian theologies of religion tend to arise precisely in the area where 'differential pluralism' overlaps with that part of the spectrum of inclusivist theologies of religion that moves toward what we might call 'differential inclusivism.'" For Heim, differential inclusivism is prepared 1) to acknowledge a genuine diversity of valid religious aims or ends, but then 2) to hold that one among these is the highest. Hence, despite his willingness to accept Griffin's classification, Heim is quick to qualify the matter. He is a differential pluralist and at once a differential inclusivist.

31. I do not mount a full-scale treatment of other particularist positions in this chapter or book because Paul Hedges has already done so brilliantly. His appreciative but rigorous critique of the particularities model sets the bar high in the TRD literature. See Hedges, "Particularities: Tradition-Specific Post-Modern Perspectives," in *Christian Approaches to Other Faiths*, ed. Alan Race and Paul Hedges (London: SCM Press, 2008), 112–135.

32. John Cobb quoted in David Ray Griffin, "John Cobb's Whiteheadian Complementary Pluralism," in *Deep Religious Pluralism*, ed. David Ray Griffin (Louisville, KY: Westminster John Knox Press, 2005), 47. Emphasis added.

33. Griffin, "Complementary Pluralism," 47.

34. Griffin, 49.

35. *The Bhagavad Gita*, trans. Laurie L. Patton (New York: Penguin Books, 2008), 155–156, 162. Translation slightly revised.

36. On the exegetical debates on this verse and the *Gita* as a whole, see Chakravarthi Ram-Prasad's stellar book, *Divine Self, Human Self: The Philosophy of Being in Two Gitā Commentaries* (New York: Bloomsbury, 2013).

37. John B. Cobb, Jr., "Multiple Religious Belonging and Reconciliation," *Many Mansions? Multiple Religious Belonging and Christian Identity* (Maryknoll, NY: Orbis Books, 2002), 23.

38. Cobb, "Multiple Religious Belonging," 23–24.

39. Cobb, 24.

40. To see his account of multiple religious participation and compare it with mine, see Mark Heim, "On Doing as Others Do: Theological Perspectives on Multiple Religious Practice"; and my "Eucharist Upstairs, Yoga Downstairs: On Multiple Religious Participation." Both are to be found in Peniel Jesudason Rufus Rajkumar and Joseph Prabhakar Dayam, eds., *Many Yet One? Multiple Religious Belonging* (Geneva: WCC Press, 2016).

41. Roland Faber and Catherine Keller, "A Taste for Multiplicity: The Skillful Means of Religious Pluralism," in *Religions in the Making: Whitehead and the Wisdom Traditions of the World*, ed. John B. Cobb, Jr. (Eugene, OR: Cascade Books, 2012), 182.
42. Faber and Keller, "Taste for Multiplicity," 182.
43. Faber and Keller, 183.
44. Faber and Keller, 202; emphasis in the original.
45. Faber and Keller, 192.

## 4. *Comparative Theology after Religion?*

An earlier and abbreviated version of this chapter was published in 2011. See John J. Thatamanil, "Comparative Theology after 'Religion,'" in *Planetary Loves: Spivak, Postcoloniality, and Theology* ed. Stephen D. Moore and Mayra Rivera (New York: Fordham University Press, 2011), 238–257. When that version was published, I was unaware of an analogous effort to mine published just a few months earlier by Reid B. Locklin and Hugh Nicholson entitled "The Return of Comparative Theology," *Journal of the American Academy of Religion* 78, no. 2 (June 2010): 417–514. Locklin and Nicholson broach therein a sophisticated vision for a "comparative theology after religion" that tracks some of the same ground I covered. I am grateful to acknowledge their work here as well as Hugh Nicholson's book, *Comparative Theology and the Problem of Religious Rivalry* (New York: Oxford University Press, 2011).

1. Daniel Dubuisson, *The Western Construction of Religion: Myths, Knowledge, and Ideology*, trans. William Sayers (Baltimore: Johns Hopkins University Press, 2003).
2. See especially Talal Asad's "The Construction of Religion as an Anthropological Category," in *Genealogies of Religion: Discipline and Reasons of Power in Christianity and Islam* (Baltimore: Johns Hopkins University Press, 1993), 27–54.
3. For accounts that emphasize that the construction of "religion" and "religions" is a product of cross-cultural encounter rather than a unilateral imposition of the West upon the rest, see especially Josephson's work on distinctive Japanese construction of religion, *The Invention of Religion in Japan* (Chicago: University of Chicago Press, 2012). David Chidester sounds analogous themes with respect to the African context in *Empire of Religion: Imperialism and Comparative Religion* (Chicago: University of Chicago Press, 2014) and *Savage Systems: Colonialism and Comparative Religion in Southern Africa* (Charlottesville: University of Virginia Press, 1996).
4. For example, "What makes something a religion and, indeed, what determines where one tradition ends and another begins are matters I will not discuss here except to say that the value of discussing them seems at times to be inversely related to the copious amount of ink that has been consumed in their discussion." See Robert McKim, *On Religious Diversity* (New York: Oxford University Press, 2012), 5. As I am one such copious spiller of ink, I must, of course, disagree with McKim's otherwise learned treatise!
5. See Paul Hedges, *Controversies in Interreligious Dialogue and Theologies of Religions* (London: SCM Press, 2010); Jenny Daggers, *Postcolonial Theology of Religions: Particularity and Pluralism in World Christianity* (New York: Routledge Press, 2013); Hugh

Nicholson, *Comparative Theology and the Problem of Religious Rivalry* (New York: Oxford University Press, 2011).

6. I borrow this phrase from Arvind Mandair. See his "The Repetition of Past Imperialisms: Hegel, Historical Difference, and the Theorization of Indic Religions," *History of Religions* 44 (2005), 288. See also his monumental work, *Religion and the Specter of the West: Sikhism, India, Postcoloniality, and the Politics of Translation* (New York: Columbia University Press, 2009).

7. Wendy Brown, *Walled States, Waning Sovereignty* (Brooklyn, NY: Zone Books, 2014).

8. I completed writing this chapter before Ted O. Vial's brilliant new book *Modern Religion, Modern Race* (Chicago: University of Chicago Press, 2018) was published. In this chapter, I argue that religion functions quite like the category race, as a mode of divide and conquer classification that impedes theological reflection. Vial makes the further and radical argument that the category "religion" is, at its origins, thoroughly racialized. There is no disentangling these categories.

9. On the momentous import of this philological discovery and its impact on ethnological racial theories, see Thomas R. Trautmann's groundbreaking work, *Aryans and British India* (New Delhi: Yoda Press, 2004).

10. Rushdie, *Ground beneath Her Feet*, 44.

11. See Trautmann, *Aryans and British India*, 168–169.

12. Trautmann, 170.

13. Trautmann, 182.

14. Trautmann, 183.

15. Trautmann, 180–181.

16. Sadly, Müller is not an unambiguous hero in this tale. Trautmann shows that Müller was himself captive to and responsible for accounts of fair-skinned Aryan invaders inevitably subduing the darker and more primitive aboriginal inhabitants of the Indian subcontinent.

17. Robert Miles, *Racism after "Race Relations"* (New York: Routledge, 1993).

18. Robert Miles and Malcolm Brown, *Racism*, Second Edition (New York: Routledge, 2003), 91.

19. Miles and Brown, *Racism*, 91–92.

20. Among these I am especially indebted to the essay just cited and the following: Arvind-Pal S. Mandair, "What if *Religio* Remained Untranslatable?" in *Difference in Philosophy of Religion*, ed. by Philip Goodchild (Burlington, VT: Ashgate Publishing Company, 2003), 87–100; "The Global Fiduciary: Mediating the Violence of 'Religion,'" in *Religion and Violence in South Asia: Theory and Practice*, ed. John R. Hinells and Richard King (New York: Routledge, 2007), 211–225; "(Im)possible Intersections: Religion, (Post-)Colonial Subjectivity, and the Ideology of Multiculturalism," in *A Postcolonial People: South Asians in Britain*, ed. N. Ali, V. S. Kalra, and S. Sayyid (New York: Columbia University Press, 2008). Taken together, these essays establish Mandair as among our foremost thinkers on the category "religion."

21. Mandair, "Repetition of Past Imperialisms," 277.

22. Mandair, 277–278.

23. Mandair, 278.

24. John Milbank, *Theology and Social Theory: Beyond Secular Reason* (Malden, MA: Blackwell Publishing, 1990).

25. It is hard to determine precisely which postcolonial thinkers fall prey to this commitment to secular critique alone and the degree of guilt to be imputed to these various thinkers. Mandair lists a variety of figures including Edward Said, Ronald Inden, and Gayatri Chakravorty Spivak, among others. See Mandair, "Repetition of Past Imperialisms," 280.

26. Mandair, 281.

27. For noteworthy exceptions to this rule, see the work of Robert C. Neville, Francis X. Clooney, S.J., and Michelle Voss Roberts. For the most sophisticated articulation of a theological program that makes comparison integral to theology as such, see Neville's *On the Scope and Truth of Theology: Theology as Symbolic Engagement* (New York: T and T Clark International, 2006). The program for theology articulated therein has been fulfilled in his three-volume *Philosophical Theology*. See *Ultimates: Philosophical Theology, Volume One* (Albany: SUNY Press, 2013); *Existence: Philosophical Theology, Volume Two* (Albany: SUNY Press, 2015); and *Religion: Philosophical Theology, Volume Three* (Albany: SUNY Press, 2015). See also Clooney's *Hindu God, Christian God: How Reason Helps to Break Down the Boundaries between Religions* (New York: Oxford University Press, 2001). For Roberts, see *Tastes of the Divine: Hindu and Christian Theologies of Emotion* (New York: Fordham University Press, 2014). See also her edited volume, *Comparing Faithfully: Insights for Systematic Theological Reflection* (New York: Fordham University Press, 2016), which seeks to integrate comparative thinking with systematic reflection on a number of classical theological loci.

28. Mandair, "Repetition of Past Imperialisms."

29. This is not to suggest that monogenetic accounts were immune to co-optation by colonial agendas. Mandair does well to demonstrate that early Indologists managed to allow for common origins between European and Indian cultures while simultaneously marking surviving Indian traditions as inferior because they have fallen away from an original and pure monotheism. The colonial project needed only the hypothesis that this original golden age of Aryan language and peoples was not preserved in India. Narratives of loss and decline were sufficient to support the need for a paternalistic colonialism that would restore to Indians their once noble cultural heritage. That said, Mandair argues that in subsequent periods of increased nationalism, the European strategy that eventually prevailed was a turn to polygenetic accounts of races and religions. See Mandair, 288–289. It is just here that Hegel emerges as a decisive figure.

30. Mandair writes that Hegel explicitly sought "to counter the influence of Indophiles such as Schelling in whose philosophy the prevailing definition of God/religion brought the origins of Oriental and Occidental civilizations unbearably close, such that the dominant vantage point of Euro-Christian identity based on its exclusionary claims to history, reason, and metaphysics, not to mention the colonial enterprise itself, would be threatened." Mandair, 289.

31. Mandair, 290.

32. This complexity has much to do with Mandair's argument that for Hegel the decisive test for a religion's maturity was to be measured by its capacity to approach the ontological proof for God's existence. See Mandair, 292–293. Traditions that have not realized the identity of being and thinking as exemplified in that argument remain deficient and trapped in earlier stages of cultural development. By appeal to this criterion,

Hegel is able to distance Indian religion from Christianity by showing that "The Indian idea of divinity was as yet 'confused,' 'monstrous,' 'terrifying,' 'idolatrous,' 'absurd,' 'erroneous'—clear evidence for Hegel that Hindu thinking was limited to thinking nothingness." See Mandair, 292.

33. Josephson, *Invention of Religion in Japan*, 1.

34. Josephson.

35. Josephson, 255.

36. Josephson, 257; emphasis added.

37. Peter Gottschalk, *Beyond Hindu and Muslim: Multiple Identity in Narratives from Village India* (New York: Oxford University Press, 2000), 136.

38. Gottschalk, *Beyond Hindu and Muslim*, 29.

39. Gottschalk, 11.

40. Gottschalk, 36–37.

41. Those unfamiliar with the Indian context may well be puzzled by the words "communalism" and "communal," which in the Indian context refer to forces and political actors who seek to pitch one community against the other typically in order to advance a right-wing Hindu majoritarianism at the expense of minority communities. The term's nearest analogue outside of India is likely "sectarianism."

42. Peter Gottschalk, *Religion, Science, and Empire: Classifying Hinduism and Islam in British India* (New York: Oxford University Press, 2013), 197.

43. Gottschalk, *Religion, Science, and Empire*, 198.

44. Gottschalk, 199; emphasis added.

45. Paulo Gonçalves, "Religious 'Worlds' and Their Alien Invaders," in *Difference in Philosophy of Religion*, ed. Philip Goodchild (Burlington, VT: Ashgate Publishing, 2003), 115–134.

46. Gonçalves, "Religious 'Worlds,'" 116; emphasis in the original.

47. Richard King, *Orientalism and Religion: Post-Colonial Theory, India, and "The Mystic East"* (New York: Routledge, 1999).

48. Gonçalves, "Religious 'Worlds,'"116; emphasis in the original.

49. Gonçalves, 117.

50. Gonçalves, 117.

51. Of course, this is not to say that becoming religiously bilingual is easily accomplished. Gayatri Chakravorty Spivak offers a rigorous account of the degree of bilingual competency required by those who aspire to take on the work of translating third-world texts. See her essay "The Politics of Translation," in *Outside in the Teaching Machine* (New York: Routledge, 1993), 179–200.

52. See Spivak, "Politics of Translation."

53. Gonçalves, "Religious 'Worlds,'" 124.

54. Gonçalves, 125.

55. Jacques Derrida, *Positions*, trans. A. Bass (Chicago: University of Chicago Press, 1981), 57, quoted in Gonçalves, "Religious 'Worlds' and their Alien Invaders," 126.

56. Derrida, quoted in Gonçalves, "Religious 'Worlds,'" 132.

57. See my book *The Immanent Divine: God, Creation, and the Human Predicament* (Minneapolis, MN: Fortress Press, 2006), 205. See also Harold H. Oliver's *Relatedness: Essays in Metaphysics and Theology* (Macon, GA.: Mercer University Press, 1984), 163–164.

58. Nagarjuna, *The Fundamental Wisdom of the Middle Way: Nagarjuna's* Mulamadhya-makakarika, Translation and commentary by Jay Garfield (New York: Oxford University Press, 1995).

59. For an important discussion of Chinese terms for "what-we-would-call-religion,"—see Robert Ford Campany's fine essay, "On the Very Idea of Religions (in the Modern West and Early Medieval China," *History of Religions* 42, no. 4 (May 2003): 287–319.

60. Campany, "On the Very Idea of Religions," 299–307.

61. Campany, 305.

62. Campany, 306.

63. Campany, 306–307.

64. More on this matter immediately later in the chapter, in our discussion of Hugh Nicholson.

65. Nicholson, *Comparative Theology*, ix.

66. Nicholson, 27. To his credit, Nicholson alertly notes that it is the early Paul Knitter he has in mind when he speaks to a certain homogenizing tendency in pluralist theologies of religious diversity. With him, I recognize in Knitter's recent discourse about a mutualist approach a new emphasis on difference between religious traditions. Whether the early Knitter should have ever been simply identified with Hick, however, is a question well worth exploring.

67. For Kathryn Tanner, see her perspicacious article, "Respect for Other Religions: A Christian Antidote to Colonialist Discourse," *Modern Theology* 9, no. 1 (January 1993): 1–18.

68. Tomoko Masuzawa, *The Invention of World Religions* (Chicago: University of Chicago Press, 2005), 315.

69. But, Masuzawa rightly observes that this premise was already made explicit in one of the founding figures of liberal Christian theology and religious studies, Ernst Troeltsch. See her discussion of Troeltsch in *Invention of World Religions*, 309–327.

70. Masuzawa, *Invention of World Religions*, x.

71. Nicholson, *Comparative Theology*, 9.

72. To appreciate how very different our notions of religious identity would look were we to begin with lives and experiences of women, see the work of Jeannine Hill Fletcher, particularly, *Monopoly on Salvation? A Feminist Approach to Religious Pluralism* (New York: Continuum, 2005).

73. Fletcher, *Monopoly on Salvation?*, 102.

74. For just such a project, see Carlin A. Barton and Daniel Boyarin, *Imagine No Religion: How Modern Abstractions Hide Ancient Realities* (New York: Fordham University Press, 2016)

75. Kwame Anthony Appiah, *In My Father's House: Africa in the Philosophy of Culture* (New York: Oxford University Press, 1993). See also his newest work, *The Lies that Bind: Rethinking Identity* (New York: Liveright Publishing, 2018).

76. Victor Anderson, *Beyond Ontological Blackness: An Essay on African American Religious and Cultural Criticism* (Continuum, 1995), 11.

77. Anderson, *Beyond Ontological Blackness*, 13.

78. Anderson, 15.

79. Anderson, 15; emphasis added.

80.  About enlargement, Anderson writes,

> Insofar as race contributes to . . . religious significations of enlargement, it contributes powerfully toward a pragmatic theology of African American religious experience. As a deep symbol, race may signify a relational moral attitude toward the world and human life beyond one's preoccupation with his/her own group. Among all the particulars that encompass the lives of African and African American peoples, race entails circles of relations. And when the symbol is reconstituted under the *sensus communis*, it signifies sympathetic filiations between families, villages, provinces, cultures, and by greater enlargement, humanity." See Victor Anderson, *Creative Exchange: A Constructive Theology of African American Religious Experience* (Minneapolis, MN: Fortress Press, 2008), 50.

81.  Anderson, *Creative Exchange*, 31.
82.  Wilfred Cantwell Smith, *The Meaning and End of Religion* (Minneapolis, MN: Fortress Press, 1991; originally published in 1962).
83.  See, for example, the work of Daniel Dubuisson, who proposes the substitution "cosmographic formations" in his vigorously argued book, *Western Construction of Religion*.
84.  David Tracy, "Comparative Theology," in *Encyclopedia of Religion*, 16 vols. (New York: Macmillan, 1987), 14.446–55.

## 5. *Defining the Religious: Comprehensive Qualitative Orientation*

Epigraph: The implied contrast in this quotation is between political conviction and religious conviction. Of the two, De Certeau argues that the latter is easier to exploit.

1.  For a fuller discussion of the terms "multiple religious participation," "multiple religious participation," and "syncretism," see my chapter, "Eucharist Upstairs, Yoga Downstairs: On Multiple Religious Participation," in *Many Yet One? Multiple Religious Belonging*, ed. Peniel Jesudason Rufus Rajkumar and Joseph Prabhakar Dayam (Geneva: WCC Publications, 2016).
2.  A public case in which multiple religious belonging proved controversial was the selection of Kevin Thew Forrester as Bishop-Elect of the Northern Michigan diocese of the Episcopal Church. Forrester's selection by his diocese did not successfully move through the Episcopal Church's consent process, which requires approval from a majority of bishops exercising jurisdiction and diocesan standing committees. A crucial factor in Forrester's failure to receive consent was his commitment to Zen practice. See *Christian Post*, https://www.christianpost.com/news/episcopal-church-nullifies -election-of-episcopal-priest-with-buddhist-ties-39962/, accessed February 16, 2019.
3.  I have learned much about the relationship between definitions and theories from Thomas Tweed, *Crossing and Dwelling: A Theory of Religion* (Cambridge, MA: Harvard University Press, 2006).
4.  Each of the italicized terms herein is a technical term that will be defined later in the chapter. As they are defined, a cumulative definition of the religious will gradually emerge.

5. Robert Cummings Neville, *Ritual and Deference: Extending Chinese Philosophy in a Comparative Context* (Albany: SUNY Press, 2008), 158.

6. Peter L. Berger, *The Sacred Canopy: Elements of a Sociological Theory of Religion* (New York: Anchor Books, 1969), 4–6.

7. For two important resources essential to such correction, see Philippe Descola, *Beyond Nature and Culture* (Chicago: University of Chicago Press, 2013); and Samantha Frost's, *Biocultural Creatures: Toward a New Theory of the Human* (Durham, NC: Duke University Press, 2016).

8. My understanding of ritual is borrowed from Robert Neville's Confucian account of ritual. See his account of ritual in *Ritual and Deference: Extending Chinese Philosophy in a Comparative Context* (Albany: State University of New York Press, 2008), 18–19.

9. On the religious import of scientific multiverse speculation, see Mary-Jane Rubenstein, *Worlds without End: The Many Lives of the Multiverse* (New York: Columbia University Press, 2014). Rubenstein's work complicates further the notion that science remains religiously neutral. That may be the way to distinguish between scientific and religious orientation, but whether such neutrality obtains is another matter.

10. See William E. Connolly, *Capitalism and Christianity, American Style* (Durham, NC: Duke University Press, 2008), 69–70.

11. See John Dewey, *A Common Faith* (New Haven, CT: Yale University Press, 1934), 79.

12. Dewey, *Common Faith*, 84.

13. My appeal to the notion of "attitude" here advanced is indebted to Steven G. Smith, *Appeal and Attitude: Prospects for Ultimate Meaning* (Indianapolis: Indiana University Press, 2005). See also his essay, "Three Religious Attitudes," *Philosophy and Theology* 11, no. 1 (1998): 3–24.

14. Peter L. Berger, *A Rumor of Angels: Modern Society and the Rediscovery of the Supernatural* (New York: Anchor Books, 1990; originally published in 1969), 61–62; emphasis in the original.

15. Berger, *Rumor of Angels*, 63–64.

16. For a noteworthy critique of Berger's conservative account of religion, see Gary Dorrien, "Berger: Theology and Sociology," in *Peter Berger and the Study of Religion*, ed. Linda Woodhead, with Paul Heelas and David Martin (New York: Routledge, 2001), 31.

17. My approach has resonances with John Dewey's program to distinguish between the religious and the religions: "The heart of my point . . . is that there is a difference between religion, *a* religion, and the religious; between anything that may be denoted by a noun substantive and the quality of experience that is designated by an adjective." See Dewey, *Common Faith*, 3; emphasis in the original.

18. See, for example, Timothy Fitzgerald, "Encompassing Religion, privatized religions and the invention of modern politics," in *Religion and the Secular: Historical and Colonial Formations*, ed. Timothy Fitzgerald (New York: Routledge, 2007), 211–240.

19. The business of determining what meanings are entailed by any given set of practices is a complicated matter because practices are polysemic; the same set of practices can house a variety of meanings. Only conversations with practitioners can determine what they take their practices to mean. Ethnography is important to theology for just this reason. For a remarkable demonstration of the promise of ethnography for

theology, see Mary McClintock Fulkerson, *Places of Redemption: Theology for a Worldly Church* (New York: Oxford University Press, 2007).

20. See Robert Ford Campany, "On the Very Idea of Religions (in the Modern West and Early Medieval China)," *History of Religions* 42, no. 4 (May 2003): 317. See also his book *Making Transcendents: Ascetics and Social Memory in Early Medieval China* (Honolulu: University of Hawai'i Press, 2009), 40–41.

21. Ann Swidler, *Talk of Love: How Culture Matters* (Chicago: University of Chicago Press, 2001) 24.

22. Swidler, *Talk of Love*, 24–25.

23. Swidler, 21.

24. Swidler, 22.

25. Swidler, 22.

26. The term neoliberalism is often hurled about, a kind of omnibus gesture to speak of features of contemporary economic life that one finds odious. In this chapter, I have in mind the specific content given to the term by Wendy Brown in her book, *Undoing the Demos: Neoliberalism's Stealth Revolution* (Cambridge, MA: MIT Press, 2015).

27. The literature exploring the theological content of economic theories and the practice of capitalism is vast. For some noteworthy books, see Marion Grau, *Of Divine Economy: Refinancing Redemption* (New York: T and T Clark International, 2004); Robert H. Nelson, *Economics as Religion: From Samuelson to Chicago and Beyond* (University Park: Pennsylvania State Press, 2001); and Kathryn Tanner, *Christianity and the New Spirit of Capitalism* (New Haven, CT: Yale University Press, 2019).

28. On the sectarian impulse, see Stanley Hauerwas, *Resident Aliens: Life in the Christian Colony*, Expanded 25th Anniversary Edition (Nashville: Abingdon Press, 2014). On the nostalgia for a lost Christendom, see John Milbank, *Beyond Secular Order: The Representation of Being and the Representation of the People* (Hoboken, NJ: Wiley-Blackwell, 2013).

29. See William Connolly, *Why I Am Not a Secularist* (Minneapolis: University of Minnesota Press, 2000).

30. Connolly, *Capitalism and Christianity*.

31. Robert H. Nelson, *Economics as Religion*, 73.

32. Jeremy Carrette and Richard King, *Selling Spirituality: The Silent Takeover of Religion* (New York: Routledge, 2005), 174.

33. Carrette and Richard King, *Selling Spirituality*, 174.

34. Linda Kintz, *Between Jesus and the Market: The Emotions that Matter in Right-Wing America* (Durham, NC: Duke University Press, 1997), 225.

35. See, for example, David R. Loy, *Money, Sex, War, Karma: Notes for a Buddhist Revolution* (Somerville, MA: Wisdom Publications, 2008).

## 6. *The Hospitality of Receiving: Mahatma Gandhi, Martin Luther King, Jr., and Interreligious Learning*

I could not have been written this chapter without the support of Lewis Baldwin. Also of great help were e-mail conversations with Vivek Pinto, author of *Gandhi's Vision and Values: The Moral Quest for Change in Indian Agriculture* (New Delhi: Sage Publications, 1998). I also owe an enormous personal and intellectual debt to the Reverend James Lawson, who was one of Dr. King's close colleagues and guides on questions of nonviolence theory and practice. I treasure our lunchtime conversations in Nashville about Dr. King and the Civil Rights Movement. Naturally, none ought to be held responsible for what remains incomplete or mistaken in these reflections.

1. On Gandhi and religious diversity, see Margaret Chatterjee, *Gandhi and the Challenge of Religious Diversity: Religious Pluralism Revisited* (New Delhi: Promila and Co., Publishers, 2005). On King's teacher's direct engagements with Gandhi, see Sarah Azaransky's groundbreaking book, *This Worldwide Struggle: Religion and the International Roots of the Civil Rights Movement* (New York: Oxford University Press, 2017).

2. I am grateful to my now former students, Dr. Joshua Samuel and Dr. Jamall Calloway, who have urged me to register the complexities entailed in working with such an ambiguous figure, one who is continually presented to western audiences uncritically.

3. On the failures of Gandhi in South Africa, see the devastating and meticulously researched work of Ashwin Desai and Goolem Vahed, *The South African Gandhi: Stretcher-Bearer of Empire* (Stanford: Stanford University Press, 2015). For example of carefully considered and a balanced critical reading of Gandhi, see Joseph Lelyveld, *Mahatma Gandhi and His Struggle with India* (New York: Vintage, 2011).

4. Some of this work has now become easily accessible to Western audiences through the publication of Ambedkar's major work with Arundhati Roy's devastating extended preface. See Arundhati Roy, *The Doctor and the Saint: Caste, Race, and Annihilation of Caste, the Debate Between B. R. Ambedkar and M. K. Gandhi* (Chicago: Haymarket Books, 2017).

5. Sudarshan Kapoor has demonstrated that far too often studies of the Civil Rights Movement focus narrowly on Dr. King's "discovery of Gandhi" and, in doing so, adopt an "elitist approach to a story which should involve the preparation of an entire people." He argues instead that "it is the experience of the African-American people and the possibilities of their prior knowledge of and experience with Gandhian methodology which are largely missing from earlier approaches to this story." See Sudarshan Kapoor, *Raising Up a Prophet: The African-American Encounter with Gandhi* (Boston: Beacon Press, 1992), 2. My focus on Dr. King in this chapter is not a return to an older elitist approach. I intend only to explore the resources that fueled his particular capacity for interreligious receptivity. Kapoor is right. We must also ask larger questions about the religious resources that empowered the African American community as a whole to learn from Gandhi.

6. Sarah Azaranksy, *This Worldwide Struggle: Religion and the International Roots of the Civil Rights Movement* (New York: Oxford University Press, 2017), 143, 149.

7. Mohandas K. Gandhi, *Gandhi on Christianity*, ed. Robert Ellsberg (Maryknoll: Orbis Press, 1991), 40.

8. Gandhi, *Gandhi on Christianity*, 41.

9. Gandhi, 37.

10. Has this call for humble receptivity been heard in Christian theology and, in particular, among Christian theologians who work in interreligious dialogue? By and large, Gandhi's call has gone unheard. One exemplary argument on behalf of hospitality,

including the hospitality of receiving, comes from the Pentecostal theologian Amos Yong, although Yong does not derive his theology of hospitality from Gandhi. What is most striking about Yong's work is his claim that "Jesus characterizes the hospitality of God in part as the exemplary recipient of hospitality. From his conception in Mary's womb by the power of the Holy Spirit to his birth in a manger to his burial (in a tomb of Joseph of Arimathea), Jesus was dependent on the welcome of others." The argument of this chapter is indebted to Yong's fine book, *Hospitality and the Other: Pentecost, Christian Practices, and the Neighbor* (Maryknoll: Orbis Books, 2008), 101.

11. Martin Luther King, Jr., *Stride Toward Freedom* (San Francisco: Harper and Row, 1958), 85; emphasis added.

12. Clayborn Carson et. al., eds. *The Papers of Martin Luther King Jr.* vol. 5, *Threshold of a New Decade, January 1959–December 1960* (Berkeley: University of California Press, 2005), 146–147; and Martin Luther King, Jr., "Letter to Dr. Harold Fey," (June 23, 1962), 2–4. Document housed in the Library and Archives of the Martin Luther King, Jr. Center for Nonviolent Social Change, Inc., Atlanta, Georgia.

13. Carson et al., *Papers* 5: 147–148.

14. King, *Stride Toward Freedom*, 89.

15. Martin Luther King, Jr., "Pilgrimage to Nonviolence," in *A Testament of Hope: The Essential Writings and Speeches of Martin Luther King Jr.*, ed. James M. Washington (San Francisco: HarperSanFrancisco, 1986), 38.

16. King, *Stride Toward Freedom*, 96–97. It is worth noting here that King specialists have called into question King's narrative of his own discovery of Gandhi in seminary. The general consensus has shifted, and most argue that King's appreciation for Gandhian nonviolence was far more gradual and a later, post-Montgomery phenomenon. This question of timing and gradually unfolding appreciation does not bear on my contention that King learned how to understand Jesus anew and afresh under Gandhian inspiration.

17. On this point, Gary Dorrien has demonstrated that King followed his Boston University teacher A. C. Knudson and held that "merit and guilt belong to individuals; they cannot be transferred from one person to another. Moreover, it is immoral to punish one person for the sins of another." Dorrien cites King on this point as saying, "'Christ's death was not a ransom, or a penal substitute, or a penal example; rather it was a revelation of the sacrificial love of God intended to awaken an answering love in the hearts of men.'" See Gary Dorrien, *The Making of American Liberal Theology: Crisis, Irony, and Postmodernity: 1950–2005* (Louisville: Westminster John Knox Press, 2006), 152. Mohandas Gandhi long held to the selfsame position and found the notion of substitutionary atonement morally incoherent and distasteful. Here we have a case not of influence but of resonance. Perhaps King's rejection of traditional theories of atonement prepared him for a Gandhian reading of the cross.

18. Martin Luther King, Jr., "Letter to Dr. Harold E. Fey, Editor of The Christian Century," June 23, 1962.

19. By way of juxtaposition, it is noteworthy that the Catholic Church's shift toward inclusivism found history making expression a full three years later on October 28, 1965, in the Vatican II document *Nostra Aetate*, or "The Declaration on the Relationship between the Church and Non-Christian Religions." That document maintains that "the

Catholic Church rejects nothing that is true and holy in these religions. She regards with sincere reverence those ways of conduct and of life, those precepts and teachings which, though differing in many aspects from the ones she holds and sets forth, nonetheless often reflect a ray of that Truth which enlightens all men. Indeed, she proclaims, and ever must proclaim Christ 'the way, the truth, and the life' (John 14:6), in whom men may find the fullness of religious life, in whom God has reconciled all things to Himself." King's creativity on questions of revelation in other religions predates *Nostra Aetate* and stands at the cutting edge of the best theological thinking of the day. The entirety of this key document is available on the Vatican's website: http://www.vatican.va/archive/hist_councils/ii_vatican_council/documents/vat-ii _decl_19651028_nostra-aetate_en.html.

20. King, "Letter to Dr. Harold E. Fey." Emphasis added.

21. Gandhi, *Gandhi on Christianity*, 33.

22. This selection is from King's milestone sermon, "A Time to Break the Silence," delivered at Riverside Church in New York on April 4, 1967, precisely a year before his assassination. See *A Testament of Hope: The Essential Writings and Speeches of Martin Luther King, Jr.*, ed. James M. Washington (San Francisco: HarperSanFrancisco, 1986), 243.

## 7. God as Ground, Singularity, and Relation: Trinity and Religious Diversity

Epigraph: Gregory of Nyssa, "The Great Catechism," *A Select Library of Nicene and Post-Nicene Fathers of the Christian Church*, Second Series, Volume V, trans. W. Moore and H. A. Wilson (New York: The Christian Literature Company, 1893), 477; emphasis added.

1. For a helpful book that summarizes and assesses a number of trinitarian approaches to religious diversity, see Veli-Matti Kärkkäinen, *Trinity and Religious Pluralism: The Doctrine of the Trinity in Christian Theology of Religions* (Burlington, VT: Ashgate Press, 2004). See also Mark Heim's remarkable treatise, *The Depth of the Riches: A Trinitarian Theology of Religious Ends* (Grand Rapids, MI: Wm. B. Eerdmans Publishing Co., 2001).

2. On hierarchical inclusivism, see Wilhelm Halbfass, "'Inclusivism' and 'Tolerance' in the Encounter between Indian and the West," in his *India and Europe: An Essay in Understanding* (Albany: SUNY Press, 1998), 411.

3. For a persuasive challenge to social trinitarianism, see Linn Tonstad's book, *God and Difference: The Trinity, Sexuality, and the Transformation of Finitude* (New York: Routledge, 2016), 12. She expresses incredulity that Christian theologians need the social trinity to interrupt the modern self-centered Cartesian individual. She writes, "Given that the defining project of postmodernity has been to make that point, one wonders who—other than perhaps certain analytic philosopher-theologians and economists (at least in their models)—considers the 'Cartesian' notion of personhood standard. Also, given that entire fields of study have managed to develop that insight apart from trinitarian doctrine, the anti-social trinitarian question remains: What do we learn from the trinity that we did not already know?"

4. The literature on recent trinitarian disputes is considerable. For an important collection of essays in which the question of social versus anti-social trinitarianism is engaged, see S. T. Davis, D. Kendall, S.J., and G. O'Collins, S.J., *The Trinity: An Interdisciplinary Symposium on the Trinity* (New York: Oxford University Press, 1999). On the question of how to read Gregory of Nyssa, see Sarah Coakley, ed., *Re-Thinking Gregory of Nyssa* (Malden, MA: Wiley-Blackwell, 2003).

5. Just as I was concluding this book, I came across Andrew Robinson's remarkable tome, *God and the World of Signs: Trinity, Evolution, and the Metaphysical Semiotics of C. S. Peirce* (Boston: Brill, 2010). I am astonished by the formal parallels between the trinitarianism I have arrived at here by way of comparative theology and his philosophical trinitarianism derived from the work of Peirce.

6. It is worth signaling that there is now a substantive interest in the trinity in centering prayer circles. See for example Richard Rohr's recent book, *The Divine Dance: The Trinity and Your Transformation* (New Kensington, PA: Whitaker House, 2016). See also, Cynthia Bourgeault, *The Holy Trinity and the Law of Three: Discovering the Radical Truth at the Heart of Christianity* (Boston, MA: Shambala Publications, 2013).

7. In a previous version of this chapter, I called this middle category "contingency." But a variety of colleagues and friends, including Catherine Keller and Robert Corrington, have pressed me to ponder whether "contingency" is the right term. They have persuaded me that "singularity" is the more adequate term.

8. Martin Heidegger, *Introduction to Metaphysics*, revised and expanded translation by Gregory Fried and Richard Polt (New Haven, CT: Yale University Press, 2014), 1–2; emphasis added.

9. Heidegger, *Introduction to Metaphysics*, 3; emphasis in the original.

10. Jim Holt, *Why Does the World Exist?: An Existential Detective Story* (New York: W. W. Norton, 2012), 23. Kindle Edition.

11. Holt, *Why Does the World Exist?*, 23.

12. Holt, 23; emphasis in the original.

13. Heidegger, *Introduction to Metaphysics*, 8.

14. Sankara, *Chandogya Upaniṣad with the Commentary of Sri Sankaracarya* (Calcutta: Advaita Ashrama, 1983), 413.

15. Sankara, *Bṛhadaranyaka Upanisad with the Commentary of Sri Sankaracarya* (Calcutta: Advaita Ashrama, 1983), 100. The translation is mine.

16. Douglas Duckworth, *Mipam on Buddha-Nature: The Ground of the Nying-ma Tradition* (Albany: SUNY Press, 2008), 97. Debate within Tibetan Buddhist traditions is often conducted exegetically. Given the enormous variety of Buddhist scriptural sources, the question is what to make of those texts in which emptiness seems to be described in rigorously negative terms—as the absence of self-existence—as opposed to texts that advance a robustly positive discourse about an underlying empty Buddha-nature. The question is which of these texts have provisional meaning (Skt. *neyartha*) and which have definitive or final meaning (Skt. *nitartha*).

17. Duckworth, *Mipam on Buddha-Nature*, 99.

18. Duckworth, 100.

19. Duckworth, 59.

20. Paul Tillich, *Systematic Theology, Vol. I* (Chicago: University of Chicago Press, 1951), 156; emphasis added.

21. Tillich, *Systematic Theology*.
22. Tillich, 271.
23. Tillich, 275.
24. Tillich, 177.
25. Mary Oliver, *New and Selected Poems, Volume I* (Boston: Beacon Press, 1992), 94; emphasis added.
26. Fr. Richard Rohr, OFM, "Irreplaceable 'Thisness,'" March 18, 2018, https://cac.org/irreplaceable-thisness-2018-03-18/.
27. This account of singularity is congruent with the Whiteheadian consequent nature of God, which receives the created world into the divine life.
28. The authoritative philosophical articulation of this understanding of emptiness as dependent co-arising is to be found in Nagarjuna's *Mulamadhyamakakarika*. See J. L. Garfield, *The Fundamental Wisdom of the Middle Way: Nagarjuna's* Mulamadhyamakakarika (New York: Oxford University Press, 1995).
29. Jay Garfield concisely characterizes Nagarjuna, the founding master of the Madhyamaka school, as holding that "emptiness itself is empty. It is not a self-existent void standing behind a veil of illusion comprising conventional reality, but merely a characteristic of conventional reality." Garfield, *Fundamental Wisdom*, 91.
30. Garfield, 245.
31. On these internal Buddhist debates, see John Makransky, *Buddhahood Embodied: Sources of Controversy in India and Tibet* (Albany: SUNY Press, 1997).
32. Robert Aitken, *A Zen Wave: Basho's Haiku and Zen* (Washington, DC: Shoemaker and Hoard), Kindle locations 118–120; emphasis added.
33. The entirety of Catherine Keller's written corpus has been substantially a thinking of relation. See *From A Broken Web: Separation, Sexism, and Self* (Boston: Beacon Press, 1988). The emphasis on relation is also profoundly articulated in the work of the Brazilian feminist ecotheologian Ivone Gebara. See especially, *Longing for Running Water: Ecofeminism and Liberation* (Minneapolis, MN: Fortress Press, 1999).

## 8. *This Is Not a Conclusion*

1. Thich Nhat Hahn, *Thich Nhat Hanh: Essential Writings* (Maryknoll, NY: Orbis Books, 2001), 58. Kindle Edition.
2. On the critical imperative to move beyond zero-sum thinking, see Richard Wright, *Nonzero: The Logic of Human Destiny* (New York: Vintage Books, 2000).
3. Ivone Gebara, *Longing for Running Water: Ecofeminism and Liberation* (Minneapolis, MN: Fortress Press, 1999), Kindle locations 1387–1389.
4. That intuition is, of course, what Keller articulates in the epigraph at the beginning of this chapter.
5. Merlin Peris, "A Note on the Etymology of 'Elephant,'" *Journal of the Royal Asiatic Society of Sri Lanka*, New Series, Vol. 38 (1993/1994), 163.

# INDEX

Whitehead, Alfred North, 235–7, 287n27
*Why Does the World Exist? An Existential
Detective Story* (Holt), 222
wisdom, reception of, 32–3, 42,
193–5, 202. *See also* hospitality of
receiving
*Without the Buddha, I Could Not Be a
Christian* (Knitter), xvi
Wittgenstein, Ludwig, 222–4

wonderment, 219, 221
Word: exclusivism and, 47, 53; ground
and, 95–6; and non-Christians, 27;
trinitarianism and, 214, 219–20.
*See also logos spermatikos*

xenophobia, 2

Yong, Amos, 284n10

**John J. Thatamanil** is Associate Professor of Theology and World Religions at Union Theological Seminary in the City of New York. He is the author of *The Immanent Divine: God, Creation, and the Human Predicament; An East–West Conversation* (Fortress, 2006). He teaches a wide variety of courses in the areas of comparative theology, theologies of religious diversity, Hindu-Christian dialogue, the theology of Paul Tillich, theory of religion, and process theology. He is committed to the work of comparative theology—theology that learns from and with a variety of traditions. A central question that drives his work is "How can Christian communities come to see religious diversity as a promise rather than as a problem?"

Comparative / *Thinking Across*
Theology / *Traditions*

LOYE ASHTON AND JOHN THATAMANIL, SERIES EDITORS

Hyo-Dong Lee, *Spirit, Qi, and the Multitude: A Comparative Theology for the Democracy of Creation*

Michelle Voss Roberts, *Tastes of the Divine: Hindu and Christian Theologies of Emotion*

Michelle Voss Roberts (ed.), *Comparing Faithfully: Insights for Systematic Theological Reflection*

Francis X. Clooney, S.J., and Klaus von Stosch (eds.), *How to Do Comparative Theology*

F. Dominic Longo, *Spiritual Grammar: Genre and the Saintly Subject in Islam and Christianity*

S. Mark Heim, *Crucified Wisdom: Theological Reflection on Christ and the Bodhisattva*

Martha L. Moore-Keish and Christian T. Collins Winn (eds.), *Karl Barth and Comparative Theology*

John J. Thatamanil, *Circling the Elephant: A Comparative Theology of Religious Diversity*

Printed and bound by CPI Group (UK) Ltd, Croydon, CR0 4YY

09/06/2025

14685660-0003